Red, White & Blind

The Truth About Disinformation and the Path to Media Consciousness

Tony Brasunas

TORCHPOST

RED, WHITE & BLIND
is a publication of

TORCHPOST
www.torchpost.com

First Torchpost edition 2023

Copyright © 2023 by Tony Brasunas

www.RedWhiteAndBlind.com

Grateful acknowledgement to the following for permission to reprint previously published material:

Excerpt from KILL THE MESSENGER by Nick Schou, copyright © 2006, is reprinted by permission of Bold Type Books, an imprint of Hachette Book Group, Inc. Excerpt from 1983 interview of John Stockwell at the Vietnam Reconsidered Conference, USC. Use by permission of King Rose Archives / Global ImageWorks LLC. Excerpt from THE MIGHTY WURLITZER: HOW THE CIA PLAYED AMERICA by Hugh Wilford, Cambridge, Mass.: Harvard University Press, Copyright © 2008 by Hugh Wilford. Used by permission. All rights reserved. Excerpt from "When Contemplating War, Beware of Babies in Incubators," by Tom Regan, is used with permission from The Christian Science Monitor, online at csmonitor.com.

Cover photo by Jenna Seegmuller

BOOK DESIGN BY JESSICA KLEINMAN

Printed in the United States of America

ISBN 978-1-66787-443-2

To my wife, Pamela,
for your love and support
on this winding, blessed journey.

CONTENTS

CHAPTER 13 330
A BALANCED MEDIA DIET

CHAPTER 14 366
THE NEW ENLIGHTENMENT

EPILOGUE 381
JOIN THE AWAKENING, OPEN YOUR MIND

Those who tell the stories rule society.

- Plato

FOREWORD

IT'S A TRUISM IN THE WORLD OF ADDICTION THERAPY, OR THERAPY OF any kind, that the treatment process begins with an acknowledgement of the problem. Well, we have a problem. A big problem. The American media, the free press enshrined not just in our Constitution but in the very fabric of our democracy, is in a state of crisis. What makes matters worse is that the people seemingly in the best position to address this problem refuse to recognize its existence. In fact, they openly champion the "health" of the system in which they are entrenched.

Unfortunately for them—but fortunately for the rest of us—the intended end user of the American press (you know, the customer that matters so much to other industries), knows better. Trust in media has never been lower. In fact it's all but evaporated, leaving the media hanging onto its former special status by a thread of credibility. And yet, media has never been more ubiquitous, or more instrumental, in shaping our perception of reality.

As a result, we're today experiencing a form of society-wide cognitive dissonance. We know in our gut that the narratives being advanced do not reflect our experience of the world. Yet we are told to obey the dictates of the media delivering them. Worse still, we are accused of a kind of dis-allegiance—to state? to society? to an unarticulated religion?—for questioning these dictates at all.

But as Tony Brasunas elegantly and systematically shows in the pages to come, there is a significant opportunity in this moment. It's charged with the energy required to refashion an essential institution like the press to meet the needs of a new era. First, however, we need to understand the problem in all its ugliness, messiness, and even in what you might call its glory.

What you'll learn from this book is just how subtly and expertly distortion has been woven into the current incarnation of our news media. You'll see that although we've only begun to have a mainstream conversation about this in recent years, the trend is one that has played out over the course of decades.

In the years following the Second World War, the American state, flush with power and loaded with resources but also burdened with the self-appointed role of maintaining global stability, deduced from these political premises that it had to do everything it could to fulfill this crucial imperative. Of course, it would turn to one of the most vibrant, sophisticated and exhilarating engines of influence in history, the American media. The media, perhaps sharing a belief in this imperative, didn't simply comply but became a full-fledged partner in the enterprise of American power.

That was then. We are governed by a very different set of circumstances today. We need the kind of change that by definition does not flow from power but is imposed upon it, to limit it, to invert the dynamic that, to an alarming extent, has resulted in the sense that we are being ruled rather than governed.

This is an important book. It's a book whose lessons you will not soon forget, least of all because Tony has experienced firsthand, as a journalist working for one of the brightest names in media, just how swiftly the hands of censorship can move. You'll learn how the CIA infiltrates a possibly all-too-willing press, how the clock face of journalism is turned by gears of the corporate machine, how facts get invented, truth gets annihilated, and stories get plucked out of thin air.

All this is to say that the time to develop what Tony calls a new "media consciousness" is now. There is not a moment to waste. For the first time in a long, long time, power is in our hands. It's up to us to use it.

Ashley Rindsberg
September 2022

INTRODUCTION

"We will know our disinformation campaign has been successful when everything the American people believe is false."

William Casey, Director of the CIA, 1981-87

VIRGINIA ROBERTS FOLDED EIGHT WHITE TOWELS INTO STACKS, ENSURING the seams lined up and the spa's floral logo appeared in the corner. She placed the stacked towels on a polished granite countertop. There were no customers, so she tied her blond hair into a ponytail and resumed reading where she had left off in an illustrated guide to massage therapy. She found the book fascinating.

I'm only fifteen, she reminded herself.

But she had a goal now: to ascend from mere attendant at the luxurious Mar-a-Lago resort to real, professional massage therapist.

A woman with pointy, black locks of hair appeared. Virginia offered the woman tea, as she always did, and asked politely whether she had an appointment. The woman didn't have an appointment, but she accepted the tea. With a friendly smile, and with a proper English accent, the woman asked Virginia several questions about the spa before she asked about her copious notes in the massage book.

With a bashful smile, Virginia shared her goal.

The woman told Virginia that her boss was a wealthy man, and as it turned out, he was looking for a massage therapist for his frequent jet trips around the world. He would pay for her training if Virginia showed the right enthusiasm for the job. The woman handed Virginia her card and introduced herself. Her name was Ghislaine Maxwell.

It was June 2000, and a three-year nightmare was about to unfold for Virginia as she followed in the path of dozens—perhaps hundreds or even thousands—of young girls who were abused by Jeffrey Epstein. Later that warm summer night, Virginia visited Epstein's Palm Beach mansion as many of the unfortunate girls did before they accompanied him to Paris, New York, London, and Little St. James, Epstein's private island in the Virgin Islands. The girls were offered as sexual property, escorts, and "massage therapists" to some of the world's most powerful and wealthy men (usually men). Millionaires and billionaires, former presidents and foreign royalty, senators and judges, hedge fund tycoons and Hollywood producers, powerful attorneys and famous actors, chairmen of boards, and CEOs of giant conglomerates. They all flew on Epstein's plush private plane. The plane was nicknamed the "Lolita Express." Ascending from a resort attendant to a professional massage therapist was not in the cards for Virginia.

Shortly after that night, as she tells the story, she was forced to have sex with Prince Andrew of England, famed attorney Alan Dershowitz,[1] and many others.[2] Those known to have flown on Epstein's jet many times include Bill Clinton, Bill Gates, Donald Trump,[3] and countless others.[4]

Non-Reporting on a Non-Prosecution

No legal action was brought against Epstein for years. The first case brought against him occurred in 2005 when a different girl's mother brought charges of sexual assault on behalf of her daughter. Many other victims came forward immediately thereafter, revealing Epstein had been running a pedophilia rape ring since at least 1993. Local law enforcement amassed a litany of evidence and multiple witnesses. It looked like a slam dunk case. Epstein faced life in prison for sex trafficking.

What ensued was one of the saddest chapters in American legal and media history. The FBI stepped in and took over the case from local Florida law enforcement. The federal attorneys heard hours of damaging testimony from the victims themselves and their families but chose to use a grand jury, which protected Epstein from the most threatening charges. Epstein's powerful attorneys, including Alan Dershowitz, who himself was a frequent traveler on the "Lolita Express," secured a highly unusual "non-prosecution" from US Attorney Alexander Acosta. It was a sweetheart deal that required him to plead guilty to *one* charge at the state level. In exchange, Acosta granted Epstein immunity and canceled an FBI probe into his activities. How was this possible?

Acosta claimed orders had "come from above" that were "above his pay grade."

National media coverage was nowhere to be found.[5] A *New York* magazine piece, "Billionaires Are Free," was one of few national pieces on Epstein at the time, and it vindicated him with a shockingly permissive "boys will be boys" attitude.[6]

And that was that. The national media uncharacteristically dropped a story about sex and famous people. Indeed, the media ran away from the matter of a major sex trafficking ring as if from an infectious virus.

Epstein had to register as a sex offender following the "non-prosecution," but eight years later, he was still somehow flying on his personal jet with "very young girls" to his private Caribbean island on a weekly basis.[7] It was as if he had never been convicted at all. The media stayed silent.

Quashing the Story Again

Years later, after Virginia finally escaped Epstein's clutches, she married an Australian and took her new husband's name, Giuffre. The birth of her daughter prompted her to overcome her shame and speak out. Virginia contacted national news organizations and penned a 139-page exposé about her experience, which was eventually submitted as evidence against Epstein and Ghislaine Maxwell.[8] In 2016, she spoke directly with ABC News host Amy Robach.

Robach was intrigued, and she took up the story. She arranged a flight to New York for Virginia, and Virginia felt confident enough to tell Robach the whole horrifying story in person and on the record. Robach recorded it all and spent hours preparing a report on the bombshell revelations. The story would finally expose Epstein for what he had done.

ABC News never ran the story. No corporate media channel picked it up despite Virginia's dogged efforts. If the main priority of American news organizations is to generate clicks and views, as many Americans believe, this story was surely a godsend. But they all ignored it. Why?

We will answer this question in this book.

Robach recalled in 2019:

> I had this interview with Virginia Roberts. We would not put it on the air. First of all, I was told, 'Who is Jeffrey Epstein? No one knows who that is. This is a stupid story.'
>
> Then the [British] Palace found out that we had her allegations about Prince Andrew and threatened us a million different ways. We were so afraid we wouldn't be able to interview Kate and Will that we... quashed the story. And then Alan Dershowitz was also implicated...
>
> She told me everything. She had pictures, she had everything. She was in hiding for 12 years. We convinced her to come out. We convinced her to talk to us. It was unbelievable what we had: Clinton, we had everything.[9]

ABC News "quashed the story" indeed. Despite Virginia's repeated efforts to tell the world, her story was never heard.

Two years—and countless young girls—later, the story finally broke in the corporate media. A low-level reporter at *The Miami Herald* named Julie K. Brown convinced her editors at long last to run a story she had spent years researching. Entitled "Perversion of Justice," the investigative piece identified over eighty girls who had been pulled into the pedophilia rape ring.[10] Brown's *tour de force* informed the nation of Epstein's and Maxwell's crimes, and the story exploded into mainstream awareness.[11] It took yet another year, but in 2019 Epstein was finally arrested. He had operated a pedophilia ring for the world's rich and famous for over a quarter century.

A Culture of Corruption

Only pervasive fraud and deceit could allow this magnitude of criminal behavior to go on this long. It wasn't one bad apple at one news organization or one attorney at one complicit prosecutor's office. Widespread corruption prevented justice from being served in 2005 and for fourteen years thereafter. Widespread corruption enabled Epstein to perpetrate his heinous crimes with impunity.

Robach's story was quashed at ABC News, but surely it wasn't the only one. We know about it because of a leaked accidental recording,[12] not because Robach came forward.[13] No major print reporters were put on the story. Julie K. Brown pursued the story out of personal interest and passion, and when her editors finally ran the story, it was the exception proving the rule.

Brown herself acknowledged this in her 2021 book, also entitled *Perversion of Justice*:

> I didn't at the time believe that any media network would have succumbed to pressure to ignore or drop such an important story. I was, however, naïve and wrong... there are news organizations that protect powerful people.[14]

How does this "pressure" affect the mainstream media's coverage of other issues? We will examine this question in this book.

As for Epstein, the media circus revealed aspects of the corruption he exploited. Before his trial, Epstein loudly told a reporter that he had dirt on hundreds of powerful men all over the world, hinting at explicit videos. The allegations flew, and the suspicions grew.[15] *Who had visited this serial pedophile rapist's island? Who had been a part of this depraved sex trafficking ring?* But few answers appeared in corporate media. Nearly as rapidly as it had exploded on the media scene, the bombshell story was gone.[16] Epstein was killed, or died, or committed suicide in prison, or secretly escaped, and the media moved on quickly from the story, running away as if from a ghost. It remains unclear to this day what exactly happened to this bizarrely omnipotent pedophile, and so contradictory are the stories of his death, it's not clear that he is dead.

What is clear is that men at the apex of the entire power pyramid of the Western World engaged in repeated sexual assault, sex trafficking, abduction, and statutory rape. It's also clear that this country's most powerful media organizations looked the other way for years. Ghislaine Maxwell finally faced a court conviction in 2022, but none of the men who participated in the despicable acts faced an iota of punishment.

For the sake of comparison, ten years earlier, in 2008, when investigations revealed that New York Governor Eliot Spitzer had interacted with prostitutes in an Albany hotel, it became an international news scandal that ran him out of office immediately. It ended his career. What he had done was unbecoming and probably illegal, but it was consensual sex between adults. The Epstein scandal was orders of magnitude larger than the Spitzer story, yet it was on the front pages for a *shorter* amount of time.

Why was this story quashed for so many years? Why wasn't it investigated extensively in the corporate media? When it did come out, how could the entire corporate media—dozens of newspapers and cable channels and magazines—drop this bombshell story so quickly?

We will answer these questions in this book.

THE NEW ENLIGHTENMENT

WELCOME TO THE ERA OF DISINFORMATION, PROPAGANDA, AND CENsorship. The horrible censorship and biased coverage of the Epstein crimes reflect but one of countless episodes of news distortion in our modern American media world. We will examine many of them in this book. Becoming accurately informed about current events today might seem impossible, but we will learn in these pages that it is actually easier than ever—if we are willing to read broadly.

We live in a time when curtains are parting, truths are being revealed, and collective knowledge is broadening and deepening. Two decades of internet expansion have unleashed an explosion of news media and delivered us into a new epoch in human communication, a brand new information age: what I call the New Enlightenment.

As we will see in this book, we were fed propaganda about the polluted water coming out of faucets in Flint, Michigan in 2014. We were misinformed by distorted news on Russia in 2018 and facemasks in 2020. We suffered from censorship when Twitter and Facebook decided what could be shared in the lead-up to the 2020 election.

Misinformation, propaganda, and censorship are formidable evils to detangle when navigating the news. We will find reasons for optimism too. Just as Hope appeared at the bottom of Pandora's Box, beneath the evils of deception and distortion lie the things they are designed to obscure: this New Enlightenment and the truths it has in store for us.

The world we know is a world in which myriad voices purporting to be news present the same event on the same day in divergent ways. Some voices shout at a deafening volume about things that matter little to us. Other voices obscure events altogether, such as the disgusting crimes of pedophiles and the powerful men whose depravity they stoked and satiated.

Whenever each voice labels the others as "deceptive," "misinformation," or "fake news," this creates a dilemma. We can choose to accept one news source as our arbiter of truth and let it distinguish the true news from the false for us. Or we can choose to read broadly and trust our own intelligence to determine the reliability of each news source and the veracity of each news report. The choice we make impacts how we consume information and how we act.

Choosing the first path—which many do—has created "reality bubbles," rigid echo chambers where a small and dwindling range of perspectives is available.

This book is for those choosing the second path.

If you're ready to acknowledge that no single news source is always right about its take on events or about which of its competitors' coverage is "fake," then you're ready to acknowledge that it's important and worthwhile to be both conscious and skeptical when consuming news. Furthermore, if you're interested in learning the history of journalism, propaganda, censorship, and media manipulation in this country, you'll discover that the slant of news events isn't exclusively chosen to deliver fair reporting nor to maximize news organizations' profits. Each news source selects its angle based primarily on a series of *filters* that steer the bounds of acceptable debate. You'll come to see that the most heavily produced news is often the most dangerously fake.

Not that fake news is new. From this country's founding, when the Freedom of the Press was enshrined in our Constitution, readers who have wanted to know the truth have had to sort through various accounts and opinions.

If you consume a narrow media diet only from one sector of the media landscape, reading this book might be uncomfortable. The stories we will investigate will likely challenge your assumption that your one source or segment of the media is always correct. We will dive deeply enough to question whether *any* source is primarily interested in accuracy or impartiality. While we can enter this New Enlightenment broad-minded, part of our social challenge is stepping outside our comfortable echo chambers.

On the other hand, if you have long had the impression that deep biases distort mainstream corporate media coverage of the news—if you already see that important perspectives are routinely dismissed, deleted, or manipulated—you will learn how, why, and by whom this manipulation is taking place.

In either event, I thank you for taking this journey toward greater awareness. The path may not always be smooth, but you will find it fascinating, worthwhile, and even transformative in how you view the world we share.

HOW TO READ THIS BOOK

THIS BOOK IS NOT A SIMPLE COLLECTION OF NARRATIVES, SUCH AS THE Epstein scandal, nor an expository analysis of corporate media filters, nor an investigative report. This book intends to be four things for you: a history, an exposé, a guide, and a pep talk.

- **History**. In my journey to media awareness, learning the *history* of media manipulation in this country has been essential to truly understanding the predicament we're in. We start with the origins of the Free Press in our Constitution, review the invention of journalism, and examine the onset of propaganda during World War I. We explore a handful of key events in the 1800s and 1900s before focusing our attention on the 2000s. Chapters 2 and 3 focus on more recent history, and then in Chapter 11 we take a deep dive into the origins of the newspaper as well as the illusory notion of "objective journalism."

- **Exposé**. A large part of this book is devoted to a thorough *exposé* of misreported events and manipulated news, such as that of Jeffrey Epstein, to demonstrate how distorted our media has become in this young decade. The manipulation is worsening too. Chapters 1, 4, 5, 6, and 7 focus on this investigation. Chapters 8, 9, and 10 delve into the new world of social media, "fact checkers," and "astroturf" independent media. You'll likely find the rise of censorship and propaganda serious concerns whether you're a Democrat, Republican, or Independent.

➻ **Guide**. Thereafter, I propose a solution—a *guide*—in Chapter 13 on how to navigate the modern media world. This Balanced Media Diet encompasses both tips on how to read and think critically as well as a concrete set of sources to read. In the old adage about teaching a man to fish, the goal of the guide is to provide you with both sources of news to consume right away and the know-how to construct your own media diet (whether or not it's pescatarian).

➻ **Pep Talk**. Finally, a *pep talk*. In Chapter 14, we step back to look at our position in the history of human knowledge. The truth is, we are not so badly off. Lies and deception by powerful people have been the rule, not the exception, for recorded human history. Today, with the growth of decentralized human communication through the internet, we are in a New Enlightenment. We have an unparalleled opportunity to experience another flowering of human wisdom and innovation.

The book is carefully organized so that you'll learn the most by reading it from front to back. Start at the start, end at the end. Every chapter is essential.

But if you'd like to read the most timely material first, read Chapters 8 and 9 first, which cover social media censorship in 2022, "fact checking," and "astroturf" independent news, as I rewrote them as the book was going to press.

If you'd like to read the book in chronological order, with the events occurring in historical order, read Chapter 11 first, then Chapters 2 and 3, and then the rest of the book.

If you're pressed for time, you might skip Chapters 2 and 3, start with Chapter 4, and read as many of the exposés as you need to understand the predicament we're in. Then, flip straight to Chapter 13 to explore the Balanced Media Diet and plan your weekly news exploration. Finally, jump to my conclusion in Chapter 14 to understand my take on where this is all going and my tips on participating in a better media world.

THE TERMS

THIS BOOK COVERS A CENTURY OF MEDIA MANIPULATION IN THE UNITED States. Many instances of *bias, propaganda,* and *censorship* will be easy to spot; others will prove sophisticated and difficult to detect. We'll look at the buildup to wars, the campaigns of national elections, the handling of the pandemic, and the covert activities of powerful organizations like the CIA. We'll confront the possibility that our media might be as distorted and "fake" as that of any country, including China, a place where propaganda dominates. Certainly the propaganda in American media sources is more sophisticated than China's—but is it less common or less deceptive?

Several key terms will be used repeatedly, and we define them here for convenience and clarity.

◈ **Bias.** All news reporting has *bias.* This is what slants, skews, filters, or manipulates news coverage depending on who's writing the report and who's publishing it. The questions we'll be investigating are, what kind of *bias* does each news source and contributor have, and what causes this *bias*? We'll distinguish three types of bias:

→ *innocent bias* - tendencies that come from the fact that journalists and editors, like all human beings, have natural blind spots based on their heritage, identity, background, and worldview.

→ *systemic bias* - distortion that originates from a news organization's ownership by a gigantic corporate conglomerate. All large corporations have interests beyond simple, candid reporting of the events of the day.

→ *nefarious bias* - covert manipulation of news reporting by intelligence agencies and other external organizations via infiltration or control.

◈ **Filter.** Each of the three *biases* above is composed of *filters.* A *filter* is a specific rule or tendency that causes *bias.* The *filters* of *innocent bias,* for instance, are the writer's race, class, political beliefs, national origin, education level, and so on. The *filters* of *systemic bias* are fascinating and often obvious in their effects, and we'll devote a full chapter to understanding these organizational screens through which news coverage is processed by professional journalists and editors. The *filters* of *nefarious bias* are rarely admitted but aren't difficult to guess: the specific, hidden agenda of the institutions controlling the news, such as launching a war, concealing racism, pushing a drug, or justifying fraud.

◈ **Propaganda.** This is the heavily produced news mentioned above. *Propaganda* is produced deliberately by governments and corporations to deceive through a mixture of dishonest statements and omissions of facts and perspectives. In a stereotypical depiction of China or the Soviet Union, *propaganda* was a one-way stream of news and views from the government to the people. In our country, *propaganda* generally comes from public relations firms, large corporate media organizations, or intelligence agencies and carries *nefarious bias* or *systemic bias*, or both. If news coverage carries only *innocent bias*, it is not *propaganda*.

◈ **Censorship.** This is the deletion of news events, perspectives, or data, or the silencing of journalists or entire news sources on account of *systemic* or *nefarious bias*—whether done by government actors or large corporations. Some people believe that only governments can perform censorship, but that narrow definition is outdated with the fusion of government and corporate power in our modern world.

◈ **The Narrative.** This is the pearl, the treasure. This is what it's all about. The *narrative* is the story we believe we are living in. The *narrative* is what *bias, propaganda,* and *censorship* aim to control. It is the background against which the media reports the news. It's *what* is happening in the world and *why*. It's the collection of facts our parents, colleagues, and friends believe about the world, or at least what we think they believe. If an athletic team is about to overcome immense adversity and win a championship against long odds, that is the *narrative* with which we turn on the television or step into the stadium. Throughout history, to those in power, control of the *narrative* has always been more valuable than money.

Speaking of money, we won't analyze wealth or power much in this book, although they are the goals of many who manipulate the news. We'll delve even less into the ultimate marriage of wealth and power sought by the most nefarious actors: social control. Wealth, power, and control are important things to research, but this book's topic is this more fundamental, priceless jewel: the *narrative*. If you can tell the people of a society what to fear and what to covet, whom to admire and whom to loathe, wealth and power will be yours.

◆ **"Fake News."** This term and its synonyms **disinformation** and **misinformation** technically refer to dishonest news and opinion published in the media. But these powerful words are most often used as slurs to discredit news reports and analysis with which one disagrees. Politicians and commentators on both sides of the political aisle employ them to reject reporting by news sources aligned with the other side. People who employ these terms rarely attempt to ascertain the actual *bias* or *filters* at play, so I call them "intellectually lazy" slurs, and they're related to another popular slur, *conspiracy theorist*, which we'll examine in depth in Chapter 2. The government and corporate media generate nearly all of the truly insidious fake news that plagues our media. There is *bias* in independent media and deliberate deception in "astroturf" independent sites, too, and we'll investigate those.

◆ **New Enlightenment.** This refers to today, our era, these last ten years and the next twenty or so years. This is an exciting, challenging epoch of unprecedented access to information. Johannes Gutenberg's invention of the movable-type press in the fifteenth century rapidly broadened popular access to knowledge and unleashed a flowering of philosophy, art, and science that led to the Enlightenment and the American Revolution. Similarly, we live in a new era of rapidly broadening access to information. Virtually anyone can share his or her experiences with the world instantaneously. This is precipitating a flowering of free thought.

◆ **Progressive, Conservative, and Reactionary.** These terms are applied in their traditional sense in this book to describe the three core political impulses that drive the ebb and flow of wealth and power.

→ *Progressive* groups and organizations seek to spread wealth and power more broadly.

→ *Reactionaries* seek to concentrate wealth and power into fewer hands.

→ *Conservatives* seek to keep the distribution of wealth and power as it is.

These impulses have been at play in all eras of human civilization. The previous millennium was primarily a progressive millennium in Western culture as feudalism and colonialism gave way to democracies and republics. In this book, we will predict what this third millennium holds in store.

Please note that the terms "progressive" and "conservative" are associated with factions of today's political parties, but that is not how I use them in this book.

One final note, on geography. This book focuses on how Americans distort the news for Americans. Foreign actors also distort some of our news—and our intelligence agencies certainly attempt to distort the news in other countries as well as in our own—but *domestic* propaganda and censorship are always most effective. Distorting a nation's news by having citizens with familiar faces tell lies to other citizens with familiar faces is easy to carry out, hard to notice, and highly effective when successful. We will touch on foreign news and foreign manipulation of our media, too, but it is not as effective nor as common and thus is not our primary focus.

WHY YOU SHOULD CARE

IF THE NEWS IN THIS COUNTRY IS HEAVILY BIASED AND MANIPULATED, why not simply turn it off and go about life as if it didn't exist? Why not treat the *bias* and *propaganda* like toxic fumes and simply not inhale? Why even try to make sense of obnoxious headlines, distorted reporting, and dishonest opinions?

The reason is simple. The news media controls the *narrative*, the background of our lives. We human beings are storytelling creatures and have been since before we could write. As American poet Muriel Rukeyser put it, "the universe is made of stories, not of atoms." The narrative is our ongoing, shared story that shapes our shared culture. The narrative tells us and our family what kind of world we are living in, what is important, what is scary, and what is wonderful. The narrative tells us and our friends which ideas to treat as benign and understandable and which ideas to treat as false and unconscionable. Going through life acknowledging that the news *does* exist binds us to the world around us.

And not inhaling is not an option. The headlines shout the day's stories, and we absorb them whether we want to or not. The narrative penetrates our hearts and minds even when we do not realize it. The narrative inserts itself into our *internal* voices—the ego and superego that guide and critique our thoughts from within, telling us we are good or bad, smart or stupid, successes or failures. Those voices are the subject of psychological analysis, but they are also affected by external voices that tell us what to value. The voices of CNN and NPR, the *New York Times* and the *Wall Street Journal,* Fox News and MSNBC, Facebook and Twitter come at us nonstop whether we'd like to quiet them or not. We cannot shut off the external voices from the media any more than we can shut off the internal voices inside our heads. And if we ignore these ubiquitous media voices, they still drive the narratives that describe our world to our friends, family, colleagues, leaders, and heroes.

What we can and must do is become *conscious* about these voices. We must become *aware* of what each media source wants us to see, think, and feel. We can learn their origins and their aims.

The goal of this book, then, is not just to instill media literacy but to ignite what we will call *media consciousness*, a state of awareness that grants the possibility of both spotting a constructed narrative and glimpsing the truth beneath it.

Our culture is at a tipping point with separate media bubbles steadily diverging. *Media consciousness* is a worthwhile goal for the sake of understanding your friends and family, comprehending the world's problems and possibilities, and surviving and thriving on a complex planet. But more profoundly, without this consciousness, your understanding of the world will be distorted, and your mental health will waver at the mercy of those who seek to manipulate your beliefs for the sake of their agenda.

Many choices you make have a profound impact on your life. At some point in your life, you will likely choose where to live, what career to pursue, whom to vote for. You'll contemplate whether or not to join a union, support a nonprofit organization, undergo invasive surgery, try alternative medicine, or take a vaccine. You'll decide whether to travel to a foreign country, attain a college degree, buy a home, or have children. Each choice will be heavily influenced by the media narrative that you are living in. Your belief about the world, its perils and possibilities, will be dictated in large part by the story you believe about current events.

Just as attaining a mature awareness about the holidays required us to recognize that Santa Claus does not exist, coming of age in American culture requires that we acknowledge that the corporate news narrative manipulates our beliefs about what is going on in our world.

Ultimately, our goal is to empower ourselves to peel back the veil on the dominant narratives in order to more easily connect with each other and more wisely make our lives' most consequential choices.

THE TRUTH WILL SET YOU FREE, BUT FIRST IT WILL PISS YOU OFF

MY PERSONAL MEDIA AWAKENING BEGAN AT THE AGE OF TWENTY-TWO. I grew up on the East Coast of the United States before I spent a year in China, where I taught English, traveled the country, and endeavored to pick up the language. As my Chinese skills improved, I noticed how the local media covered events very differently from the American media. The UK handed the wealthy island of Hong Kong to China while I was there, and the differences in the headlines at the time were stark. The American media covered the event with concern for the people of Hong Kong and the freedoms of the Press and Speech that they enjoyed. The Chinese media published stories that were uniformly celebratory and triumphant. While I didn't yet notice the manipulation in the American coverage, the naked propaganda in the Chinese media taught me my first lesson in news distortion, and it confused and angered me: the Chinese media simply never covered or discussed any concerns of the people of Hong Kong. I saw their place and my place in a media narrative.

I returned to the United States in time for the 2000 presidential election, the second one for which I was old enough to vote. I followed the presidential campaigns closely and became fascinated by American politics. For the first time, I noticed distortion in news coverage. The fact that the two wealthiest and most politically-connected candidates, George W. Bush and Al Gore, received virtually all the media coverage, intrigued and infuriated me. Meanwhile, the candidate who seemed to me the most inspiring, capable, and popular—Ralph Nader—was routinely insulted if given any attention at all. Even when his events attracted over 10,000 people, the mainstream media treated the Nader campaign as if it were of no interest to anyone. I attended Nader events and wrote about what I witnessed for the benefit of friends and family. Why wasn't this capable candidate getting a fair shake?

Three years later, during the buildup to the Iraq War, I was a young blogger deputized by the *San Francisco Chronicle* to cover an appearance by a senator named Joe Biden. By this time, I had a slightly broader understanding of the media. Biden spoke at a fancy, downtown hotel. He was an articulate and forceful speaker at the time, and he expounded at length, advocating for an invasion. He almost convinced me, but nowhere did he mention the potential cost to the Iraqi people in lives and environment for a war that was ostensibly for their benefit. I found this troubling. I wrote up my report, and the piece was published, except for the part finding fault with Biden's case for war. Once again, the corporate media infuriated me, and this time, I grew curious as to how this censorship was occurring. Who had chosen to strike that section from my article? In a subsequent piece for the *Chronicle*, which happened to be about the phenomenal growth of Craigslist, a reference to George W. Bush was deleted prior to publication. That experience made it clear that the major newspapers were willing to provide endorsements by omission, and I looked for it in other sources.

I published an online political magazine of my own in San Francisco at the time, focusing primarily on issues that didn't get into the big papers, such as ownership of media, election fraud, and the underlying stories about the Iraq War, third parties, 9/11, and domestic surveillance. I noticed censorship and propaganda distorting virtually every major story in the corporate media, and it inspired me to look more deeply. I learned to distinguish everyday editorial decision-making—which is not censorship—from imperiously silencing viewpoints or entire stories on account of *systemic* or *nefarious bias*, which is indeed *censorship*.

In 2016, I wrote about the Bernie Sanders campaign for *Huffington Post*. I witnessed the way the corporate media treated Sanders and his supporters. It was eerily reminiscent of the way Ralph Nader's campaign had been treated sixteen years before. CNN, NPR, the *Washington Post*, and the *New York Times* ignored and denigrated the campaign. I noticed how effectively that manipulation deceived people about Sanders. In my articles, I pointed out the stark difference in outlook between those regularly reading a broad media diet that included independent media and those only taking in corporate media news. I wrote about it until, that is, my writings were censored by *HuffPost*. I recount those events in Chapter 4. It was the third time—but by no means the last—that the corporate media infuriated me.

I wrote this book to open the eyes of Americans about the ways our corporate media is censored, biased, and deliberately distorted, and how detrimental this is to our individual happiness and to our shared future as Americans. If I spark a conversation as to how we can become more thoroughly and truthfully informed citizens, then I've achieved my goal. While I am a longtime progressive, and I wrote about the Sanders campaigns out of both interest and support, I wrote this book because I'm more committed to transparency and uncovering the truth than I am to any political party or candidate.

The task of writing this book became both easier and harder as I went. I witnessed systematic censorship and narrative management in 2020 and 2021 that I had never envisaged and could not ignore when writing this book. New examples of news distortion and propaganda emerged daily that I felt I needed to include, and at times I wondered whether I would ever complete this book. Yet, my thesis became easier and easier to illustrate. Far more journalists than I expected became complicit in news distortion. While there are many journalistic heroes out there, the majority of corporate media journalists and editors who I've met on my journey are not, in fact, idealists striving to hold the powerful to account or tell the underlying truth about events. Most journalists in the corporate media, in my experience, are ordinary professionals seeking career stability and advancement, hoping perhaps someday to be famous and wealthy media personalities.

Today, the corporate media controls the narratives that appear on cable television and mainstream newspapers more tightly than ever. Some people see this control, some don't, but the clear trend across this great nation of ours is that people are noticing this deception, this comprehensive bias, and it is for them I spent three years researching and writing. This deceit forms a set of blinders that obscures the true state of our world, leaving us in a deceived state I call "red, white, and blind." It simultaneously befuddles Americans and angers us, stoking our collective thirst for alternatives, hastening the rise of independent media. This is how I know the New Enlightenment is here. With or without this book, *media consciousness* is already sprouting among us, dismantling manufactured narratives, dissolving consensus reality, and preparing us for a better, more honest world. It is both scary and exciting. Let's dive in.

DARE TO THINK FOR YOURSELF

TWO CHALLENGES WILL ARISE ON THE PATH TO *MEDIA CONSCIOUSNESS* as you turn these pages. First, you'll wonder how you can overcome despair once you see the propaganda-riddled predicament we're in. Secondly, you'll wonder how you can rise to the occasion, find time in your day, become informed about current events, and, despite the difficulties, walk a path toward understanding the news.

To address the first challenge—despair—I'll remind us of the benefits of *media consciousness*. Awareness of underlying truths awaits. *Media consciousness* makes us healthier individuals as well as more knowledgeable and more collaborative members of our families and communities.

To address the second challenge—walking the path—we'll explore a Balanced Media Diet guide in Chapter 13. The Diet is a diverse set of media sources that allows anyone with thirty minutes a day to attain awareness of current events. Following the Diet will also grant knowledge about the biases in news coverage and the underlying truths they aim to conceal.

In my experience, reading broadly doesn't bring on depression. Rather, witnessing the ways propaganda distorts our news media leads to an invigorated mind that increasingly enjoys considering opposing ideas. Much as a balanced food diet scares us at first but ultimately leads to strength, health, and vitality, broadening our media diet enables us to listen not just to *what* is said but to *who* is saying it and to *how* it aims to make us feel. This listening will stimulate our minds and broaden our awareness.

We aren't alone. A media awakening is unfolding all over the country. Media censorship and propaganda are increasing but so is awareness of this distortion. This isn't the first book on this, and it won't be the last. It has become cliché lately to say a battle is being fought for the minds of Americans, but that's because it's true. This battle is part of a larger war going on all across the world in this era of accelerating technology, globalization, and wealth inequality. This war is between, on the one hand, *reactionaries* who seek greater *centralization* of power into the hands of national and global governing bodies, something that the internet and globalization enable. Opposing them are those whom I call *progressives* who seek *decentralization* of power and a return of sovereignty to smaller communities and individuals, things that the internet also enables in a way never before possible. Will the internet enable a small new set of rulers to *centralize* global power and run the world, or will its extraordinary ability to distribute information and knowledge fuel an enlightenment? The former could happen using modern surveillance, facial recognition, monitored biometrics, controlled social media, and manufactured media narratives. The latter, however, could establish a new *decentralized* world of smaller, freer, more autonomous communities and nations. The presence or absence of Free Speech and a Free Press will in part determine the outcome of this great power struggle.

The propaganda besieging us will increase as this war wages and as the New Enlightenment unfolds. The first Enlightenment, the one that was ushered in by the movable-type printing press 500 years ago, toppled the centralized power of monarchs and popes, and it unleashed a magnificent flowering of literacy and publishing that advanced human potential. Prior to the printing press, there were only an estimated 50,000 books in existence in all of Europe; after its invention, within just fifty years, more than twelve million books were in people's hands. That time witnessed the unprecedented spread of philosophy, democracy, and written constitutions, including our own groundbreaking Bill of Rights that guarantees the rights of all people freely to speak, write, and print ideas that run counter to the government's interests.

Today, as we'll see in the pages of this book, these freedoms are under grave attack, and we are at the inflection point. We must understand this. This new Age of Information, birthed by the internet, has the potential to advance those remarkable rights and to thereby create another magnificent flowering of human culture. Just as the serfs and peasants in medieval Europe did in the 1500s, we Americans must utilize this new power to communicate with one another, and, as the Enlightenment motto goes, to *sapere aude*, "dare to think for ourselves." It is our time to claim the knowledge, creativity, and sovereignty over our own affairs that are our inalienable human rights. It is our time to understand what distorts our vision of the world. It is our time to see clearly.

Disclaimer

THIS IS A BOOK ABOUT TRUTH AND ACCURACY, BUT IT'S ALSO A BOOK about current events. Current events will change between now, when I'm putting the final touches on the manuscript, and now, when you hold this book in your hands. This pains me to admit as a perfectionist who goes to great lengths to research and confirm everything I write, but it is so. This book is rigorously sourced with notes beginning on page 385.

Nevertheless, inaccuracies will surface in this book about truth. Please reach out to me whenever you find that things have shifted since I signed off on the manuscript so that I can issue corrections online and in any future print editions. Thank you.

1

UNIFORMITY AND OBEDIENCE

"Any dictator would admire the uniformity and obedience of the American media."

Noam Chomsky

SHI ZHENGLI HAILED A CAB ON A CROWDED SHANGHAI STREET. SHE climbed inside and urged the cab driver to hurry. Traffic was thick, but she needed to get to the train station. She absolutely *had* to catch the next train to Wuhan.

A virologist and expert on bat coronaviruses, Shi had been attending a conference in the Pearl City when a phone call arrived that would change her life. "Drop whatever you're doing and get back to the lab," ordered her supervisor, the Director of the Wuhan Institute of Virology. "You need to be here. You need to deal with this."

It was the evening of December 30, 2019. Two mysterious viral samples had arrived at the Wuhan lab earlier that day from a nearby hospital. Doctors at the hospital reported seeing patients with an unusual type of pneumonia. The doctors requested the assistance of the lab, which was nearby and fortuitously was China's most sophisticated virology center.

Shi was no small fish in the pond of Chinese virology. As director of the Institute's Center for Emerging Infectious Diseases, she had led cutting-edge research in her lab for years. Her work focused on viruses and engaged in "gain of function" experiments—efforts to engineer viruses to be more transmissible, more deadly, or both. The ostensible reason to do this dangerous research was to predict possible evolutionary paths of viruses in the wild and be prepared should a deadly strain emerge. A great deal of this type of research, however, has historically been done[1] to create biological weapons[2] for use in unconventional warfare,[3] so the true purpose of the research was not clear.

In particular, Shi had been working for years on isolating coronaviruses from bats in caves in distant Yunnan Province and performing "gain of function" experiments on these viruses, combining them, and genetically modifying them, via cutting-edge, viral manipulation technology. The work was intense and controversial. It was also prestigious and partially funded by the United States.

Shi jumped out of the cab and slipped into the station just in time. She caught the train. As she looked out the window, it accelerated away from the Shanghai station and wound its way west through the city's suburbs. Soon, she was deep in the Dabie Mountains of Anhui Province. She spoke via phone with her subordinates at the lab, discussing methods to discern whether the pathogen discovered in the nearby hospital, which appeared to be a new virus, had in fact escaped from her lab.

Gain of Function, Loss of Reason

The week that followed was the most stressful time of her life, Shi later told *Scientific American*. The new virus was infecting many people in Wuhan. She spent hours examining its characteristics to determine whether it was an organism she had created. She was horrified, she was anxious, and she didn't sleep for days.[4]

According to the Chinese media, test results showed that there was no match between the viral samples provided by the hospital and the viruses that Shi had harvested from horseshoe bats in distant Yunnan Province.[5] What was unclear was whether the hospital samples matched any of the viruses that Shi's team had *created* through its "gain of function" research. What was less clear was whether the Chinese media would tell the world the truth either way.

An English zoologist named Peter Daszak was also tirelessly working, half a world away. He had overseen the American funding of Shi's controversial work in the Wuhan Institute of Virology (WIV) for years.[6] Daszak stood to lose significant money and reputation—his entire career perhaps—were it discovered that the virus had actually been created by research that his organization, EcoHealth Alliance, had been funding via grants[7] from the United States National Institutes of Health (NIH).[8]

Daszak reached out frantically to friends in labs around the world. He pulled together a team that could declare that the virus *couldn't* have escaped from Shi's laboratory and *must* have emerged naturally in a food market in a nearby district of the city.[9]

Published with much fanfare in the United States and Britain, Daszak's team's paper asserted that there was no evidence for anything other than the "natural zoonotic" theory, whereby the virus had jumped organically from bats to humans via an intermediary animal, such as a pangolin. "We stand together to strongly condemn conspiracy theories suggesting that Covid-19 does not have a natural origin." They dropped the *conspiracy theory* slur in a scientific paper, just like that. "We declare no competing interests," the paper added.[10]

What was not disclosed in the paper nor in corporate media coverage was how closely Daszak had worked with the WIV and how many competing financial interests he had had in the paper's verdict. Neither the paper nor the media mentioned that two signatories on the paper worked directly for him and that he had pushed many of the other signatories into signing.[11] Daszak had even covertly edited parts of the paper to conceal his role in its writing. All of that information slowly slipped out in smaller corporate publications and independent media, but the mainstream media never revealed Daszak's role at the WIV.[12]

Why would that be? What might explain this oversight? In this book, we will examine the *biases* that led to this *censorship*.

An Eroding Narrative

The central argument made in Daszak's team's paper was fairly weak. It asserted essentially that the mutations present in the virus were too unusual for human ingenuity to have invented. Far from proof, this wasn't even rigorous logic given the current state of virus manipulation technology. Nevertheless, the paper and a resulting *Nature* article[13] were enough for corporate media trendsetters like NPR and the *New York Times*, and they thereafter reported on the virus as if it were of natural origin, treated other ideas as "debunked conspiracy theories," and generally discounted the need for further inquiry.[14]

President Trump, then Secretary of State Mike Pompeo, then Senator Tom Cotton, then evolutionary biologists Bret Weinstein and Heather Heying, and many, many others began to suggest the virus had a lab origin.[15] The *New York Times* called this a "fringe" "conspiracy theory" in an article that sarcastically ridiculed suggestions that the virus could have originated in a lab.[16] Entitled, "Pompeo Ties Coronavirus to Chinese Lab Despite Spy Agencies' Uncertainty," the *Times* piece didn't leave the question open, catalog divergent opinions, or provide actual evidence one way or the other. Instead, it repeatedly implied one side was right and the other was wrong.[17] It quoted unnamed "sources" and unnamed "American allies." And that article was enough. It set the tone—as the *Times* often does—for the entire American media landscape. For the rest of 2020, the corporate media's unscientific rush to judgment kneecapped scientific inquiry into the virus. The NIH even gave EcoHealth Alliance *more* money to fund more risky virus manipulation research later in 2020.[18]

The "lab leak hypothesis," as it was called, was neither debunked nor a conspiracy, but it *was* a theory. It was quite a plausible theory. The WIV had harvested more bat coronaviruses than any other lab in the world, and the pandemic had broken out in the exact city where the lab was located. But suggesting a laboratory origin elicited attacks and censorship on social and independent media, which chilled debate on this critical question. Influential independent talk show host Joe Rogan outlined the evidence for a lab origin in September of 2020; he was denounced as a "conspiracy theorist" by Media Matters.[19] Fernando Castro-Chavez, a molecular biologist with hundreds of scholarly citations, wrote a widely distributed article that analyzed the gene sequence of *sars-cov-2*, revealing telltale "furin cleavage sites" that strongly suggested human manipulation and a lab origin; his interviews were taken down on YouTube.[20] Independent health program *The Highwire* presented doctors discussing the likelihood of a lab origin; its videos were taken down by YouTube and its press release privileges were revoked by PR Newswire.[21] Financial and cultural blog *Zero Hedge* asked the same questions;[22] it was labeled a "far-right website" that "amplifies conspiracy theories" and was removed by Twitter and delisted by Google.[23] Even a Chinese virologist claiming he had proof that the virus was created in the lab was banned from Twitter.[24]

As plausible as it was, the theory elicited fierce attacks in corporate media and sudden censorship on social networks. It became a hot potato no one wanted to touch. One had to admit that the virus had evolved naturally, leaping from animals to humans in a market, following the scientific phenomenon known as "zoonosis." This fancy word told the beginning, middle, and end of the story.[25] The narrative was not to be questioned.

Seeing Unicorns in Wuhan

It took a full year for things to change. Early in 2021, the CDC director himself resigned and provided his honest opinion: the virus emerged in a lab.[26] This emboldened a few corporate media outlets to publish modestly open-minded analyses, including a pivotal piece in *New York* magazine that summarized the evidence in favor of the "lab leak hypothesis," including the telltale discovery of furin cleavage sites in the virus's genetic code.[27] Similarities to other manipulated viruses continued to emerge.[28]

Meanwhile, no direct evidence emerged for the natural "zoonosis" theory. This theory required three things: an "intermediary" animal host to enable viral transmission from bats to humans, evidence of early antigen activity in the market workers, and a plausible trail of evolution in the virus's genetics. None of this ever emerged, not in 2020 nor in 2021.[29] Only indirect and inconclusive evidence supported the "zoonosis" theory, such as data analysis on the locations of the first known cases. Further unsettling for wet market "zoonosis" supporters were revelations that the Wuhan lab's experimentation on bat coronaviruses was not rigorously secured. Shi's lab carried out its work at biosafety level 2 (BSL-2) when such work is generally performed at BSL-3+ by international virologists. Richard Ebright, a Rutgers University microbiologist, likened the conditions in the WIV to "the biosafety level of a US dentist's office."[30] So now the world knew: the NIH had funded "gain of function" research at the WIV; that research was on precisely the types of bat coronaviruses that formed the backbone of *sars-cov-2*; the virus bore striking similarities to other lab-created viruses; and that work had been carried out in an insecure fashion. Nevertheless, the "lab leak" remained off-limits in most corporate media. Brief mentions of the CDC director's opinion, the lax safety standards, or the furin cleavage sites would surface but disappear quickly.

This was *narrative management,* something we will explore thoroughly in this book. The corporate media repeated one narrative over and over—making it dominant—while minimizing or concealing facts contradicting it.

Puncturing the narrative, molecular biologist Alina Chan of MIT collaborated with Matt Ridley, bestselling author of *Genome,* to publish a 2022 book carefully examining the virus's origin.[31] In an interview on independent media channel *Rising,* Chan pointed out that the discovery of the NIH's "gain-of-function" grants to the Wuhan lab in 2018 was "like uncovering a 2018 proposal for putting horns on horses in a lab, and then, at the end of 2019, seeing unicorns in Wuhan."[32]

Peter Daszak was the man who perhaps most vehemently rejected a lab origin of the virus, but a colleague of his was just as adamant. NIAID Director Anthony Fauci testified repeatedly to Congress at the time that the zoonosis theory was an *absolute certainty.* There was zero question about it in his mind. The very suggestion of a lab origin was "preposterous," he declared.[33] "The most ridiculous majestic leap I've ever heard of."[34] Fauci also refused to acknowledge publicly that his organization had funded Daszak's EcoHealth Alliance and Shi's risky "gain of function" research. Going further in an interview with MSNBC, Fauci declared not only that the virus was certainly of natural origin but that those who disagreed with him on the matter disagreed not with him but with *science itself.*[35] It was a claim of infallibility, the way a dictator or pope might respond to criticism. Much of his credibility would turn on this remark, which he repeated many times.

Censorship Kills

The month of August 2021 wreaked havoc on the credibility of both the *Times* and Fauci. Evidence emerged that the newspaper had accepted millions of dollars in payments from the Chinese government to run coverage approved by the Chinese on topics concerning China.[36] Additional published evidence proved that the NIH had in fact funded the research[37] and that Fauci and other officials had coordinated with media organizations[38] to discredit scientists supporting the lab leak theory.[39] As public opinion shifted toward the lab leak theory, cracks appeared in many experts' statements.

Fauci, for one, changed his tune when speaking to CNN.[40] He claimed he had "always kept an open mind" about a lab origin. President Joe Biden, who had never publicly questioned the "zoonosis" theory, responded to public outcry and requested an intelligence review. The intelligence agencies came back three months later without a conclusive finding, but there was a consensus across the agencies that the lab leak theory was plausible.[41] The *Lancet* itself, the prestigious medical journal that had published Daszak's team's original paper "strongly condemning conspiracy theories" about the virus's origin, changed course in 2022 and deemed a lab origin possible.[42]

Yet, the idea was *still* treated in the corporate media as "dangerous misinformation." Even after countless doctors, innumerable scientists, and fully 72% of the American public declared belief that the virus had originated in a lab, the corporate media ridiculed the idea if it mentioned it at all.

Why would this be? The scientific community was not certain about the virus's origin, but the *New York Times,* CNN, NPR, and MSNBC all silenced and censored one side of a scientific debate. Why?

We will investigate this question in this book. It is essential to understand how and why news narratives are managed. Censoring mere questions about the origin of *sars-cov-2* impaired scientific study of the virus at a time when open inquiry might have saved thousands of lives.

Well into 2022, the *New York Times* was still distorting this story. A February 27, 2022 piece, "New Research Points to Wuhan Market as Pandemic Origin," purported to present conclusive evidence to support its long-held side but in fact ran over the same ground. What was new were some fancy graphics depicting an analysis of known data. It was interesting, but in no way did the piece provide what the headline promised, proof about the provenance of the virus.[43] The *Times* has not run a neutral story on the topic yet, let alone a story acknowledging the preponderance of evidence favoring a lab origin. Why?

This censorship harms humanity to this day.

A NEW KIND OF SILENCE

"WE CAN'T COMPLETE THIS REQUEST. THIS LINK HAS BEEN IDENTIFIED by Twitter as potentially harmful."

These were the words on a tweet on my feed in October of 2020. It was just weeks before the presidential election. The link in the tweet was a *New York Post* article revealing new details about Joe Biden's alleged involvement in a Ukrainian corruption scandal and his son Hunter's potential role in it.[44]

But I couldn't follow the link nor could I retweet it. Twitter disabled everything about the tweet.[45] I visited the *New York Post's* own Twitter account.

Tweets are not available right now.

The entire account was disabled.

On Facebook, the story was suppressed as well.

Was the story true? What was established at the time was that Hunter Biden had been hired by the Ukrainian energy firm Burisma in 2014 and paid at least $600,000 annually for sitting on the company's board and otherwise doing relatively little. All media sources acknowledged that Burisma had been under domestic investigation for corruption at the time, and a man named Viktor Shokin, Ukraine's Prosecutor General, had been leading the investigation.[46] It was also verifiable fact that Shokin had been abruptly fired during the investigation of Burisma. What was unclear was whether Shokin had been fired because of a request by the Biden family.

There was more. Joe Biden had boasted about getting Shokin fired in a talk he gave to the Council on Foreign Relations in 2018, so that part was no longer in dispute. The CFR is a powerful, CIA-connected think tank[47] generally focused on analyzing international events (and, more often than not, providing justification for the United States to go to war). In his remarks to the CFR, Biden declared that as vice president in 2015 he had been at a meeting in Ukraine with senior officials who were urgently requesting a $1 billion loan guarantee.

On that day, Biden said, he forced the firing of Shokin. "I looked at them and said, 'I'm leaving in six hours. If the prosecutor is not fired, you're not getting the money.' Well, son of a bitch. He got fired."[48]

So, in October 2020, as I tried to follow that tweet, the only part of this putative corruption scandal that remained unclear was *why* Biden had forced the firing of Shokin and whether Hunter had communicated to his father that Burisma wanted Shokin fired *before* the actual termination had taken place. This one missing link was what the *New York Post* article claimed to establish. The *Post* had apparently obtained an email from April 2015 in which Ukrainian officials thanked Hunter for arranging a meeting with his father in Washington D.C.[49]

Doublespeak & Distraction

The *Post* maintained it had received this email from someone who had found it on one of Hunter Biden's laptop computers in a repair shop. The laptop's provenance was under dispute, and while there was no evidence it had come from anywhere other than Hunter Biden's own possession, a piece appeared a week later in the *Washington Post* entitled, "Insisting that the Hunter Biden Laptop is Fake is a Trap. So is Insisting that It's Real."[50] The headline's bizarre doublespeak presaged a nonsensical assertion in the article: "We must treat the Hunter Biden leaks as if they were a foreign intelligence operation—even if they probably aren't."

The piece insinuated that *anything* that ran counter to the establishment narrative should be *presumed* to be disinformation even if evidence suggests otherwise.

The mainstream establishment narrative was that the Bidens didn't engage in corruption in Ukraine.[51] Thus, according to the article, any evidence to the contrary should be considered "fake news." It was a perplexing angle to say the least, as it essentially invalidated the notion of investigative reporting. If articles that run counter to the mainstream narrative are suppressed, you do not have a Free Press.

Why would a newspaper as prestigious as the *Washington Post* instruct its readers this way?

Four days earlier, National Intelligence Director John Ratcliffe had publicly stated that the emails obtained by the *New York Post* "had nothing to do with Russian disinformation."[52] Furthermore, neither of the Bidens disputed the emails' authenticity when asked directly.

But none of that mattered. As we will see throughout this book, the hand of the intelligence agencies often manipulates important stories in the mainstream media via *nefarious bias*. In this case, the *Washington Post* used a letter signed by a gaggle of former intelligence agents suggesting that while there was no actual evidence, Russia *might* have been behind the discovery of the emails and the laptop, and thus the story *should* be censored. "We want to emphasize," the letter stated, "we do not know if the emails... are genuine or not, and we do not have evidence of Russian involvement... but [we're] suspicious of Russian involvement."

And that was it, enough for the *Washington Post*. The newspaper ran with the letter's doublespeak, and the mainstream media followed, calling the revelations in the emails "disinformation" and "Russian operations" even if they "probably weren't."[53] The notion that Russian agents had conspired to plant Biden's laptop in a repair shop was simply passed along based on *biased* coverage by the *Washington Post*. It was a conspiracy theory that didn't need evidence.

And then the story just went away until after the election.

Why? How did *nefarious bias* distort this mainstream media coverage?

As for the tweets, they remained censored. The account of the *New York Post* remained disabled for sixteen days, until the eve of the election.

After the election was won by his father, Hunter Biden made an unusual appearance on CBS's *Sunday Morning*. Show host Tracy Smith asked about the laptop. Hunter declined to confirm or deny that the laptop was his, holding up his hands. "Who knows?" He shrugged.[54]

Tracy Smith pressed him further. Hunter Biden just smiled quizzically. Maybe it was his, maybe it wasn't. Maybe it was planted by Russia, maybe it wasn't. He declined to clarify.

Six months later, when Ben Schreckinger's meticulous book *The Bidens* was published, the world learned the truth: the laptop and the emails were all genuine.[55] Six months after that, the *New York Times* and *Washington Post* finally, quietly admitted it.[56] The gaggle of intelligence agents with their tendentious assumptions had been wrong. Russia had not been involved.

The censorship, of course, had already done its damage. Twitter's and Facebook's suppression of authentic reporting curtailed our Free Press on the eve of an election.[57] And the episode revealed something more important to our understanding of our modern news world. Social media censorship of this story had a larger impact than the mainstream media's insistence that it was "fake." A handful of employees at Twitter and Facebook were able to shut down the story, prevent its dissemination, and all but remove it from public awareness. They banned the story, and the rest of the establishment media simply followed suit and dismissed it.[58] Social media assumed more power than the news organizations themselves in this instance, a trend that has accelerated in the years since.

With the origin of the virus, the corporate media screened, censored, and manipulated the flow of news and information about consequential events. Now, on the eve of the nation's quadrennial general election, the social media companies performed the manipulation and censorship. We no longer have to worry only about the *sources* of the news but also about the *filters* placed on the news by monopolistic technology corporations.

A PHANTOM MENACE

HIGH ON A RUGGED MOUNTAINSIDE IN AFGHANISTAN, A TALIBAN fighter pulled the trigger, firing a Russian hand-held rocket launcher at a United States military compound half a mile away. With a thunderous explosion, the rocket slammed into the compound, injuring a dozen US soldiers and killing two. It was a ferocious and bold strike, financed by Russia. President Trump had gone too soft on Putin, and American soldiers were paying the price. Trump's popular idea of negotiating a withdrawal from Afghanistan looked foolish and premature.

It was July 2020. The election race between Biden and Trump was heating up, and the *Washington Post, Wall Street Journal,* and *New York Times* all reported on the attack, quoting numerous eyewitness accounts as well as diplomats who spoke on the record about a program whereby the Russian government "paid bounties" to the Taliban for attacks on American soldiers.[59]

The only problem was that none of that had happened.

There was no attack, no rocket launcher, no explosion. There were no eyewitness accounts nor diplomats speaking on the record. There was no evidence of any of it.

There was only the *New York Times* article speculating that these attacks were happening, speculating that Russia was funding them, quoting un-named "intelligence sources," and placing the alleged horrors at Trump's feet. "Russia Secretly Offered Afghan Militants Bounties to Kill US Troops, Intelligence Says" ran the headline.[60]

The *Post* and *Journal* echoed the *Times* like dutiful mockingbirds, publishing supporting pieces with a similar lack of actual evidence. "Russian Bounties To Taliban-Linked Militants Resulted In Deaths Of U.S. Troops, According To Intelligence Assessments" was the *Post's* headline.[61]

Not only was there no evidence that these attacks were happening, the attacks were objectively unlikely. Trump was publicly advocating a *withdrawal* from Afghanistan at the time, so why would Afghani troops launch a new attack that would provoke American troops? Precious little evidence of casualties emerged on the ground, and even if these unlikely, unproven attacks were taking place, there was no evidence that Russia was involved. It seemed odd that Taliban fighters, who solemnly swear to defend their country against foreign invaders, would need any incentive from Russia to attack occupying American forces.

But the *Times* story was picked up by the *Post* and the *Journal*, followed by news outlets around the country, and each outlet amplified the story despite its lack of evidence, logic, and named sources. Troop withdrawal from Afghanistan was something the *Times* and *Post* had already editorialized against, so it was plausible the papers were simply putting out a biased interpretation of events on behalf of some group that didn't want troops withdrawn from Afghanistan.[62] This is *propaganda*.

The story was in fact speculation about an unproven conspiracy—that Russians were paying Afghanis to attack Americans.[63] But the story was permitted to circulate freely on both Twitter and Facebook as well.

Why wasn't it suppressed as other unproven "conspiracy theories" were? Far more evidence supported the allegations about the Bidens' corruption in Ukraine, yet that story had been suppressed. Why?

If they justified the censorship as an effort to prevent the spread of questionable news on the eve of an election, why the double standard? Why did Facebook and Twitter, in particular, get involved on behalf of one candidate?

That was the summer of 2020 when, for perhaps the first time, the power that social media giants Facebook, YouTube, Twitter, and Google wielded over the news narrative rivaled the power long held by the establishment media.

Once in office, half a year later, the Biden administration and the corporate media quietly acknowledged that the evidence had been "insufficient"[64] and "far from conclusive"[65] about the whole thing—the "bounties," the Russian guidance, and the alleged attacks.

How could the corporate media deceive the American public about such an important matter? Why did these newer corporations behave so similarly to the corporate news organizations?

THE PROMISE OF A FREE PRESS

THE FOUR STORIES WE'VE EXPLORED EACH END WITH QUESTIONS rather than conclusions. These are the questions we will explore in this book. Much like the Epstein crimes we examined in the Introduction, each of the stories in this chapter present an event that was covered in a partially accurate but deeply biased manner. Together, these four stories sketch a picture of the distortion in today's American media—the bias, censorship, and propaganda that endanger our cherished Free Press.

We will examine and distinguish the different types of *bias* that led to this censorship and propaganda in the next several chapters. Before we do, it's important to remember the essential role of a Free Press in a free society. The role of journalist is the only non-political occupation directly mentioned in the US Constitution. The roles that journalism plays in maintaining a free and democratic society are ineffable and profound. These are the duties the press must play in an open and sustainable democracy:

1. **Watchdog.** The press must hold the powerful to account by investigating and reporting on misdeeds. In both government and corporate settings, the press should try to vet and expose the true viewpoints and hidden aims of both those in power and those who aspire to power. This role is the most important, the one that prompted Thomas Jefferson to say, "Left to me to decide whether we should have a gov-

ernment without newspapers or newspapers without a government, I should not hesitate a moment to prefer the latter." A Free Press is the best safeguard against tyranny, and the stifling of a Free Press is one of the earliest indicators that tyranny is on the horizon. Unfortunately, the Watchdog role is the role our corporate media most clearly abdicates today. This is a key reason for the rise of independent media.

2. **Smorgasbord.** The press should provide a broad array of viewpoints on current issues rather than be confined to the views of only one class or political persuasion. Most importantly, abundant viewpoints that differ from the government's must be allowed. Democracy depends on the open consideration of a wide variety of opinions prior to official debates and votes. Unfortunately, the variety of viewpoints offered in corporate media has dwindled for decades. Corporate consolidation throughout the twentieth century and into the first decade of the twenty-first reduced media diversity and necessitated a rise of independent media to fulfill this role. A diverse Smorgasbord is necessary for important minority viewpoints to be considered. The Constitution doesn't mention "professional journalists." *Everyone* is free to print pamphlets, make websites, write letters, or distribute emails to inform and persuade fellow citizens.

3. **Bulletin.** The press should provide citizens with a basic list of recent and upcoming events. While this role is less important than the other two, it is nonetheless essential that the citizens of a democracy are accurately informed in a timely fashion about political events, natural disasters, and military conflicts. Analysis and opinion about these events are covered by the press's other roles; this role is the simple notification that events important to the citizenry have happened or are scheduled to happen.

Those are the three indispensable roles of the press. In this book, we'll examine how and why the corporate and independent media are fulfilling—or abandoning—these duties and whether their failings are deliberate or accidental. On a practical side note, you'll know you're enjoying a balanced media diet when your media sources fulfill these three duties.

Wolves in Sheep's Clothing

According to the American Press Institute, the purpose of journalism is to "provide citizens with the information they need to make the best possible decisions about their lives, their communities, their societies, and their governments."[66] Many professional journalists and deans of journalism schools speak proudly of their field as a crusading profession and trumpet their assiduous discharging of the three duties of the press. Academics who study the media see its role as socializing citizens and shaping our mainstream culture. Sociologists value news as a utility to empower the informed. They refer to our culture as "a 'mediated' culture where media reflects and creates culture."[67]

In practice, however, as we've seen in this chapter, much of mainstream corporate media is something far different. While great journalism does still take place at corporate media conglomerates, mainstream media outlets typically just reiterate the line of other corporate media sources, promoting in chorus the official story—even if it's unreliable, unverified, or wholly untrue. Twenty-first-century mainstream media delivers to Americans, in the average case, half-truths replete with bias and misinformation masquerading as truth, and, in the worst case, censorship and outright propaganda about news of paramount importance.

As the saying goes, "the wolf in sheep's clothing is more dangerous than the wolf." As we will see in this book, biased mainstream media posing as objective is more deleterious to American democracy than is independent media even with its own biases.

In the cases we've examined so far, journalists often simply passed along the words of sources who wanted to deliberately manipulate citizens' minds for political or personal reasons, including the words of elected officials, intelligence agents, and corporate public relations representatives.

The public—you and I—must take it upon ourselves to decipher what is left out of the story. A balanced media diet, and the *media consciousness* such a breadth of perspectives engenders, is the best way to do this. It is for this reason so many alternative voices are emerging.

The transformation underway in American consciousness is unfolding precisely because the public's necessary expectations of the media go unfulfilled. Rather than broadening and transforming itself, the corporate media behemoths today push and pull viewers into habitual echo chambers, knowing full well that people are more comfortable and more easily satisfied hearing what they want to hear. In this way, the corporate media is ripping us apart as a society rather than performing the press's essential roles in a democracy.

One way we know the corporate media is failing in these roles is the success of independent journalists. Julian Assange's success in revealing important truths and misdeeds around the world—and the dangerous ways the establishment have persecuted and imprisoned him—provides ample evidence of the corporate media's failings in all three of its roles.[68] Assange's story and journalistic work present a complex and compelling case, and we examine it in detail in Chapter 12. Were Assange not in prison in 2020, how much more might we have known about Epstein's associates, the origins of covid, and social media censorship?

This book is for those who are inspired to leave the comfort of echo chambers, if only for a few hours a week, and walk a path to *media consciousness*. Not only will this consciousness help you become better informed, but it will help you notice misinformation in the legacy media. No one media conglomerate or esteemed pundit should entirely form a person's perspective, and no large media outlet should survive that abdicates its prescribed roles in favor of deliberately deceiving its readers.

An Invisible Hand

We will also examine the rise of social media. As we saw in the Hunter Biden laptop story, legitimate investigative journalism is now censored by tech corporations Google, Facebook, and Twitter as often as by the legacy corporate media behemoths. Social media often wields power over the news narrative that equals or surpasses the power of cable news networks, magazines, and newspapers. For this reason, and because of the essential importance of Free Speech and a Free Press in a functional democracy, we will pay particular attention to the censorship executed in social media today, as it poses a clear and present danger to our democracy as well as to modern science.

> *"Whoever would overthrow the Liberty of a Nation, must begin by subduing the Freeness of Speech."*
> —Benjamin Franklin

Some will argue that when, say, Google's YouTube deliberately suppresses a particular viewpoint, it does not violate constitutional Free Speech because Google is a private company rather than an arm of the government. We will address this in detail in Chapter 9 and show that, for several reasons, such censorship violates constitutional speech. Even outside of constitutional concerns, *any* kind of censorship, whether practiced by a government, a church, or a corporation is a danger to science, democracy, and other bedrock cultural values upon which our society is built. This book presents an analysis of the manipulation of news narratives in America by powerful social and corporate media corporations. In this analysis, censorship plays an enormous role alongside disinformation, propaganda, and bias.

Social media and corporate media are blinding Americans to the true state of the world, and this book also presents the optimal solutions to this predicament. On an individual level, a Balanced Media Diet and *media consciousness* are the best available paths forward. At the institutional level, for the insidious problems of censorship and disinformation, the best solution is a sensible regulatory framework.

Through their new monopolies, Facebook and Google amassed towering power before most Americans noticed their potent roles in society, and they must be regulated more strenuously. There are two relevant regulatory models—*publisher* and *utility*—and we must choose one. The *publisher* regulatory model allows a corporation (for instance, a book publisher) to print only what it wants to print and to retain some intellectual property rights on what is published; these corporations are fully liable for anything illegal they publish, such as libel, and they may not attain a monopoly in any large geographical area. The *utility* model frees a corporation (a phone company, for instance) from any liability for what is said over its network and allows monopoly market share in some instances; these corporations may not choose who gets to speak or what may be said on their networks. In short, Facebook and YouTube and the others *either* get to censor, demote, promote, "shadowban," and silence certain users, *or* they get immunity from legal prosecution for what users post, but not both. While both models have some appeal, we'll see that the *utility* model is the best fit for these corporations. Independent media is coming of age and increasingly fulfilling the key roles of the press. It is largely through social media channels that news is now distributed. These channels must not act as thought police.

FOR EVERY GALILEO, THERE WILL BE AN INQUISITION

MANY PUNDITS IN CORPORATE MEDIA TAKE TIME OUT OF THEIR BUSY days to decry the existence of independent media. This is increasing as the New Enlightenment arrives. Rachel Maddow, for instance, on MSNBC, has told her viewers not to trust news or perspectives that don't carry the imprimatur of mainstream media.[69] Don't do your own research, a similarly anti-intellectual *New York Times* piece suggested in 2021. "Critical thinking ... isn't helping," the piece declared,[70] warning readers that they would come to incorrect conclusions if they started reading independent media and thinking for themselves. Independent media threatens traditional establishment media power, so they disparage it.

These pundits purport to be protecting you from disinformation or errors in judgment, but the underlying goal is to maintain their hold on the news narrative. They will always recommend that you don't trust your own mental faculties to compare the perspectives and findings of their publications with those of independent media. Better to trust them and their chosen experts, they will say. Much as the Roman Catholic Church did five hundred years ago when the first Enlightenment was arriving, the powerful media corporations today would prefer it if you didn't read too broadly nor think for yourself.

They neglect to mention that Free Speech and a Free Press—and the free thought and free inquiry they engender—are prerequisites for a functioning democracy. A multitude of divergent news sources is precisely what the framers of the Constitution envisioned. The ferment of oppositional ideas rolling off of printing presses was common in the Age of the Enlightenment that birthed our American Revolution and Constitution. The concept of "objective journalism"—that there could be a neutral accounting of daily events—wasn't even considered by America's founders; the notion is barely one hundred years old and was invented at about the same time as propaganda. We will explore in Chapter 11 the era in which "objective journalism," combined with sophisticated propaganda, took control of the news narrative. Objectivity is not bad, of course. The ineluctable problem lies in determining whose accounts are objective.

Free Speech and a Free Press are necessary preconditions for science and democracy. With them in place, the search for truth, the quest for solutions to societal problems, and the pursuit of happiness are not only possible but likely natural occurrences due to innate human instinct and longing. Without them, it is impossible to arrive reliably at the truth about anything because powerful interests who prefer the status quo will conceal the purpose of their activities. For every Galileo, there will be an Inquisition. It is thus far better to have many diverse sources of news and analysis—both corporate media and independent media, in today's world—than to hope and pretend that one set of news sources will always be truthful.

The term *corporate media,* for the sake of this book, refers to the big media news channels and publications funded and run by billionaires and large corporations. *Independent media* essentially refers to everything else: smaller publications, bloggers, podcasters, and independent social media journalists.

The *New York Times* generally dismisses concerns about censorship, and as the historic leader of narrative management in the United States, the *Times* leads the charge *against* the New Enlightenment. The *Times* is the nation's largest daily newspaper and perhaps the world's most prestigious, one that styles itself "the paper of record." The *Times* is an organization we will spend significant time examining in this book, although no segment of the corporate media will be spared. The *Times* didn't cover Epstein's pedophilia ring when it mattered or the American connections to the Wuhan lab. It raised doubts not about Twitter's censorship of fellow New York newspaper the *New York Post* but about the Hunter Biden revelations themselves, effectively abetting the censorship. The *Times* extravagantly promoted the anonymously-sourced story on the "Russian bounties" and never retracted it. It has run negative pieces that implicitly justify, rather than oppose, censorship of anti-establishment journalists such as Lee Camp, Del Bigtree, and others, as we'll explore later. Its biased reporting served to control one of our nation's most precious treasures: the *narrative*.

We are a species that makes sense of the world through stories. Our religions are essentially stories that we tell each other to describe our existence. We find meaning every day in the stories we share with each other about why we're here, what we're doing, what we hope for, and what we fear. The *narrative* is this same set of stories told at a societal or national level. The *narrative* is thus the water in which we swim as we seek to understand our place in the flow of human events.

When examining the news narratives of the Trump presidency in retrospect, it's almost as if an invisible hand managed the narratives. This invisible hand, it turns out, isn't so invisible when one begins to look. We start our examination of that concealed force now by turning the clock back to a pivotal decade, the 1960s.

A NOTE FOR REVIEWERS

IF YOU'RE PREPARING TO REVIEW THIS BOOK, THANK YOU! PLEASE TAKE a moment to consider whether the publication in which you plan to publish your review is one that practices the techniques of distortion documented in this book.

To ensure that your review does not in fact become propaganda to dismiss legitimate inquiry into the functioning of our media, please ensure that your review answers at least these four questions:

1. Did you read the whole book?

2. Are you basing your review on the entirety of the book or just on one or two parts of it?

3. Are you making any use of the slur "conspiracy theorist" in your review? I explain why this term is an anti-intellectual epithet in a note following the next chapter.

4. What parent organization is the ultimate owner of your publication?

Ok, that's it. Four questions. Not too much to ask, I hope. Thank you very much indeed for your time and for your review.

2

A HISTORY OF LIES

"You don't need to manipulate Time *magazine, for example,*
because there are Agency people at the management level."

William Bader, The Church Committee

IT WAS A BRIGHT, SUNNY DAY IN DALLAS. PRESIDENT JOHN F. KENNEDY
waved at onlookers from the open seats of a black convertible limousine. The
limo slowly turned a corner. Gunshots rang out, and the president's head
slumped forward. Blood ran down the right lapel of his charcoal blazer. His
wife, Jackie, wearing a pink hat and coat, reached over to touch her husband's
head.

Minutes later, the rest of America learned of the assassination, the defining
domestic political event of the twentieth Century. The murder shook the nation's political and moral conscience to its foundations. The event wouldn't
be alone, for as Shakespeare wrote, "when sorrows come, they come not single spies, but in battalions." Mysterious assassinations would take the lives of
Robert F. Kennedy, Martin Luther King, Jr., Malcolm X, and other prominent leaders in the ensuing years. Nixon would resign over Watergate. Coups
with covert American support would topple governments in Chile, Ethiopia,
and Angola. Unsettling events unfolded, seemingly piling conspiracy on top

of conspiracy, and for the first time, Americans endured an era of censorship and disinformation in the corporate news media. Much of this media manipulation, we now know, was undertaken by intelligence agencies of our own US government.

Investigative journalism, government whistleblowers, and a remarkable set of Congressional hearings in the wake of the turbulent years (1963-1974) exposed this extensive corporate media distortion. In this chapter, we explore these revelations in order to understand one type of media bias, *nefarious bias*.

The Church Committee

In 1970, a captain in Army Intelligence by the name of Christopher Pyle turned whistleblower and kicked off an era of government revelations. Pyle described for the public an extensive, covert domestic military spying operation on American citizens. Pyle disclosed that, for instance, plainclothes intelligence officers attended every US political protest that attracted more than twenty people.[12]

Several years later, investigative journalist Seymour Hersh also revealed widespread secret surveillance of American citizens. His bombshell exposé[3] focused on the CIA's interventions[4] in Chile[5] but also touched on other CIA activities.[6]

The sobriquet "conspiracy theorist" was born in this era. It was a new label, a tag the corporate media attached to Americans who attempted to explain the underlying forces behind the coups, assassinations, domestic spying, and other conspiracies that had unfolded over a single tumultuous decade. This epithet is an important element of American censorship and propaganda, and we'll examine its use in depth at the end of this chapter.

This era of "conspiracy theories" reached a crescendo in 1974 and led to a Congressional inquiry in 1975. The Church Committee, led by Senator Frank Church, a Democrat from Idaho, was a series of groundbreaking hearings that delved into the unsettling revelations, suspected conspiracies, and perceived overreach by the executive branch and by the CIA, NSA, and IRS over the preceding decade. The stated goal of the committee was to determine who knew what when—before, during, and after—the many coups and assassinations.

What resulted was breathtaking: the largest series of official disclosures of clandestine government activities in national history. The committee uncovered:

◈ *Operation Shamrock*, a CIA program monitoring Americans' phone and telegram conversations over three decades.

◈ *Operation MK-Ultra*, an extensive program of mind-control experiments in which CIA agents and scientists attempted to brainwash Americans with a bizarre and horrifying variety of techniques over several decades.

◈ *Cointelpro*, an FBI operation that covertly infiltrated, sabotaged, and discredited feminist, socialist, antiwar, and Black political organizations for twenty years.

OPERATION MOCKINGBIRD

THOSE REVELATIONS WERE BOMBSHELLS THAT ROCKED THE NATION'S conscience, confirming the presence of government conspiracies that many Americans had long deemed impossible, unthinkable, or paranoid. Many "conspiracy theorists" were proven correct, at least partially. But it was another stunning disclosure of the Church Committee hearings that is most useful and relevant for this examination of media manipulation in the United States, a revelation that changed Americans' understanding of our ostensibly impartial news media.

Near the end of the hearings, as some of the final discoveries were released, the American people learned of Operation Mockingbird. This operation was a secret campaign run by our intelligence agencies to influence major media organizations and control the reporting of the news. Under Mockingbird, the CIA recruited leading American journalists into a network of paid correspondents to present news, analysis, and viewpoints that the CIA sought to amplify.[7] The CIA also founded newspapers, magazines, student associations, cultural organizations, and entire publishing companies as fronts to manipulate opinion and facilitate domestic and international spying. Through this operation, the CIA infiltrated and manipulated mainstream news media organizations, news coverage, and political opinion for at least three decades.

This extensive network of propagandists and spies worked so well that the influence of these organizations and journalist-spies over political campaigns both here and abroad grew in concert with covert actions by other operating units of the CIA. In many cases, leading journalists at major newspapers and television networks both in the US and abroad were recruited into the program via clandestine interviews. In other cases, the CIA recommended that the news media organizations hire certain new journalists. As a third option, the Agency directly placed its own agents into employment positions at media organizations with the (usually covert) knowledge and blessing of organizational ownership. Whatever route each particular journalist took to join the program, *Operation Mockingbird* cultivated deep relationships with them. Their ranks included some of the country's most prominent journalists, hosts, and writers. These secret relationships with the CIA often lasted decades.

All of this directly violated the Smith-Mundt Act of 1948, which prohibited government propaganda within the United States. The law was meant to highlight a difference between "free" American news media and the propaganda-driven media of the Soviet Union. Smith-Mundt remained the law of the land until it was repealed under President Obama in 2014 as we'll examine later.

THE MIGHTY WURLITZER

IT REMAINS DIFFICULT EVEN TODAY TO KNOW THE PRECISE NUMBER OF journalists who were, are, or have been part of Mockingbird. The number is probably in the thousands. Investigative journalist Carl Bernstein published a landmark article in *Rolling Stone* in 1977 entitled "The CIA and the Media," which assiduously detailed the Church Committee's revelations about Operation Mockingbird.[8] Bernstein pointed out that in the 1950s and 1960s alone, at least 400 journalists were part of this CIA propaganda operation, although he repeatedly said that the number was "probably much higher." We know approximately $1.1 billion (in adjusted 2022 dollars) was spent on this program *each year*, much of it in direct payments to journalists and writers. That buys a lot of writing. In the words of the Church Committee:

> The CIA currently maintains a network of several hundred foreign individuals around the world who provide intelligence for the CIA and at times attempt to influence opinion through the use of covert propaganda. These individuals provide the CIA with direct access to a large number of newspapers and periodicals, scores of press services and news agencies, radio and television stations, commercial book publishers, and other foreign media outlets.[9]

This galaxy of subservient journalists came to have its own nickname within the CIA: "The Mighty Wurlitzer." A Wurlitzer is a pipe organ, one of the largest musical instruments ever created and the largest of the many organs installed in music halls in the first half of the twentieth century. These organs could play an enormous range of sounds, and at impressive volumes, essentially allowing a single player to create the sounds of an entire orchestra.

Frank Wisner, carrying the title Deputy Director of Plans at the CIA when he oversaw the inception of Operation Mockingbird in 1948, recruited well-known journalists at most of the nation's largest media organizations as well as minor journalists across the American media landscape.[10] He eventually nicknamed the system after a Wurlitzer, believing he could play any "note" at any time and disseminate any news report—be it true or false—throughout the country and the world.[11]

In *The Mighty Wurlitzer: How the CIA Played America*, published by Harvard University Press in 2008, Professor Hugh Wilford describes the initial attitude of media organizations toward Mockingbird:

> Many of the United States's best-known newspapers cooperated with the CIA as a matter of policy. Arthur Hays Sulzberger, publisher of the *New York Times*, was a good friend of [CIA Director] Allen Dulles and signed a secrecy agreement with the Agency, although he delegated liaison duties to subordinates so as to give himself plausible deniability. Under the terms of this arrangement, the *Times* provided at least ten CIA officers with cover as reporters or clerical staff in its foreign bureaus, while genuine employees of the paper were encouraged to pass on information to the Agency...

Another eminent news executive on friendly terms with Dulles was William Paley of CBS, whose new president, Sig Mickelson (later chief of the [CIA-funded] Radio Free Europe), was in such constant telephone contact with CIA headquarters that... he installed a private line that bypassed the CBS switchboard. Among the services provided to the Agency by Paley and Mickelson was a "recruiting-and-cover capability" like that offered by the *New York Times.*[12]

Operation Mockingbird was an immediate, smashing success. Wisner rarely ran into trouble hiring or placing a journalist or a senior editor in any of the nation's major publications or television networks. The Wurlitzer came to life with a symphonic start in the 1950s and continued to add notes, pipes, sounds, and range throughout the 1960s and into the 1970s.

In *Katharine the Great: Katharine Graham and Her Washington Post Empire*, a book about a longtime owner of the *Post* and that paper's many connections to the CIA, author Deborah Davis adds to our picture of Wisner's Wurlitzer and its speedy success:

> By the early 1950s, Wisner had implemented his plan and "owned" respected members of the *New York Times*, *Newsweek*, CBS, and other communications vehicles, plus stringers, four to six hundred in all. Each one was a separate "operation," requiring a code name, a field supervisor, and a field office, at an annual cost of tens or hundreds of thousands of dollars—there has never been an accurate accounting. Some of these journalists thought of themselves as helpers of the agency, some simply as patriots who wanted to run stories that would benefit their country; some did not know where their information was going, or did not know information they received was "planted" with them. The Agency considered all of them to be operatives... Wisner discussed with [Philip Graham, publisher of the *Washington Post*] which journalists were for sale and at what price ("You could get a journalist cheaper than a good call girl," the former Agency man said, "for a couple hundred dollars a month"), how to handle them, where to place them, and what sorts of stories to produce.[13]

Carl Bernstein's groundbreaking piece provides further details into the fruitful relationship between Wisner and management at the *Washington Post*:

> When *Newsweek* was purchased by the Washington Post Company, publisher Philip Graham was informed by Agency officials that the CIA occasionally

used the magazine for cover purposes, according to CIA sources. "It was widely known that Phil Graham was somebody you could get help from," said a former deputy director of the Agency. "Frank Wisner dealt with him." Wisner, deputy director of the CIA from 1950 until shortly before his suicide in 1965, was the Agency's premier orchestrator of "black" operations, including many in which journalists were involved. Wisner liked to boast of his "mighty Wurlitzer," a wondrous propaganda instrument he built, and played, with help from the press. Phil Graham was probably Wisner's closest friend. But Graham, who committed suicide in 1963, apparently knew little of the specifics of any covert arrangements with *Newsweek*, CIA sources said.[14]

While the *Washington Post* and CBS played major parts in Mockingbird, many accounts we have today clearly show that the *New York Times* was from the start the most useful—and most used—media organization. The close friendship between CIA Director Dulles and *Times* publisher Arthur Hays Sulzberger accelerated the relationship between the two powerful organizations, and the prestigious paper proved a reliable vehicle for Mockingbird news dissemination. Sulzberger was publisher of the *Times* from 1935-61, and Dulles was Director of the CIA from 1953-61, so they were consistent at the top as well.

When the Church Committee solicited testimony from the CIA about Mockingbird, officials gave unusually forthcoming testimony about certain aspects of the operation, but they all went to great lengths to minimize two components of the operation. They obfuscated the overall *number* of journalists participating. And they were reticent about the extent to which it operated as a vehicle for *domestic* propaganda as well as for international influence and espionage. The hearings revealed repeated inconsistencies in their answers.

At first, the CIA suggested that only "several dozen writers" participated and that the entire operation targeted only international audiences in countries at risk of "going communist." But by the time the hearings were complete and the findings were published, albeit partially redacted, and investigative journalists like Bernstein were able to pore through the released documents, a different reality emerged. It became clear that at least hundreds—and probably thousands—of journalists had participated in some way and many wrote for American audiences.

The simplest way to determine the breadth and depth of Operation Mockingbird would have been for the Church Committee to summon prominent journalists to testify to Congress. This never happened. Despite startling evidence of expansive CIA use of journalists, the Senate Intelligence Committee and its staff chose not to question a single reporter, editor, publisher, or broadcast executive whose CIA relationship was detailed in the files.

To restate this, Congress only questioned people on one side of the arrangement. This massive flaw in the hearings is perhaps why Bernstein subtitled his article, "How America's most powerful news media worked hand in glove with the CIA, and why the Church Committee covered it up."

The CIA also endeavored to present the operation as undertaken only for foreign cover and never for the purpose of disseminating propaganda to domestic audiences. They were largely successful at controlling this part of the inquiry. Bernstein reported many felt the CIA was neither fully honest nor forthcoming:

> Some members of the Church committee and staff feared that Agency officials had gained control of the inquiry and that they were being hoodwinked. "The Agency was extremely clever about it and the committee played right into its hands," said one congressional source familiar with all aspects of the inquiry. "Church and some of the other members were much more interested in making headlines than in doing serious, tough investigating. The Agency pretended to be giving up a lot whenever it was asked about the flashy stuff—assassinations and secret weapons and James Bond operations. Then, when it came to things that they didn't want to give away, that were much more important to the Agency, Colby in particular called in his chits. And the committee bought it."[15]

In their well-researched 2006 book, *Static: Government Liars, Media Cheerleaders, and the People Who Fight Back,* authors Amy and David Goodman delved deeply into the extent to which Mockingbird was employed covertly to disseminate disinformation in the United States.[16] They found that the news wire services were often witting or unwitting conduits.

> One way that the CIA would knowingly route propaganda back to the United States was when it placed stories on the wire services, which were picked up all over the world, including the United States. The Associated Press estimated that in 1977 its material reached half the world's population. The CIA was actively placing false information through the AP, UPI, and Reuters.

The Church Committee's investigation into the use of journalists was supervised by two past and future intelligence officers, William Bader and David Aaron. Both were soon promoted to bigger and better things. Bader would go on to high-level intelligence work at the Defense Department. Aaron would become deputy to Zbigniew Brzezinski, President Jimmy Carter's national security adviser. They were neither fringe nor brief members of the intelligence community. But as supervisors for the Church Committee investigation, both became alarmed at the Operation Mockingbird revelations.

The CIA flatly refused to provide Bader and Aaron with information on all of the journalists involved in Mockingbird, which is why the full number remains unknown. After persistent requests, the CIA produced brief summaries on 400 such journalist-agents, with names and publications redacted, and agreed to provide full information on twenty-five. So, Bader and Aaron reviewed the provided summaries and selected what they hoped would be a representative twenty-five.

From the limited files they received back, the truth became crystal clear. For three decades the CIA had developed and maintained relationships with journalists in the most prominent sectors of the American press corps, including the broadcast networks, the two major newsweekly magazines, and five of the nation's largest newspapers. Despite the omission of names and affiliations from the 25 files—each was "between three and eleven inches thick"—the information was sufficient to tentatively identify either the journalist, his affiliation, or both, particularly because so many of them were well known.

"There is quite an incredible spread of relationships," Bader reported to the senators. "You don't need to manipulate *Time* magazine, for example, because there are Agency people at the management level."[17]

The full committee's final report only scratched the surface.[18] Bowing to the CIA's preferences, it falsely presented Mockingbird as utilizing only a narrow scope of media professionals. It minimized mention, for instance, of the recruitment of clergy and college professors. Senator Gary Hart, who sat on the committee, lamented its shortcomings. "The report hardly reflects what we found. There was a prolonged and elaborate negotiation [with the CIA] over what would be said."

Both Bader and Aaron urged further investigation by the Senate's new permanent CIA oversight committee. Such a deeper dive never occurred.

Bernstein concluded:

Obscuring the facts was relatively simple. No mention was made of the 400 summaries or what they showed. Instead the report noted blandly that some fifty recent contacts with journalists had been studied by the committee staff—thus conveying the impression that the Agency's dealings with the press had been limited to those instances. The Agency files, the report noted, contained little evidence that the editorial content of American news reports had been affected by the CIA's dealings with journalists. Colby's misleading public statements about the use of journalists were repeated without serious contradiction or elaboration. The role of cooperating news executives was given short shrift. The fact that the Agency had concentrated its relationships in the most prominent sectors of the press went unmentioned. That the CIA continued to regard the press as up for grabs was not even suggested.[19]

What we know for certain is that for at least 25 years, the CIA depended on a network of journalists and agents inside media organizations to manipulate the American mainstream media on topics both foreign and domestic. The operation was codenamed "Mockingbird" because of its goal: to be able to place a single article or talking point in one publication, and then listen to all of the "owned" journalists at other organizations mimicking the point of view in their respective publication in a fashion similar to mockingbirds singing call-and-response in the trees.

This mockingbird strategy has two great benefits. First, it drastically reduces the amount of covert, compromising communication that has to happen behind the scenes when rolling out a new story or redirecting coverage of a current story. The communication is essentially out in the open; no secrets are needed. One mockingbird issues the call in a prominent publication, such as the *New York Times* or *Washington Post*, and that article itself is sufficient communication to request a response from other mockingbirds.

Second, this rapid repetition of the same viewpoint, coverage, or analysis maps nicely onto the propaganda techniques pioneered by Edward Bernays and Walter Lippmann in the 1920s and 1930s, which we'll examine later. We human beings are deeply social creatures, frequently checking in with our communities to see if the way we see the world jibes with our friends and peers. This innate desire to see the world similarly makes us easily manipulated when we hear the same viewpoint multiple times from apparently distinct sources. A story heard once may make little impact and be mentally dismissed; a story heard many times from different sources is generally incorporated as truth by an uncritical mind.

The only thing remaining unclear today is whether these mockingbird activities and relationships ever truly ceased.

DO THOSE BIRDS STILL SING?

THE EXISTENCE OF OPERATION MOCKINGBIRD WAS REVEALED BY THE Church Committee. It has been declassified, demystified, and documented in detail. It happened. Intelligence agencies placed writers and editors at American news organizations with assignments to ensure that the goals of the government and of the various intelligence organizations were well represented or dominant in coverage of issues and events.

The question that remains is whether Operation Mockingbird—or something like it—continues today, and if so, what that means for the bias, propaganda, and censorship we see in our news media today. Which news is "fake" and which news is "real" if much of it is manipulated by agents of our intelligence agencies?

The purported end of Mockingbird came on February 11th, 1976, when incoming CIA Director George H. W. Bush made the following declaration as his first public action:

> Effective immediately, the CIA will not enter into any paid or contractual relationship with any full-time or part-time news correspondent accredited by any U.S. news service, newspaper, periodical, radio or television network or station.[20]

At the time of the announcement, the CIA claimed the policy would result in termination of less than half of its relationships with a mere fifty US journalists still affiliated with the Agency. The full number of journalists was never disclosed during or after the Church Committee hearings, so there was no way to know whether this claim that "only" fifty journalists remained in the program was accurate. The text of Bush's announcement noted that the

CIA would continue to "welcome" *voluntary* or *unpaid* cooperation from journalists. Thus, many relationships were permitted to remain in place.

And that's the final word on Mockingbird, at least publicly. Information on any successors to it remains classified.

Signs of Survival

If Operation Mockingbird was so successful, and if propaganda is no longer illegal in the United States, why would we assume Mockingbird manipulation is no longer going on? We will see throughout this book that there are ample reasons to believe this type of media manipulation remains fully operational and has in fact substantially increased.

Before we consider longer examples of Mockingbird-style manipulation, here are several smaller signs that the birds still sing:

- ↦ **Still Recruiting.** Scott Shane, a major *New York Times* writer, was recruited by the CIA in 1979, three years after George H. W. Bush's declaration. After returning from graduate study in England and Russia, Shane received an odd letter with instructions to call a certain phone number. "I called the number," he recalled in 2018. "The woman who answered confirmed that the letter was from the Central Intelligence Agency."[21] Shane today claims he turned down the CIA's interest, but it is curious that he thereafter enjoyed swift success as a journalist at the *Baltimore Sun* and the *New York Times,* traveled frequently to Russia, and penned countless articles specifically about the CIA and NSA. Today, he still writes for the *Times* and regularly covers propaganda-laced topics such as alleged Russian interference in American elections. His career looks very much like a Mockingbird career.

- ↦ **"You've Got To Be More Careful About It."** Sig Mickelson is often referred to as "the man who invented TV news." A broadcasting pioneer, he served as president of CBS for over a decade. Mickelson was asked in 1985 whether he believed, despite the revelations about Operation Mockingbird, that the CIA was *still* covertly working with reporters. His answer:

Yes, I would think probably for a reporter it would continue today. But because of all the revelations of the period of the 1970s, it seems to me a reporter has to be a lot more circumspect when doing it now or he runs the risk of at least being looked at with considerable disfavor by the public. I think you've got to be much more careful about it.[22]

↦ Just An Internship. Prominent CNN anchor Anderson Cooper today stands at the apex of the corporate media ladder. He interned with the CIA for not one but two summers while a student at Yale, in 1988 and 1989.[23] Like Scott Shane, above, he claims he chose not to pursue a career with the Agency and instead chose to become a journalist. Curiously, he had no journalistic training or experience at the time. His subsequent rapid ascent as a television journalist in the ensuing decade saw him travel to Myanmar and Vietnam, anchor news shows at ABC, and in 2001, become one of CNN's famous faces. Today, he hosts presidential debates and anchors his own show. His career has all the markings of a Mockingbird career.

↦ War Propaganda on Public Radio. Eight Psychological Operations ("PsyOps") Army soldiers were secretly placed at NPR[24] and CNN[25] in 1999 to work as interns during the Kosovo War.[26] PsyOps is a nickname for the military unit whose personnel are trained in the production and dissemination of propaganda. Christopher St. John, Commander of a PsyOps unit with 1,200 soldiers and officers stationed at Ft. Bragg, North Carolina, said the cooperation between his unit and the news networks was "a textbook example of the kind of ties the US Army wants with the American media."[27] NPR eventually admitted with obvious embarrassment that the unit did indeed place PsyOps soldiers there as interns and that they had worked from six weeks to four months on its flagship programs *All Things Considered* and *Morning Edition.*

↦ Fake News in Iraq. In 2003, and throughout the Iraq War, the US military secretly paid and placed fake articles in Iraqi newspapers.[28] The articles appeared to be written by everyday Iraqis who supported the US invasion but were, in fact, written by American PsyOps soldiers and intelligence agents. "Here we are, trying to create the principles of democracy in Iraq," said a Pentagon official who opposed the practice in vain. "Every speech we give in that country is about democracy. And we're breaking all the first principles of democracy when we're doing it."

→ **A Facade of Objectivity.** A 2008 report found most "military analysts" appearing on CNN, MSNBC, and other television networks to give ostensibly objective analysis on the Iraq War and the War on Terror are actually employed by the Pentagon. "Hidden behind an appearance of objectivity," reported the *New York Times*, "is a Pentagon information apparatus that has used analysts in a campaign to generate favorable news coverage for the administration's wartime performance."[29] This continues to this day, with networks like ABC, NBC, and Fox News routinely bringing in, for instance, John Brennan as an "expert national security analyst" without mentioning his lifelong career in the CIA.

→ **Pentagon Targets Public Opinion.** As if having their generals and intelligence agents regularly pose on TV as neutral analysts wasn't enough, a 2009 investigation by the AP found that the Pentagon and intelligence agencies spend over $4 billion annually to influence public opinion.[30] A staff of over 27,000 employees work daily at tasks such as placing pro-war propaganda in mainstream newspapers, television shows, and social media under fake names like "Hometown News Network."[31] The true source of the biased opinion pieces and propaganda is rarely disclosed.

→ **Udo Ulfkotte.** This German journalist worked for 25 years as assistant editor of one of Germany's largest newspapers. He blew the whistle in 2014 and revealed his long relationship with the CIA. In explosive interviews that were mostly censored both in European and American media, Ulfkotte explained how CIA operatives trained him to write exclusively pro-American and anti-Russian stories, at times forcing him to publish the works of intelligence agents under his own name.[32] Noncompliance ran the risk of being fired, he revealed, but the mandate to manipulate the news finally became intolerable to him. He spoke out because he feared people in high places were agitating for war with Russia and that journalists, by conforming to CIA pressure, were playing a role in this potentially horrendous crime against humanity. When asked if Germany was the only country whose media was rife with CIA infiltration, Ulfkotte replied:

> No, I think it is especially the case with British journalists, because they have a much closer relationship. It is especially the case with Israeli journalists, of course, [and] with French journalists. . . . It is the case for Australians, journalists from New Zealand, from Taiwan, well, many countries . . . like Jordan for example.[33]

Ulfkotte's story, despite its importance, was never told in the German or American media. He wrote a book to finally reveal the full story, but it has been brutally censored in English-speaking countries. At the time of publishing this book, a search on Amazon for his title, *Journalists for Hire: How the CIA Buys the News*, brings up a page that alternates every few weeks between "currently unavailable" and one copy available for $1,309.50.[34]

➻ **Ken Dilanian.** One of the clearest indications that Mockingbirds still sing today is the story of this prominent reporter for the *Los Angeles Times*. Dilanian was abruptly outed in 2017[35] on account of a FOIA request to the CIA.[36] The CIA rarely fulfills FOIA requests—another of the many laws the organization generally disregards—but this one produced a surprising series of email exchanges. The released emails cover only a few months in 2012. But from even such a small sample, it is clear that Dilanian not only showed articles to the CIA prior to publication and made changes to them after Agency requests, he actively wrote propaganda supporting CIA agendas. "I'm working on a story about congressional oversight of drone strikes that can present a good opportunity," Dilanian wrote in one email to the CIA, explaining that what he intended to report would be "reassuring to the public" about CIA drone strikes.[37]

➻ **The Steele Dossier.** This single document, perhaps the most important document in American politics during the 2010s, is itself evidence of immense intelligence agency manipulation of mainstream media. The Steele dossier was used as justification to spy on high-ranking officials in the Trump administration and to assert that the entire administration was an asset of Russia and Vladimir Putin. We now know the document was created by British and American intelligence agencies, its source was a longtime Clinton family public relations consultant named Charles Dolan, it was based on opposition research funded by the Democratic National Committee, it was deliberately amplified by the FBI and CIA, and it was faithfully passed along as fact by many journalists in the mainstream corporate media[38] for four full years.[39] The Steele dossier presents a perfect picture of Mockingbird manipulation of the press. The dossier's reputation continued to plummet in 2021 and 2022, including when Igor Danchenko,[40] the Russian who gave Dolan's information to Christopher Steele, was indicted for lying[41] to the FBI.[42]

THE DANGERS OF PROPAGANDA

THE SMITH-MUNDT ACT OF 1948 ACKNOWLEDGED THE DANGERS OF DO-mestic propaganda in a free society and prohibited it. During the decades of the Cold War, the prohibition of propaganda was used frequently to highlight the differences between life in the free, capitalist, democratic West and life in the authoritarian, communist dictatorships of Eastern Europe, China, and the Soviet Union. Some US government agencies were permitted to publish propaganda and disinformation in *other* countries to fight against communism, but domestic propaganda was strictly prohibited.

Thus, for over 60 years, disseminating propaganda was illegal in the United States. Therefore, most of Operation Mockingbird was illegal. The revelations of the Church Committee prompted Congress to strengthen the Smith-Mundt Act in the 1970s. It was strengthened again in the 1980s.

In 2013, it was repealed. The Smith-Mundt Modernization Act of 2012, passed as part of the National Defense Authorization Act of 2013, and signed by President Obama, removed the prohibition[43] on domestic propaganda.[44] The justification for doing so was flimsy, but the corporate media sounded precious few alarm bells. The ostensible reason the president gave for lifting this long-standing ban was to allow government agencies to fight the dissemination of disinformation from *other* countries. What it did in practice was permit the government to covertly release to its citizens news reporting of its own creation. The act didn't allocate a funding mechanism to actually pay American government agencies to propagandize the citizenry, but that was remedied when Congress passed the 2017 National Defense Authorization Act, which included the Countering Foreign Propaganda Act, also signed by Obama. This law set up a grant program to fund any organization engaging in "countering propaganda and disinformation."[45] One particularly concerning aspect of this second law is that it allows these agencies to produce unattributed propaganda, thus preventing US citizens from learning the source of the reporting.[46]

The problems here should be obvious. The government now selects agencies to "counter propaganda" or writes unattributed news stories of its own. This is a major step toward the model of the Soviet *Pravda* and the Chinese *Renmin Ribao* in which there is only one legal version of the facts, the government's version. It is a 180-degree turn away from the essential Watchdog and Smorgasbord roles of the press envisioned in the Constitution. As we have already discussed, a Free Press sustains a functioning democracy by supporting and maintaining open political debate and free expression. The government cannot control the funding for the news organizations, or countless conflicts of interest immediately arise.

Two arguments are used to justify this dangerous practice of government propaganda and state-sponsored media manipulation. Unsurprisingly, large corporate media channels most frequently and forcefully argue these perspectives. The first claim is that countering foreign propaganda is so important and difficult that it requires our government to "fight fire with fire," to use "any means necessary," including commandeering private media channels to covertly broadcast its own spin on global affairs. Some suggest startling ideas, such as revoking our constitutional rights to Free Speech and privacy.[47] Those who hold these ideas, who harbor undue fear of foreign media, typically have little awareness of domestic media manipulation.

The second argument is a more grandiose notion. A society must have a coherent version of its past, present, and future in order to coalesce as a governable society. Only a shared myth can glue a large, diverse nation like ours together. The government is best placed, this argument goes, to craft this "shared story" and tell it to the American people, even when—particularly when—the story isn't wholly truthful.[48]

These arguments are not completely without merit, and indeed, in the former Soviet Union, North Korea, and China, for instance, these twin claims form the foundation of propaganda policy. Here in the United States, however, with our essential right to free expression and our cherished tradition of open political debate, I do not see how either claim comes close to justifying, from a practical or ethical standpoint, the formation of deceptive systems of storytelling to manipulate citizens' minds. It is all any government's propaganda organization has ever claimed: it is countering the propaganda of *other countries* and simply trying to broadcast our own poor government's perspective on the issues.

Widespread awareness of the government's side of the story has never been at risk. When the government's message is truthful, it has no trouble communicating it to the American people. It is defending governmental *lies* that has become more difficult in the New Enlightenment era, where independent media can often produce more original sources and offer more convincing accounts of events. This is why the government engages in covert propaganda.

As for other countries deceiving Americans via propaganda, many are certainly trying, just as our intelligence agencies try to manipulate the minds of people in virtually every foreign country. There is simply no proof that this has had the impact of homegrown propaganda, and those who believe otherwise likely don't appreciate the sophisticated domestic distortion underway today. I aim in publishing this book to elucidate this. Russia and China and many other nations do try to deceive Americans, but it is Americans speaking with American accents on American corporate media who are most effective at misinforming Americans. If the American democratic system and Free Press survive the unfolding of the New Enlightenment, it is unlikely this will ever change.

As for the claims that Russia swung the 2016 or 2020 elections, the evidence simply doesn't support the claims. The Muller Report uncovered many attempts, but in 2016 Facebook was the primary conduit for Russian influence, and not even $100,000 of ads and boosted posts were purchased.[49] It was a crude effort. Consider the countless millions spent by both American parties to sway American minds.[50] The Clinton campaign alone raised over $1 *billion*.[51] Russian media and intelligence did try to sway the election—as did many other countries interested in who calls the shots in the USA—but the foreign efforts were merely a drop in the bucket. We'll delve deeply into the misinformation that plagued the 2016 election in Chapter 4; suffice it to say, the primary purveyors of misinformation were not *foreign* news sources or intelligence agencies but rather our very own.

On the path to *media consciousness*, foreign news and perspectives play an important role. To gain a balanced perspective on the world and on what our government, military, and corporations are actually doing, we should neither fear nor trust foreign news sources more than American ones. Every source has its biases.

We turn now to these biases and how they bend media coverage of the news.

But first, we must understand one more important term, a powerful phrase used by pundits to discredit all who dare to investigate the corporate media's deceptive practices.

EXTRA

WHAT IS A CONSPIRACY THEORY?

"People of the same trade seldom meet together...
but the conversation ends in a conspiracy against the public."

Adam Smith

A BRIEF NOTE ABOUT AN EPITHET.

This is an era of rapidly expanding access to information, similar to the time when Johannes Gutenberg invented the movable-type printing press. That monumental invention struck fear in the hearts of feudal lords and Catholic clergy as it revolutionized free thought in Europe, germinated the philosophical flowering of the Enlightenment, and birthed modern science. At that time, the Catholic Church was civilization's most powerful institution, and its exalted elite were terrified by the prospect that ordinary people might read, write, and publish information themselves, that monks copying Bibles by hand might no longer be the only ones writing books, that they, the elite leaders, might lose control of history, information, and knowledge.[52] They were scared of losing control of the *narrative* that people told themselves about the life they were living.

That last part—as mentioned earlier—is the most important. Humans have always been storytelling creatures. Power over the human story is the most formidable power granted to those who control the flow of information. It is tantamount to power over humanity itself.

This book invites you to look at the prevailing narratives of our modern era, consider their mixed veracity, and question the role of those who construct and manage these stories. The printing press was invented in the year 1440, and within just thirty years, a wonderful little thing called the Spanish Inquisition began. Its goal was to root out "heretics" and "blasphemers."[53] It arrested, tortured, and killed innocent people ostensibly to protect the good Christian people of Europe from what today might be called "dangerous misinformation." In retrospect, we know the Inquisition was simply a desperate measure undertaken by the Catholic Church to maintain its power.

Despite the Inquisition, over the ensuing century, unsanctioned information spread rapidly. The Renaissance of art and music was soon flowering, and the Reformation that would pose a decisive challenge to the Church's infallibility was underway. Furious, the Catholic Church's high bishops stepped up their Inquisition, and its reign of terror metastasized throughout the entirety of Europe as well as to the New World where European colonists forcibly conquered and converted the peoples of the Americas. Then, as today, the spread of information generated a backlash.

"Witches" were burned at the stake, "blasphemers" were tortured, "heretics" were stoned to death. All for the unforgivable crimes of thinking for themselves and speaking freely. This continued for two centuries as the Church strove to keep its monopoly on the narrative. Little by little at first, and then in a sudden storm of revolutions in the 1700s, the regions of the New World threw off their colonial masters and established nations of their own, endowed with religious freedoms.

Here in the United States, after enduring censorship, persecution, and peremptory arrest, our founders wrote in the Constitution's First Amendment the core *progressive* freedoms for the new nation: the Freedom of Speech, the Freedom of Assembly, the Freedom of the Press, the Freedom of Religion, and the Freedom to Petition the Government. These five freedoms were placed prominently in the nation's founding document exactly because of the centuries of *reactionary* tyranny brought by the Church and others to suppress the flowering of free thought, science, and democracy. Thereafter, as we'll see in Chapter 11, the Freedom of the Press waxed and waned as it survived the country's first two centuries. Newspapers, followed by radio and television, gave Americans ever-increasing access to the most important news and information of their day.

While still vastly more diverse and inarguably better than the model of the Middle Ages, this model remained similar in one crucial way: it was a centralized, top-down dissemination of information, and it still frequently deceived Americans about the world they lived in. Five centuries after Gutenberg, the next revolution in the sharing of information neared.

To Coin a Phrase

When the defining domestic political event of the twentieth century took place—the assassination of President John F. Kennedy in 1963—many ordinary Americans had questions about the events. Who had killed this beloved president? How had it been accomplished seemingly so easily? Many were not convinced by the theory that a single gunman had been responsible. These people were about to learn that they were guilty of the unforgivable crime of questioning the *narrative*. Like the "witches" and "heretics" of a prior era, they were soon branded with an epithet.

The CIA first applied the phrase "conspiracy theories" in a 1967 document examining criticism of the Warren Commission.[54] In true Mockingbird fashion, the *New York Times* and other newspapers around the country took up the phrase promptly. It became the modern version of "blasphemer." Anyone who questioned the dogma of the day received this new label. This book is not about the presidential assassination, and I don't take a position on what did or did not occur that day. I am concerned with the birth and growth of the anti-intellectual slur of our modern era.

In the words of political scientist Lance deHaven-Smith, in his book *Conspiracy Theory in America*:

> The term "conspiracy theory" did not exist as a phrase in everyday American conversation before 1964 ... Since then, the term's prevalence and range of application have exploded. In 1964, the year the Warren Commission issued its report, the *New York Times* published five stories in which "conspiracy theory" appeared. In recent years, the phrase has occurred in over 140 *New York Times* stories annually.[55]

Today, this epithet falls on virtually anyone who questions establishment narratives.

The New Enlightenment is still in its infancy. We are perhaps where the Renaissance was just as the priests of the Inquisition were first hauling "blasphemers" onto the rack. Free thinkers find each other more easily than they did in that era, and this is revolutionizing ordinary people's ability to learn and share information. It is a time of awakening. Many people today are thinking more broadly and more critically than they have before.

It is therefore no coincidence that the high priests of our time—the wealthy opinion makers on corporate news television—go to such lengths to vilify anyone who questions their narratives. Because many people now question the top-down dissemination of news from corporate media, corporate news must defame anyone in any place of prominence who does so as not just wrong but as a liar of such perfidy that he or she must be ostracized and censored.

Just as medieval serfs, colonists, and natives in the New World lived in an era when high bishops and Catholic priests denounced and silenced "blasphemers" and "heretics," we live in an era of "fake news" and "disinformation." There are "conspiracy theorists" who are denounced by the high executives of social media and silenced by the propaganda masters in the intelligence agencies. Alternative viewpoints are "fake news." The bravest skeptics, investigators, and truthtellers are "conspiracy theorists."

An Invitation

I invite you to consider that the term "conspiracy theorist" is, at best, intellectually lazy, and, at worst, a disingenuous attempt to silence someone who asks uncomfortable questions. George Orwell, in his brilliant and prescient novel *1984*, used a slur similar to "conspiracy theory" to castigate free inquiry: *thoughtcrime*.[56] Merely thinking a wrong thought, in Orwell's dystopia, indicates mental weakness, unstable paranoia, or punishable heresy.

As an author and journalist who asks uncomfortable questions, I would like to extend my humble request to anyone reading or reviewing this book. If you use this epithet, take a moment to consider why. Much of the time, it might be to call in the power of the corporate media propaganda machine to marginalize or invalidate a line of inquiry. Perhaps you are trying to win an argument without engaging with it. Maybe you wish to reject an uncomfortable idea without considering it.

On the other hand, if you are open to fairly considering all ideas and to thinking freely for yourself, please feel free to wear the term "conspiracy theorist" with pride. The Center for Inquiry initiated "National Blasphemy Day" in 2009 to encourage people to embrace the idea of blasphemy and to examine and critique religious dogma; it celebrates a kind of intellectual bravery that was much more difficult to muster 300 years ago, but the point remains: to embrace a slur meant to disparage free thought.[57] There is little intellectual risk today in declaring oneself a blasphemer. Embracing the term "conspiracy theorist" today takes courage.

Conspiracies happen all the time. Powerful people get together to talk about their shared interests, and sometimes, they act on what they talk about. That's what a conspiracy theory considers. *Are powerful people acting together covertly in their interests and not in mine? Is what they're doing illegal or unethical?*

Economist Adam Smith famously said back in 1827, "People of the same trade seldom meet together...but the conversation ends in a conspiracy against the public."[58] Conspiracies, like other crimes, are a part of human life.

Just consider what we now know about the Iraq and Afghanistan wars,[59] the Iran-Contra scandal, and even leaded gasoline,[60] lightbulbs,[61] and prescription opioids.[62] Censorship and propaganda hid activities that were extremely profitable to a small number of people but irrevocably harmful for millions of others.

The corporate media only attaches the term "conspiracy theory" to theories of wrongdoing that contradict their dominant narrative. The theory that George W. Bush and Dick Cheney postulated—that Saddam Hussein had biological or chemical weapons but was hiding them and lying about them—was never labeled a "conspiracy theory" in 2003, although that's what it was. The theory that Donald Trump worked covertly with Russians to win the 2016 election was never labeled a "conspiracy theory" in 2017, although that's what it was.

One aim of this book is to examine our trust in the giant American media corporations that control mainstream news. They have repeatedly disseminated propaganda created by the very institutions that are launching wars everywhere, diminishing our freedoms and rights, impoverishing our species, and destroying our richly abundant planet. Many wars and harmful cultural changes over this past century have been launched on false premises and biased narratives. The top-down dissemination of information must be thoroughly challenged if we are to live in a better world that honors the core *progressive* freedoms our Constitution promises.

In this time of great awakening, I hope you'll consider supporting free thought rather than attacking it. The Church leaders might call you a blasphemer for reading a new Bible or sharing an idea you came up with on your own. But you'll be part of the Renaissance rather than the Inquisition.

3

BIAS, INNOCENT OR NEFARIOUS

"Propaganda is making puppets of us.
We are moved by hidden strings
which the propagandist manipulates."

Everett Dean Martin

WE ALL NOTICE BIAS IN THE NEWS. THERE IS THE POLITICAL PARTY BIAS we see when changing channels from, for instance, Fox News to MSNBC. There is the cultural and social bias we see when tuning into media channels long connected to a certain segment of the population. And there is a particular establishment-vs.-anti-establishment bias we notice when moving back and forth between corporate media and independent media.

All media organizations have a *bias*, naturally, as all content is ultimately reported, written, edited, and promoted by human beings. We have inherent biases in how we see the world and interpret phenomena. This kind of bias we refer to in this book as *innocent bias*, as it's an innate part of human nature and an inevitable part of news reporting. Race, gender, ethnicity, age, nationality, and all other intrinsic human traits contribute to *innocent bias*.

The journalist, or editor perhaps, isn't deliberately attempting to distort the story, but *innocent bias* plays a role nonetheless in how the story is written and presented. That doesn't mean it doesn't matter—it *does*, and you should pay close attention to this kind of bias in the news you consume, particularly if you're accustomed to viewing news only from people with innate biases similar to your own.

The Mockingbird-style infiltration of our media organizations is a bird of an altogether different feather. This bias we examined in the previous chapter. It is a calculated slant in analysis, a carefully twisted version of an important event, or an entire persistent narrative about a series of events. Government organizations, such as the CIA, surreptitiously introduce this bias into news reporting to alter the public's perception of world events. This kind of bias we call *nefarious bias* in this book. *Nefarious bias* is not the result of innate, human variation playing out in news reporting but rather a deliberate, disingenuous attempt to distort the news, to limit viewpoints, or to deceive viewers. There is always a hidden agenda to *nefarious bias*. Sometimes this agenda is easy to guess, such as launching a war; sometimes it's difficult to ascertain, such as why the lab origin of *sars-cov-2* has been concealed for so long. *Nefarious bias* is the intentional use of censorship and propaganda. Operation Mockingbird was responsible for propagating certain news stories and censoring others to further a hidden agenda for at least 25 years. Serving their own objectives, this insidious bias serves to alter global perceptions about events, places, and people.

In addition to *nefarious bias* and *innocent bias,* there is a third type of bias—*systemic bias*, which we'll also describe in the next chapter along with innocent bias. We'll consider establishment and anti-establishment bias as we delve into the origin of "fake news" in Chapter 5. For the remainder of this chapter, we explore instances of *nefarious bias* playing out in our national media and observe that Operation Mockingbird was likely not shut down in the 1970s but simply recalibrated, reassigned, and redefined.

COMMUNISTS EATING BABIES
FOR BREAKFAST

JOHN STOCKWELL WAS A SENIOR OPERATIONS DIRECTOR IN THE CIA. After thirteen years managing covert operations in Vietnam, Congo, and Angola, he left the agency and described what he experienced.[1] He led a covert CIA operation in Angola that fought on the side of Apartheid South Africa against a socialist government backed by Cuban troops. In an interview in 1983 with news anchor Clete Roberts, Stockwell recalled managing three teams in Angola dedicated to separate tasks: covert operations, intelligence gathering, and propaganda. After mentioning the activities of the first two teams, he explained the role of the third.

> **Stockwell:** Another thing is to disseminate propaganda to influence people's minds, and this is a major function of the CIA. Unfortunately, of course, it overlaps into the gathering of information. You have contact with a journalist, you will give him true stories, you'll get information from him, you'll also give him false stories.
>
> **Roberts:** Do you buy his confidence with true stories?
>
> **Stockwell:** You buy his confidence and set him up... You also work on their human vulnerabilities to recruit them in a classic sense, make them your agent, so that you can control what they do, so you don't have to set them up by putting one over on them. So you can say, 'Here, plant this next Tuesday.'
>
> **Roberts:** Can you do this with responsible reporters?
>
> **Stockwell:** Yes, the Church Committee brought it out in 1975, and... Bernstein put the article in *Rolling Stone* a couple of years later.

In order to convince the world that the Apartheid South African side were the good guys in a war against Cuban-backed communists in Angola, Stockwell's propaganda team would feed fictional stories about barbaric Cuban atrocities to reporters who were either CIA assets themselves or who were unwitting journalists watching the news wire waiting for stories. All stories carried the CIA's view, its *nefarious bias*, Stockwell recalled, and approximately one out of every five stories was wholly false, including, for instance, stories of Cubans eating babies. The stories would percolate through African media and wind up in European and American newspapers as well. As we saw in the last chapter, the global wire services serve as useful vehicles for placing Mockingbird propaganda into American media outlets. Today, social media also serves this "conduit" role.

Stockwell directed his propaganda team to distribute a mixture of truth and falsehoods to journalists. The reporters would then disseminate the stories via their respective news outlets.

Stockwell: We would take stories which we would write and put them in the *Zambia Times* and then pull them out and send them to [one of the] journalists on our payroll in Europe. But his cover story would be that he got them from his stringer in Lusaka who had gotten them from the *Zambia Times*.

We had the complicity of the government of Zambia ... to put these false stories into [their] newspapers. But after that point, the journalists, Reuters, and AFP, the management, was not aware of it. Now our contact man in Europe was, and we pumped just dozens of stories about Cuban atrocities, Cuban rapists. In one case, we had the Cuban rapists caught and tried by the Ovambo maidens who had been their victims, and then we ran photographs that made almost every newspaper in the country, of the Cubans being executed by the Ovambo women who had supposedly been their victims.

Roberts: These were fake photos?

Stockwell: Absolutely. We didn't know of one single atrocity committed by the Cubans. It was pure raw false propaganda to create an illusion of Communists, you know, eating babies for breakfast. Totally false propaganda.

Roberts: Was this sort of thing practiced in Vietnam?

Stockwell: Endlessly. A massive propaganda effort in Vietnam in the 1950s and in the 60s, including a thousand books that were published, several hundred in English, that were also propaganda books sponsored by the CIA. Give some money to a writer, write this book for us, write anything you want, but on these matters make sure you write this line.

Roberts: Writers in this country? Books sold and distributed in this country?

Stockwell: Yeah, sure. English language books, meaning an American audience as a target, on the subject of Vietnam, on the history of Vietnam, and the history of Marxism, and supporting the domino theory.

Roberts: Doesn't the CIA flatly deny this? They've admitted there is some propaganda, but their position is that it's all outside the United States, not in the United States. Isn't that true?

Stockwell: While we were running this Angolan operation, and pumping these stories into the world and US press, exactly at that time, Bill Colby, the CIA Director, was testifying to Congress, assuring them that we were extremely careful to make sure that none of our propaganda spilled back into the United States. And the very days that he was giving this false testimony, we were planting stories in the *Washington Post*...

Roberts: So you planted stories in the *Washington Post* by bringing a man from abroad. You had no difficulty? You got right past the editor with it?

Stockwell: Yeah.

Roberts: Is this common? Is it easy?

Stockwell: It's easier than you would think.

That was the 1970s. Communists eating babies for breakfast. Operation Mockingbird in full swing.

Now, let's jump forward a few decades and see if things were different.

THE AMBASSADOR'S DAUGHTER

AN ARABIC WOMAN IN A BLACK HEADSCARF SAT ON A WOODEN CHAIR, testifying before Congress. Tears ran from her eyes. She wiped her cheeks and recounted what she had witnessed. She had seen soldiers maraud into a hospital in her native Kuwait. She had seen them break down the doors. She had watched them kill defenseless patients. She had stared helplessly as they tore infants from incubators and left them on the cold floor to die.

Her testimony to Congress continued. Her name was Nayirah—she didn't give a last name—and she was a hospital volunteer in Kuwait. The Iraqi army had invaded her homeland, she recounted emotionally, and committed horrific Nazi-esque atrocities. They were ripping babies from incubators for God's sake.[2]

That evening, Nayirah's testimony about the babies and the incubators appeared on every American evening news channel. It was October 10, 1990. Over the ensuing week, President George H. W. Bush mentioned "babies torn from incubators" on eight different occasions.[3] He called immediately for war.

There was one problem. The American people weren't interested in intervening in this little war. Sure, fighting had broken out between Iraq and Kuwait, two Middle Eastern countries thousands of miles away. *What concern is it of ours?*

Whether or not President Bush had assured Iraq that the US *wouldn't* intervene if Iraq invaded, as independent media reported at the time,[4] Iraq had invaded the small nation. And whether or not Saddam Hussein had been an ally of the US until this point mattered even less to everyday Americans. *This is not a war we need to join.*

But the shocking stories that Nayirah told—the babies and the incubators—and the breathless coverage given to the story by mainstream television and newspapers—turned the tide of public opinion in favor of launching a military attack on Iraq.

The only detail that the news reports left out about Nayirah's story was that it was fiction.[5]

Nayirah wasn't a hospital volunteer. She was the daughter of the Kuwaiti ambassador to the United States. She hadn't been in Kuwait at the time of the invasion. She was living with her father in a posh condominium in Washington D.C. The whole story, from her false identity to the made-up incubators, had been created by a D.C. public relations firm named Hill & Knowlton.[6]

But few knew that at the time, only those reading alternative news. There was no public internet at the time, no social media, no independent voices with a platform or virtual megaphone the way these exist today in this dawning New Enlightenment.

For most Americans, the truth would only emerge years later.

At the time, the story was reported as truthful in one newspaper, then the rest, Mockingbird-style. People who only weeks before had regarded Kuwait as the repressive regime that Amnesty International had labeled "harshly authoritarian" for jailing and torturing dissidents and journalists, suddenly learned it was a freedom-loving place that America needed to liberate. Whether it had been the CIA or a different arm of the executive branch that had hired Hill & Knowlton for the job, the *propaganda* was created to advance a hidden agenda. This is the definition of *nefarious bias.* The hidden agenda was to justify an American invasion of Iraq. The propaganda was disseminated broadly, and it percolated quickly through the corporate media, becoming the dominant *narrative*, the thing people talked about and argued about. This is how distortion is used to create and manage news narratives.

The public was persuaded, at least to some extent. Tom Regan, a columnist for the *Christian Science Monitor*, wrote a brave piece years later, remembering the buildup to the war:

> I can still recall my brother Sean's face. It was bright red. Furious. Not one given to fits of temper, Sean was in an uproar. He was a father, and he had just heard that Iraqi soldiers had taken scores of babies out of incubators in Kuwait and left them to die. The Iraqis had shipped the incubators back to Baghdad. A pacifist by nature, my brother was not in a peaceful mood that day. "We've got to go and get Saddam Hussein. Now," he said passionately.[7]

And three months later, that's what the military did. A biblical storm of bombs—one of the heaviest aerial bombardments in military history—terrorized the Iraqi people. More than 1,000 sorties dropped nearly 100,000 tons of bombs on the country, and the ensuing war, famous for its introduction of "precision bombs," killed somewhere between 60,000-150,000 Iraqi soldiers as well as another 100,000–200,000 civilians, according to BBC estimates. These are likely undercounts.

All to save babies who never existed.

Nefarious bias always has a hidden agenda behind it. In this case, the hidden agenda was bombing Iraq and carving up the nation's energy resources to the tremendous benefit of weapons and energy corporations. Agents in the intelligence community hired a public relations firm to create the propaganda before the mockingbirds of the corporate media repeated the message.

WEAPONS OF MASS DISTRACTION

TWELVE YEARS LATER, A DIFFERENT PRESIDENT BUSH IN THE WHITE House issued another urgent cry to invade Iraq.[8] The new president, along with his vice president, Dick Cheney, Secretary of Defense Donald Rumsfeld, Secretary of State Colin Powell, and National Security Advisor Condoleezza Rice declared in sudden unison in August 2002 that Iraqi President Saddam Hussein was an imminent threat to the world.

Saddam was developing "weapons of mass destruction," they swore, and it was of the utmost urgency that we attack Iraq, again, to defend the United States.

A new war in Iraq had approximately zero support among the American populace. The idea was even less popular than it had been in 1990. The notion that Hussein had these dangerous weapons appeared neither certain nor sufficiently grave to justify destroying the country and sending Americans to fight and die.

Then the narrative management began. Stories appeared in all of the major corporate media sources, echoing the urgency and danger proclaimed by the White House. A string of articles in the *New York Times* painted Saddam Husein's weapons stockpiles as dangerous.[9] One writer in particular at the *Times* by the name of Judith Miller penned successive articles pushing the White House line.[10] With information that apparently no one else had, she published pieces where unproven allegations ran as disingenuous headlines. "Iraq Said to Try to Buy Antidote Against Nerve Gas"[11] landed on the front page. Then, "Defectors Bolster U.S. Case Against Iraq, Officials Say."[12] Journalists in other media outlets published similar articles, and soon the corporate media as a whole was analyzing things the same way: whether or not it was "legal," it was our duty for the sake of global peace to invade, and our path toward war was legitimate, necessary, and ethical.

The opinion of the American populace as a whole, nevertheless, remained firmly against a new invasion, and this time, a powerful protest movement against an invasion of Iraq sprang up rapidly. A new device called the Internet was available, and millions of people signed online petitions opposing war. In fact, on February 15, 2003, the largest collective mass action in world history occurred as millions of people took part in anti-war marches in hundreds of major cities around the world.[13]

In the White House, undeterred by the unprecedented global opposition, when asked how confident he was that Iraq had "weapons of mass destruction,"[14] CIA Director Bob Tenet said, "It's a slam-dunk case."[15] At the UN, Colin Powell announced to the world that Iraq had these dangerous weapons: "What I'm about to tell you are not assertions," he swore, staring into the camera. "They are facts and conclusions based on solid intelligence."[16] The term "weapons of mass destruction" was repeated endlessly by everyone who appeared on camera. When FBI Director Bob Mueller stepped before the cameras, he proclaimed soberly, "Iraq's weapons of mass destruction program poses a clear threat to our national security."[17]

The corporate media passed these assertions along as gospel. There was no doubt that these officials were telling the truth, wrote Judith Miller and others at *The New York Times, Washington Post,* and the rest. There was no doubt that Iraq was manufacturing chemical, biological, and even nuclear weapons, they said. There was no doubt that this was a clear and present danger to the United States; there was no doubt that a military invasion was justified. It was as if a set of talking points had been planted in the media. These phrases seemed to echo endlessly around in a small chamber, regardless of public opinion or dissent.

Precious little dissent was heard in corporate media despite the astonishing national and global outcry. A study by the media watchdog FAIR identified 1,617 on-camera pundits on the six major television networks who provided news or opinion about Iraq. Antiwar voices comprised only 10% of these sources, and just 6% of non-Iraqi sources, and a tiny 3% of US sources. In terms of government and military sources allowed on air, the numbers were even smaller:

> Of a total of 840 US sources who are current or former government or military officials, only four held anti-war opinions: Sen. Robert Byrd (D-WV), Rep. Pete Stark (D-Calif.), and two appearances by Rep. Dennis Kucinich (D.-Ohio). Byrd was featured on PBS, with Stark and Kucinich appearing on Fox News.[18]

We know what happened next. A long and hellish decade of war again tore Iraq apart, the site of the cradle of human civilization. A bombardment of terror that many in the media adoringly called a campaign of "shock-and-awe" ultimately took the lives of over a million Iraqis, wounded several million more, and caused still more untold millions of human beings to flee their home, their towns, and their country. All in the name of preventing the use of "weapons of mass destruction."

Thousands of Americans too were killed, wounded, traumatized, or poisoned by experimental depleted uranium weaponry, scarred by the violence they witnessed or committed, or afflicted with PTSD. Perhaps the least-told part of the story is the impoverishment of American domestic and social programs for the sake of sending trillions of dollars overseas for wars based on lies. In their 2008 book *The Three Trillion Dollar War: The True Cost of the Iraq Conflict,* two Nobel Prize-winning economists, Linda J. Bilmes and Joseph E. Stiglitz, sorted through the swamp of lies told by politicians and a compliant media in the lead-up to the war. They named their book after their estimate on the war's true financial costs.[19]

A secret, extravagant $540 million Mockingbird-style propaganda campaign created fake news to instill support for the invasion. This was but one more brutally unnecessary expense.[20] Employing hundreds of people for years, the program created soap operas, movies, terrorist videos, and fake news reports that aired in Arabic across the Middle East, purporting to be domestic, Iraqi content.[21] It was an astonishing campaign of disinformation that included suppressing Google searches and distributing videos on CDs that would secretly track people who inserted the discs into their computers.

No significant "weapons of mass destruction" program was ever found in Iraq. Not before, during, or after the invasion, or indeed during the subsequent occupation that continues today. But evidence of a rapacious seizure of oil and gas—and control of a critical swath of Middle East land—was everywhere. Even the Iraqis who survived were terrorized, grieving their dead, and trying to cope with the poisoning of their land by the American military's use of depleted uranium.

The media during the buildup and prosecution of these wars was certainly fraught with the *innocent bias* described above. Corporate media always presents hawkish support for wars, and pacifists only appear on independent media. There are some differences in corporate media between left-leaning and right-leaning media, something we'll look at in later chapters.

But what is important to see from these two examples is the pervasive presence of *nefarious bias* at these momentous junctures in history. A large population was led into one war after another. Would greater *media consciousness* among the American populace have prevented these wars? It's one of the questions that drove me to write this book. These wars caused the deaths of millions of people and benefited only a very few. The mass deception was based on, in the first case, propaganda to elicit anger about babies in incubators, and in the second case, propaganda to elicit fear about weapons of mass destruction. In both cases, during the war's buildup, and during the wars themselves, corporate media meticulously and successfully managed the narratives in the news.[22]

Those two wars occurred before I had taken many steps on my personal, ongoing journey toward *media consciousness*. Now, let's take a look at a type of manipulation that unfolded during my personal awakening to the insidious presence of *bias, censorship,* and *propaganda.*

IMMUNIZED AGAINST THE TRUTH

AN AFRICAN NEWBORN GASPS IN A SQUALID HOSPITAL IN LESOTHO. A midwife gathers the infant girl into her arms and rushes to an intensive care room. The baby is barely breathing and urgently needs oxygen. Six newborns already share the intensive care room's single oxygen tank through rigged stethoscope tubes. There are no more tubes.

The desperate newborn slowly asphyxiates.

The infant's mother waits anxiously in the maternity ward. The midwife finally returns, informing the mother that her baby didn't make it. The mother utters a heartrending cry of sorrow.

Two days later, the mother undergoes a traditional rite of grief.

A neighbor shaved Matsepang Nyoba's head with an antiquated razor. Blood beaded on her scalp. Tears trickled down her cheeks, but not because of the pain. She was in mourning, and this was a ritual.

Two days earlier, her newborn baby girl had died in the roach-infested maternity ward of Queen Elizabeth II, a crumbling sprawl that is the largest hospital in Lesotho, a mountainous nation of 2.1 million people surrounded by South Africa.[23]

What the miserable mother likely didn't know was that the oxygen tube that would have saved her baby girl's life cost a mere $35. She also couldn't have known that Bill Gates and his Global Alliance for Vaccines and Immunizations (GAVI) had donated thousands of dollars to the hospital but for expensive vaccines and pharmaceuticals, not for inexpensive interventions such as oxygen tubes.

A *Los Angeles Times* article, "Unintended Victims of Gates Foundation Generosity," provided an uncommonly bold look at the actions of one of the world's more secretive and powerful billionaires. Matsepang Nyoba and her daughter's story appeared in December of 2007. The piece served as a reminder that despite their generally woeful track record, American corporate media outlets have produced many high-quality investigative articles over the decades. This type of coverage has dwindled to nearly nil in the twenty-first century, but I would be remiss in compiling the many deliberate and accidental failures of the corporate media that I do in this book were I to completely omit examples of quality work. Every once in a while investigative corporate journalism is solid, even sparkling.

We'll examine some of the high points of the era of "objective, professional journalism" in Chapter 11.

This *Los Angeles Times* piece is peppered with statements that flatter Gates and the work of GAVI on public health in Africa. But the authors also covered the numerous ways that Gates's efforts have proven counterproductive. They cited data showing that Gates Foundation interventions have not reduced overall infant mortality in Africa.

> As successful as vaccination drives have been in curbing targeted diseases, 2006 data, the most recent available, show a paradoxical relationship between GAVI funding in Africa and child mortality. Overall, child mortality improved more often in nations that received smaller than average GAVI grants per capita. In seven nations that received greater than average funding, child mortality rates worsened.[24]

Locked Out of the Gates

It is said that "the exception proves the rule." Other than that single two-part investigation by the *Los Angeles Times* in 2007, there has been essentially no negative coverage in corporate media over the past twenty years about Bill Gates or his worldwide vaccination efforts. Is this a coincidence?

Nefarious bias isn't only a tool of governments, intelligence agencies, and profiteering corporations. Gates, the world's second richest man, and Jeff Bezos, its richest, are wealthier than most nations, and they have the power to deliberately distort the media as well. We will discuss Bezos's opportunistic purchase of the *Washington Post* and its corrosive effect on corporate media coverage later, but the efforts of Bezos to manipulate the media pale in comparison to those of his rival Seattle billionaire.

Even during his messy 2021 divorce, which was rife with accusations about his longstanding friendship with Jeffery Epstein, Gates enjoyed gentle treatment in corporate media. He was just a generous nerd in a sweater who wanted to save the world.[25]

Independent media hasn't been as friendly. In November 2021, independent news magazine *MintPress News* released a revelatory report on the money that Bill Gates and his many foundations have provided directly to media organizations. The meticulous investigative reporter Alan MacLeod unearthed records showing that Gates has bankrolled hundreds of media organizations in both this country and abroad to the tune of over $300 million.[26] In today's era of shrinking corporate media advertising revenue and employment consolidation, $300 million buys a lot of writers and editors. The *MintPress News* noted the white-glove treatment Gates has received from international media, noting that the Microsoft co-founder was even christened 'Saint Bill' by *The Guardian*. As it turns out, *The Guardian* has been the second biggest recipient of Gates's largesse, receiving a cool $12.9 million from the billionaire.

The largest beneficiary? NPR. The radio network has taken in $24.3 million from Gates. Have you ever heard a negative word uttered about Gates on public radio?

Media corporations also receiving Gates's largesse include PBS, CNN, NBC, *The Atlantic,* and New York Public Radio, as well as the major news outlets in European countries: BBC and *The Daily Telegraph* in the UK, *Der*

Spiegel in Germany, *Le Monde* in France, and *El Pais* in Spain, and many, many more. Gates even sponsors *Al Jazeera*, in Qatar.

Not stopping at the media organizations themselves, Gates also underwrites professional journalism associations and investigative journalism centers to the tune of $52 million. According to MacLeod's reporting:

> The foundation also puts up the money to directly train journalists all over the world in the form of scholarships, courses and workshops. Today, it is possible for an individual to train as a reporter thanks to a Gates Foundation grant, find work at a Gates-funded outlet, and belong to a press association funded by Gates. This is especially true of journalists working in the fields of health, education, and global development, the ones Gates himself is most active in and where scrutiny of the billionaire's actions and motives are most necessary.[27]

No News is Good News

Negative coverage of Bill Gates and his various initiatives remains rare in corporate media. In 2020 and 2021, as the covid pandemic dominated the news, negative coverage of the Gates Foundation was censored in both corporate and social media. Gates himself, who has no medical or vaccinology training and holds no college degree, was interviewed frequently as an expert on CNN, MSNBC, and NPR and was always presented as an intelligent man—or even an expert—selflessly trying to help. Never did corporate media mention that Gates was funding the media itself nor that he had a financial stake in the pharmaceutical and technology corporations making money from the pandemic.

As the pandemic wore on, Tim Schwab, another independent investigative reporter, managed to publish another exception to the rule, albeit not in corporate media. *The Nation*, a venerable and mildly anti-establishment magazine, published "While the Poor Get Sick, Bill Gates Just Gets Richer" that documented the fabulous wealth Gates was accruing by profiteering off of vaccine development, farmland acquisitions, and the widespread use of remote learning in schools. Not only was Gates raking in billions during the pandemic, Schwab revealed, but he was doing so in secret, allowing the billionaire to maintain a beneficent image.[28]

For its part, the Gates Foundation claims to be open about its activities, but it makes public very little about what its grant money is used for. The \$319 million tabulated by the *MintPress News* report is thus a serious undercount, as it only counted donations made directly to press organizations or to clearly-identified media campaigns. This means thousands of grants and sub-grants having some media element were not counted. MacLeod acknowledged this and used as an example the Gates Foundation's multifarious partnership with Paramount, the media behemoth that controls *CBS News*, Viacom, *MTV, VH1, Nickelodeon, BET*, and many other subsidiaries:

> The Gates Foundation was paying the entertainment giant to insert information and PSAs into its programming ... Gates had intervened to change storylines in popular shows like *ER* and *Law & Order*. However, when checking the grants database, "Viacom" and "CBS" are nowhere to be found, the likely grant in question (totaling over \$6 million) merely describing the project as a "public engagement campaign aimed at improving high school graduation rates and postsecondary completion rates specifically aimed at parents and students," meaning that it was not counted in the official total.[29]

In a powerful show of narrative management, Gates is using his millions surreptitiously to manipulate the storylines of television shows.[30] The billionaire generated his original riches in the 1990s as a zealously monopolistic CEO who was prosecuted for anticompetitive practices. Today, he is still making billions, but due to his foundation's infiltration of corporate media and a decade of sculpted PR, many see him as a wise, if awkward, philanthropist giving his wealth away.

Nefarious bias doesn't always spread disingenuous propaganda; sometimes it conceals important facts. In the case of Bill Gates, the hidden agenda is keeping the world unaware of a billionaire's activities so that his wealth and power can grow.

THE NATURE OF DISTORTION

WE COULD FIND DOZENS OF SIMILAR INSTANCES OVER THE YEARS OF *NE-farious bias.* In particular, the buildup to wars, the issues at stake in elections, and the emergence of national crises are the times that this insidious bias is most heavily used. These are also the times this bias can most readily be seen if one watches closely.[31]

Preparation for war is the time when public opinion is most commonly arrayed against the imperialist establishment goals of the military and intelligence industrial complexes. In addition to the wars mentioned above, which took place after the official Mockingbird era, the buildup to the Vietnam War, which occurred during the height of the Mockingbird era, was justified in the national media on account of an event that never occurred. The Gulf of Tonkin Incident, an alleged attack by North Vietnam on US Naval vessels in a sea off the coast of Vietnam, was fabricated by our intelligence agencies.[32] The false story was passed along in perfect Mockingbird fashion through the American media and resulted in Congress passing the Gulf of Tonkin Resolution[33] that started a war that bitterly divided the nation, killed at least 50,000 American soldiers, and annihilated somewhere between two and three million Vietnamese and Cambodian people.[34] Launching wars generally requires heavy narrative management.

National elections are another time when *nefarious bias* surges. Citizens sense they have some power and pay closer attention to the news. One can observe *nefarious bias* at work in corporate media, as the *narrative* is often manipulated to make one candidate, say, Pete Buttigieg, appear more likely to win than another, say, Bernie Sanders, who establishment interests dislike.

National crises also often bring out *nefarious bias* in our corporate news. The egregiously biased coverage of the pandemic, which we examine in this book, was fraught with *nefarious bias.* Sometimes, this *nefarious bias* plays out not by distorting what you read but by censoring what you might have read, as in the case of facts that say, Bill Gates, does not want you to know.

Is There a Cure?

If any of this seemed unbelievable before reading these first few chapters, I imagine it doesn't any longer. This is the nature of narrative management, which consists primarily of *censorship* and *propaganda*. A government attempts to shift the opinions of its people in order to attain certain goals. It happens in this country as it does in every other. The tools of modern narrative management can quickly sway opinion when used with precision on an unaware audience.

Globally, news distortion of this type is sophisticated roughly in proportion to a country's historic power and wealth. A well-educated citizenry requires more sophisticated propaganda. In China, for instance, the propaganda is strong but neither as subtle nor as complex as this country's. A salient difference is the great variety of media sources that exist in wealthy countries like the United States, which gives a sense of a diversity of opinion even when the same corporations own almost all sources of news.

Despite its insidious nature, there is a cure for the malady of media manipulation. The rise of truly independent media is the most powerful and promising development in the world of information right now—both here and abroad—and it is the primary topic of the second half of this book. As humanity develops *media consciousness*, we will increasingly see through the endless misinformation that leads to such calamitous loss of life.

The assassination of John F. Kennedy in 1963 and the tumultuous American decade of assassinations and coups that followed led to the revelatory Church Committee that in turn forced upon many Americans a recognition that *nefarious bias* permeates our news media. Operation Mockingbird is officially a thing of the past, but its methods of narrative manipulation appear to be alive, quite well, and quite poisonous.

Now, we return to the modern era to look at an equally important type of bias, *systemic bias,* and how it caused the most profound moment thus far on my personal journey toward *media consciousness*. I was censored while covering the pivotal 2016 election.

4

IT'S NOT ABOUT THE MONEY, IT'S ABOUT THE MONEY

"The media is the most powerful entity on earth.
They have the power to make the innocent guilty
and to make the guilty innocent."

Malcolm X

I CLICKED 'REFRESH' ON MY BROWSER. THE ARTICLE DISAPPEARED. A blank, white screen stared back at me.

I refreshed the page again.

An error page appeared this time. *500. Internal Server Error. The system encountered an unexpected problem.*

I refreshed the page a third time, and the top of the page filled with the standard *Huffington Post* header and navigation bar. But where the article that I had written had appeared mere moments ago, there were only a few short words. *Page Not Found. Error 404.* Below the words was a button: *Visit the homepage.*

My article was gone.

I clicked on my author icon and loaded my author page. The other articles that I had written for *HuffPo* were listed. My most recent article was nowhere to be found.

I attempted to log in to the contributors' portal, to see if perhaps the piece had been unpublished for some reason.

That username or password is incorrect.

My credentials no longer worked.

The article had gone live the night before, and it had been up for about eight hours by my calculations. It had received at least 50,000 views but probably many more. Fifty thousand was the number of views I saw before going to bed.

It was July 2016, three months after I had been brought on board at the *Huffington Post*. The Democratic National Convention was a short week away, and the divisions between the Bernie Sanders and Hillary Clinton camps remained stark.

A Question of Privilege

A *HuffPo* editor named Hayley Miller had first approached me in early April. She was interested in a piece I had written about the Democratic Primary. At the time, social and corporate media were throwing around the word 'privilege' easily and frequently, usually to insinuate that everyone should support Hillary Clinton. Clearly, for most everyday people, the *privileged* position was having sufficient income or wealth where a voter *could* support Clinton. Not needing a higher minimum wage, canceled student debt, tuition-free public college, and universal healthcare—the things that the Bernie Sanders campaign was demanding—seemed to me to be the more privileged perspective.

So, I wrote a short piece spelling this out. I wasn't attempting to encapsulate the entire race or say anything particularly profound. I entitled the piece, "Please Recognize Your Privilege If You Can Afford Eight Years of Hillary Clinton and the Status Quo."[1]

The article attracted more attention than I'd expected. Twitter and Facebook users shared it extensively. Miller reached out to me via a private message. She asked if she could publish it at *Huffington Post*, and she offered to make me a regular contributor.

I accepted her offer, and over the next few months, I wrote numerous articles about the primary. I was one of only two writers at *Huffington Post* covering the historic race from the perspective of Sanders supporters. My pieces regularly generated thousands of likes and shares while attracting tens or hundreds of thousands of views. Several of my articles were featured on the front page.

As the race proceeded through April and into May, several primary elections between Clinton and Sanders were fraught with "irregularities," and allegations of election fraud grew. I wrote two articles on the severe problems in the vote counts—one about Arizona and New York,[2] the other about California.[3] One was cited in a lawsuit brought to the Department of Justice by an election integrity group named Citizens' Oversight Projects. That piece, "Exit Polls are the Thing Wherein to Catch the Conscience of Elections," summarized the allegations and cited mathematical calculations based on the exit poll numbers, which did indeed suggest something amiss with the way the electronic machines were counting the votes.[4] It deserved real scrutiny, I thought, and I gave it the attention that I could.

The Smell of Suppression in the Morning

June arrived and brought with it the momentous California primary that witnessed many more allegations of election fraud. I wrote about that as well, particularly given my front-row seat as a California resident. My articles covered other important elements of the race, too, such as the candidates' different fundraising, the purpose and plans of the "superdelegates," the meaning of Democratic Socialism, the protests at Standing Rock, and more.

None of those articles generated any negative attention from *Huffington Post* editors that I was aware of. I received no critical communication.

Then, that evening in mid-July before the Democratic Convention, I wrote an opinion piece suggesting that the widespread perceptions about *dishonesty* and *scandals* surrounding Hillary Clinton made her a riskier candidate against Donald Trump than the widely trusted Sanders whose popularity was increasing rather than diminishing at the time. The piece was entitled "The Deeper Reason Many Intelligent Progressives and Independents Will Not Support Hillary Clinton," and in it, I made a last call to convention delegates to consider nominating Sanders over Clinton.[5] Neither candidate would arrive at the convention with a clear majority of earned delegates, I argued, so it would be the choice of the convention delegates—the "superdelegates"—that would determine the nominee. Sanders was also faring better against Trump in head-to-head polling. I argued to the best of my ability that Bernie was the better candidate for the general election.

That morning, after repeatedly clicking the refresh button on my browser to no avail, and finding that my credentials no longer worked to log in, I realized I wasn't just censored, I was sacked. I would never again write for *Huffington Post*.

I also learned that many people on alternative news sites were discussing my piece. They were speculating as to why it had been taken down. One site had a cached copy of the article, and it was being copied and pasted on smaller independent news sites. Since I was no longer able to access the *Huffington Post* contributor platform, I published a copied version of the piece on my personal blog at Medium.[6] I put a link to it on Twitter before I got on the plane to go to Philadelphia for the convention. Frankly, I was quite angry about the suppression, but I was also confused. I wanted my call to the "superdelegates" to be available for reading and discussion.

Narrowing the Discussion

The article went viral on Twitter. It became my most widely read piece of the year. Many people came up to me at the convention and mentioned that they had read the piece and agreed with it. Perhaps it was that well-written and well-argued, but more likely it was the "Barbara Streisand effect," whereby something suppressed receives more attention because of the attempt to censor it.[7] This phenomenon is salutary in a propagandized nation like ours.

Whatever the case, I was left uncertain as to why I had been censored and sacked, and that uncertainty was the first seed of curiosity that led to the book you hold in your hands. The question has driven me. *Where does this censorship originate?*

Perhaps I was sacked at *HuffPo* because of the content of the piece. In laying out the case that Sanders was more trusted than Clinton, I briefly enumerated some of the more controversial scandals in the Clintons' past. Or perhaps I was sacked because the executive editors were under orders to narrow the popular discussion as the convention began. As we'll explore in Chapter 12, many commentators who were insufficiently supportive of Clinton were terminated at that very time at corporate media outlets. Perhaps the establishment had wanted a broad array of perspectives during the early phase of the primary, so as to draw in as many people as possible, but no longer wanted the perspective of Sanders's supporters at the convention.

It was ironic, then, that their censorship had directly contributed to the piece's broad popularity.

As mentioned earlier, everyday editorial decision-making is not censorship. Many news sources edit what their writers write or speakers say, and if writers and editors communicate, revise, and come to agreements, it isn't censorship. On the other hand, if a writer is entirely prevented from presenting a particular story or analysis—or is terminated for even trying—and when it's done by a corporate media outlet prone to both *systemic* and *nefarious bias,* it is indeed *censorship.*

I was canceled, to use a modern term, and never given an explanation nor an opportunity to revise or publish anything else. I reached out directly and repeatedly to Hayley Miller, and to others at *HuffPo,* but received no response. A letter that a lawyer sent on my behalf to *HuffPo* brass resulted in a terse response without explanation that quoted a vague passage of a Terms and Conditions document.

My piece was censored, and I was never told why. In retrospect, it was probably not on account of *innocent bias* nor *nefarious bias* but rather on account of the third type of bias that we explore in this chapter: *systemic bias.*

Let's examine one more case of *systemic bias* before we delve into how it works.

NO STANDING ON STANDING ROCK

SEVERAL MONTHS LATER, NATIVE AMERICANS FROM THREE HUNDRED tribes set up camp together on a windswept, North Dakota prairie. In a bit-ing, November cold spell, they pitched a vast array of tents on a swath of land just inside the Standing Rock Sioux Reservation. It had been over a century since members of so many tribes had come together with a shared cause, set aside differences, and stood as one. Thousands of other human beings, native and non-native people of every race, place, and background, from around the country and around the world, had journeyed to pitch camp and support the tribes. The purpose was to stop a proposed oil pipeline from crossing pristine land, violating native sovereignty, and endangering a precious watershed. United, they called themselves "Water Protectors." Their numbers swelled to nearly 10,000 as Thanksgiving Day approached.

In the predawn hours of November 20, 2016, dozens of Water Protectors stepped onto Backwater Bridge, a crossing over a small river. The bridge was state-owned, and security forces had deliberately strewn it with debris that prevented emergency and other traffic from coming and going to the Protectors' camp. The debris also prevented the protestors from getting to the site where the pipeline was under construction. In the darkness, the Water Protectors began to clear the bridge.

Phalanxes of hired security guards and body-armored state police appeared almost instantly over a crest. Attack dogs barked. Police vehicles revved their engines. One jeep rolled into view, carrying a water cannon. A minute later, the water cannon came to life, splitting the subzero night air with streams of frigid water. The Protectors howled and shrieked as the water struck them on the bridge, drenched their clothes, and froze in their hair. People screamed and recoiled in disgust. Then, the unexpected happened: with an intrepid and defiant joy, one Water Protector called out to the military police for a bar of soap. With a shared purpose, they all pushed on, clearing the bridge.

Then came the rubber bullets. Like baseballs of frozen rubber, the bullets struck the Protectors in the head, shoulders, chest, and groin. Pepper spray came in gusts. The flash of concussion grenades, temporarily deafening and blinding, exploded amongst those on the bridge. Chaos ensued. The Protectors at this point were simply trying to survive.

A young woman named Sophia darted out of the network of tepees in the village, carrying a large shield and several bottles of drinking water down to the bridge. She had already made several such deliveries of supplies to the Protectors on the bridge. She was wet and tired, but she pushed on. As she neared the bridge, she lifted the shield to protect her own face and torso from the projectiles, but it was too late. A searing explosion struck her deaf and blind, and pain like lightning tore a jagged gash up her left arm.

The next thing she knew, she was staring up into a pale, dawning sky, her sight and hearing returning gradually as pain shot through her left arm. A young man told her a concussion grenade had been fired directly at her. Most of her arm was blown off.[8]

Sophia was placed in a fellow protestor's truck and rushed to a hospital where shrapnel was removed from her arm and torso.

Muddying the Waters

Independent media outlets published pieces written by journalists on the ground that evening. Eyewitnesses repeated that the traumatic injuries from the water cannons and flashbang grenades on the Backwater Bridge were the result of police use of dangerous but nonlethal combat weaponry.

Reports appeared in the corporate media too, but they weren't nearly so clear in their versions of events. Perhaps this was because they weren't published for several days or because the corporate media outlets for the most part didn't send any journalists.[9] The *New York Times*, without a reporter on the ground, ran a story on November 24th that muddied the waters significantly. The piece, "Cause of Severe Injury at Pipeline Protest Becomes New Point of Dispute,"[10] cast doubt as to where Sophia was at the time of the attack, who caused her injury, and whether grenades were used at all. Through extensive use of paraphrased statements—not actual quotes—from a single police officer, the piece presented the police's account as the credible one. The officer's statements were printed with a simple "he said" at the end of each statement:

> Around the time of the explosion, Lieutenant Iverson said, officers fired sponge and beanbag rounds at three people who had shielded themselves behind a length of plywood near a burned vehicle on the bridge. The three were thought to be acting suspiciously and refused orders to emerge, he said ... officers did not use concussion or flash grenades at any time. Instead, officers used tear gas, pepper spray canisters and what are known as stinger balls ... he said.

Were you to read only this and other corporate media accounts, your conclusion would likely be, *Well, that's terrible that this ardent protester got hurt, but hey, we can't be sure what happened.*

On the other hand, Sophia's father, who arrived in North Dakota on the 23rd, released a precise and lucid statement on Sophia's behalf while she was still in intensive care. It was printed in many independent media journals, including *Indian Country Today*:

> At around 4:30 a.m., after the police hit the bridge with water cannons and rubber bullets and pepper spray, they lobbed a number of concussion grenades which are not supposed to be thrown at people directly, at protesters, or protectors, as they want to be called. A grenade exploded right as it hit Sophia in the left forearm, taking most of the undersurface of her left arm with it. Both her radial and ulnar artery were completely destroyed. Her radius was shattered and a large piece of it is missing. Her medial nerve is missing a large section as well. All of the muscle and soft tissue between her elbow and wrist were blown away. The police did not do this by accident—it was an intentional act of throwing it directly at her. Additionally, police were shooting people in the face and groin intending to do the most possible damage.[11]

A few quotes from this statement appeared in the *Times* piece, but they were dwarfed in length and emphasis by several paragraphs attributed to the police officer.

Whatever you believe about the Protectors, the Native Americans, the militarized police, and the corporate goals of Energy Transfer Partners; whomever you believe was to blame for Sophia's destroyed arm; whether you supported or opposed the pipeline itself—the important point for our purposes is to understand how and why the corporate media distorted the story. Outlets like the *Times* scrupulously took the side of the energy corporation and police as if by *instinct*. My writing in the *Huffington Post* was also censored as if by *instinct*. In this chapter, we examine this *instinct*.

There were no obvious lies in the *Times* piece. Every dubious assertion of the police's version was followed by the words, "he said." Yet, by focusing on the police's version of events, by amplifying its viewpoint with more graphic details, and by paraphrasing quotes rather than using unedited words, the *Times* manipulated the news. Obfuscation is one type of news distortion.

The article's title is itself disingenuous. "Cause of Severe Injury at Pipeline Protest Becomes New Point of Dispute," uses the passive voice, which reduces its immediacy and suggests that what is newsworthy is not that a young woman's arm was blown away while peacefully exercising her right to assemble, but rather that there's a *dispute*. The dispute is newsworthy, not someone's grievous injury. Even the photo included with the article was confusing: a shadowy portrait of unidentified silhouettes on a foggy night.

The *Times* runs so many stories each day that many readers only scan the headlines and photos. This fact is an essential point in understanding the impact of corporate news as a whole. Headlines are crafted to spin the story from the outset.

No newspaper is obligated to cover every single occurrence on the face of the Earth. But the *Times* ran no article simply reporting the injury. It ran only this piece guiding its readers into uncertainty. The *Times* writers boosted one side of the story enough to suggest parity between the accounts and to suggest a particular conclusion, even if, in this case, that conclusion was indecision.

Unbiased reporting of injuries sustained by demonstrators at, for instance, Selma, Alabama in 1965, led to significantly deeper sympathy among the public for their cause. By not sending a reporter and by not reporting the injury in a straightforward way, the *New York Times* prevented its readers from developing sympathy for the demonstrators.

THE WAR FOR YOUR MIND

THE NEWS COVERAGE OF STANDING ROCK PROVIDES A HELPFUL SNAPshot of the state of today's media world, even if the events took place more than five years ago. There were accounts of the events in both corporate media and independent media, and the accounts diverged widely. This split in coverage caused a split in nationwide opinion.

In this war for the minds of the nation, both sides ultimately claimed victory. While the pipeline went through, and oil now flows through metal tubes beneath the prairie and under the Missouri River, the Standing Rock Sioux Tribe and a coalition of other tribes declared groundbreaking success in challenging and changing the national news narrative about Native Americans. A report published in 2018 entitled *Changing the Narrative about Native Americans*[12] called the Standing Rock movement a success since the "movement's core organizers controlled the narrative and refused to let opponents and mainstream media define their movement."

Of course, the success of a protest movement isn't only determined by what people *think* about it. The power of the mainstream corporate media is enormous, and the wealth to be gained from the pipeline won the day, as it did in Iraq. But the words of the *Changing the Narrative* report presaged something grander than a pipeline or a war: the rise of independent media. The consciousness that the tribal leaders possessed about narrative control heralds the unfolding of the New Enlightenment.

Many Americans still trust corporate media more, but the balance has steadily been shifting over the past 20 years toward those who place more trust in independent media. When asked in 2014, for the first time, a slim majority reported mistrust of the mainstream corporate media.[13] When asked again in 2020, the number had dropped to 40%, with only 9% of Americans reporting "a great deal" of trust in the corporate media and 31% indicating "a fair amount" of trust; a striking 33% reported "no trust at all," and the remaining 27% reported "not very much."[14]

A year later, in 2021, polling revealed that the trend had accelerated. Just 29% of people reported general trust in corporate media compared with a massive 44% who did not. Twenty-seven percent were unsure.[15] The unfolding demographics were as stunning as the plummeting trust in the corporate media. Trust is even lower among those under the age of 50.[16] We already live in a country where people accept unilateral corporate media narratives with less trust and regularity than their parents. This too heralds the dawn of the New Enlightenment.

Increasingly, younger Americans turn to independent news sources— that is, those not owned by billionaires or the nation's five giant "infotainment" behemoths. Numbering in the thousands, these myriad self-sustaining sources of news in many cases report and analyze current events with a quality and accuracy that exceeds that of the corporate media. These independent news sources pose a true danger to the exalted power of *narrative control* that organizations like CNN and the *Times* have for so long enjoyed.

As for CNN, a network that was once a central authority on the news of the day, viewership has declined precipitously in this decade. After the pandemic and the 2020 election brought more viewers, the ensuing years have not been kind. Viewership peaked at 2.2 million daily viewers in 2020, plummeted to 1 million midway through 2021,[17] and was just 550,000 in January of 2022.[18] These numbers bounce around as news events come and go, of course, but the overall trend is clear. MSNBC lost 34% of its viewers over the same time period. Fox News, 12%. CNN's dire hit was likely exacerbated by revelations late in 2021 that leading anchor Chris Cuomo used his primetime show to protect his brother, New York Governor Andrew Cuomo, from allegations of sexually assaulting staffers[19] and forcing elderly covid patients into nursing homes.[20] Network news on ABC, CBS, and NBC are faring little better, with leading morning news shows like ABC's Good Morning America, which attracted nearly 2 million viewers in 2012, dropping below 900,000 in 2022.[21] CBS and NBC have lost even more viewers.

The corporate media is thus losing, slowly but surely, its most valuable asset, Americans' trust. The *New York Times* is the nation's leading media organization. It featured numerous articles on Standing Rock but didn't actually have a reporter on location. This may have been due to an oversight, an innocent matter of priorities, an intentional decision to reduce sympathetic or honest coverage, or the *instinct* which we mentioned above that we explore in this chapter. Whatever the case, the *Times'* coverage set the media agenda for the nation and favored the gas and oil corporations that simply wanted the Water Protectors to go away, preferably without media attention.

The corporate media giants will not let their formidable power and status go without a fight, and we as a nation are suffering their death throes. They are trying to survive by silencing, vilifying, and marginalizing independent sources of news and opinion. This trend is accelerating. Legacy publications sustain hits to their legitimacy every year. A *Times* podcast on ISIS and Al Qaeda[22] in 2018 turned out to be fictional.[23] A funder of the paper's coverage of China in 2020 turned out to be the Chinese government.[24] As their credibility erodes, they lash out ever more fiercely at the independent media organizations gradually replacing them.

In the words of Jordan Schachtel, one of the influential independent journalists we'll highlight in our Balanced Media Diet, the corporate media is like the mafia:

Think of the legacy press as something akin to a Mexican cartel. It's all about retaining dominance over the space. They don't want anyone from the outside coming in, so they resort to modern day book burning and intimidation.[25]

A central realization underpinning the science of propaganda is that the power to control a society's *narrative* about its present is tantamount to controlling that society's future. This is why there is a war on for your mind.

One Perspective vs. The Truth

In an era not long ago, countries behind the Iron Curtain used endless propaganda to persuade their citizens that the life they enjoyed was superior to that in the West. That war for people's minds ultimately didn't go well. Today, the establishment news organizations of the American corporate media, with their longtime stranglehold on American public opinion, strive to convince you to fear independent media.

It may not go well. Americans today already have profuse news sources of every stripe and slant, a tapestry of perspective, analysis, and opinion that provides a diversity of narratives and opinions. This profusion is enabled and enhanced by the internet, and it increasingly serves the roles that the press must for a democracy to thrive. The corporate media dinosaurs do own just about every sizable news outlet that money can buy, and they desperately want to put the genie back in the bottle and regain control of the narrative. They want to dictate to us every day *who* we are, *what* we should fear, *whom* we should admire, and *where* our nation and planet are going. The new era of independent media is revealing the lengths these organizations are willing to go to regain control. They're not worried about independent media lying to you; they're worried about independent media telling you the truth.

Independent media is, of course, wrong about things too sometimes. There's essentially no floor to the journalistic standards that a group of independent writers or a lone blogger might choose to meet. It can be difficult at first to discern the competent sources from the incompetent ones. The legacy media organizations seize upon these difficulties to scare away as many Americans as possible.

Independent media sources also have *innocent bias* because they're human organizations. But few suffer from *nefarious bias* or *systemic bias,* and this insight will be important as we construct our Balanced Media Diets later in this book. Another benefit of independent media is that people generally take its reporting and analysis as just one perspective, not as The Truth. This makes an enormous difference on the path to *media consciousness.* When we attempt to form a coherent sense of the world, corporate media professes to purvey everything we can and should know, but as the analysis in this book shows, it too provides only one perspective, and usually the perspective favored by billionaires and those who profit most from this country's current distribution of wealth and power. This is the biggest problem with corporate media, and the reason so many Americans are in a state of constant deception: corporate media suffers not just from *innocent bias* but from *nefarious bias,* too, and from an additional type of bias we now define, *systemic bias.*

THE THIRD BIAS: SYSTEMIC BIAS

WHAT WE'VE CALLED "INNOCENT BIAS" THUS FAR IS RESPONSIBLE FOR many distortions in partisan news sources. The mockingbird model propagates news with a *nefarious bias* easily witnessed at times of particularly significant decision-making—such as during the buildup to wars and the emergence of a deadly virus—when the interests of the expanding American empire run counter to the interests of the populace. But the majority of media news bias is *not* of this nefarious kind. Most of the time, simple reporting of the news by corporate media is done on the ground by innocent, ambitious journalists, filtered up through media ownership channels, and broadcast in a produced, digested form to viewers and readers around the country.

So, how can we account for the way the media distorts the truth about relatively mundane current events, such as this story about police and protestors in North Dakota? What determines what is covered, how it is covered, and what is left out?

Casual media observers might assume that it's basic profit economics. This superficial theory holds that economic interests and the pursuit of profits dictate how media companies determine coverage and slant. News outlets, this theory goes, choose what stories to cover—and how to cover them—based on the number of viewers or clicks each will get. The adage "if it bleeds it leads" encapsulates this theory of editorial decision-making, and those who subscribe to it even assume that they're being a bit cynical by alleging that the news isn't actually covered based on objective "newsworthiness" of a particular event.

It turns out this is not the case at all.

Money *is* a primary consideration for editors and news organizations owned by billionaires and giant corporations, as they all are these days, but not through choosing news that will generate clicks and views. The important distinction to understand—and what gives this chapter its title—is that news stories are reported in a way that supports the *larger profit motive* of the parent conglomerate. Stories are omitted or distorted if they run counter to this larger profit drive of the parent organization. They're concerned with making money, but first and foremost, the goal is to protect the veneer of honesty and objectivity while building support for the parent corporation's agenda. That's where the real power is asserted, and that's where the real money is made. The corporate media's true objective is control of the narrative. This power enables it to shape our perspectives and manipulate our fears and angers. This power generates far more money than increasing clicks on an article.

"The business of a New York journalist is to distort the truth, to lie outright, to pervert, to vilify, to fawn at the foot of Mammon, and to sell his country ... for his daily bread ... We are the tools and vassals of rich men behind the scenes."
—Publisher John Swinton, 1833

For instance, the *Washington Post* could have attracted a large amount of attention and clicks by fairly covering the Alabama labor movement's attempt in April of 2021 to unionize the workers in an Amazon warehouse for the first time. But Amazon founder, Jeff Bezos, the world's richest man, owns the

Post, and he doesn't want Amazon workers to unionize. So, the story was not covered in a way that would have maximized attention and clicks but rather in a way that best served the larger financial and power interests of Amazon.[26] This *filter* greatly outstripped in importance any drive for the *Washington Post* to make money via attracting attention to its coverage.

All major corporate media outlets are owned by large transnational conglomerates, each of which has its own set of concerns, interests, and desires to expand its own wealth and power. To fully understand the way news media as a whole is covered, we have to understand the way news media is *filtered*.

Noam Chomsky and Edward Herman explored this question in their groundbreaking 1988 book *Manufacturing Consent: The Political Economy of the Mass Media*.[27] They examined an enormous quantity of corporate media reporting on a handful of controversial topics. They brilliantly distilled a coherent way to understand how corporate media bias works. We're going to take some time here to understand Chomsky and Herman's important insights.

During their extensive study, they identified five primary lenses through which news reporting is *filtered*. These lenses, which in this book we will update for the twenty-first century and call *filters*, serve to emphasize certain issues, spin other issues, and remove entirely certain other issues from the media. By comprehending these five filters, we can understand the third type of *bias* in our corporate media: *systemic bias*.

Chomsky and Herman's model does have shortcomings, which we'll discuss in a moment, but it remains a highly useful part of the analysis of this book. As an aside, please consider reading *Manufacturing Consent* along with Edward Bernays's book *Propaganda* mentioned earlier. These two books provide important background to understanding my analysis in this book.

The Five Filters of the News System

In this book, the term *filters* refers to updated versions of the lenses that Chomsky and Herman identified in *Manufacturing Consent*. These filters form the basis for a sophisticated understanding of how propaganda and censorship function in modern news—what I call *systemic bias*. Let's examine each of the five filters, and how they work in today's media world.

1. ***The Interests of Ownership.*** Nearly all corporate media outlets are owned today by five giant, transnational conglomerates, and any news coverage that runs counter to the parent corporation's clear interests will be filtered. Any large media organization that reaches a large audience had to raise investment capital at some point and thus has brought along with itself the interests of large investment capital. The example of the *Washington Post* and Amazon, mentioned above, is an obvious case. The *Bloomberg News* policy of not reporting on Michael Bloomberg's enormous wealth, scandals, or personal life choices serves as another clear example. Slightly more subtle would be NBC News supporting the drive to start a war in Iraq in 2003, given parent corporation GE's potential profits from the sale of weapons technology and military equipment. Another subtle but salient case is MSNBC reporting unfairly on Bernie Sanders, who has called frequently for the breakup of media conglomerates and the public regulation of internet service providers as utilities; these proposals would endanger the profits of MSNBC's parent conglomerate, Comcast.

2. ***The Interests of Elite Sources.*** In order to write stories on a daily basis that capture popular attention and explore world events, media organizations generally want to interview and quote wealthy and powerful people in government and business. Thus, journalists seek what is called "elite access." An organization with this access can often quickly obtain newsworthy quotes and interviews with powerful people who are in the news. Writing stories that are critical of elite sources can lead to being denied access or "frozen out" the next time a big story comes around, so there is substantial institutional risk to alienating powerful people or running stories that oppose their preferences or interests. These stories will be filtered.

3. ***The Interests of Advertisers.*** Most media organizations, regardless of who owns them, earn the majority of their revenue from advertising, so they're unlikely to cover news that runs counter to their advertisers' interests. If such "controversial" news is covered, the angle they take will be one that advertisers favor. This puts advertisers in an extraordinarily powerful position, and often prevents media organizations that boldly cover things like labor movements or drug scandals

from becoming profitable in a competitive media environment. Essentially, all corporate media outlets avoid topics that are controversial or run counter to the interests of large corporations that have a substantial advertising budget.

4. ***Avoiding Outcry.*** Corporate newsrooms often welcome controversial and scandalous stories (so long as other filters don't apply), but they avoid covering stories that will generate deeply negative reactions, such as sustained social media outcry, boycotts, lawsuits, or legislative action. Even if the story is true, these negative reactions can immensely harm a news organization's reputation—even its survival. "Outcry" here means negative attention organized by powerful private interest groups like churches, think tanks, social justice groups, and labor unions. The media organization and its parent corporation fear sustained outcry, and this fear is a formidable deterrent to covering certain topics or employing bias in the wrong direction.

5. ***The Dominant Narrative.*** This, the final filter, is the least obvious but the most powerful. News reporting that runs counter to the dominant news *narrative* of the day will be filtered, distorted, or omitted. In the original version of their filters, Chomsky and Herman called this filter "anti-communism," as that was a dominant story of the time; in the 2010s, Chomsky updated this by saying this lens had become the "war on terror." In 2020 and 2021, the dominant narrative was the "dangerous pandemic." If we think of news narratives as rivers, and journalists and politicians as fish, any reporting that swims against the stream will be filtered.

These five filters of *systemic bias* demonstrate clearly that attracting viewers to earn money is important, but that the corporate ownership's underlying profit and power motives are what truly determine news coverage. Stories that would generate a lot of viewers—and a resulting bump in advertising revenue—are not covered when they might cause a larger loss of money, power, or control for the corporate conglomerate. This is why the Epstein story, as just one example, was censored for so long.

Sometimes, contradictory opinions and voices are offered in corporate media for the sake of engagement because these outlets must maintain the interest of their most privileged audiences. But in general the growth and protection of the parent conglomerate's power is far more profitable than the popularity any single investigation or new perspective might bring. This is the ever-present power of *systemic bias.*

One example is the case of Seymour Hersh. Hersh is one of the most decorated and respected independent investigative journalists in American history. He broke the earth-shattering story of the My Lai Massacre in Vietnam in 1969. He exposed the torture at Abu Ghraib Prison in Iraq in 2004 before it was common knowledge. He revealed the countless flaws in the story of the alleged killing of Osama bin Laden in 2011.[28] Hersh was not likely to go down easily, but *systemic bias* struck even for him. In 2010, he wrote a book on Dick Cheney, chronicling the secret prisons, killing squads, and private bank accounts that Cheney had arranged[29] around the world in his bloodthirsty paranoia after 9-11.[30] The book would have interested many people had it seen the light of day. But President Obama initiated a crackdown on journalists and whistleblowers at the time,[31] and the book was never published.[32] The second and fourth filters—Elite Sources and Avoiding Outcry—were responsible for this decision.

Another example is the way coverage unfolded so painfully slowly during the water poisoning scandal in Flint, Michigan, something we'll explore in detail in Chapter 11. *Systemic bias* was in effect from top to bottom. The second and third filters—Elite Sources and Advertisers—were responsible for most of the omissions and distortions in the coverage of the issue. At Standing Rock, the Ownership and Elite Sources filters reduced or removed altogether sympathetic coverage of the Water Protectors.

MORE THAN MERE MONEY, MORE THAN MERE CONSENT

IT IS FASCINATING—AND PERHAPS DEPRESSING—THAT A MODEL DEvised in the 1980s still so accurately describes how news is filtered and suppressed in today's corporate media. But much has changed in the decades since Chomsky and Herman published their findings, and the intervening years have revealed two major shortcomings in their work.

The first shortcoming is that they focused only on *systemic bias*. They did a fabulous job distilling these filters, and their work remains highly relevant, but they talked very little about *innocent bias* and didn't examine *nefarious bias* at all. For all their detailed study, Chomsky and Herman looked only superficially at Operation Mockingbird and similar types of deliberate, covert media distortion. They rarely looked for evidence of actual censorship or covert collaboration among journalists, editors, and government actors. We must examine the interplay of all three types of bias to understand news distortion in our country today.

The other shortcoming of *Manufacturing Consent* is that its analysis is ultimately shallow. Certainly one imperative of the corporate media in America as a whole is to "manufacture consent" for the agenda of the billionaires, the US military, and the largest corporations. This was a groundbreaking insight distilled over years of study that even today far too few Americans grasp. But "consent" is not the ultimate prize for which media corporations compete. As we've already seen in this book, the *story* we are living in—the composite beliefs we have about our lives—not only determines our consent for policies but *predicts our future behavior*. It is control of the narrative for which the corporate media behemoths most ardently strive.

The true ferocity of the war for our minds can be seen from this larger perspective. The managers of the narrative don't pursue just our *consent* but rather our full participation in the fear, anger, and hope they weave into their manipulated stories. The distortion through *systemic* and *nefarious bias* seeks to strip us of our basic mental faculties of reason and rationality and replace them with emotion.

The Freedom of Speech and the Freedom of the Press are first principles of our nation because they enable participatory democracy and evidence-based science, bedrock values of the first Enlightenment. *Systemic* and *nefarious bias* threaten our society's first principles. Propaganda is anathema to democracy. Censorship is the enemy of science. Yet, censorship and propaganda are precisely the tools corporate media use today to deceive us and, ultimately, to undermine the blossoming of this New Enlightenment.

We can't simply rely on the Constitution and its guarantees to protect systems that have been overrun by powerful interests. As citizens, we must know and *exercise* our rights in order to preserve our precious democracy. As we've seen so far in our exploration, many who control the dominant narratives are in powerful positions and stand directly to benefit from those narratives and the pressures of *systemic bias* that cause other narratives to be excluded.

Systemic Bias in the Org Chart

The filters of *systemic bias* aren't only at play when corporate media organizations select which stories to print and which to ignore. *Systemic bias* also determines hirings, firings, and promotions. A journalist whose reporting or perspective tends to threaten advertisers' interests, say, or undermine the dominant narrative, will be passed over for promotion or simply never hired.

Thus one of the most poisonous effects of *systemic bias* is the culture it creates in news corporations of mental cowardice and self-censorship. As independent news analyst Russell Brand said about the coverage of the Epstein crimes and the length of time it took for the justice system and the media to pay attention: "It would take a culture of corruption" to hide it for so long. "There wouldn't just be a single bad apple for a decade," he remarked.[33] "Clearly, the problem wasn't that the pedophilia existed. The problem was that it was discovered." After two decades, *systemic bias* finally failed.

This culture of corruption is an important component of *systemic bias* since it leads to censorship and distortion that it is *instinctive* rather than conscious. Editors and writers will instinctively know what should and should not be filtered in news reporting by simply living in the culture of corporate media establishments. When my writing at *Huffington Post* was taken down, three of the filters played a role— Ownership, Elite Sources, and Avoiding Outcry—but probably in an instinctive rather than a conscious way.

In a fascinating interview with Andrew Marr of the BBC in 1996, Chomsky explained this clearly.[34] Chomsky had penned an article asserting that all journalists at all major corporate media organizations perform essentially the same role and report from the same narrow range of viewpoints. Marr opened the interview by asking Chomsky to explain this analysis. Marr then challenged his assertions.

> **Marr:** I was brought up, like a lot of people, post-Watergate, to believe that journalism was a crusading craft and that there were a lot of disputatious,

stroppy, difficult people in journalism. And I have to say, I think I know some of them.

Chomsky: Well, I know some of the best and best-known investigative reporters in the United States—I won't mention names—whose attitude towards the media is much more cynical than mine. In fact, they regard the media as a sham ... It's perfectly true that the majority of journalists who are trained have it driven into their heads that this is a crusading profession, adversarial, "we stand up to power." It's a very self-serving view actually. On the other hand, in my opinion, and I hate to make a value judgment, but the better journalists, and the ones who are commonly regarded as the *best* journalists, have quite a different picture, and I think a very realistic one.

Marr: How can you know that I'm self-censoring? How can you know that journalists are self-censoring?

Chomsky: I'm not saying you're self-censoring. I'm sure you believe everything you say. But what I'm saying is, if you believed something different, you wouldn't be sitting where you're sitting.

In an analysis similar to Chomsky's, author Anand Giridharadas, a prominent commentator on MSNBC and writer for the *New York Times*, revealed that the guardrails for journalists are enforced both overtly and covertly. In a 2020 interview on the independent news show *Rising*, he revealed to hosts Krystal Ball and Saagar Enjeti that, in some instances, elite journalists are directly told by media executives what to cover and what not to cover.[35] They are sometimes told specific questions to ask and specific questions not to ask. At times, he explained, it gets to the point where commentators on mainstream media shows are literally texting with billionaires under the table while on the air.

But Giridharadas concluded by describing what he sees as the more common corrupting influence: innate mental habits that lead to intellectual cowardice. To reach elite positions, journalists have instinctively learned to be cautious about, for instance, advocating for Medicare for All, which the giant pharmaceutical corporations oppose, questioning the need for another war, when the weapons and energy corporations generally support wars, or investigating election fraud, when powerful politicians (the ones who won) don't want it explored. Instinctively and honestly supporting an agenda is useful in manufacturing consent for it. Thus, the defining quality of the non-Mockingbird journalists who reach elite positions in the corporate media world is that they write and speak in ways that do not trigger the filters of *systemic bias*. The Mockingbird journalists, meanwhile, manage the narratives with *nefarious bias.*

Thus, the produced, digested form of news that is broadcast by corporate media to Americans is almost entirely created by people in one of three groups: those who just happen to honestly support dominant narratives, those with long-standing intellectual cowardice, and those professionally tasked with deceiving the public.

5

RED NEWS, BLUE NEWS, FAKE NEWS, TRUE NEWS

"The conscious and intelligent manipulation of the organized habits and opinions of the masses is an important element in democratic society. Those who manipulate this unseen mechanism of society constitute an invisible government which is the true ruling power of our country."

Edward Bernays, *Propaganda* (1922)

THE STANDING ROCK MOVEMENT THAT LED TO SOPHIA WILANSKY'S DIS-membering had started much earlier that year, in March 2016. A Sioux elder by the name of LaDonna Brave Bull Allard set up Sacred Stone Camp at about the same time I was brought on board at *Huffington Post*. The movement grew concurrently with the campaigns of the 2016 presidential candidates. While neither Hillary Clinton, Donald Trump, nor any of the many other Republican candidates said much about the Standing Rock movement—and the corporate media filtered news about it—one candidate spoke out vocif-erously in favor of the Water Protectors from the outset. He supported the movement and decried even the attempt to use the land for corporate goals as a violation of Sioux Nation sovereignty.

Bernie Sanders was virtually alone in doing so among major elected officials, but that, of course, wasn't new territory for Sanders. He had been a lone or nearly-lone voice in Congress for years, opposing things like the Iraq War, privatization of federal services, corporate monopolization of the media, homophobia, racial injustice, open borders, and trade deals that shipped jobs overseas.

At the outset of his campaign, Sanders was also virtually alone in believing he had any chance at the nomination.[1] He was a relatively unknown senator from a small state, and he wasn't even a registered Democrat but rather an independent who called himself a Democratic *Socialist*.[2] He refused corporate campaign contributions and instead raised money directly from American citizens. Few in the Democratic Party brass or on corporate media editorial boards expected him to win even 10% of the vote nationally.

A candidate the establishment disliked, Bernie Sanders nevertheless grew extraordinarily popular among the American populace. This makes his campaign for president useful for our analysis. We will examine the agenda that the corporate media followed and the ways their coverage differed from simply reporting the news or simply maximizing profits and readership. Using various types of distortion, the corporate media went to extraordinary lengths to diminish the appeal of the Sanders campaign.

It was a remarkable year, and I wrote about it with a front-row seat. Sanders supporters created an independent news media world that for days and weeks at a time provided an alternative narrative to the one pushed by the corporate media. The Sanders campaign obviously "connected" across the country as it drew enormous crowds to arenas and stadiums and raised historic amounts of money directly from everyday people. When the Democrat-leaning, mainstream corporate media sources—what we'll sometimes call "Blue News"—lose control of the narrative, the steps they take to regain control are fascinating to analyze. This period of 2016 is instructive in analyzing how *bias, censorship*, and *propaganda* distort our media world, and we will focus on Bernie Sanders and his "revolution" in this chapter.

FEELING THE BERN

AFTER A SURPRISE DEAD HEAT IN IOWA, SANDERS CRUISED TO A LARGE victory in the 2016 New Hampshire primary. It was only February, but the campaign suddenly had momentum. It began to pose an actual threat to a presumed Clinton nomination. The corporate media could have simply covered this development as compelling national news. The story was certainly newsworthy, and it generated abundant clicks and views as I discovered in writing about it. The only socialist senator was touring the country decrying oligarchy, tyrannical billionaires, and manipulative media monopolies and making unheard of promises about things like a $15 minimum wage, student debt forgiveness, tuition-free public college, and Medicare for All. "Feel the Bern" became the campaign's slogan, and soon, it was winning primary elections in not-so-radical places, like Michigan and Utah.

But clicks and views are not the corporate media's foremost priorities. *Systemic bias* filtered these stories at places like NPR and the *New York Times*. It became evident to Sanders supporters that the corporate media was trying to stop him.

The media watchdog organization Fairness and Accuracy in Reporting (FAIR) pointed out in March of 2016 that the *Washington Post* had run 16 negative articles about Sanders in a single 16-hour period.[3] I knew it was bad, but this seemed impossible to me until I went and actually read the sixteen-article barrage of March 7th. Reading piece after piece, the collection served as an early indictment of that particular newspaper's pretensions to impartiality. The media assault took place just after Sanders had won three state caucuses by comfortable margins on the eve of a pivotal primary in Michigan. The *Post* calls itself a "paper of record," like the *New York Times*, and professes high journalistic standards. Also like the *Times*, the *Post* had recently been acquired by a billionaire. In fact, Jeff Bezos, who had purchased the paper, had taken a larger stake in the *Post* than Carlos Slim had with the *Times*. Bezos had also made his opposition to a Sanders nomination public, and yet the paper's readership was asked to believe that his ownership had no effect on coverage. Bezos may never have directly requested the articles. This is how *systemic bias* works. Direct orders to journalists are rarely needed.

The *Times,* at least, endeavored to maintain a veneer of neutrality. It balanced every four or five negative pieces about Sanders with something positive.[4] But the *Times,*[5] too, along with virtually every newspaper and magazine owned by the five large media corporations—which is basically all of them—suppressed[6] or attacked Sanders[7] on multiple occasions.[8] It was as if there was a tune played in concert by the pipes of a mighty Wurlitzer.

The Blue News outlets favored most by Democrats—NPR and MSNBC—were the ones most thoroughly supportive of Clinton and dismissive or hostile to Sanders. As we'll see in Chapter 12, a chapter devoted to banned journalists that might surprise you, many journalists at Blue News establishments were fired for showing insufficient support for Clinton at this time. I was but one of many.

Modern-Day Mockingbirds

We might not have known the extent to which the media actively opposed a Sanders nomination were it not for a historic leak of internal emails. International transparency organization WikiLeaks released a trove of emails between the Hillary Clinton campaign and high-ranking members of the Democratic National Committee (DNC).[9] The DNC was the organization running the primary between Sanders and Clinton, and its leadership howled about the *timing* of the release of the emails. The *authenticity* of the emails was never challenged.

The leaked internal communications revealed active collusion between the DNC, the Clinton campaign, and journalists at many of the country's most prestigious media outlets. One set of emails revealed that the Clinton campaign received debate questions in advance.[10] Another set of emails disclosed that a ranking official in the DNC specifically requested that a debate moderator force Bernie Sanders to confirm or deny holding Jewish religious beliefs in order to divide and diminish support for his campaign.[11] As a whole, the emails painted a compelling picture of sustained and concerted media *bias* to hurt Sanders.

Perhaps the biggest revelation was a list in one email of some 45 media personages—journalists, columnists, editors, and television hosts—whom the Clinton campaign called "friendly,"[12] "safe" or "malleable."[13] These media pros were in frequent communication with the campaign via private channels. Several *New York Times* writers, for instance, gave Clinton "veto" power over what was included in an interview. Other writers agreed to run articles by her prior to publication.[14] There is no record or claim that the Sanders campaign received any such privileges.

Maggie Haberman of *Politico* and the *New York Times* was singled out in the emails as a particularly "safe" and "malleable" writer by the Clinton campaign. Campaign spokesman Nick Merrill wrote to campaign manager Robby Mook:

> As discussed on our call, we are all in agreement that the time is right [to] place a story with a friendly journalist in the coming days that positions us a little more transparently while achieving [our] goals ... we feel that it's important to go with what is safe and what has worked in the past, and to a publication that will reach industry people for recruitment purposes. We have had a very good relationship with Maggie Haberman of Politico over the last year. We have had her tee up stories for us before and have never been disappointed.[15]

The leaked emails[16] also revealed the historic decision that the Clinton campaign and the DNC made to boost the candidacy of Donald Trump and several other Republican candidates.[17] In a document called "Our Goals & Strategy," dated April 15, 2015, a campaign strategist informed John Podesta and the rest of the campaign's senior staff of the plan:

> We need to be elevating the Pied Piper candidates [Donald Trump, Ted Cruz, and Ben Carson] so that they are leaders of the pack and tell the press to [take] them seriously.[18]

Thereafter, throughout the entirety of the primary, the corporate media elevated Donald Trump, and he received hours and hours of television coverage, effectively free advertising.[19] During 2015, before any votes were cast in the primaries, Trump received about six times more live network news airtime than what was given to Clinton and fifteen times more than the paltry minutes given to Sanders.

One of the most glaring examples of collusion and bias on the part of the corporate media took place when the largest state, California, was about to vote. On a day when no one voted, on the day *before* six primary elections were to take place, including the huge California primary, the Associated Press and NBC made an extraordinary declaration: Hillary Clinton had won.[20]

It was a stunning bit of narrative management. First, it was untrue: Clinton still didn't have enough delegates to clinch the nomination. Second, it was a media concoction: Clinton had won no new votes on the day, and the declaration was based on a dubious private survey of superdelegates, who don't vote until the convention. Third, and most egregious, writing headlines like this is voter suppression: announcing on the eve of an election that one candidate has already won is meddling in that election. Sanders had actually been faring better on election-day voting throughout the primaries; Clinton had been enjoying an edge in vote-by-mail and early voters. These facts revealed growing support for Sanders and made it still less excusable to call any race prematurely. But there it was, coordinated *bias* and *propaganda* on the part of the corporate media establishment.

It wasn't just traditional media outlets colluding. As we will see in upcoming chapters, internet behemoths Google, Facebook, and Twitter now have as much—and in some ways more—power over shaping the narrative than do traditional media outlets. Trust in corporate media is declining, but independent media spreads most quickly through search engines and social media. So, the internet companies act as much like gatekeepers as do, for instance, the editorial board of Fox News, NPR, or the *New York Times*.

We'll look more at their biases and intentions in a bit, but it's worth mentioning one thing here since it indicates Google's intentions were already clear in 2016. Google created a search engine "widget" that popped up when anyone searched on "Hillary Clinton," "Bernie Sanders," "Democratic primary," or related terms. Search results would display this widget at the top and show the current delegate count for the two potential nominees, with one significant feature: it counted "superdelegates" who hadn't voted yet. Superdelegates are members of the DNC, ranking officials, and lobbyists who get the enormous privilege of voting on the nominee of the party at the convention. Their votes count with the strength of roughly 10,000 voters. Superdelegates vote at the convention, not before, yet the Google widget counted them throughout the primary *as if they had already voted*; this gave the impression to anyone who visited Google for information on the primary that Hillary Clinton had an enormous lead.

THE RISE OF
ALTERNATIVE VOICES

THOSE WERE BUT A SMALL SAMPLING OF THE MANY EGREGIOUS INCI-
dents of media bias and collusion in favor of an establishment choice—in this
case, Hillary Clinton—by corporate media outlets. One subset of the American population is incurious supporters of establishment Democrats who read
Blue News outlets loyally and might contest that this *bias* exists. For everyone
else, pointing this out doesn't create a scandal or controversy. It's like saying
water is wet.

It's not a controversy, and it's not shocking. This is known bias. All sources
have their *bias*, and news outlets controlled by billionaires and reporters who
themselves are millionaires are likely to have a particularly strong bias toward
candidates and movements that advance or protect the interests of millionaires and billionaires. The issue is that these Democrat-leaning Blue News
establishment sources—and Republican-leaning Red News sources as well—
present themselves as The Truth rather than as purveyors of one perspective.

The twentieth century effectively took the nation from an infinite number of voices down to six, and that suited the establishment just fine. That
was the news media environment that existed in this country at the turn of
the century, the era of 9-11, and the time of the first Iraq War. Establishment
corporate media had a lock on the narrative, and those who didn't agree had
few places to go. In 2004, when Howard Dean led a less famous but no less
dramatic incipient campaign within the Democratic Party, he was taken out
with the notorious "Dean scream" moment.[21] This was in fact a disingenuous
act of microphone stripping by CNN that made his enthusiastic address to
supporters look insane. Those in the campaign knew it was a dishonest video,
but they had nowhere to go to get the word out; what they witnessed was not
discussed on NPR, written up in the *Washington Post,* or placed on the wire
by the Associated Press. So most Democrats had no idea that the video of
Dean "screaming" had been manipulated. His presidential campaign ended
then and there. There wasn't even a scandal.

The rise of independent media has begun to erode their narrative control
and their ability to call their reporting The Truth. This trend surfaced with

Obama's campaign in 2008 as the era of social media kicked off in earnest. By the time 2015 rolled around and unleashed on the nation the Bernie Sanders revolution, people's use and comfort with the internet, Facebook, Twitter, and YouTube had considerably increased. The technology to share content—including real-time video—had improved so substantially that genuine alternative sources for live news emerged in this country for the first time.

Social Media Grows Up

The Sanders campaign's groundbreaking ability to raise money via direct personal contributions through the internet is still reverberating through the PowerPoint presentations of political strategists. Corporate fundraising had dominated every major campaign for decades, until that year. Establishment political strategists and pundits still don't fully understand its ramifications.

In the same way, the Sanders campaign's use of the internet and social media built on the successes of the Dean and Obama campaigns before it, and it continues to transform our political process and how people learn about current events. An entirely novel source of news came of age in 2016. People were not just consuming and sharing news media—they were *becoming* the media. Bloggers and podcasters were showing up at political events with nothing more than a smartphone, witnessing events and asking candidates questions, editing their own audio and video, and uploading directly to Twitter, Facebook, and other channels. And that was that. It was news, and it was true, and it was published, and it was available for everyone.

When I was in Philadelphia for the convention, shortly after being censored by *Huffington Post,* the articles I published in independent media and the videos I posted to Facebook frequently received thousands of views and shares. A conference attendee told me on the lawn outside the convention center that all Sanders campaign volunteer delegates[22] had been stripped of their credentials and banned from the convention floor in order to make the audience look supportive of Clinton on television. I tweeted this out, breaking news that had been filtered out in corporate media.

I was just one of many. Some of those who were kicked out of the convention became journalists themselves that night, posting videos of their accounts of what had happened, and their unquestionably authentic accounts influenced the national narrative throughout the convention despite the corporate media's attempts to silence it.

Throughout that 2016 primary—as well as in the early stages of the 2020 primary four years later—the corporate media often lost control of the national narrative. Internet journalists with memes, hashtags, live reporting, and diverse, original analysis often provided more compelling and more truthful content, particularly for those with an even mildly balanced media diet.

Months before the convention, when a young Black woman held up a banner saying "We have to bring them to heel" at a Hillary Clinton campaign event just before the South Carolina primary, a Twitter hashtag captured the event better than the corporate news reports.[23] *#WhichHillary* underscored Hillary's perceived inconsistency on issues such as criminal justice and racism, and the fact she lost her temper with the young woman became not just newsworthy but a topic for analysis. The hashtag received over 400,000 tweets that day.[24] It became the day's narrative. Corporate media talk shows and nighttime comedy shows discussed an issue they had largely avoided to that point.

Twitter suppressed *#WhichHillary* the next day.

At another point in the campaign, a small, brown finch serendipitously landed on Bernie Sanders's lectern while he was addressing a rally of 11,000 people in Oregon. The hashtag *#BirdieSanders* was born. On Twitter, Facebook, and Instagram, repositories of videos, photos, and commentary appeared instantly as people all over the country uploaded media. This instant trove of commentary and coverage provided both independent media and corporate media alike an entire narrative, complete with creative assets, that dominated the corporate news cycle for several days. *#BirdieSanders* was suppressed eventually too.

A month later, with Sanders catching up to Clinton in pledged delegates, the corporate media narrative was that Sanders was "too negative" in his campaign messages and should "tone down" his critiques on issues like Wall Street corruption, climate change, and student debt relief. This happened on the eve of the crucial New York primary. Joel Benenson, a longtime Clinton staffer, publicly accused Sanders of "running a very negative campaign."[25] He suggested that the Clinton campaign would refuse further debates with Sanders unless the Vermont senator "toned down" his speeches.[26]

In response, Sanders supporters created *#ToneDownForWhat* and posted thousands of tweets under the hashtag, which changed the conversation from the perceived nature of Sanders's "negative" rhetoric to Clinton's perceived shortcomings.

> Are you kidding me @HillaryClinton?
> If you can't handle Sanders' tone, good luck dealing with Trump or, I dunno,
> ISIS. #ToneDownForWhat
> - @Meowdeleine

Social media and internet media like this were so effective that it often frustrated corporate media pundits unaccustomed to pushback on their mighty editorials and televised pontifications. They smeared Sanders supporters as "aggressive" and "mean" when the only characterization that was supported by data was greater enthusiasm for their candidate. All sides included negative voices. What was truly "aggressive" about Sanders supporters was that they were ridiculing the corporate media's distortions and errors and creating rival news sources.

EVERYONE'S A RACIST, EVERYONE'S A BRO

MEANWHILE, ON THE REPUBLICAN SIDE, THE SITUATION WASN'T ENtirely different. Presumptive nominees received the imprimatur of the party establishment: first Jeb Bush, then Ted Cruz, then Marco Rubio. Dominant "Red News" outlets praised them, gave them airtime, and held them up as "electable." But each was outshone in turn by an upstart campaign by Donald Trump and by the independent online media his supporters created. Trump's rallies eclipsed the other candidates' just as his supporters' own independent news narrative increasingly eclipsed corporate news narrative inevitably critical of Trump.

Independent media was setting the news narrative on both sides of the aisle. Whether one liked it or not, a new type of news media came of age in the United States in the summer of 2016.

This development scared some Americans. It thrilled others. Supporters of Trump and Sanders were likely the most excited, and those closely affiliated with one of the two political parties were likely most alarmed. Also nervous were the pundits, columnists, and editors at establishment corporate media whose priceless control of the daily narrative was eroding. The party brass worried they might lose control of their respective parties; the media types worried they might irrevocably lose control of the narrative. They all needed a way to regain control of the news. Ignoring the internet media renaissance instigated by Sanders and Trump proved ineffective. The actions they took next are fascinating.

> *"It is easier to fool someone*
> *than to convince them they've been fooled."*
> —Mark Twain

First, the corporate media doubled down on negative caricatures to smear the candidates and their supporters. With Trump supporters, the corporate media went with "white supremacists" as the narrative. They were called "Trumpers," and they were painted as unintelligent, White, racist, and—if the narrative of the day enabled it—violent, angry, and gullible. If a small scuffle broke out at a rally of 15,000 people, the scuffle would be covered rather than the fact that 15,000 people had turned out who wanted political change. The central message was *fear*, and the content was name-calling and insinuation rather than substantive analysis.

With Sanders, the narrative coalesced around a term, "Bernie Bro."[27] Quintessential Blue News journal *The Atlantic* coined it, and it proved irresistible to the Mockingbird media.[28] Pundits on NPR, MSNBC, and CNN seized on it in their opinion pieces, kicking off a years-long campaign to paint Sanders supporters as predominantly young, White men who were "aggressive," "vitriolic," and "mean."[29] It was odd that the caricature was so similar to how Trump supporters were smeared, but few pointed this out in the corporate media. How could a single demographic be behind groundbreaking national campaigns on both sides of the aisle? Those supporters (and many were neither male, White, nor young) were creating their own media to keep one another informed about the progressive campaign's goals and progress.

Bernie Made Me Male

The "Bernie Bros" narrative was particularly, demonstrably false. More of Sanders's under-45 supporters were actually women.[30] This created powerful counter-narratives. The *#BernieMadeMeMale* and *#BernieMadeMeWhite* hashtags became smash hits as women and people of color shared with sadness, sarcasm, or anger how the corporate media attempted to make their support of Sanders invisible.

There were some differences between how the dominant Red News and Blue News networks covered the candidates. While both campaigns benefited from insurgent, snowballing campaigns on social media, Sanders never received much coverage in any corporate media outlet. Trump, on the other hand, managed to garner swaths of free airtime on mainstream corporate news. Trump was usually portrayed in a negative light, to be sure, but he skillfully turned this to his advantage, a living embodiment of PT Barnum's axiom: "There is no such thing as bad publicity." Corporate media enhanced Trump's outsider appeal by attacking him repeatedly while showing contempt for Sanders with neglect.

What was unclear was why Blue News networks like NPR, MSNBC, and even ostensibly serious progressive media outlets like *The Young Turks* would devote more coverage to Donald Trump than to Bernie Sanders. It was one thing to watch CNN and Fox News devote airtime to Trump's empty lectern in anticipation of his speeches, but in the summer of 2016, the Blue News networks spent hours depicting Trump as crude, scary, fascist—a bogeyman. Meanwhile, they generally omitted Sanders altogether. Tuning into Red News network Fox News and conservative talk radio also revealed a fascination with an enemy, but it was Hillary Clinton rather than Sanders who was reviled. Partly this was due to the fact that Clinton was generally ahead in delegates for the nomination, but it also happened following Sanders victories, unveiling *systemic bias* in favor of the establishment candidate.

Rarely on Red News or Blue News channels did anyone ask why so many people on both sides of the political fence were so eager for change that they would rally to an old Jewish socialist with bad posture, on the one side, and a corrupt reality TV star who wore makeup on the other. It was never considered that these candidates might be popular *because they represented fundamental change.* I'm fairly certain this is why my articles—including my piece on privilege which the *Huffington Post* first published—were enormously popular. The corporate media was absolutely awash with *systemic bias* and *nefarious bias* favoring establishment candidates as it always is during national election seasons. When people discovered that there was an alternative, many piled out of the corporate media bus.

The "Bernie Bros" and "white supremacists" narratives found little success in suppressing the impact of independent media in 2016. At best, these canards succeeded in dividing the two parties internally. On the left, the nonsensical lies about Sanders supporters drove chasms between casual supporters of Clinton and Sanders, thereby making unity more difficult after Clinton was eventually nominated. The coverage of Trump's ascent similarly divided the GOP. These slur-based narratives however were by no means a sufficient remedy to the increasing diffusion of independent news narratives. The publishers of corporate media knew this. They needed something more to stop the rise of independent media.

THE BIRTH OF "FAKE NEWS"

BOTH CAMPAIGNS SENT SHOCKWAVES THROUGH THEIR RESPECTIVE PO-litical establishments. Stunning the elite, political media pundits and long-time party strategists, the Republican Party at its convention in June of 2016 nominated Donald Trump for president. His victory was seen as a surprise, but it was also a landslide. The following month, in a much more closely contested convention in Philadelphia, the Democratic Party nominated Hillary Clinton, who had edged out Bernie Sanders 54%-46% in pledged delegates. The convention was marred by WikiLeaks's release of the trove of emails mentioned above, which revealed widespread collusion, voter suppression, and election rigging on the part of the DNC in favor of Clinton. DNC chair Debbie Wasserman Schultz resigned during the convention in disgrace. Nonetheless, Sanders accepted defeat, gave a rousing concession speech, and in a show of unity campaigned vigorously for Clinton after the convention and throughout the months leading up to the November general election.

On both sides of the aisle, unexpected eruptions of anti-establishment passion had dominated the primary season. While Trump was successful in winning his adopted party's nomination, Sanders did not quite succeed in securing his. Broad and deep discontent with the political status quo was evident in both parties.

Neither campaign would have been possible without this new coming-of-age of independent internet media. In earlier eras, the mainstream media's chosen narrative would have been the one and only dominant narrative, and most Americans' opinions of candidates and campaigns would have been successfully managed. But 2016 was different.

A New Ghost Appears

The general election approached, pitting against each other the two least popular candidates in the history of approval polling. Perhaps to distract Americans from this sorry state of affairs, a terrible new specter appeared: *fake news.*

The corporate media alerted the American citizenry to be on the lookout for this devious, new evil. *False* accounts of events were now rampant. America faced an epidemic of *fake news.*

Pundits insinuated that this dishonest reporting surfaced online and infested all platforms. The results of the primary and general election were blamed on it,[31] rather than on any interest in political change.[32]

Fake news.

With the country divided, and on pins and needles in anticipation, all virtuous, mainstream media channels commenting on the election issued warnings in unison.

Fake news.

The new ghost was bemoaned, condemned, vilified, and blamed for the sorry state of ... everything. Our shambolic democracy and our national culture's moral failings. It was a media meta-narrative in its ascendancy. It was a problem that everyone in media boardrooms dutifully denounced. It was a scourge that all journalists with a column in a big newspaper lamented or warned about.[33]

Outside those boardrooms and columns, other interpretations of the term surfaced. Writers in independent media recognized the term quickly as a new justification for censorship. *Who exactly would determine which news was "fake" and which news was "true?"*

For supporters of Trump and Sanders, the term had immediate appeal in a different light. What better label could there be for the perpetual negative coverage their candidate had received from the likes of CNN, MSNBC, NPR, Fox News, the *New York Times*, and the rest? When the *Times* and the *Guardian* of London and countless other corporate media outlets reported that Trump had suggested someone should assassinate Hillary Clinton,[34] what better label for those reports could there be than "fake news?"[35] Trump had simply said supporters of the Second Amendment would have to find ways to prevent the passage of restrictive gun control legislation if Clinton were elected, but that wasn't how his words were reported.[36]

Fake news.

DEMOCRACY DIES IN DARKNESS

TICKER TAPE RAINED DOWN FROM THE CEILING OF THE MANHATTAN Hilton late on the night of November 8, 2016. Donald Trump stepped forward and gave his victory speech to a stunned corporate media that had only just called the election. His speech was short and conciliatory. Hillary Clinton did not make a concession speech, apologizing that she had not prepared one.

The DNC voiced its assessment that "fake news" and "Russian interference" were the reasons for Clinton's loss rather than any shortcomings of her campaign, strengths of her opponent's campaign, or the anti-establishment mood of the electorate.

And the corporate media ran with it. *Fake news.*

When Clinton made her concession speech the next afternoon, it was less conciliatory in tone, and Blue News outlets such as the *Washington Post, Vox,* CNN, MSNBC, and NPR steadily shifted their tone toward the DNC's complaints. Editorials decried[37] alleged Russian interference.[38] Analysis pieces declared that "fake news" on social media had swung the election.[39] Trump's victory might be illegitimate, they suggested. Alongside the same media channels' longstanding warnings that Trump was a white supremacist and secret fascist—and that his supporters were too—this narrative fostered hysteria in loyal Democrats as the inauguration neared.

Trump fired back, to the delight of his supporters. In his first press conference as president-elect, Trump refused to call on a CNN reporter. He called the corporation "fake news," lobbing the grenade they had constructed back at the corporate media.[40] This enraged the journalists and media executives who were attacking him. CNN and the *New York Times* doubled down. They denounced Trump's actions in refusing to call on a reporter as a threat to the First Amendment. Once again, they warned that Trump was secretly a fascist who would likely attempt to become an authoritarian dictator and shut down news organizations that criticized him.

Nevertheless, Trump's words began a process that ultimately defanged this new weapon that had been used to marginalize independent media.[41]

The Enemy of the People

Trump never became a fascist nor banned newspapers, at least to my knowledge at this moment, but no apologies were ever made. The term *fake news* also did not die. Both sides continue to use the term, one as a label for questionable articles in independent media, the other as a label for corporate media articles rife with *bias*.

The corporate media coverage of the extraordinary campaigns of 2016 thus set the scene for four years of division. Red News and Blue News media sources espoused almost entirely different versions of reality. When Trump tweeted a month into his presidency, "*The Fake News media (@nytimes, @NBCNews, @ABC, @CBS, @CNN) is ... the enemy of the American people,*" he summarized succinctly one side of the debate. The tweet also egged on his adversaries, as he so often does, by using the term "enemy of the people," a famous phrase used in dictatorial regimes. Neither Trump nor Biden after him did anything to bridge the divide on the definition of *fake news*.

Use of the term in Blue News corporate media during Trump's term in office positively exploded. Warnings about *fake news*—and its new synonyms *disinformation* and *misinformation*—appeared exhaustively, continuously, and repeatedly. The purpose was ostensibly to suppress inaccurate accounts of important events. In reality, it was a pretext for censorship of news that ran counter to corporate media narratives. These labels were the weapons of choice for corporate media outlets bent on seizing back control of the news narrative from independent media.

The *Washington Post*, for instance, took on a new alarmist slogan in the aftermath of the 2016 election, "Democracy Dies in Darkness." The paper promoted itself as resolute defenders of the First Amendment. Yet, it encouraged the censorship of independent media that occurred on both the right and the left, in both independent journalism and on social media, during the years of the Trump administration. Particularly during the cataclysmic year of 2020, as we'll address in the next chapter, censorship spread throughout social media. The censorship was done not by the White House or by MAGA-hat-wearing rioters in the streets but rather by the giant tech companies of Silicon Valley that have quietly ascended to the role of arbiter of public debate in our public square. The corporate media has been at best silent on this encroaching censorship, but most of the time it cheerleads and calls for more. As we'll see, many mainstream publications that claim to fear fascism and to uphold the highest principles of freedom—Freedom of the Press, Freedom of Speech, Freedom of Assembly—support censorship in order to control the narrative.

Weaponized Labels

At first glance, *fake news* seems like a danger worth fighting against—and worth being protected from. Who wants to read disinformation or false reporting? The world is a complex place as it is, everyone seems to have an ax to grind, and we're all too busy to read a dozen accounts of a city council meeting or foreign trade deal. *Screen out the lies, please*, a reasonable citizen might request, *and just print the true stuff*.

But an examination of the use of these terms reveals that they were never intended as useful labels to protect honest citizens from wholly false coverage or stories with a few small lies.

News that is wholly false is hardly a new phenomenon. Full-on specious articles like "Man Gives Birth to Dog" that run in *The National Enquirer* and other tabloids have been around forever and pose no serious threat to anyone's power or position. These stories have migrated online as clickbait with outrageous titles and excessive ads. That's not what they're combatting when they say they're protecting you from *fake news*.

Nor is the problem news articles that contain a few lies but mostly tell the truth. *That's what corporate media coverage is.* As we've already seen and will continue to see in this book, news coverage of important issues by CNN, ABC, Fox News, and the rest generally consists of segments that are largely true but contain a few key tendentious omissions and distortions. That's their *bias*, and corporate media has no interest in protecting you from their dishonest reporting. That would be painting with too broad a brush.

The goal of these terms, simply put, is to hide narratives that they don't control.

The labels conceal a disingenuous manipulation of our human instinct to learn and understand the world around us. We have evolved to trust stories told to us by people we know. This narrative style of history is as old as human civilization itself and is the way history and information were passed along for centuries in pre-literate human society. Many Americans in 2016 formed new direct lines of trust, communication, and storytelling that were not intermediated by corporate media. We told each other the news directly, and we trusted reports more that we heard in person for good reason: it's harder to lie in person. This term *fake news* asks Americans to remove any instinctual trust they might have established in independent sources and return that trust back into the hands of the mainstream corporate media. The terms' true, modern goal is to help the large media corporations regain control of the narrative that they lost many times during the anti-establishment campaigns of Donald Trump and Bernie Sanders. The terms are tools to minimize, marginalize, and silence independent media. Corporate media doesn't just want to *suppress* independent voices, they want Americans to *fear* them.

The thing is, it didn't work. What they attacked with this term was the internet itself, independent media creators, and the rise of alternative sources of news narratives—all of which are stronger today than they were in 2016. Trump's appropriation and use of the term to counter distorted reports about him revealed that the term *fake news* was also sloppy. It takes just a few demonstrable lies in, say, the *New York Times* or MSNBC for attentive viewers to turn this powerful term around. And this is exactly what happened as Trump's first term came to a close. As the corporate media distorted and censored news about the origin of covid, Hunter Biden's laptop, nonexistent attacks in Afghanistan, and Jeffrey Epstein's sordid deeds, the corporate media itself was unveiled as a leading source of *fake news*. It had backfired.

Within four short years, the term *fake news* failed to attain its cynical goal, and it was replaced. Today, the terms *misinformation* and *disinformation* serve the same purpose—to make Americans fear narratives that the corporate media does not control.

But independent news isn't something to fear. Every source has its *biases*. We just have to understand them. What we Americans need is not disingenuous labels nor managed narratives but instead the *media consciousness* to discern *bias* in news reports. A Balanced Media Diet and the strength of our own independent minds are sufficient for understanding the world around us.

6

MANAGING THE
NARRATIVE

---

*"Ownership of the media is always in the
hands of the perpetrators."*

Aleksandr Solzhenitsyn

BERNIE SANDERS RAN FOR PRESIDENT AGAIN IN 2020. JUST BEFORE
American society went topsy-turvy over covid, the Vermont senator launched
a populist campaign similar to his 2016 candidacy, and it gathered tremendous support as the primary season opened. Unlike in 2016, when he had
faced only one opponent, Donald Trump was in the White House in 2020,
and nearly two dozen candidates mounted serious campaigns for the Democratic nomination.

This campaign, too, is worth our inspection. It shows that the passive fil-
tration of corporate news by *systemic bias* is not the only phenomenon taking
place when it comes to news distortion. Active manipulation of the narrative
by corporate and social media giants and other *nefarious bias* also takes place.

Sanders never quite led the sizable pack of candidates in 2019, but this
changed as the new year arrived. A January 10, 2020 poll found Sanders in the

lead in the first state to vote, Iowa.[1] The *New York Times* published several articles on efforts by the Democratic Party to "Stop Sanders,"[23] and the perspective was repeated Mockingbird-style in other Blue News outlets. A narrative took shape: Sanders was described as popular only with small subsets of the population, such as young, White people, and he was portrayed as too divisive a figure to defeat Donald Trump. These descriptions were in fact biased and false. Data showed that Sanders was quite popular with people of color as well as with both longtime Democrats and Independents, making him the candidate most likely to defeat Trump according to many calculations. What was rarely mentioned was the danger Sanders posed to the establishment. A Sanders presidency could threaten the powerful positions of large media corporations, which Sanders decried as too powerful; the giant drugmakers, which Sanders called profiteers; and the Wall Street banks, which Sanders described as corrupt. The narrative manipulation ramped up more quickly than it had in 2016.

Elizabeth Warren was running too. Calling out similar political issues, albeit with less conviction and a shorter track record, the senator from Massachusetts claimed the second largest share of progressive support in the polls. She was a woman, and some Democrats believed a woman could defeat Trump and even possibly heal the scars of the 2016 rift between Clinton and Sanders supporters.

Coverage of Warren in Blue News channels was often positive and suffered far less *systemic bias* than did coverage of Sanders. MSNBC, *The Washington Post*, NPR and many others ran positive stories about Warren, and she became a favorite of wealthier Democrats with a liberal bent. Warren did not connect, however, with younger and poorer Americans the way Sanders did, nor with people of color. Warren's polling numbers in other demographics had kept up with Sanders through the fall, but as January arrived, Sanders pulled ahead of her by eight points. In Iowa, Sanders led Warren by six points, which was a large lead in such a crowded field.[4]

Meanwhile, the negative narrative about Sanders continued apace, and he received next to no positive coverage in Blue News corporate outlets. As the two leading "progressives" in the race, Warren and Sanders had said only positive things about each other through 2019 and well into January 2020. That changed abruptly on a chilly January day.

Playing the Queen of Clubs

The first votes to determine the Democratic nominee were to be cast on February 2nd. As the date of the pivotal Iowa Caucus neared, the final televised debate on January 14th took on crucial significance. On the eve of that debate, trailing Sanders in the polls by a widening margin, having said nothing negative about him until that point, Elizabeth Warren dropped a bomb.

She played the sexism card. Warren claimed that Sanders had told her that a woman couldn't win the presidency. Sanders actually saying this was virtually inconceivable. It was also implausible that Warren would have said nothing about it until that moment had Sanders, in fact, said this. Sanders and the entire nation had just watched a woman, Hillary Clinton, beat him for the nomination and win the popular vote for president in 2016. Clinton had narrowly lost the electoral college. Warren claimed that Sanders had said in 2018 that a woman couldn't win the presidency.[5] As for whether Sanders *wanted* a woman to become president, he was on record encouraging women to run for president for *three full decades*. He had told countless prominent female politicians they could become president. He had even encouraged Warren herself to run in 2015.[6]

It was never likely that Sanders would have thought this, let alone said it. Most independent media journalists recognized the claim quickly as implausible and desperate. An unbiased set of journalistic institutions might have, at least, requested evidence that Sanders had made such a remark before broadcasting it to the world. But the corporate media went the opposite way.

In near unison, the megaphones of the news behemoths presented what was, at best, a hotly contested rumor as fact. Narrative management was dialed up. The opportunity to bolster the insinuation that the Sanders campaign and its supporters were sexist was not squandered.

CNN, as host of the big debate the following evening, was in a unique position to set the record straight. They could have investigated what was likely a dishonest interpretation of a private conversation between the two candidates. Instead, CNN amplified Warren's allegation in several ways. First, the network ran the unverified quote in the title for its coverage, utilizing the headline to assert Warren's allegation: "Bernie Sanders Told Elizabeth Warren in a Private 2018 Meeting that a Woman Can't Win, Sources Say."[7] By putting the "sources say" bit at the end of the headline, CNN deliberately mini-mized the possibility in the reader's mind that it was unverified, partly because the brain processes words in order and partly because the ends of headlines are often cut off on social media and news feeds. Rather than neutral reporting, this was narrative management.

Additionally, CNN's article provided only Warren's side of the story in its first six paragraphs. The first two paragraphs set the scene—a meeting in 2018 in which Warren told Sanders she was going to run for president. The entire third paragraph was a simple statement: "Sanders responded that he did not believe a woman could win." No attribution, no corroboration, no evidence. Just the unverified, unlikely, unproven, sexist comment. This was disinforma-tion spread by CNN. The terms "sexist" and "sexism" appeared five times in the piece, pushing an association between Sanders and sexism.

The *bias* was thick, reminiscent of Hillary Clinton's collusion with corpo-rate media in 2016. Moreover, the timing and presentation of the allegation fit so well into CNN's schedule leading up to the debate that it reveals *nefari-ous bias* at play on the part of CNN editors and possibly collusion between CNN and the Warren campaign.

The rest of the media was little better. In mockingbird fashion, the *New York Times* ran a similar article, with a similar structure, similar set of para-graphs, and a similar headline, "Warren Says Sanders Told Her a Woman Could Not Win the Presidency."[8]

But the starkest moment of narrative management by CNN came the next evening.

When Did You Stop Beating Your Wife?

On stage, CNN debate moderator Abby Phillip pushed a question at Sanders twice. The clear intent was to distort viewers' impressions. She addressed him:

> CNN reported yesterday—and Senator Warren confirmed in a statement—that in 2018 you told her that you did not believe that a woman could win the election. Why did you say that?

She didn't ask neutrally, "Did you say that?" She asked, "*Why* did you say that?" This is what's called a "loaded question" in law and rhetoric. Just to answer the question is to agree to its incriminating premise. A famous leading question used humorously in law schools goes like this: "When did you stop beating your wife?"

Sanders duly denied the allegation. "As a matter of fact, I never said that."[9] He spoke at length, taking the time to enumerate the many reasons Warren's story made no sense: He had urged Warren herself to run in 2015, he himself had campaigned for a female candidate who had won the popular national vote by 3 million votes in the last election, and the rest.

Abby Phillip asked him to clarify. "So you never said it?"

"That is correct," Sanders replied. "I never said that."

Phillip then turned to Warren. "Senator Warren, what did you think *when* Senator Sanders told you that a woman could not win the election?"[10]

You couldn't have made it up if it hadn't happened. A second egregious loaded question by a news source that professes neutrality.

In the words of independent journalist Matt Taibbi, writing in *Rolling Stone*:

That *"when"* [by the moderator] was as transparent a media "fuck you" as we've seen in a presidential debate. It evoked memories of another infamous CNN ambush, when Bernard Shaw in 1988 crotch-kicked Mike Dukakis with a question about whether he'd favor the death penalty for someone who raped and murdered his wife, Kitty.

This time, the whole network tossed the mud. Over a 24-hour period before, during, and after the debate, CNN bid farewell to what remained of its reputation as a nonpolitical actor via a remarkable stretch of factually dubious reporting, bent commentary, and heavy-handed messaging.[11]

As the debate went on, when Sanders or Warren spoke, CNN displayed messages under the screen (called "chyrons") to enhance the narrative management:

◆ "Warren supports a new trade deal with Mexico and Canada; why is Sanders's opposition to it wrong?"

◆ "Sanders's proposals would double federal spending over a decade; how will he avoid bankrupting the country?"

◆ "Does Sanders owe voters an explanation of how much his healthcare plan will cost them and the country?"[12]

Bernie Bros and the Russian Bots Under the Bed

Despite CNN's efforts, the Warren allegations didn't go anywhere. In a reprise of 2016, large swaths of the population didn't buy what the corporate media was selling.[13] If anything, the polls showed the opposite, that the whole affair had backfired on Warren's campaign. Sanders expanded his lead in Iowa and actually pulled into his first national lead over Biden only days after Warren's sneaky browbeating. Sanders's lead over Biden was a thin 1%, but his lead over Warren grew to nine points.[14] Even among women, Warren's ploy had fallen flat.[15] Despite CNN's narrative management, independent media saw through it,[16] and Bernie's supporters ignored the attack.

It was more evidence that for all its sophisticated tools and extensive reach, corporate media's ability to control the narrative is waning. Independent media wields increasing power in setting the narrative, or, at least, in accepting or rejecting narratives pushed by the corporate giants. Independent voters were not convinced that Sanders had turned into a secret sexist overnight, and it appeared many were turned off by Warren's dishonest deployment of the sexism card. Nevertheless, the narrative continued apace in the mainstream media. Warren's theatrical refusal to shake Sanders's hand at the debate was explained the very next morning by Blue News outlet *Vox* as a distraction from "talking about sexism."[17]

The Iowa Caucus arrived two weeks later, and as we explore below, the results deflated Warren's campaign further while bolstering Sanders. Narratives cropped up to oppose the Sanders campaign that were mostly old media narratives recycled from the previous campaign: Bernie Bros and Russian Bots.

The "Bernie Bro" canard, recycled from 2016, attempted to portray the Sanders movement's greatest strength—its enthusiastic and numerous supporters—as a dangerous flaw. Analysis performed on thousands of political tweets on Twitter showed that all candidates had a roughly equivalent number of obnoxious supporters:[18] about 1% of tweets by each candidate's supporters were negative or offensive. Bernie had more *total* supporters, so there were, by extension, more negative Sanders supporters. Surveys reviewing the 2016 cycle also showed that Bernie's supporters were no more aggressive online than Trump's or Clinton's.[19] As for demographics, more women than men supported Sanders, and more people of color supported Sanders than any other candidate. Nevertheless, the corporate media hammered on the

"Bernie Bros" smear, month after month. The science of propaganda predicts that if a narrative is repeated often enough, and without forceful repudiation, it will steadily persuade people and eventually be accepted by the majority as truth. You can't fool all the people all the time, but well-crafted propaganda that is broadcast repeatedly will eventually fool most of the people most of the time.

The ugliest of the many corporate media attacks on the Sanders campaign came on nominally-left network MSNBC after Sanders's convincing victory in Nevada. Host Chris Matthews addressed the nation by comparing the win to Hitler's invasion of France.[20] Sanders is of course a Jew whose family died in the Holocaust, yet comparing his success to that of the Nazis was not below a corporate media outlet bent on smearing him. The point of these smears and *bias* was to stop Bernie at all costs.[21]

Alongside the "secret sexist" narrative, the Bernie Bros slur, and the comparisons to Hitler's blitz, Sanders was also red-baited. This distasteful act was done with a similar dearth of evidence. Sanders was a Russian stooge, "Putin's puppet," or whatever the writers at NPR or the *New York Times* could come up with.[22] In one instance, corporate media outlets simply passed along unsourced "intelligence agency analysis," mockingbird-style, that suggested that Sanders was receiving aid and support from the Russian government.[23] The scant "evidence" provided was some quoted passages from Russian newspapers recounting the truth about the 2016 primary—that it had been manipulated by the DNC to favor Clinton and stop Sanders. That foreign media was truthful was apparently the problem. The propaganda was similar to the allegations that had been used for four years on anyone that the Democratic Party establishment opposed, from Donald Trump to Tulsi Gabbard to Jill Stein to Mitch McConnell.

As we'll examine at the end of this chapter, the entirety of *#Russiagate* had been shown by the end of 2019 to be an evidence-free "conspiracy theory," but nonetheless, Sanders was associated with it as his numbers in the polls rose. Those poll numbers continued to rise leading right up to the primary's first contest, the pivotal Iowa Caucus. The narrative was slipping out of the hands of the corporate media, but not for long.

A VICTORY SHROUDED
IN SHADOW

"IOWA, YOU HAVE SHOCKED THE NATION," CRIED THE BOYISH PETE BUT-
tigieg from atop a podium on a chilly Des Moines evening. It was February
2, 2020, the day of the momentous Iowa Caucus, the very first election of
the Democratic Presidential Primary. A broad smile crossed the South Bend
mayor's face as he basked in the surprised applause of his supporters.

"By all indications, we are going on to New Hampshire *victorious!*" he declared.[24]

The crowd roared.

The only problem was that Buttigieg was losing.[25]

In the released vote count at that point in the evening, Bernie Sanders had
28.3% of the vote. Elizabeth Warren was in second with 25.5%. Buttigieg was
back in third with 23.9%. And only a minuscule 1.87% of the vote was in.
How could Buttigieg claim he had won?

Elsewhere in Iowa, Sanders and Warren and the other presidential candidates made typically positive and confident albeit uncertain pronouncements
about the results. Only "Mayor Pete" declared victory.

Everyone was wondering, *does he know something the rest of us don't?*[26]

The nation would undergo two full, excruciating days before learning that
the answer to that question was *yes*. Every few hours, a few more official results trickled out from the Iowa Democratic Party.[27] Citizens were tantalized,
1-3% of the vote at a time. Caucuses don't have ballots. There were no votes to
count. There were just the 1,765 caucus sites' tally sheets to add up. In prior
years, the results were released the night of the caucus.[28] Even more strange
than releasing the count so slowly was the fact that halfway through the tor-
turous count, the Democratic National Committee (DNC) stepped in and
took over. As voters wondered what Buttigieg had meant, the reporting about
the count stalled repeatedly.

It was no secret that the DNC desired that someone other than Sanders
become the nominee. Just as in 2016, when Sanders had run against Hillary
Clinton, there had been multiple "Stop Sanders" meetings convened by DNC
brass. Sanders' ability to raise all his campaign money directly from individual

voters rather than from large corporate contributions enabled him to support policies such as Medicare for All and breaking up big media—ideas that were anathema to the pharmaceutical and media corporations, respectively. Sanders's policies, despite being overwhelmingly popular, were threats to the DNC's ability to raise money from these corporations. Thus, Sanders threatened to undercut the DNC's business model of raking in corporate contributions to fund operations and candidates' campaigns. The question on my mind at the time was, could the DNC be behind the stalled release of results?

In another era, we might have known no more about the strange counting of the Iowa vote. But this was 2020, and independent media flexed its muscle. In the hours after Buttigieg's unexpected victory cry, independent journalists reported that a little-known technology company named Shadow had created a phone app that had been inserted into the caucus counting procedures. This app handled the counting and submission of vote totals instead of the paper records that had been used in prior years. Unbeknownst to most campaign staff until the eve of the caucus, this app had allowed the DNC to monitor the vote totals throughout the evening before they were reported from caucus sites and before they were released to the public. This revelation demonstrated that the DNC could have paused the release of the vote totals on the evening of the caucus, perhaps because they didn't like the way the results were going.

The app's existence had been kept secret for months. Even on the day of the caucus itself, Blue News corporate media barely mentioned it. Independent investigative journalists revealed that Tara McGowan, the CEO of Shadow's parent company, Acronym, was in fact a wealthy and well-connected supporter of the Buttigieg campaign. McGowan initially denied knowledge of the Shadow app, but as evidence emerged, she owned up to it. Numerous other connections emerged between Shadow and the DNC establishment. In addition to CEO McGowan, the CTO, the COO, and the Chief of Product at Shadow were all former Hillary for America 2016 campaign staffers. Shadow had extensive political connections to both the Buttigieg campaign and top-ranking officials in the DNC, the very organization that opposed a Sanders nomination.[29] The corporate media did not report on these relationships or the use of the app until these facts were uncovered by independent media and discussed at length on social media.

To the supporters of Sanders and the other candidates, the issue wasn't that the entire Shadow executive team had supported Hillary Clinton. The problem was that there was no legitimate need for an app for this purpose. No app like this had been used in the past, and the simple recording of each caucus's results that had always been done on paper could have been handled by a centralized spreadsheet, Google form, or something similar and more transparent while still ensuring the (obviously low) level of security provided by this app.

Whether or not the developers at Shadow deliberately designed the app to enable cheating on caucus night, the software that they created sent data to unidentified IP addresses throughout the night[30] and allowed remote adjusting of the reported caucus results. The app also enabled remote viewing of vote totals prior to submitting reports to the central offices as well as adjusting vote totals after they were submitted. These capabilities hadn't existed before. So, there were "means, motive, and opportunity" for the DNC to adjust the voting totals prior to release. Perhaps they just needed to ensure that any adjustments they made were mathematically undetectable; this would explain the strange, long delays in releasing the results.

Where there's smoke, there's usually fire, but it isn't the aim of this book to establish whether the results were, in fact, manipulated. I exhaustively compiled the evidence on that question in a piece I published at the time, which I humbly recommend you read.[31] The concern now is, why were these vital questions never asked in the corporate media?

The answer is twofold. First, the Elite Sources filter of *systemic bias* prevented questions about the validity of the reported results because it implicated the DNC. Second, allegations of election fraud fall in a special category in American corporate media—the "third rail"—topics which are often directly managed by *nefarious bias*.

A Shadow Cast Over Election Fraud

As it dawned on me that the DNC had possibly manipulated the vote totals, the next question crossing my mind was, what process would Americans tolerate in a primary? Four years earlier, in the aftermath of the 2016 primary, Sanders supporters sued the DNC, claiming the primary had been rigged to assure Clinton's victory. The DNC's lawyers used a strange, spectacular defense in the case. They didn't argue that the primary had been fair, nor even that it was slightly unfair but not rigged. Instead, they argued that even if it had been rigged, the DNC was entitled to do so and to run the primary as they liked. They were not bound by any rules in selecting their nominee; there was no "fair" or "unfair." The DNC could, they claimed, choose their nominee in a smoke-filled room and then legally conceal this information.[32] They thus made the unexpected argument that the primary couldn't be rigged, per se, since there were no rules governing it. Perhaps this lawless approach is indeed how the DNC chooses its nominees—perhaps even in a smoke-filled room—and perhaps that is what Buttigieg knew on that February night. He declared victory perhaps because DNC officials had told him he was going to win. The process had been changed to enable an app to dictate the results, and no one in corporate media cried foul.

The Blue News corporate media also hadn't reported on that court case. Independent media outlets uncovered the story,[33] and after the astonishing case buzzed around the internet for a while, *Salon* and *Newsweek* eventually ran stories.[34] A group known as Project Censored included it in their "25 Most Censored Stories" of 2017 because the coverage was so sparse.[35]

Thus on February 3rd, the night of the 2020 Iowa Caucus, the DNC likely knew they could get away with manipulating the vote totals if they needed to ensure that Sanders didn't win.[36] If they needed to find a covert way to do so, the Shadow app was an ideal tool.

The corporate media managed the narrative around this pivotal first caucus in one other key way. Before the caucus took place, on the eve of the election, a leading poll by the *Des Moines Register* was quashed.[37] It wasn't just any poll. The *Des Moines Register* poll has long been considered the "gold standard" for predicting the winner of the peculiar Iowa caucus. It was the only poll in the country that had correctly predicted the winner of every caucus for three entire decades. On the eve of February 2, 2020, this poll showed Sanders beating Buttigieg by six points. The poll was never reported to the public. Its results were quietly leaked five days *after* the caucus.

The *Register* said they spiked the poll because someone from the Buttigieg campaign called into the paper and claimed one of the pollsters had omitted Buttigieg's name one time from one of the questions. This unverified complaint was evidently enough for the *Des Moines Register* to cancel their thirty-year-old, gold-standard poll.[38]

The corporate media also did not discuss Buttigieg's history with the American intelligence services.[39] He had collaborated with the NSA and CIA during a deployment in Afghanistan, and military intelligence had been a significant part of his short military career.[40]

Stealing the Momentum

The main prizes of the Iowa Caucus are momentum and media buzz. The delegates at stake in the small state—just 41 in all—are inconsequential next to the aura of success and legitimacy that halos the winner of the very first contest. Thus, despite being behind on the night of the caucus, and losing in all metrics not managed by the app, Buttigieg was awarded by the media the true spoils of victory. During the two long days of vote counting, the media narrative was that Buttigieg had shocked the nation and gained momentum. Countless articles appeared about his surprising performance and growing popularity. No national corporate media pieces investigated whether the Shadow app could have been used to rig the caucus. Narrative management was dialed up: Buttigieg had shocked the nation; Sanders had underperformed.

With this buzz in the air, the DNC released a large batch of caucus numbers on Wednesday afternoon, taking the total to 97%. The results put Sanders on top, Buttigieg just behind in second, and Warren in a distant third. With just 3% of the vote remaining to be released, the *New York Times* elections tool projected a Sanders victory with 95% certainty.

But the day was not over.

At 9 p.m., Buttigieg appeared in a "Town Hall" event on CNN. He stood before a live audience to answer their questions. It was the first time he had taken questions from everyday people since the caucus. Would he finally be asked about his premature victory declaration?

Before allowing a single question from the audience, host Chris Cuomo opened the event with some "real time" news.[41] Cuomo informed Buttigieg and the world that another 2.8% of the vote had been released at that very moment. Cuomo smiled as he delivered the news—news Buttigieg ostensibly didn't know. Buttigieg was now in the lead, beating Sanders by 0.1%.

Rather than facing uncomfortable questions about his premature declarations, Buttigieg got to deliver another victory speech. This time, live on CNN. The media moment could hardly have been scripted better for "Mayor

Pete," the former military intelligence officer. He accepted the upset victory on live television. It was quite a coincidence, indeed, that those final votes were released during the first moments of his first live appearance on CNN, just weeks after a CNN debate moderator had fired loaded questions at Sanders and published Warren's allegations of sexism.

Cuomo never asked Buttigieg about the app, its connection to his campaign, the changing of votes, the spiked *Register* poll, or his premature victory speech. Those questions weren't part of the narrative. Buttigieg had shocked the nation with a stunning, narrow victory; Sanders wasn't as popular as his rallies and poll numbers suggested.

Both *propaganda* and *censorship* were used in this case, and both *systemic* and *nefarious bias* were in effect. The propaganda boosted Buttigieg's candidacy via the CNN Town Hall and bestowed visibility and vindication. The censorship killed the pre-election poll and also quashed investigations of possible election fraud.

Judging by the narrative used, what mattered most in this case to the orchestrators of *nefarious bias* was that the aura of victory from the Iowa Caucus was awarded to someone not named Bernie Sanders. The corporate media treated Buttigieg as the victor right up until the eve of the next contest, New Hampshire, which Sanders won. Sanders also went on to win the following contest, Nevada, showing a popularity that eclipsed his candidacy in 2016. Nonetheless, the narrative continued that he was dangerous, sexist, angry, and unpopular. When a narrative must continue in the corporate media, it will continue, regardless of the facts.

Nine months later, CNN quietly published some investigative journalism. They released a report finding that, indeed, the DNC was responsible for creating the app, forcing its use, and delaying the release of results for two days after the caucus while their software "processed" the data.[42] Of course, by that time, the 2020 Bernie Sanders campaign was long over.

A WELL-FUNDED CABAL
OF POWERFUL PEOPLE

BERNIE SANDERS WAS STOPPED IN 2020 AS HE HAD BEEN IN 2016. THE corporate media played no small role in these feats. We have examined Sanders's two candidacies for president in depth because together they demonstrate the immense power that the corporate media behemoths wield in constructing the news narratives that paint the backdrop of American life.

This power is tantamount to controlling our democracy. Would Sanders be president today had the media covered all candidates and elections fairly? It's beyond the scope of this book to prove such speculation, but certainly the narrative that was crafted in 2016 that Sanders was radical, angry, and sexist was managed and sustained—despite copious evidence undermining its premises—for as long as was needed to harm his chances of winning elections.

Vast power to control the news is in the hands of nondemocratic media corporations who actively manipulate public perception. As I mentioned in Chapter 1, the press in our democracy has three true and indispensable duties: watchdog, smorgasbord, and bulletin. The corporate media today doesn't merely abdicate these roles but abuses them to an extent that harms our democracy. This abdication and abuse are the primary reasons that independent media is growing in depth, quality, and viewership. The internet's availability combined with people's growing awareness that the media is lying to them are fueling the New Enlightenment, a revolution in global awareness.

The owners of the corporate media see this, and they are not going to sit idly by as their immense power wanes. Ending the campaigns of anti-establishment candidates like Bernie Sanders demonstrates this. Several other efforts are underway today to delay the rise of independent media and fight the inevitable unfolding of this enlightenment.

The Media Matters

One organization with a starring role in opposing the New Enlightenment and the rising power of independent media is Media Matters. This group was founded by David Brock, a controversial figure with a track record of dishonesty and political manipulation. With money from the DNC, the Clintons, George Soros, and other wealthy funders, Brock set out in the early 2000s to "closely monitor and counter conservative commentators and journalists when they make mistakes."[43] Democrats at the time viewed it essential to challenge the power of the Republican-leaning Media Research Center, which regularly documented and published reports showing "liberal bias" in the corporate media. Media Matters sought to do this in reverse, to disprove the existence of a "liberal bias" and fight the ascendancy of Fox News.

This oppositional stance sounds legitimate and helpful in a polarized media environment, but when we review their track record, something more troubling emerges. For a decade, the organization earned respect for the fresh data analysis it provided on bias in media reporting. Its "War on Fox News" provided useful criticism. But before long, it became clear that the organization wasn't any more committed to the truth than the Red News sources it vigorously criticized. It provided useful data and reports precisely when that data supported its version of the story: that conservatives dominate American media, and that conservative viewpoints are dangerous. It had a bias and agenda of its own, and its bipartisan credibility disintegrated altogether during the 2016 election. The group effectively became an arm of the Clinton campaign, assisting in its collusion with Blue News journalists and attacking Sanders and then Trump with biased reports.

That was telling, but what is most relevant for our examination of narrative management is what happened immediately *after* Clinton's loss in 2016. In sync with that campaign's claims that "fake news" had cost it the election, as we discussed in Chapter 5, Media Matters changed its entire *raison d'etre* on a dime. The organization pivoted away from countering Red News sources like Fox News, and it began to target instead independent media sources and "fake news."[44] The organization brought in a new president, Angelo Carusone, who announced that the organization's new focus would be "the alt-right, conspiracy theories, and fake news." Independent media that challenged dominant narratives would be in its crosshairs.

This is precisely the pivot going on throughout the legacy media world right now, particularly at places like NPR, the *New York Times*, the *Washington Post*, and internet magazines that follow their lead. The managers of the narrative view their primary adversaries no longer as competitor corporate media outlets but rather the new media sources who can set the narrative independently. Slurs such as "alt-right," "radical left," "conspiracy theory," and "fake news," as we document throughout this book, are used by those seeking to control the narrative rather than allow a Free Press to flourish.[45] NPR's new "disinformation team," announced in 2022, is a perfect example.[46] The goal is not to protect you from lies but rather to undermine narratives they don't want you to consider.

In its 2017 strategic plan, leaked by an internal staff member, Media Matters declared its new primary goal was to expose and discredit "propagandists" and purveyors of "disinformation." Two of its specific goals were as follows:

Internet and social media platforms, like Google and Facebook, will no longer uncritically and without consequence host and enrich fake news sites and propagandists.

Trump will be defeated either through impeachment or at the ballot box in 2020.[47]

And with that, David Brock and Angelo Carusone embarked on a journey to censor social media and independent news in order to defeat Trump. Media Matters began to "partner with" Facebook, Twitter, and Google in 2017 to take down tweets, posts, and videos, and to ban and blacklist sites.[48] Many pundits in the corporate media applaud this work without considering its ramifications. Allowing a clearly partisan organization to convince, coerce, or compel social media companies to ban ideas and censor specific speakers is not a protective act for our democracy but rather censorship. What is unclear is whether this organization, paid by and acting on behalf of powerful politicians to limit the speech of private citizens,[49] crossed the First Amendment line and violated protected speech; we'll take a deeper look at this question and the controversial Section 230 in Chapter 9.[50]

Either way, this suppression has gone from bad to worse in the years since 2017. Media Matters and organizations like it have succeeded in banning countless citizens and groups from social media. What were dozens of banned sites has mushroomed into hundreds, perhaps thousands. The true extent of censorship, once it begins, is difficult to calculate. By 2021, Facebook alone had banned over a billion accounts,[51] including thousands of "right-wing" groups[52] and "misinformation purveyors."[53]

The aim of Media Matters is not free and open democracy but rather the elimination of competition for control of the narrative. Contrary ideas must be discredited as "disinformation" or "conspiracy theories."

The organization seems to have succeeded in both of its stated goals.

The Great Conspiracy to Save Democracy

Generally, the American people are difficult to convince of the existence of a covert conspiracy if the mainstream media does not want its existence known. Those who manage the narratives have a century of experience with the arts of propaganda and can usually manipulate the news and discredit voices whom they deem a threat.

But much like the belated CNN investigation that uncovered DNC responsibility for the Iowa fiasco, an article appeared many months after the 2020 election that confirmed suspicions that a secret, extensive, and powerful collaboration at the top of corporate and social media worked to ensure the election of Joe Biden.[54]

Appearing in *Time* magazine, the article was a significant work of narrative management on its own. "The Secret History of the Shadow Campaign That Saved the 2020 Election" clocked in at a hefty 7,000 words, and it endeavored to both reveal and justify expansive use of censorship and propaganda by a powerful "cabal" ensconced throughout the American media power structure.[55]

Author Molly Ball recounts in the piece the actions of "a well-funded cabal of powerful people ranging across industries and ideologies, working together behind the scenes to influence perceptions, change rules and laws, steer media coverage and control the flow of information."

Change laws? Steer media? Control information? This was quite a set of revelations for the thoroughly establishment *Time*, the magazine that had once anchored Operation Mockingbird and famously hosted CIA men in its executive management. If its Blue News bona fides were in question, this piece was a clincher.

Ball reveals concerted efforts to push CEOs of social media giants to censor opinion pieces, news stories, and even whole accounts that didn't support Biden. She described these unusual clandestine measures taken to manipulate opinion of the candidates with a tone of celebration: "They were not rigging the election; they were fortifying it."

The piece explained how this group held regular secret meetings to coordinate and change the outcome at the polls via planting reports in mainstream news, controlling opinion on social media, and changing electoral laws. The article went to great pains to present such manipulation and censorship as positive, healthy, protective actions that supported both journalism and democracy. The implication was that our free and open democracy had to be suspended in order to save it. Ultimately, the article spun a concerted covert effort to elect one candidate as a benevolent effort to defend democracy.

This clandestine collaboration meshes well with the facts revealed by Google whistleblower Zach Vorhies in his bombshell book *Google Leaks*, which we will examine in detail in Chapter 8.[56] Reading Vorhies's book, I was surprised to learn that Google's algorithms worked against Trump both before and after the 2016 election. Political preferences are coded into search results on both Google and YouTube. This enhanced the censorship and propaganda of the mainstream corporate media. Whether or not our democracy needs a grand conspiracy to save it, control of the narrative extends to the new social media giants of our era.

The Internet Death Penalty

It would have been nice to see the Biden administration, upon taking office, reverse the corporate media trend toward censorship. But perhaps the biggest indicator that secret work to extend censorship, propaganda, and narrative management is underway has been the Biden administration's disturbing actions. In one telling week in July 2021, the White House signaled in three ways their desire for authoritarian control of both social media and the corporate news. First, on July 16, Biden said that Facebook was "killing people" by allowing certain information his administration disliked about covid, vaccines, and lockdowns to appear on its site.[57] There was no evidence for this claim that Facebook was killing people, so it seemed to be a warning shot at Facebook that the administration could bring executive action unfavorable to the tech behemoth. The same day, Biden said, "The only pandemic we have is among the unvaccinated."[58] There was no evidence for this claim either. In fact, most scientific evidence contradicted this claim since both vaccinated and non-vaccinated people numbering in the thousands were in the hospitals at the time. "If you get these vaccines, you won't get covid," Biden added three days later.[59] Again, by his own definition, Biden was disseminating scientific misinformation.

The second disturbing act came just a day after this warning to Facebook. On July 19, Biden Press Secretary Jen Psaki made the administration's deeper desires clear. In a White House news conference, she urged the social media companies to ban people for spreading misinformation, whether it was about covid or *about anything else.*[60] This wasn't just inching closer to the First Amendment line. This was grabbing a pole vault and leaping over it. The only requirement for this censorship, she said, would be that the person was "spreading misinformation." This meant that someone talking about, say, the lab leak theory about covid's origin in 2020 would have been permanently banned from social media since at that time that theory was considered misinformation.

Gunning for the gold medal in the pole vault, Psaki went further. The third disturbing act had an Orwellian twist. Psaki indicated that Biden didn't only want social media platforms to ban users for saying improper things on their platform but also to ban users who said improper things *on other platforms.* Psaki was requesting all platforms simultaneously silence anyone who said something deemed false by the government. She even hinted that this would include not just social media but things like email and text messages as well. Independent media termed her proposal "the internet death penalty."[61] Wherever this idea came from—whether it was Psaki, Biden, Media Matters, or the CIA—the notion that a user, group, or news organization could be instantly banned from the entire internet would diminish our Free Speech to something resembling the liberties granted in China and North Korea. Psaki indicated the government would like to be able to single out users and gag them. If the actions of Media Matters were in a gray area with regard to First Amendment speech protections, this chilling speech by the White House crossed directly into unconstitutional territory before crossing the next border into authoritarian dystopia.

It was something I honestly never thought I would hear when I began writing this book. The summer of 2021 witnessed the executive branch of the US government seeking to utterly silence citizens whose voices it did not like.

I took an afternoon off from writing to consider whether publishing a book that might be censored was a worthwhile use of my time.

I came back to this project inspired. I realized that the "internet death penalty" is the epitome of killing freedom to save it. Worse, it is killing *democracy* to save *control of information*. I couldn't think of a more meaningful way to spend my time than notifying Americans of this. Our First Amendment exists precisely because authoritarian rulers always seek to manage the flow of information. Even if you personally like and trust Biden and Psaki—or you personally like and trust Donald Trump, or Bernie Sanders, or Ron DeSantis—would you want to hand the terrifying power of censorship to the next administration not knowing who the next president might be?

No, no citizen in their right mind would do that.

Nevertheless, those are the dystopian lengths to which the current administration and its party leaders seem willing to go to maintain control of the narrative.[62] To protect their favored perspective, they will seek an internet death penalty.

For the remainder of this chapter we will look at two additional kinds of narrative management: narratives that frequently change and narratives that die quick deaths.

First, a narrative that frequently *changes* induces a type of *hysteria* in people who pay close attention to the news and *amnesia* in those who don't. This type of media propaganda is called *gaslighting*, and it creates confusion via a constantly *shifting* narrative. *Gaslighting* profoundly affects a person's ability to perceive reality. The term *gaslighting* comes from an old black-and-white Ingrid Bergman film called *Gaslight* in which a woman is psychologically tortured by her husband to the point that she no longer knows what to believe and loses faith in her own ability to discern reality.[63] Narrative management is called *gaslighting* when it induces in citizens a mental fog that weakens their brain's ability to think clearly about a topic and decipher fact from fiction. In these events, the narrative ultimately becomes "trust the government" or "trust the experts" rather than discern reality on your own. The remedy for *gaslighting*, as with other types of narrative management, is a Balanced Media Diet and *media consciousness*. Let's look now at an example of *gaslighting*.

VIRTUE HAS A VEIL,
VICE A MASK

IN TIMES OF NATIONAL PANIC, THE MAINSTREAM MEDIA ALWAYS TELLS us to trust the experts. The month of March 2020 kicked off just such a time. Reports emerged daily about a deadly new virus, scary stories popped up on social media, and hysteria swept the country. The leading medical expert featured in the corporate media was Dr. Anthony Fauci, Director of the National Institute of Allergy and Infectious Diseases (NIAID). Fauci became the face of the American response to the coronavirus.

Midway through March, with few confirmed cases but the country on pins and needles, Fauci sat for an interview with *60 Minutes*.[64] Questions about the wearing of facemasks permeated the national media. The narrative at the time was that masks were *not* helpful in fighting the virus. Earlier that week, the hosts of *Good Morning America* on ABC News had ridiculed mask wearers as anxious, uninformed, and scientifically obtuse.[65]

Here was Fauci, the trusted expert, seated and available for questions on national television. The host put it straight to him. "There's a lot of confusion among people—and *misinformation* out there—surrounding facemasks. Can you discuss that?"

"Right now in the United States," Fauci replied, "people shouldn't be walking around wearing a mask." He emphasized that masks were not useful for healthy people and instead should be used to prevent ill people from spreading the virus.

> When you're in the middle of an outbreak, wearing a mask might make people *feel* a little bit better, and it might even block a droplet, but it's not providing the perfect protection that people think that it is, and often there are unintended consequences of people ... fiddling with the mask and touching their face.[66]

Fauci instructed the nervous nation that masks were of no significant assistance in preventing the spread of the virus and could in some cases cause healthy people problems. "When you think about masks, you should think about healthcare providers needing them, and people who are ill," he concluded. There were decades of studies on the use of masks to prevent the spread of viruses, and the studies were inconclusive at best; some found harmful effects from extensive use of masks.[67]

News sources across the country dutifully broadcast Fauci's instructions, which confirmed the existing narrative, and the matter of masks was dropped—for two months, that is. As summer approached, with lockdowns descending and confusion reigning everywhere, Fauci changed his tune. Medical masks were suddenly essential in preventing the spread of the virus, he said.

Are You Lying Now, or Were You Lying Then?

The news narrative shifted with him on a dime. As always with *gaslighting*, there was no middle ground: you were with Fauci or against him. Another month went by, and in an interview with *The Street* in June, Fauci declared that not just medical masks but *any* mask—be it a N95 mask, a surgical mask, or any handmade piece of cloth with a band—was essential in stopping the virus. The narrative shifted with him again. Casually, almost in passing, Fauci admitted that, well, yes, he had chosen to lie to the American people earlier in the year, telling the nation that he had chosen to deceive them because he had been concerned that "healthcare workers [didn't have] ... the equipment that they needed."[68]

The corporate media commented on neither the lie nor the narrative U-turn, simply passing along the new guidance and an implicit command to follow it and not ask questions. The normal human reaction to being lied to is shock, and a doctor knowingly misleading people about an illness would be on many people's short list of unethical behavior. But the *gaslighting* narrative was "trust the experts," and so the shock was sublimated into mild curiosity. Dr. Fauci acknowledged his lie casually. He wasn't contrite or apologetic. He didn't even suggest that he'd been wrong or dishonest. He did not beg the nation's forgiveness for lying or apologize for risking millions of lives. He didn't promise not to do it again. He was *gaslighting*, and the media simply passed along his contradictory comments with, at most, mild curiosity.

"Who controls the narrative controls the world."

— Caitlin Johnstone

Fauci claimed he was "following the science" and that he issued new guidance "as the science changed." But he said other things privately. Journalists from the *Highwire*, *BuzzFeed*, and the *Washington Post* submitted Freedom of Information Act requests and received thousands of pages of emails to and from Fauci.[69] A close look at the emails revealed that many of his messages had been deceptive and that he had generally believed masks to be less effective than he had expressed publicly.

Whatever might be the ultimate truth about the efficacy of masks in reducing the spread of a coronavirus—a question that is beyond the scope of this book—Fauci was clearly *gaslighting* the nation, and the corporate media enabled it. This was done repeatedly and consistently on account of *systemic bias*. I don't know whether Fauci was concealing incompetence, ignorance, a drive to dehumanize people, or an interest in prolonging the pandemic. What I know is that neither his lie nor his *gaslighting* were ever called out by the mainstream media because the narrative was "trust the experts." Many independent media journalists, on the other hand, pointed out Fauci's dishonesty[70] and inconsistencies.[71]

A Voice of Sanity

At the bottom of the Pandora's Box of evils unleashed during the pandemic was a profoundly hopeful force: the ascendancy of independent media. Analysis of Fauci's deception that couldn't appear in the corporate media because of *systemic bias* was abundantly available in independent media. Had the nation's leading medical authority been lying in March, or in June? Or both, or neither? In simply asking this question as well as openly inquiring whether masks were helpful or not, the New Enlightenment unfolded a bit more in 2020. If masks actually prevented the spread of the virus, Fauci's lie in March had cost lives. If, on the other hand, Fauci was telling the truth about masks back in March—and his leaked emails later showed that this was more likely the case—then this lie in June fed a yawning political divide in the country. This analysis, again, occurred only in independent media.

The *New York Times* didn't analyze both sides. CNN didn't summon Fauci for a follow-up interview. The medical authority had lied to the nation in a time of confusion and fear, but none of our ostensibly rigorous bastions of journalism were alarmed. Few even called it a "lie," though his words fit the dictionary definition to a tee: "to make an untrue statement with intent to deceive." Independent media news shows, on the other hand, such as the increasingly popular shows run by Joe Rogan and Jimmy Dore, pointed out to their audiences (which often rival or surpass the viewership of CNN) the strange nonchalance with which Fauci explained his decision to lie, his unrepentance, and the likelihood he would therefore lie again if he saw fit.

Fauci's position on masks continued to gyrate, and with it the *gaslighting* narrative moved. In 2021, everyone was instructed to mask all the time, then outdoor masking was unnecessary, then two masks were recommended, then only non-vaccinated people needed to wear masks, then the vaccinated needed masks too. Children didn't need masks, as they were at a low risk of infection and transmission, but then children needed to wear masks at all times, then only indoors. The narrative changed so frequently that many people succumbed to the "gaslit" state concerning masks.[72] *Media consciousness* is essential in the face of this type of narrative management.

Systemic bias plays a major role in "trust the experts" narrative management. Elite sources such as Fauci are instinctively protected from media scrutiny. Managing the narrative, in this case, meant ensuring Fauci's integrity was never called into question. Thus, the narrative changed as often as necessary to follow Fauci's remarks—masks are foolish, masks are optional, masks are necessary, masks are no longer needed, masks are needed indoors but not outdoors, two masks are better than one, the type of mask matters, the type of mask doesn't matter, et cetera.

The power and flexibility of narrative management enabled this narrative to change constantly while the narrative that Bernie Sanders was dangerous and radical could endure unchanging despite the facts for five years. At other times, news narratives neither endure nor change frequently but simply disappear altogether.

WHEN A NARRATIVE DIES

TWO NARRATIVES WERE USED BY THE CORPORATE MEDIA MORE THAN any others during Donald Trump's presidency. Prior to covid, the stories that seemed to go on forever were, to use their famous hashtags, *#Russiagate* and *#MeToo*. Both of these stories received extraordinarily broad coverage for months and years but collapsed in quick succession during the spring of 2020 as the pandemic began and the presidential election neared. The narratives vanished so quickly it was as if they had never existed. This type of narrative management induces *amnesia* about false narratives used in the past in order to preserve credibility in the next narrative.

The *#Russiagate* allegations were at their very base a theory—a *conspiracy* theory if we're precise—that members of the Russian government plotted secretly with the Trump campaign to manipulate the 2016 election in Trump's favor and that Trump himself was either in the pay of the Kremlin or an actual Russian agent. The theory grew and grew as 2017 and 2018 unfolded—allegedly involving figures as disparate as Tulsi Gabbard, Mitch McConnell, Jill Stein, Rex Tillerson, Scott Bannon, and Bernie Sanders. It received wall-to-wall coverage on Blue News channels like MSNBC month after month. Rachel Maddow, in particular, staked her credibility on the story, covering it daily. During one six-week period in 2017, Maddow covered Russiagate more than all other stories, *combined*.[73] At one egregious moment, she warned her viewers that Russians were hacking the power grid of the Midwest during the winter months to freeze the homes of farmers.[74]

None of these theories was ever proven. When Special Counsel Robert Mueller presented to Congress in May 2019 the results of a massive, two-year investigation that attempted to prove Trump-Russia collusion, his ultimate conclusion was:

> The investigation did not establish that the members of the Trump campaign coordinated or conspired with the Russian government in its election interference activities.

So, after years of incessant tirades and insinuations in the Blue News corporate media about Russia, and after years of investigations led by a former

FBI Director, there was nothing, no bombshells, no proof, no indictment of a single American for collusion with Russia.[75]

All that survived was evidence that Russia, on its own, had attempted to sway the election via propaganda techniques, and that those efforts had ultimately had little effect.

The allegation that Russia had hacked the DNC servers to leak emails during the 2016 primary couldn't be proven either. The DNC never allowed the FBI to actually look at its servers, and the company the DNC themselves brought in to prove Russian infiltration, CrowdStrike, was unable to establish that the hacks had happened at all, let alone had resulted in the theft of the emails.[76] A dubious "fact check" by the AP claimed to support CrowdStrike but merely confirmed that the FBI didn't inspect the servers directly and instead inspected "forensic evidence" provided by the DNC's hand-selected firm,[77] which was a bit like the FBI performing a murder investigation without inspecting the crime scene and instead carefully studying "forensic photographs" of the crime scene provided by a company hired by a prime suspect. It was not a convincing investigation and certainly not enough to prove the extraordinary claim of Russian culpability.

The Endless Conspiracy

Nevertheless, in 2019 and into 2020, the conspiracy lived on. As late as March 2020, with Bernie Sanders still leading the race for the Democratic nomination, corporate media reported with a straight face that via "as yet undetectable methods" Russia would hack the 2020 election and that Bernie and Trump would likely benefit.[78] There remained no evidence of any of these "undetectable methods" (it was unclear how anyone had detected an undetectable method), and the conspiracy theory was growing long in the tooth. Nonetheless, it survived in news narratives month after month, propped up by a stream of warnings from unnamed intelligence sources.

In the summer of 2020, everything about *#Russiagate* suddenly changed. The Senate Select Committee on Intelligence transcripts were released, revealing the fact that senior intelligence officials had generally had little confidence in the allegations about Russia yet had lied repeatedly on national television.[79] The corporate media had been a simple propaganda conduit for the story.

The fateful summer of 2020, with most people distracted by the covid pandemic, also brought the news that President Barack Obama and then-Vice President Joe Biden had attempted to criminally prosecute incoming National Security Advisor Michael Flynn in 2016 for initiating diplomacy with Russia on the grounds that it was evidence of a conspiracy. In other words, far from being rife with Russian agents when entering office, the Trump administration was deliberately handicapped by the Obama administration. Obama leveled criminal attacks on Flynn and sent instructions to the FBI to investigate him, based on alleged ties to Russia that didn't exist.[80] Charges against Flynn were finally dropped in the summer of 2020.[81]

As 2020 wound to a close, the final nails in the *#Russiagate* coffin were driven in.[82] The Steele dossier, the underlying document that shaped much of American politics for nearly four full years, was finally and thoroughly discredited. First, corporate media acknowledged that the dossier had been funded not by Republicans or the British but by the Clinton campaign and the DNC. Then Igor Danchenko, the primary source for the dossier, was indicted for lying to the FBI. Those still paying attention learned that not only had the dossier's creation been funded by the Clinton campaign, but Danchenko had worked with longtime Clinton advisor Charles Dolan to concoct its salacious and false contents, including several fictional meetings between Trump and Russian prostitutes.[83]

By late 2021, the corporate media was quietly retracting articles about the dossier[84] and acknowledging that the Trump-Russia collusion theory had been false.[85] The whole thing—the grand conspiracy—was acknowledged as a tale written by the DNC with the help of several intelligence agents in the waning weeks of the Obama administration. The underlying document used to architect the conspiracy narrative was a bogus report devised to damage Trump, and the corporate media played along for years. The Steele dossier will go down in the annals of narrative control alongside Colin Powell's vial of an undisclosed substance that he held aloft in the UN as proof of Iraq's weapons of mass destruction.

When a narrative is dropped, it is gone, silently and quickly, and the next scandal or story takes center stage. Did the corporate media spend any time on this? Did the *New York Times* examine why their most prestigious journalists had pushed a phony and incredibly dangerous story for years? Did Rachel Maddow apologize for years of disinformation? Were there widespread *mea culpas* and apologies for misleading the public? No. They all moved on quickly to the Biden-Trump election, then to covid and vaccines, then to Putin and Ukraine. This swift transition between stories, coupled with the emotional outrage of the next story, cultivates short attention spans, confusion, and amnesia—the things necessary to maintain credibility and control over the narrative.

Reviewing its substance, the *#Russiagate* narrative had served its purpose by the summer of 2020. Its purpose was, first, to obscure the true reasons for Trump's victory and Clinton's loss in 2016, and second, to weaken Trump's presidency by painting his administration as not just corrupt (which would have been easy to prove with real facts) but as actual traitors and criminals compromised by Russia. This worked to demonize not just Trump but the entire nation of Russia, too, and to further entrench the power of a military-industrial complex bent on creating tension and selling arms.

There was *innocent, systemic,* and *nefarious bias* all at play in the endless promotion of this fictional conspiracy. When analyzing *nefarious bias*, it is essential to remember that intelligence agencies like the CIA have their own agenda quite separate from what is presented in the news. When unproven reports from unnamed intelligence sources are presented as fact in the corporate media, an ulterior agenda is always at play. As you cultivate *media consciousness*, you will begin to notice these unproven reports and decipher the ulterior agendas on your own.

For some Americans, the collapse of *#Russiagate* destroyed what was left of the corporate media's credibility. Certainly, trust in the media among conservatives and supporters of Trump was driven to new lows. But in other ways, the narrative worked. By dominating news cycles for years, *#Russiagate* distracted Democrats from considering both the real reasons for Trump's victory and the corruption in the DNC revealed by the WikiLeaks emails. It also allowed the corporate media to reestablish its role in the eyes of many Democrats as the arbiter of truth and tar independent progressive news sources as irresponsible.[86] As with so many repeated news narratives, this one's damage was permanent. Many people to this day believe that Trump conspired with Russia to steal the 2016 election. This fact made demonizing Russia during the disastrous proxy war in Ukraine far easier. More people believe Trump conspired with Russia than believe Iraq ever had "weapons of mass destruction," although the two claims enjoy a similar level of evidence. As the saying goes, it is easier to fool someone than to convince him he has been fooled.

When a narrative is no longer feasible, when its story begins to run in reverse, it is quietly dropped regardless of how many years it has served as a mantra. And its damage is rarely repaired.

Believe Some Women

In pursuit of generally noble goals, the *#MeToo* movement attempts to reduce sexual assault and harassment and related shame and stigma by encouraging women to step forward, share their stories, name names, and press charges. The corporate media amplified this movement for many months, with expansive and frequent coverage of *#MeToo* campaigns and their aims. This came to an abrupt halt in the summer of 2020, similar to *#Russiagate*.[87] The minute that the mission of the movement ran counter to a desired narrative, it was dropped from public discourse.

As a movement, *#MeToo* had been around for over a decade before it attained its peak momentum in October 2017. Allegations of Hollywood producer Harvey Weinstein's hundreds of sexual crimes were published in the *New York Times*, and the entire media immediately jumped on board, amplifying the hashtags *#MeToo* and *#BelieveWomen* on social media as well. The coverage prompted many more women in Hollywood, in corporate business towers, and in political capitals to come forward with personal stories of sexual harassment and assault. The national news narrative was that women were routinely subjected to sexual assault and harassment and that it was time to listen to their stories. Women spoke out, stories were shared, and men in high places lost reputations and sometimes careers. The *Times* won a Pulitzer Prize for its coverage. *Time* magazine named "The Women Who Broke the Silence" the People of the Year for 2017.

The narrative came to another crescendo a year later, in the fall of 2018. Congress was holding Supreme Court confirmation hearings for Trump nominee Brett Kavanaugh. A woman named Christine Blasey Ford came forward and alleged that Kavanaugh had sexually assaulted her when they were teenagers. In this case, they were both young, and there was no evidence of assault beyond the woman's testimony, so it was a thorny issue that divided opinion. Nevertheless, the *New York Times* and the *Washington Post* trumpeted, "*#MeToo*" *and* "*#BelieveWomen*," standing on principle that women should always be believed and that cases of false accusations are too rare to matter.

Then came the summer of 2020. A woman came forward with allegations of rape by a powerful man, and the initial reaction to her story on social media was, as expected, "*#BelieveWomen*" and "*#MeToo.*" People jumped on board in solidarity, listened to her story, and called on the media to question the man whom she alleged had raped her. The man she accused was a particularly powerful man, a longtime US senator, a man who was the presumptive presidential nominee for the Democratic Party. Her name was Tara Reade. His name was Joe Biden.

At the time of the alleged rape, Biden had already been an adult for many years and was already an elected congressman; there was corroborating evidence beyond just Reade's story; the allegation was of a much more invasive kind of sexual assault than what had been alleged by Christine Blasey Ford; and there was a clear power dynamic at play since Biden had been Reade's boss at the time.

Nevertheless, rather than drop Biden, the entire Blue News corporate media dropped *#MeToo.*[88]

First, the story was ignored. Reade was interviewed only on independent news shows *Rising* and *Democracy Now* while every outlet of the mainstream corporate media waited.[89] Every channel had been eager to interview Ford the day she came forward with her allegations in 2018, but Reade was for weeks only seen on independent news shows. Why would no one—not one—of the many left-leaning media channels interview her? Why was that? Reade's stated preference was *not* to go on a Red News network for fear of being seen as playing politics. Why wasn't Biden asked to comment on the allegations for *a month* during the Democratic Primary as voters in many states were choosing between Biden, Sanders, and other candidates? Why did the media fail to do its *watchdog* duty of holding the powerful to account and, instead, patiently await this powerful politician's indication he was ready to speak about alleged misdeeds?

After several more victories over Bernie Sanders in primary contests, Biden permitted the media channels to ask him about the matter. The corporate media then eagerly asked to interview Reade, but at that point, Reade made a groundbreaking choice of her own. She chose to be interviewed not by a

Red News or a Blue News network but by an independent journalist. She sat down with Megan Kelly, a news host who had formerly worked at both NBC News and Fox and who had struck out on her own.[90]

Reade finally found a smidgen of power in the situation. She told her story on her own terms. To me, it was another small but hopeful sign that the New Enlightenment is upon us. Three decades earlier, a woman by the name of Juanita Broaddrick attempted to come forward with extremely credible allegations of sexual assault by Bill Clinton,[91] but the corporate media was able to shut her out entirely.

Reade's allegations were convincing to many, but when Biden finally addressed them by denying her claim that he had sexually assaulted her in the Capitol Building when he was a congressman and she was one of his aides, the corporate media shifted the narrative. In an instant, the entire *#MeToo* narrative about women with allegations of sexual assault switched from one in which women should be believed to one in which men must be allowed to tell their story first and receive due process.

Regardless of your opinion as to which approach to sexual assault allegations is best and most ethical, watching a presumably principled stand on the part of corporate media evaporate like morning fog when the allegation came from the wrong person at the wrong time was telling.[92] The *#MeToo* movement and its *#BelieveWomen* narrative were amplified when it was useful and dropped when it was inconvenient.

What was stunning in this case was the double collapse of arguably the two biggest news narratives of the Trump administration. Both were dropped in the same month, further undermining the corporate media's credibility.

A LONGING FOR TRUTH AND FREEDOM

ULTIMATELY, THE GOAL OF CORPORATE MEDIA—AND, INCREASINGLY, social media as well—can be summarized as *managing the stories that the American population believes*. The purpose of this work is *to advance the agenda of the largest corporations, wealthiest families, and most powerful arms of government.* Managing narratives generally uses the techniques of censorship and propaganda pioneered by Edward Bernays and Walter Lippmann in the 1920s, which we'll examine in Chapter 11. The techniques require, first, a carefully constructed narrative about both the world people live in and the problems people face. Second, this narrative must be repeated over and over, ideally with no contradictory information diluting its strength in order for it to be adopted first as "probably true" by citizens and then accepted broadly as default reality. Any news outlets with opposing viewpoints should be silenced, discredited, or marginalized lest the persuasive power of the narrative diminish.

When the people believe this all-important story to be true—as indicated by opinion polling—the narrative can die.

These techniques have proven virtually unstoppable for a century, until this era. Today's phenomenon—the rise of independent media—is fueled by two tremendous forces: the unquenchable and innate desire of all humans to know the truth, and the constant and evolving distribution of information by the internet to those who seek it. These twin forces increasingly conflict with the age-old power of centralized narrative control and propaganda, and this conflict is one of the crucial battles in a burgeoning global war between the centralization and decentralization of political power. Those who seek to further centralize power in a technocratic elite seek to advance narrative control; they censor independent media with slurs like "fake news" and "disinformation." The vast majority of people, on the other hand, increasingly thirst for the decentralization of knowledge and truth that the internet enables; they seek to protect and advance the ability of all people to think and act freely. This vast majority and its will to freedom is bringing about the New Enlightenment.

7

THE PIPES OF THE MODERN WURLITZER

"Journalism is printing what someone else does not want printed. Everything else is public relations."

George Orwell

THE MAN SPOKE STERNLY. HE LOOKED ME IN THE EYE. "美国最好不要惹中国," he said. *The United States better not mess with China.*

I stood beside him, gazing at the placid waters of Cuihu Lake.

He turned to me, to check that I understood.

I nodded.

He offered me his open bag of peanuts. I took a few, snapping the shells between my fingers and tossing the nuts into my mouth. We were in a public park in Kunming, the capital city of China's subtropical Yunnan Province.

"你們認為你們仍然可以欺壓我們嗎?" he asked, crushing and discarding shells onto the pavement. *Do you think you can still push us around?*

It was April 2, 2001, and I'd been in China for two months. I had been enjoying my second visit to the country when, on April Fool's Day, a US Navy EP-3 spy plane collided in midair with a Chinese fighter jet. The collision occurred just off the coast of Hainan Island, approximately five hundred miles from where I was standing.

The man had approached me kindly as many strangers did in China in those days. Precious few foreign faces dotted the city's streets back then, and people were curious. I felt at times like an animal in a zoo when strolling the streets of smaller cities.

I assured him to the best of my ability about American intentions before I left the park's tree-lined banks and walked around the corner to seek both sides of the story. I strolled past the newspaper stands on street corners where headlines bellowed about an "act of war."

I bought a copy of the 人民日报 (*People's Daily*) before I stepped into a tiny 網際吧 ("internet cafe").

Although the internet was not yet widely used in China, a segment of the population adopted it early, used email, and visited websites. The authorities viewed computers very positively at that time—as signs of modernization and development—and few internet resources were censored. I sidled down a narrow aisle in a cramped den of whirring computers, bulky monitors, power cords, and bottled water. Deep in the computer cave, I sat in front of a blocky monitor. After a few clicks of the mouse, I was at *CNN.com*, staring at the news headlines from a faraway land.

The websites of the American corporate media offered their narrative of the event, and it flowed easily into my mind. I'd been raised and educated on the American viewpoint of such matters. Good propaganda, like good brick-laying, always prepares a spot to add more.

After an hour, I stepped back into the sunlight. With my handy pocket dictionary, I challenged myself to read the front page articles of the Chinese paper. As I absorbed the Chinese media's narrative about this international event, it made my brain spin. The coverage couldn't have been more different. The Chinese viewpoint wasn't difficult to understand. The Chinese papers vilified the notion that the US could freely fly spy planes directly over Chinese sovereign land. I, too, was surprised that the American spy plane had flown over Chinese land.

Over the next few days, I talked to people on the streets, in the market, on buses, and in the tutoring sessions I taught. I found everyday people more open to talking about politics than normal. The issue ran on the front pages for weeks. Many asked me my opinion, an American in China.

A Tale of Two Nations

It would take years for the full story to come out, and even longer for me to ascertain which side's reports were closer to the truth.

At the time, in the American media, howls of outrage echoed from every corner. How could a plane that had not gone into Chinese airspace—and that was only flying a "routine surveillance route"—be deliberately brought down, perhaps even shot out of the air? The assumption was that the Chinese were lying and that the American plane had been doing nothing wrong and was illegally attacked.

The Chinese media was equally outraged: *How could the American military fly spy missions "directly over China" and so blithely invade our sovereign territory? Will they never respect our borders?* The assumption was that the Americans were lying and the plane had gone down by accident, but there was a secondary narrative in the Chinese media I was able to discern: in case the Americans were telling the truth, it would have been completely legal under international law for China to shoot the plane down had the "patient" Chinese military saw fit to do so.

As it turns out, gazing back now with the luxury of time and research, we know the Chinese media was closer to the truth. Learning this was one of many steps on my own path to awakening and *media consciousness*. The US plane was, in fact, spying on Chinese activities south of Hainan Island. Chinese planes scrambled to confront it. There are no credible records of a shoot down. The evidence suggests instead that a Chinese plane accidentally clipped the larger American aircraft due to pilot error.[1] The Chinese media obscured the role its planes might have played in the crash, but the US media's coverage was more deceptive in that it obscured entirely the problem of the US plane's presence there in the first place while alleging the more warlike offense of intentional shootdown.

The one thing I did know as I sat reading the American propaganda for the first time was that the Chinese media was deceptive. In my first stint in China, chronicled in my book *Double Happiness*, I learned that most Chinese people know their media lies. Chinese people have decades of mistrust of centralized government media dating back to the Cultural Revolution of the 1960s.

耳聽為虛眼見為貴
"Trust what you see, not what you've heard."
— Chinese Proverb

What I didn't know yet was the level of trust most Americans had in their media. When I wrote emails back home to inform friends and family that I was safe, they responded that they were worried about me and aghast at China's actions. They all assumed—no, *knew*—that the American media's reporting was factual and balanced, that the American media was free of deliberate bias, and that if there was bias in one American publication, it would be balanced out by the honest journalism in others. They were curious about my thoughts, but they assumed the American media wouldn't deliberately distort the truth and, thus, believed that the Chinese had intentionally shot down the plane.

This was one of several early steps in my personal journey that led to the book you hold in your hands. The Chinese media was not reporting the full story, but many Chinese people knew it wasn't the full story. Many were fiercely patriotic, like the young man eating peanuts, but most assumed their news was not reporting the whole story.

Americans, on the other hand, were not as overtly patriotic, but they displayed what I sensed was a more implicit ignorance with their certainty about the veracity of their own media.

Although this is changing today at the dawn of the New Enlightenment, millions of Americans to this day still believe that their favorite news source—be it ABC, the *New York Times*, Fox, or NPR, for instance—is reporting events truthfully and honestly to the best of its editors' and reporters' ability. Many Americans have continued to believe this even after the revelations of Operation Mockingbird—indeed, even after the lies that led to two wars and millions of deaths in Iraq, and after the revelations of the Afghanistan Papers. This mental state that we'll call "red, white, and blind" is a state of confusion and amnesia similar in some ways to the mental condition of the weaker member of an abusive relationship. It is an ongoing forgetfulness about repeated, rampant deception, and it muddles an awareness of reality.

Most Americans, for instance, will say they support peace even after their mainstream news source of choice—their trusted arbiter of truth and lies—

has supported every war that the United States has engaged in during their lifetimes. They don't notice the contradiction, or they notice it in a fuzzy uncomfortable way for a moment before getting back to the scandal of the day or, indeed, listening to the next pro-war pundit on their screen.

The *New York Times* distorts the truth as frequently as the Chinese media, only in subtler ways that masterfully elude its readers' notice. This is a marvel of modern propaganda, perhaps an unparalleled achievement in the history of news media. As a whole, the American corporate news media—Wisner's "Mighty Wurlitzer"—is by far the most sophisticated propaganda machine ever created.

It is difficult for Americans, even for those aware that their corporate media is a conduit for propaganda, to remember that our mainstream media has the same goal and effect as the Chinese and Russian government media.

FAKE NEWS, FAKE SOURCES

TWO DECADES LATER, IN ANOTHER PART OF CHINA, PROTESTS BROKE out for democracy and freedom. The "Umbrella Movement" in Hong Kong was a period of massive pro-democracy protests spanning the island city in 2019 and 2020. These protests mattered to me a great deal as I had been in China in 1997, the year Hong Kong had been transferred to China. I had spent quite a bit of time in the "Fragrant Harbor" at the time of the handover.

As the Umbrella Movement overtook the island, the *New York Times* and *Washington Post* frequently interviewed grassroots protestors on the ground. One man, Kong Tsung-gan, appeared regularly in the corporate American media. Kong provided the American media with insight into the motives of the protests and the threats posed to Hong Kong's political system by mainland China. He was interviewed and quoted again and again.

There was just one problem. Kong Tsung-gan didn't exist. He was a fabricated media persona and social media presence. He was an alias used at times by an Amnesty International worker named Brian Kern, an American based in Hong Kong.[2] The methodical independent journalist Max Blumenthal uncovered the fact that Kern had been posing as Kong for five full years, speaking to the local media and publishing articles and books in the local press.[3] Meanwhile, in reality, Kern was a White guy organizing protests,[4] and, it would seem to one accustomed to identifying such actors, an *agent provocateur* working with the CIA or other western intelligence agency. Very Operation Mockingbird for him to be quoted again and again, under a fake name, in places like the BBC and the *Guardian* of London. An *agent provocateur* is someone who infiltrates an organization or movement to push it to do more violent or illegal activities in order to expose the organization to arrests and criminal charges and thereby neutralize it.

We don't hear the term "fake sources" very often. Certainly, we hear the term "fake news" more. The latter is used to marginalize independent media reporting, but devising fake sources is, in fact, a more sophisticated tool used in modern American propaganda. Let's examine two other instances of "fake sources" where prestigious corporate news narratives were based on the words of suspicious or altogether fake persons.

➦ **Capitol Riots: John Sullivan.** Shortly after the "Stop the Steal" election fraud protests and breach of the Capitol on January 6, 2021, CNN aired footage from inside the Capitol. The video was provided by an unusual attendee of the protests, a young man named John Sullivan, who was interviewed on CNN by the Anderson Cooper and paid $35,000 for his footage.[5] The problem was, Sullivan wasn't an election fraud protestor at all. He was a Black Lives Matter activist. Or was he? He had appeared at BLM protests in Utah in 2020 under the name "Activist John." But the Black Lives Matter movement had repeatedly disowned him, saying he was known to push protestors to be more violent.[6] They suspected he was an *agent provocateur*. And that's what he had done during the "Stop the Steal" breach as well—egged on the protestors to push farther into the building, to force the doors, to become more violent. Videos show Sullivan shouting repeatedly to the protestors, "It's our house motherf___s!" and "We're going in!"

Much like Brian Kern, above, Sullivan's role in various protest movements appears to be to infiltrate and provoke the protest from within, ratcheting up the violence to either justify intervention by law enforcement or provide material for a particular news narrative.[7] Whether or not Sullivan is an asset of an intelligence agency, his checkered past in various protest movements on different sides of the political spectrum was never mentioned on CNN or NBC. How precisely CNN found him and why they promoted him was unclear as well. He seemed to show up at the perfect time; his presence egged on the protestors to enter the Capitol; and his footage was used by the corporate media to present the events as more dangerous than they were.

↪ **ISIS: Shehroze Chaudhry.** The *New York Times* launched a new podcast in 2018. With much fanfare, they proclaimed that their new darling, *Caliphate*, represented "the new modern *New York Times*." *Caliphate* delved into the nitty-gritty reality of Al Qaeda, ISIS, and other terrorist groups in the Middle East. The podcast repeatedly interviewed Shehroze Chaudhry, a Canadian who had traveled to Syria and joined ISIS as a radical recruit to their cause. Chaudhry told *Caliphate* his harrowing stories over multiple episodes: he had risen in the ranks of ISIS, witnessed executions, and even executed people himself as one of the organization's "terminators." It was riveting stuff, and the *Times* podcast became quite popular. The media corporation congratulated itself on its "ambitious, rigorous, hard-nosed reporting." In one interview, editor Sam Dolnick gushed:

> We're taking our audience to dangerous places they have never been, and we're doing it with more transparency than we ever have before.[8]

There was only one problem. It was fiction. Chaudhry had never traveled to Syria, nor joined ISIS, nor performed executions.[9] All-star *Times* reporter Rukmini Callimachi, who supervised the show, turned out to be either painfully naive or willfully deceptive,[10] and given the track record of the *Times* in covering the news of the Middle East, the latter seemed the more likely. In either case, for over two years, the *Times* deceived its audience. Again.

Fake sources lead obviously to fake news. Only brilliant narrative management can induce the "red, white, and blind" state that cleanses readers' minds of the frequent sins of deliberate deception. For the remainder of this chapter, we'll examine the dominant Red News and Blue News outlets and how as a whole they divide and deceive Americans, lull them into a deceived state, and keep them there.

TODAY'S MIGHTY WURLITZER

THE VAST ARRAY OF NEWS SOURCES IN THE UNITED STATES PROVIDES both real and managed diversity of opinion to American readers. The variety of styles appeal to different tastes and outlooks. This diversity is what enables the American corporate media world to attain its sophistication. While, most of the time, the various voices vociferously disagree within a defined range of opinion, when the entire array of apparently different voices agree on something—that an election was fair, say, or a documentary was disinformation—most people accept it as the undisputed truth. With the decades of development of propaganda techniques, this constellation of sources, which now includes social media, has raised news narrative management to an art form. Or, in the words of a famous CIA man, a musical symphony.

Frank Wisner, Deputy Director of the CIA at the time, famously evoked a "Mighty Wurlitzer" when describing the CIA's collection of front organizations, "owned" media, and planted reporters who were assembled as part of Operation Mockingbird. As described earlier, a Wurlitzer is an enormous pipe organ that can play a huge range of sounds at full volume. Wisner declared that with the resources at his disposal he could at any time disseminate any news report, be it true or false, throughout the country and around the world.

The following pages are a review of some of the largest and best known components of this Mighty Wurlitzer, its biggest and loudest pipes, and how they function today to attract, persuade, and maintain their respective target audiences.

The New York Times: Delusions of Candor

With its thousand employees, forty-two global bureaus, and heavy hundred-page weekday issues, the *New York Times* brings an astounding breadth of resources to doing what it does best: telling its left-leaning, affluent, urban audience how and what to think. To please, flatter, and keep its target audience, its editorial tone is elevated, patient, and studied, almost whispering to a reader as she flips or surfs its pages, *you're intelligent, you're reading the New York Times.* So broad is its daily news section and so lengthy its articles that readers get the impression that every angle must have been considered, that true journalism must be occurring, that with all of the sentences and paragraphs and sources surely no salient facts are missing.

The "Gray Lady," indeed, does great work some of the time. The more local, the less political the piece, the better its coverage. In every issue, there is usually at least one truly brilliant feature or example of stellar professional journalism; cultural treatises on cultural topics like sports, music, and theater are typically of high quality.

It's the articles on political and global events that suffer its thick *bias*. This newspaper has been wrong about national politics so frequently that no serious analysis can conclude the errors have been from honest mistakes or only innocent bias. At the outset of World War II, the *Times* reported that Poland invaded Germany, rather than the other way around. Ashley Rindsberg, who penned the foreword to this book, chronicles this and a century of these deceptions in his magisterial 2021 book *The Gray Lady Winked: How The New York Times's Misreporting, Distortions, and Fabrications Radically Alter History.*[11]

For regular readers, however, it can be easy to forget the errors—and the *Times* helps you forget by moving on quickly from crisis to crisis. The underlying methodology that produced the distortions is never fixed, because the distortions weren't mistakes. The *Times* has supported every single free trade deal that weakened the American middle class by shipping jobs overseas.[12] They've endorsed every war that the military-industrial complex has shown interest in launching over the last century, and not just the overt ones, as in the case of the Iraq Wars, but the covert wars, too, with their support of the military destruction of places like Yugoslavia, Libya, and Sudan. In the past few years, they've amplified lies about chemical weapons attacks in Syria, concealed a genocidal war in Yemen, and obscured the causes of coups in Venezuela and Bolivia. Thanks to the Afghanistan Papers, we know the *Times* joined the deep state in disseminating fifteen years of lies about the illegal annihilation of Afghanistan.[13] After all of these "mistakes," will things change? Why would they? They'll engineer narratives that support the next war too.

It is important to point out that the *Times* is the country's, and probably the world's, most prestigious newspaper. This is why we are spending so much time examining its coverage, and this is why its section in this chapter is the longest. The *Times* sets the agenda for the American media world, and thereby, in many cases, the world's.

Not coincidentally, the "Gray Lady" was known to be Mockingbird's biggest asset. The personal relationship between *Times* publisher Arthur Sulzberger and CIA Director Allen Dulles enhanced the burgeoning power of both organizations. Because the paper sets the agenda for the media world, it holds power over that precious, precious thing we keep mentioning, the *narrative*. This jewel, Bernays recognized, is what gives our lives meaning. It is what holds our society together.

The *Times* doesn't just report news, it directs your mind, organizes your worries, channels your desires, and paints the backdrop of your life. The *Times* called the Mexican election of 2006 for the conservative Calderon before any results were in. It decided the 2016 movement at Standing Rock was too complicated for you to understand. It provided rankings of the 2020 Democratic candidates before any votes had been cast so as to focus your attention on Kamala Harris. In 2020, it focused your anxiety on whatever state or country had the worst covid case trends in order to instill anxiety and produce consent for government lockdowns. In 2021, despite its intellectual aura, it discouraged free thinking.[14]

While its prestige, national and international, is formidable, the *Times* has amassed its greatest power among its core audience of wealthy urban Democrats. Its deafening voice, like that of the Wizard of Oz, literally configures the window of acceptable debate for Democratic politicians and pundits. Certain topics are promoted, others are discouraged, and many are simply outside the realm of permitted discussion. In this way, it governs what we call in this book Blue News narratives. Certain perspectives will be repeatedly highlighted, day after day, while other perspectives will be mentioned in passing, demoted, or ignored altogether.

Times opinion columnists become famous and powerful parts of the Democrat establishment even if they're frequently incorrect. Lying and mistakes never lead to demotion or dismissal so long as the errors are in the interests of the powerful. Paul Krugman opined at the end of 2020 that stimulus checks of $2,000 to Americans suffering from the lockdowns were unnecessary, a stance that made no sense if one believes in the economic concept of stimulus, which he does.[15] Several months later, he dismissed fears of inflation as overblown. He was simply performing repetition, mockingbird-style, of talking points put out by DNC brass. In a vacuum, his opinions made as much sense as his column at the outset of the century declaring that the internet would affect our society to the same extent as the fax machine. Like many of his compatriots at the *Times*, Krugman has been wrong too many times to count, but as we'll see in the next chapter, getting things badly wrong doesn't matter for corporate media journalists, so long as their errors enhance their organization's management of the narrative.

While the Democratic Party once counted the working class as a core constituency, the DNC has shifted[16] and made the Democrats the party of affluent urbanites, and the paper has shifted its tone to cater to wealthier interests. Today, the *Times* features lavish Style and Entertainment sections, and the ads target city dwellers with the means to, say, purchase high-end brandy or travel to Kauai or Tuscany.

The primary competition for this audience is no longer other newspapers or cable television news but rather the increasing quantity and quality of online independent media. Sensing this threat, they attack, ridicule, and undermine independent media sources. The *Times* will tell you that watching YouTube news shows, for instance, will turn you into a racist or misogynist. They vilified Young Turks Network founder Cenk Uygur as a racist after he *sarcastically* told David Duke, "sure, you're not a racist!"[17] They ran hit pieces on popular independent journalists with growing audiences, like comedians-turned-journalists Joe Rogan,[18] Jimmy Dore, and Lee Camp.[19] Meanwhile, they repeatedly buried Tara Reade's credible allegations of sexual assault against their preferred candidate, Joe Biden.[20]

Times culture reporter Taylor Lorenz was caught lying about audio social media site Clubhouse in 2020. She claimed to have heard a slur that hadn't been uttered, then later admitted her mistake, but the damage was done. Her goal had been to smear the growing alternative social media site. Clubhouse facilitates free political discussion outside the purview of the *Times* and outside the reach of the censors at Facebook and Google. Lorenz had also concealed her profession to get into the Clubhouse room before she lied about what she heard there.[21] When caught in these lies rather than honorably apologize, she simply locked her Twitter account to prevent criticism.[22] There was nothing to apologize for. She was doing her job.

Earlier in 2020, *Times* opinion editor Bari Weiss famously disparaged Democratic presidential candidate Tulsi Gabbard as an "Assad toady," a talking point put out by DNC brass who wanted Gabbard out of that race. Weiss appeared on Joe Rogan's show, and Rogan challenged her about this attack. Weiss had to actually ask for the definition of the word "toady."[23] She hadn't even known the word but had used it anyway. She was just doing her job.

As detailed in the previous chapter, it's often telling to look at how Blue News sources have handled the Bernie Sanders phenomenon, as his candidacy appealed directly to the base of the Democratic Party but was not favored by the DNC. An ensemble of *Times* writers leveled repeated disingenuous attacks at the supporters of Sanders, calling them "awful,"[24] "abusive,"[25] and "angry."[26] In fact, an impartial analysis found that all candidates had an equal proportion (about 1%) of support from people who wrote offensive things on social media.[27] Sanders simply had far more total supporters.[28] This oversight wasn't an error. It was a lie. The real reason his supporters were called an "obnoxious" "army" was because they had the audacity to respond to the columnists' articles, tweets, and posts in sufficient numbers to change the narrative.[29] This pushback was new, and the *Times's* power comes precisely from its one-way dissemination of the narrative. This privileged status is what they are so terrified of losing.

I could make a list like this for every corporate media source in the country. They make the same tendentious transgressions and errors-that-are-not-accidents. In this book, I pick on the *Times* because it is the biggest and the strongest and because it presents itself as the most rigorous, principled, respected, and factual news source. The *Times* is simply the leading mouthpiece for narrative management.

Still, at the end of the day, this newspaper has my admiration. I have to join Edward Bernays and stand back and admire the most sophisticated and brilliant propaganda instrument ever created. The brilliance of the *New York Times* is unparalleled in history. It deftly convinces by hook and by crook many of the nation's most intelligent and generous people—including many citizens most able and most willing to sacrifice to help the poor and advance the ideals of democracy and justice—that the status quo is the best we can hope for and Americans need only oppose the DNC's villains: Republicans. The true stroke of brilliance is how the *Times* makes its readers feel smart and compassionate. To sublimate the progressive instincts of a wealthy nation into signing off on ever-expanding wars abroad, lockdowns and poverty at home, and censorship of dissent is no mean feat. The *Times* pulls it off with style.

Fox News: The Allure of Outrage

With "Fair & Balanced" as its slogan, Fox News Channel was founded by Rupert Murdoch and Roger Ailes (from MSNBC) in 1996. Its declared goal was to counter the "liberal bias" of the mainstream media at the time, including the *New York Times* and CNN. In the decades since, the channel has succeeded in giving voice to conservative ideals, and while neither fair nor balanced, the network has broadcast legitimate conservative critiques of government policy by hosts such as Tucker Carlson and Laura Ingraham.

Compared to the *New York Times*, which was founded in 1851, Fox had to work hard to build an audience. It nonetheless succeeded within a few years and had cornered a majority of the Red News market by the year 2001. Where conservative viewers and Republicans are concerned, and among rural viewers as well, it wins in the ratings. In fact, Fox News has enjoyed the highest ratings among cable news networks in the United States for over a decade now.[30] While the *New York Times*, and to some extent CNN, manage the daily national news cycle and the window of acceptable debate on issues for the nominally left side of the political spectrum, Fox News has become the standard bearer, arbiter of truth, and manager of the window of acceptable debate for the nominally right side of the spectrum. Fox is not truly conservative—just as the *Times* is not truly progressive. We have to follow a Balanced Media Diet to include perspectives from true political philosophies.

With slick graphics, loud sounds, attractive blonde hosts, "breaking news reports," and endless scrolling chyrons, the station can be almost hypnotic in its visual effect, and that's no accident. You're not meant to think freely while watching Fox; you're meant to drink up the outrage and thirst for more. The appeal to its audience is its simultaneous claim to be both the victim of a biased "liberal media" and the champion of patriots—the voice defending traditional American values. To Fox News hosts and viewers, the mainstream left media consists of urban elites who denigrate the history of the country, malign conservative ideals, and ignore the concerns of the average family. With these twin appeals to its viewers, the network feeds a slowly boiling anger and fuels an emotional call to action that attracts its viewers the way a charismatic politician lures voters.

Outrage instills a mix of anger and fear, and in this emotional state, the loud graphics allow the underlying messages of reducing social programs, gutting government regulation, cutting taxes for the wealthy, transferring power to large corporations, and ultimately speeding the transfer of wealth from the poor to the wealthy to proceed uninhibited. Whether these values are truly conservative is certainly up for debate, but not on Fox News.

While all corporate media networks promote their parent company's economic and influence interests via *systemic bias*, Fox was more guilty than most in building the narrative that fanned the flames of war in the lead-up to the disastrous invasion of Iraq. An incisive 2003 study found that all networks misinformed their viewers by implying that Saddam Hussein had "weapons of mass destruction" and was involved in 9/11, despite the fact there was no evidence for either implication, but viewers of Fox were the most misinformed.[31] Up to 80% of Fox viewers, according to the study, believed one or both of these unproven things. Worse, the study found that the more someone watched Fox News before and during the war, the less they knew about the causes of the war, and the more they supported the American side. This is literally the goal of propaganda, and it evokes the words of CIA Director William Casey: "We will know our disinformation campaign has been successful when everything the American people believe is false."[32]

With his boyish looks and brash remarks, Tucker Carlson is Fox News's most popular anchor. In 2021 and 2022, his popularity soared, making him the most popular news personality in the country.[33] His nightly rants cover everything his followers crave to hear about, from unpopular overseas wars to unpopular vaccine mandates to unpopular critical race theory lessons in schools. Carlson speaks often about the border, immigration, inflation, and free speech. As with his network—and the corporate media as a whole—his words are not always truthful. In 2020, after Carlson said on air that former model Karen McDougal was "extorting" President Trump over her allegations of an affair, McDougal sued Fox. With some embarrassment, Fox lawyers had to argue in court that Carlson's show was "opinion" rather than "news," and that "reasonable people" would not take Carlson's show as "factual."[34]

Carlson's show, nonetheless, provided important facts and media balance during the Trump presidency, particularly during the lockdowns and mask mandates of 2020. As we've documented in this book, the media atmosphere constricted tightly around several incorrect narratives about covid that were configured by CNN and the *New York Times*. Fox was often the lone voice in the mainstream corporate media questioning the politically-driven version of science that justified the flawed response to the covid pandemic. This showed that some genuine balance of opinion does remain in corporate news media. For this reason, and because it is important to learn to see through false narratives, corporate news media remains in the Balanced Media Diet that I propose in this book.

The problem with Fox is that their coverage of the news, cloaked in bright patriotic colors and a victim mentality, disguises an underlying movement detrimental to its viewers' political and economic interests. Just like the *New York Times*, it protects its corporate owners' wishes by maintaining a single narrative—in this case, that Democrats are the source of all evil. The dissemination of news is top-down, and it excludes exposure to multiple points of view, especially views that threaten the power, prestige, and wealth of those who work to centralize power. This agenda prevents Fox from serving the *watchdog* role that it claims to serve. It holds the powerful to account no more than does the *Times*.

MSNBC: Snobbish Indignation

Also founded in 1996, MSNBC forms the mirror image of Fox News in the American propaganda menagerie. A gnarly merger between Bill Gates's Microsoft and General Electric's NBC News minted a news network that today sets the tone for outrage among Democrats.

In much the same way that Fox built its audience by encouraging a perception of media bias, MSNBC grew by suggesting that the media as a whole had a dangerous, right-leaning bias on account of widespread corporate control of media voices. The network, in its early years, offered news and analysis that featured legitimate progressives with strong and often brilliant critiques of American policy.

Hosts such as Phil Donohue, Ed Shultz, Krystal Ball, and Ashleigh Banfield built a network that eclipsed CNN within a few short years of its founding. MSNBC soon rivaled the leader in ratings, Fox News, in the number and loyalty of its viewers, and held up the other side of the narrow political spectrum that defines permitted, "mainstream" political thought in this country.

Its audience is not entirely different from that of the *New York Times*, but from the start, it targeted and won viewers younger than the typical wealthy urban and suburban *Times* subscriber. The appeal MSNBC made about media bias worked as well as Fox's, which seems strange upon initial analysis. How could people agree both that the media has a left-leaning bias *and* a right-leaning bias? The answer, of course, is that the corporate, mainstream media has *systemic bias* and *nefarious bias* against both legitimate right and legitimate left critiques. Thus, viewers on both sides can be convinced that the establishment media's censorship and propaganda are arrayed against them.

Before long, MSNBC found itself an integral part of that corporate establishment. GE made billions from the second Iraq War[35] and had, at best, a waning interest in the legitimate criticism the network's hosts were leveling at that war.[36] So, as we will explore in the next chapter, MSNBC fired far more hosts on political grounds than either the *Times* or Fox.

Indeed, a surprisingly large number of principled hosts were sacked during MSNBC's second decade. Phil Donohue, Ashleigh Banfield, Krystal Ball and several others were purged. The network grew in stature and importance but maintained its appeal to progressives and liberals with a quieter anger— a more subdued, condescending outrage. It appealed to mainstream liberals without inspiring them to fight for labor movements or general strikes that might effect progressive change. The Fox News outrage provides a disguise that enables it to propagandize its viewers into accepting things like deregulated industry, broadening wars, and incessant upward transfers of wealth and power. So, too, MSNBC's faux outrage enables it to propagandize its viewers into accepting a watered-down liberal movement that focuses mostly on identity politics and blames all ills and injustice on Republicans. "Vote Blue No Matter Who" is a common chorus of MSNBC pundits. MSNBC's underlying agenda is that of its parent corporation—supporting the ongoing reactionary trend of concentrating wealth and power at the top. The faux outrage conceals the fact that MSNBC, too, is abdicating its primary *watchdog* duty— the duty for which the press is singled out in the Constitution.

And that's what we've seen recently from MSNBC. Four years of faux outrage about Russia and Trump that cloaked the fact that the network had canceled its progressives. There was precious little genuine left critiques of poverty, working class debt, wealth inequality, environmental destruction, or racial oppression. And by intentionally omitting actual, honest analysis as to *why* Trump won in 2016—working class desperation—the network propagandized its liberal viewers into accepting a hawkish reactionary with authoritarian tendencies named Joe Biden in 2020.

The post-Trump era has not been kind to MSNBC. Its most popular host, Rachel Maddow, lost her favorite target when the former game show host left office. Declining ratings have prompted several shakeups of the network's programming.

Nicole Wallace, perhaps the network's most reactionary host at the time, was promoted and given a two-hour daily slot. This revealed that the network is interested in guiding its viewers away from independent media and anti-establishment ideas and back to the corporatist view, matching the paths advocated by Joe Biden. Wallace has a remarkably complete resumé when it comes to narrative management—there is public footage of her lying about virtually every major story in this book: she called investigations into the origin of covid a "conspiracy theory," labeled the Hunter Biden laptop "Russian disinformation," referred to non-existent "mountains of evidence" for the story of Russian bounties in Afghanistan, and called the Steele dossier "totally true, fact-based information."[37] With Wallace in the ascendancy, all remnants of the Bernie Sanders progressives are gone. The discussion on the network in 2021 and 2022 pitted anti-Trump Republicans against pro-Biden Democrats; a narrower range of political opinion would be difficult to devise.

This lack of viewpoints is, of course, disguised well by the photogenic Maddow. Like Tucker Carlson at Fox, Maddow is MSNBC's most famous anchor, and she regularly feeds her audience's outrage on topics like, well, primarily Trump and Russia. There haven't been a lot of other issues for Maddow. With the collapse of *#Russiagate*, rather than acknowledge her errors, Maddow's show became weekly rather than daily. Maddow was also sued for false statements.[38] With an argument shockingly similar to the one used by Carlson's lawyers at Fox, the lawyers for MSNBC fought the lawsuit by claiming that no one takes Maddow's show as factual news, and "reasonable people" know the show is only for entertainment.[39] Whether that's true about her viewers is debatable.

Unsurprisingly, Maddow's defamatory statement was accusing someone of being a Russian asset. In this case, she sanctimoniously called the entire conservative OAN News Network "really literally Russian paid propaganda." She had no evidence for this claim, so her lawyers made the revelatory argument in court that Maddow's statements are intended as opinion and entertainment. The judge agreed and let Maddow off the hook,[40] dealing another body blow to the network's credibility.[41] We thus had in one year lawyers for both Fox and MSNBC declaring that their most popular shows were opinion and entertainment rather than factual news. Little wonder, then, that trust in corporate media continued to sink in 2022.

The power and pull of networks like MSNBC and Fox are waning in favor of independent media, and this terrifies corporate media. Like the *Times,* MSNBC attacked independent media star Joe Rogan for endorsing Bernie Sanders in January 2020. The outrage was fierce since Rogan has a powerful voice outside the control of corporate media.[42] Ostensibly, the problem was that Sanders shouldn't accept an endorsement from Rogan, who has said things—or simply had guests on his show who have said things—that were politically incorrect. But the underlying issue was that Rogan's endorsement had eclipsed their own. MSNBC's second most popular host, Morning Joe, Joe Scarborough, with his supercilious but predictable endorsements, had less pull than another Joe who had only a successful series of YouTube videos behind him. The times they are a-changin'.

A year later, MSNBC went after Rogan even harder when he had the audacity to ask a doctor on his show whether the benefits of giving the experimental covid vaccines to children outweighed the risks. This question interested many Americans at the time. But MSNBC couldn't present both sides of the question fairly on account of the massive advertising largesse it receives from the drugmakers Pfizer, Johnson & Johnson, and Bayer. Instead, Maddow, on her show, had to present only the drugmakers' pitch. She stared into the camera and deadpanned to her viewers: "The vaccine stops the spread of the virus, stops it cold. It will end this pandemic."[43]

There was no evidence for this claim, and there is now voluminous evidence to the contrary,[44] but, predictably, neither she nor MSNBC have ever issued a correction. In another chapter in the unfolding of the New Enlightenment, many people learned only on independent media that the injections didn't stop transmission or infection.

On the one hand, Americans have MSNBC, and networks like it, funded by advertisers and riddled with *systemic* and *nefarious bias* on account of narrative management. On the other hand, we have countless independent media channels that are not bound by such constraints and must appeal to the true interests of everyday people for their survival. This dynamic is draining viewers from corporate media every day just as it forces independent media to improve.

CNN: Propaganda Central

The biggest corporate news network in the world, CNN was founded by Ted Turner in Atlanta way back in 1980, the year Ronald Reagan was elected. Now owned by WarnerMedia, which in turn is a subsidiary of AT&T, the network plays an essential role in the American corporate media landscape by purporting to occupy the "center" between the Democrat-filled MSNBC and the Republican-filled Fox. It uses this position in the "center" to style itself as an authoritative "fact-based" network when in fact it is the opposite. Not having to appeal to a specific subset of the population enables CNN to more purely disseminate propaganda than its competitors. More active and former intelligence agents appear on CNN as pundits than on any other network, and the narratives favored by the military industrial complex can reliably be found on the network—as well as the narratives preferred by the giant pharmaceutical, fossil fuel, and financial corporations. In this way, CNN is the closest American equivalent to the Soviet *Pravda* or the Chinese *People's Daily*.

As the "centrist" channel, CNN is played endlessly in airports, hotel lobbies, and dentists' waiting rooms across the country as simply "the news." Throughout the 2010s, CNN carried a Democrat bias but provided unrivaled coverage of Trump's rallies during the 2016 presidential race. Blanket coverage of many of his speeches ran unedited airtime that was denied to other Republicans. This helped Trump solidify front-runner status in the primary. The network then joined the Blue News networks in attacking Trump and the administration throughout his presidency. The network lent uncritical credence to *#Russiagate* and the attempted impeachments. This Blue News bias has increased during the Biden administration.

Larry King, a pillar of the network who hosted an interview show for 25 years, left CNN in 2013. Looking back on the reasons he left, he said in a

2018 interview that CNN had become an entertainment network rather than a news network.

> CNN stopped doing news a long time ago ... They do Trump. FOX is Trump TV, and MSNBC is anti-Trump, all the time. You don't see a story—there were vicious winds and storms in the Northeast the other day—not covered on any of the three cable networks.[45]

When restarting his interview show that year on RT, the Russian-controlled network, King explained his reasons for moving away from CNN: "I'd rather ask questions of people in power than speak on behalf of people in power."[46]

All corporate media news organizations are acutely aware of the interests of their largest advertisers, and that is doubly true of CNN. We've already explored the influence of the big weapons corporations on coverage of wars. The giant drug corporations might influence these networks even more, as we've already seen with MSNBC. CNN receives its largest funding from the drugmakers through advertising and direct sponsorship of shows. The largest settlement in the history of the US Justice Department was the $2.3 billion settlement Pfizer paid after it fraudulently pushed a drug called Bextra that harmed thousands of people.[47] There has been scant mention of this disaster on CNN,[48] and it was never mentioned in 2020 when show after show covered Pfizer's request for experimental approval of its covid vaccine.[49] The FDA does not grant experimental approval of new drugs if an effective treatment for the disease already exists, which might be why corporate media—and CNN in particular—attacked the drug ivermectin so fiercely. CNN went out of its way to label the drug a "horse dewormer."[50] The science at the time on ivermectin's effectiveness as a treatment for covid was mixed,[51] but its inventor was awarded the Nobel Prize for medicine for its use in humans, and over three billion doses had been safely administered to people over three decades.[52] Ivermectin is for humans, yet CNN repeatedly referred to it as "livestock medicine" and a "dewormer."[53] The network even doctored footage of Joe Rogan, who used ivermectin to treat himself and discussed it on his show, to make his face look greenish and sickly when he spoke about it.[54] This was *nefarious bias*. Rogan, in response, interviewed chief CNN medical correspondent Sanjay Gupta on his show, and in an unusual moment of candor, Gupta admitted that CNN had lied about ivermectin.[55]

While the notion of "war profiteers"—corporations raking in millions from war—is very rarely mentioned in corporate media, the notion of profiteering off of diseases and pandemics is *never* mentioned. "Drug profiteering" is certainly as immoral as war profiteering and likely as common; it just isn't discussed. We'll talk about these *perverse incentives* later in the book.

For CNN's credibility and viewership, 2021 was a particularly bad year. Worse than obviously distorted coverage of Joe Rogan and ivermectin, a secret recording of CNN Technical Director Charlie Chester surfaced revealing that the network's goal for over a year had been to remove President Trump. The network used "propaganda," according to Chester, to promote Joe Biden and tarnish Trump. "Our focus was to get Trump out of office," Chester remarked. "I came to CNN to be part of that."[56]

Chester also revealed that CNN promoted a *biased* investigation into Congressman Matt Gaetz (R-Fla.) because Gaetz was someone the DNC wished to remove from office.[57] The investigation insinuated Gaetz had participated in sex trafficking during a 2018 trip to the Bahamas when, in fact, the women he and some friends traveled with on the vacation were all over the age of 18.[58] Nevertheless, CNN ran the story for several days. (The *New York Times* pushed this tawdry story too, without pointing out the lack of evidence.[59])

Listening to Chester's revelations about CNN's political objectives brought me back to Cuihu Lake and the spy plane incident. I wondered whether Americans' trust in CNN would plummet to the levels of mistrust Chinese people feel for their media. I wondered whether it would wake Americans up from our deceived "red, white, and blind" state. I don't have an answer yet, but things have gotten worse for CNN.

A few months later, the world learned that millionaire CNN anchor Chris Cuomo had used his primetime show to shield his brother, New York Governor Andrew Cuomo, from allegations ranging from sexually harassing staffers to forcing covid patients into nursing homes. Andrew resigned from office shortly thereafter. Chris was fired. By year's end, the scandal engulfed the network's president, Jeff Zucker[60] too. He resigned in disgrace over favoritism and sexual misconduct in February of 2022.[61] The network appeared to be in collapse when parent corporation AT&T spun off Warner Brothers and created a merger with Discovery, promising an overhaul of CNN. Time will tell what shape our intrepid American *Pravda* will take when it's reborn.

NPR: Soothing Superiority

Founded in 1970, National Public Radio differs from these other news sources in that it's not owned, at least not directly, by billionaires or one of the five transnational conglomerates. It remains government-owned, and its many member stations are generally owned by public universities or local governments. The network always notes and emphasizes this difference. It lends an independent air and serious tone to NPR's presentation of news. The network covers many stories with nuance, expert interviews, and eclectic audio clips in ways that are simply not available from other mainstream news sources.

NPR also cultivates an honest—even struggling—image, with frequent fundraisers and no-frills transitions between shows. This earnest and indigent image is the stated justification for accepting funding or "underwriting" from the same large corporations that fund the corporate media. This creates something of a tortured justification: the network provides superior coverage of the news because it doesn't accept advertising; because it doesn't accept advertising, it cannot sustain itself without donations from individuals; because those donations are not sufficient, it must accept corporate funding; even after accepting that funding, it maintains its claim to a separate and superior existence. It's funded by the same corporations as the corporate media but claims to be different and better.

By many measures, NPR is financially secure and doesn't need such frequent appeals to its listeners. Perhaps the fundraisers are held so frequently to justify accepting more corporate money. NPR's annual revenue exceeds $300 million, its assets and copious endowment now approach $800 million,[62] and it attracts generous corporate underwriting from brands eager to associate themselves with its wealthy audience. It even runs its own network of space satellites from Earth stations in its Washington, D.C. and St. Paul, Minnesota network headquarters. Nevertheless, it cultivates an image of destitution, something that has helped it attract an unwavering group of supporters.

NPR also has a history of receiving lavish donations from many of the largest and oldest foundations in the country. One example is the Robert Wood Johnson Foundation (RWJF), which underwrites many NPR programs. Listeners aren't notified that this is a Johnson of Johnson & Johnson, one of the nation's largest pharmaceutical corporations. When J&J spends thousands advertising on CNN, there might be a "Sponsored by Johnson & Johnson" message; when

RWJF underwrites NPR programming, no listener is notified of the under-writer's interests in coverage of, say, the side effects of an immensely profitable covid vaccine or the $2.2 billion it paid to settle a fraud case where it repeatedly pushed a risky schizophrenia drug on children and the elderly.[63]

Another such foundation is the billion-dollar Ford Foundation, which has historically been a conduit for "left gatekeepers" funding.[64] The "left gate-keepers" are media organizations that the CIA funded during the Operation Mockingbird era.[65] They pretended to be providing Americans on the left side of the political spectrum with honest news and analysis but were actually disseminating propaganda supporting capitalism and establishment politics; their funding came via foundations to cloak the true source of the money. A history of this phenomenon is beyond the scope of this book, but in summary, the CIA created front organizations, such as the Congress for Cultural Free-dom, which in turn founded publications or funded existing news sources for the sake of domestic and international propaganda. The CIA deemed foun-dations like Ford "the best and most plausible kind of funding cover."[66] Op-eration Mockingbird was, of course, shut down, at least publicly, but much NPR coverage sounds to this day like "left gatekeeping."

Similar to the *New York Times*, NPR covers news with a cultured tone de-signed to appeal to urban liberals and wealthy members of the managerial class who, in this case, commute to work in their cars. People in any other country would suspect immediately that a government-founded media outlet would be strongly biased, but most Americans are, again, naive about the role pro-paganda plays in their lives. Many listeners earnestly believe NPR covers the news fairly. The network enhances this reputation by going out of its way to make listeners feel intelligent as they're deceived. But gone are the days when, say, Noam Chomsky or Malcolm X appeared on public radio. Actual citizen control of stations is a thing of the past; the "public" in public radio doesn't mean what it used to. Instead, we have a network that runs the same headlines as corporate media, that interviews the same set of experts, that ignores strikes and labor movements, that supports wars and conceals coups, that censors topics like vaccine injuries and election fraud, and that uses dulcet tones to engineer consent for the same agenda as the more obviously corporate outlets.

Whereas the "everyman" talk radio shows mentioned below are designed to appeal to Republicans, NPR's audience is Democrats, and it provides news with a strong Blue News bias, favoring the establishment "centrist" wing of the party. As with the *Washington Post*,[67] a telling point was NPR's coverage of the popular but anti-establishment Bernie Sanders. On the eve of the 2020 Iowa Caucus, for instance, with Sanders enjoying an edge in the polls in the nation's first primary, NPR subtly boosted Buttigieg at the same moment the *Des Moines Register* canceled its gold-standard poll. NPR stations around the country ran a piece from WGBH's *The World* interviewing students in Iowa.[68] Two of the students happened to support Pete Buttigieg while the third supported no one "because no candidates of color remain in the race." No mention of the leading candidate at all. And no mention of Tulsi Gabbard or Andrew Yang either, the two remaining people of color still in the race since they were the other anti-establishment candidates. Instead, *The World* interviewed another student from the Sunrise Movement. As an organization, Sunrise had endorsed Sanders, but his name wasn't mentioned. Instead, they managed to find a Buttigieg supporter inside the Sunrise Movement who named the environment as her highest priority but who admitted on air, "my candidate isn't the most progressive with the climate." The final person they talked to supported "anyone who can beat Trump," and, specifically, Buttigieg. Sanders was the candidate leading in the polls, strongest on environmental issues, and endorsed by Sunrise, yet he was never mentioned. NPR's agenda, like that of the *Post* and the rest of the Blue News channels at the time, was to promote Buttigieg and marginalize Sanders.

Like the *New York Times*, NPR sees its competition increasingly coming from independent online news media, and when they can't ignore or silence independent news sources, they attack them. After the *Times* ran a hit piece on popular independent news host Lee Camp,[69] NPR ran a similar piece, calling Camp a "shrill" "useful idiot" "ranting" like "an angry fifteen-year-old."[70] They refused to interview Camp live, likely out of fear that their smears wouldn't work live or that he would say something incongruous with their narrative.[71] NPR performs the same narrative management—and is rife with the same *nefarious* and *systemic bias*—as the rest of the corporate media. As mentioned earlier, like CNN, NPR has quietly hosted PsyOps agents on both of its flagship shows, *Moring Edition* and *All Things Considered*.[72]

It's easy to forget China's crude propaganda when listening to the often brilliant and more subtly deceptive journalists and experts on NPR, but the goal is the same: the management of the narrative. The best propaganda is creative, interesting, and mostly true, and NPR's editors never forget this.

Talk Radio: Everyman Allure

After Fox News, the leading place for conservative-leaning analysis and re-porting of the news has been talk radio, with its wide availability to anyone anywhere with a simple radio. People in their cars like to listen to news and analysis, and whereas NPR broadcasts Blue News narratives on the FM band, talk radio broadcasts Red News narratives on the AM band.

Rush Limbaugh and Sean Hannity were the top two talk radio hosts in 2020, and their style of outrage-based, conservative critique remains popu-lar, particularly as there is generally no one else speaking with any authen-ticity to the issues that working class people experience across this country.[73] These hosts generally distribute subtle but effective propaganda and narrative management. The message is often scapegoating immigrants and blaming Democrats for most ills rather than advocating genuine labor movements to confront the powerful or citizen mobilizations to defend liberty and win a more just society for all Americans.

The same young sources of independent news that threaten the *New York Times* and Fox News threaten the talk radio hosts too: independent online news sources that are not filtered nor controlled by the five corporations that control everything else we hear, read, and see.

Washington Post & Wall Street Journal: Meet Your New Owners

The *Washington Post*, and to a lesser extent the *Wall Street Journal*, play pow-erful second fiddles to the *New York Times*, mostly following its lead but occa-sionally setting the national media agenda and tone on their own. This made them bargains when they were recently purchased by powerful billionaires.

Billionaires are increasing their power at an alarming rate. Amazon's Jeff Bezos, the world's richest man at the time of this book's publication, pur-chased the *Washington Post* in 2013 for $250 million.[74] Whether or not this was a good deal for the Graham family, who had owned and run the paper for 80 years, the sum was pocket change to Bezos. With a tiny percentage of his net worth, he acquired the priceless ability to shape the national debate on things important to his growing power and wealth: taxation, labor law, social media regulation, data privacy, data storage, oversight of intelligence agencies, and more. Amazon was seeking contracts at the time worth tens of billions of dollars to handle data storage for the CIA. IBM had also bid to host this priceless data, and there was a struggle between the two corporations for the contract. Shortly after the *Post* came under its control, Amazon won the contract. In fact, the deal expanded at that point, and Amazon won not just the right to host the CIA's data but the data of all 17 agencies that comprise the United States intelligence community.[75] The dangers inherent in a single undemocratic corporation hosting the most sensitive data of the American government and its citizens are beyond the scope of this book to contemplate but must be examined in short order if we are to preserve our Fourth Amendment right to privacy.

The issue of labor unions is also of critical importance to Bezos. Amazon's enormous network of warehouses is run by low-wage workers well positioned to unionize and exact some of the giant corporation's absurdly untaxed annual profits.

Amazon might have won the right to host the CIA's sensitive data without the *Post* as its cheerleader, but it certainly didn't hurt. As for labor unions, not only has the *Post* run countless hit pieces about the country's most famous labor organizer, Bernie Sanders—including the 16 pieces in 16 hours mentioned in Chapter 5—but the paper has run zero negative pieces about Amazon itself, despite Amazon now being the nation's largest corporation.

Half a dozen years earlier, the *Wall Street Journal* was purchased from the Bancroft family of Boston. The family had controlled the paper for over a century, including the proudest time in its history when the *Journal* became the nation's first national paper in the 1950s and 1960s. For decades, the *Journal* was considered by many the country's most reputable news source. The buyer was Rupert Murdoch, one of the handful of rapacious billionaires who today control our corporate media landscape. His News Corp, which owns Fox News and dozens of other media properties gobbled up the *Journal's* parent company, Dow Jones & Company, and in a short time, the paper had tuned its editorial slant to complement the role of Fox News.[76] Together, these News Corp entities hold down the Red News party line on political issues, managing the dominant narrative, and drawing the lines of acceptable debate for conservatives on social issues, environmental issues, personal freedom, and taxation.

RED, WHITE, AND BLIND

THOSE ARE THE MAJOR, DOMINANT PIPES OF THE DAZZLING AMERICAN media Wurlitzer. Often, they're played in concert, other times in counterpoint. While some Americans still believe that our corporate news is free of propaganda and censorship, an increasing number of Americans, like their Chinese counterparts, realize the tune played by the organ is manipulated.

But even when we know the tune is manipulated, when we know *bias* distorts our perception, none of us is able to see through all of the propaganda all of the time. The organ's music is sophisticated, and each channel composes its tune to appeal to a certain sector of American society. Therefore, we are all in a state of deception to some extent; we are all "red, white, and blind." To get closest to the truth, we need to counter the censorship and centralization of information by actively seeking voices that question or oppose the dominant narratives. This book proposes a Balanced Media Diet in Chapter 13 so that we can hear a variety of points of view, learn to recognize narrative management, and determine the truth independently.

The *New York Times* doesn't want you to think critically.[77] They'd like to do that for you, but our human capacity to consider divergent ideas is one of our most powerful capabilities. We must cultivate this capacity in order to thrive during the dawning of the New Enlightenment. I wrote this book to encourage Americans to read more broadly, see that they are in a state of deception, and awaken their minds' inherent capabilities.

When I stood on the banks of Lake Cuihu after the EP-3 went down over China, I was on a profound inner and outer journey in China. But my journey to thinking critically about the voices of the media had only just begun. I am still on this journey, and I am writing to share some insights from where I am. This journey is a mental voyage, and like any voyage it challenges us, strengthens us, angers us, and ultimately makes us more knowledgeable. When we sit down and truly listen to opposing ideas and unfamiliar tunes of the Wurlitzer, we learn. This is the journey to *media consciousness*.

Some in the corporate media say that the influence of their propaganda pales in comparison to the effect that *foreign* propaganda has on the minds of Americans. Russian influence and Chinese influence, they say, is broad, deep, and pernicious. There is scant evidence of this. Some Chinese voices might have appeared in American media when the EP-3 went down, or during the questions about the origin of covid, or when Jeffrey Epstein was arrested. But those voices scarcely set the tone let alone managed the narrative. As for Russia, the vast majority of *#Russiagate* accusations and coverage—the party polarization, political witch hunts, and heated controversy over ideological issues—were driven by our domestic media. The effect of Russian attempts to manipulate social media or swing elections is thin on the ground and led mostly to calls for election integrity and for social media companies like Facebook to be more transparent about proceeds from Russian accounts.[78] Compare those effects—a few thousand social media posts and calls for transparency and integrity—to the powerful, daily manipulation of narratives funneled through the incessant, buzzing headlines of the American corporate media, where American news anchors speak American English to deceive their fellow Americans. Foreign manipulation of American media is real, but it is a minor piece of the puzzle. Foreign countries don't manage the narrative, guide our hopes and fears, or set the tone of our public lives. The ubiquitous distortion originating right here at home is what we must recognize first on the path to a truthful view of the world.

The multifarious pipes of the Mighty Wurlitzer are the forces that have made this nation "red, white, and blind."

We turn now to the newer tools of narrative management, the pipes that are replacing the Mighty Wurlitzer: search engines, "fact checkers," "astroturf" independent media, and social media censorship.

8

CENSORSHIP CENTRAL

"There are a great many people who have a vested interest in maintaining the stupidity of the American public."

Gore Vidal

IN THE EARLY YEARS OF THE INTERNET, AND UP UNTIL ABOUT TEN YEARS ago, all websites, apps, portals—all direct interactions with the internet itself—were a threat to the corporate media's narrative management. Sharing a cute kitten video might not seem subversive, but the ability to create your own content and instantly set it before the eyes of millions of fellow human beings was an earthshaking development. Before the internet, doing this required access to the great conduits of the media corporations.

The power of everyday people to publish news accounts and distribute their own opinions has precipitated a global consciousness awakening akin to the Renaissance and the Enlightenment, which were sparked by Gutenberg's press in 1440. That consciousness awakening led to the American and French Revolutions as well as to revolutions in science, philosophy, art, music, and law.

Today's enlightenment enables collaborators to publish multiple angles instantaneously. These collaborators might not be affiliated with any organization or government nor live near each other. This has birthed independent media and what we now call online social media.

Several social media companies have grown to the point that they eclipse all others and rival the power even of the legacy media corporations. This is due to the burgeoning power and appeal of independent media. Americans increasingly know that the corporate media is distorting the news through propaganda and censorship, and they turn to independent media. Facebook, for instance, has a business for exactly one reason: its users freely publish independent media that it then owns. Facebook, Instagram, YouTube, Google, Twitter, Apple, Amazon, and a small handful of others now act as portals through which a majority of Americans interact with the news narratives of the day. These towering corporations hold the greatest promise—and pose the greatest peril—to a world in which independent news is broadly accessible, all voices are free of censorship, and the New Enlightenment blossoms.

At the same time, censorship poses the gravest threat to democracy and science. Propaganda and bias are bad, but censorship is the one attack that Enlightenment values cannot withstand. Whether it comes from a government, a church, or a monopolistic corporation, even well-meaning censorship is a poison pill for a free society. It is therefore crucial to understand the growing use of censorship in social media, and this is what we will examine in this chapter.

The End of the Beginning

Search engines and social media platforms were originally truly open fora. The sites were generally run by Silicon Valley nerds as libertarian meccas, offering a grand democracy of ideas, free speech for all, and access to the world's information. Equal weight was given to populist, anti-establishment thinkers as to establishment journalists and government officials. The New Enlightenment took flight in the early years of the internet.

This state of affairs began to shift a decade ago under the dubious pretense of fighting "fake news." Since 2016, the year I was censored at *Huffington Post,* these platforms' algorithms have been overhauled repeatedly to promote establishment voices over others. As we saw in the political campaigns that year, the media giants were terrified when alternative and independent media took over the news narrative for days at a time, propelling Donald Trump to the Republican nomination and very nearly catapulting Bernie Sanders on the Democratic side. That terror was so intense that it led to four years of anti-Trump hysteria at outlets like MSNBC. That terror forced the corporate social media giants to heed the mockingbird call and deploy the term "fake news" to ban and censor users. The goal is to scare as many people back to establishment corporate media as possible. In 2020, the situation grew worse with intense narrative management around the pandemic, the "Stop the Steal" protests, and the duplicitous QAnon narrative.

In May of 2016, several whistleblowers at Facebook kicked off a series of revelations about the tech giants' new participation in narrative management. These whistleblowers revealed that Facebook's "Trending Topics" box was not in fact a simple list of the topics that were most talked about on the site but was instead a list of topics covertly curated by elite staff members. These select staffers were told never to allow certain topics to trend but "to artificially 'inject' selected stories into the trending news module even if they weren't popular enough to warrant inclusion—or in some cases weren't trending at all." In particular, they "routinely suppressed news stories of interest to conservative readers."[1]

These internet destinations where people come to connect with one another and learn about the world have become the nerve center of narrative management: Censorship Central.

Whereas most people once typed directly into their browser's URL bar the address of the news or information website they wanted to visit, most Americans now simply open up their social media homepage or app and read the articles that the social media sites' algorithms determine will be interesting, safe, and agreeable for them. In this way, social media sites have become the Wurlitzer of the modern day. The covert filters of *systemic bias* not only live informally in the minds of journalists and editors but are now directly encoded into the algorithms of the news purveyors themselves.

Three of these corporations now surpass the power of the legacy media outlets, and we will devote this chapter to examining the roles Google, Facebook, and Twitter—and their subsidiaries—play in manipulating and distorting the world's news. These corporations and the government agencies that assist and collaborate with them are looking for ways to reinforce or even replace the filters used by the legacy media corporations and Operation Mockingbird.

In 2018, online manipulation crossed an important line in the sand. Controversial independent news creator Alex Jones was banned simultaneously by YouTube, Facebook, iTunes, and Twitter. It was a trial balloon for the social media corporations and whatever government agencies behind the scenes crave the power of censorship. Jones is deeply admired and trusted by his fans but openly reviled and ridiculed by most mainstream commentators and a majority of the population. He was no doubt seen as an easy figure to attack first. I don't personally recommend Alex Jones as a news source, but at the time, I joined principled Free Speech advocates decrying this "internet death penalty," the coordinated censorship of an unpopular voice. But the principled voices were not heeded, and it set a dangerous precedent. Those of us who warned what it could lead to have unfortunately been proven correct.

As we prepare to delve into the increasing use of censorship in our country and the dangers posed currently to Free Speech, it's worth remembering what censorship and Free Speech really are. Free Speech is not simply allowing people to disagree. It's the tolerance of the expression of unpopular or disgusting ideas specifically because the dangers posed to a free society by authoritarianism are greater than the dangers posed by unpopular or disgusting ideas. In the words of Noam Chomsky:

> If you believe in freedom of speech, you believe in freedom of speech for views you don't like. Goebbels was in favor of freedom of speech for views he liked. So was Stalin. If you're in favor of freedom of speech, that means you're in favor of freedom of speech precisely for views you despise.[2]

While some social media censorship has been done secretly in ways that are not obvious to everyday visitors, some of it has been explained and implemented publicly. Because there is a hidden agenda that is at least partly deliberate, this is *nefarious bias* and not just *systemic bias.*

We examine now the extent to which the largest of the social media portals censor and deliberately distort the news.

Google & YouTube
The World Through Rose-Colored Glasses

THE FIFTH BIGGEST CORPORATION IN THE WORLD, THE PORTAL TO THE world's information, Google might just hold more power over how the global population thinks than any entity in history. Perhaps the Catholic Church had a greater hold on the epistemology of the Western World at the apex of its power in medieval times. That's about it. Google wields incalculable power when it comes to control of what we've called the narrative, and for this reason, we will spend a bit more time analyzing its role in distorting the news than the other social media corporations.

When we search the internet for information—to find the symptoms of a disease, say, or the lyrics to a song, or the reasons people voted for Donald Trump—Google has 92% of the market share *worldwide* and 89% of the market share here in the United States.[3] Many believe that to discover the truth about something is to "google it." That's how Google wants it. The curated Google News page, for its part, is the fifth biggest news site in the world, with over 500 million monthly visits.[4]

Legend has it that Google was founded by Larry Page and Sergey Brin in a garage in Menlo Park, California in 1998. The reality is a little different. The CIA and NSA dumped money into a project called Massive Digital Data Systems in 1993, and in 1995, this intelligence agency project funded Brin and Page's work on data queries, search algorithms, and digital surveillance.[5] The two computer scientists were still graduate students at Stanford at the time. By the time Google was legally incorporated in 1998 (in a friend's garage), Brin and Page had already received hundreds of thousands of dollars from groups connected to the intelligence agencies and the military's Defense Advanced Research Projects Agency (DARPA). Google is an intelligence agency project turned into an immensely powerful and profitable public corporation.

The connections between Google and the Department of Defense, CIA, and NSA don't end there. In 2003, Google customized its search engine for use by these same intelligence agencies, expanding the mass surveillance they had built into their original algorithms. In 2004, the CIA-funded Keyhole became part of Google, enabling the development of high-resolution satellite surveillance that eventually became known as Google Earth.

The list goes on, as cataloged in Nafeez Ahmed's meticulous exegesis "How the CIA Made Google."[6] I recommend his piece if you're interested in learning more. Suffice it to say, the intelligence agencies have been heavily involved in Google's development and have helped shape the corporation as it continues to grow and dominate aspects of our lives.

For everyday Americans, it might seem that none of this matters. You see a friendly, colorful page with an input box offering the world's knowledge in under a second. It *is* a miracle. What you don't know, even if you suspect it, is the amount of data about you that they store and track, and the sophisticated *bias* applied when they compose the results that are returned. This is not open access to the world's knowledge. This is a tracking system wrapped around lists of filtered information. It is what the CIA asked Brin and Page to create. The two programmers succeeded beyond the Agency's wildest dreams.[7]

A New Pipe in the Organ

As with all corporate news sources in the Mighty Wurlitzer, Google plays a powerful and essential role in the control and management of the news narrative. It is a new and fantastic pipe in the organ, and it grows daily in importance.

Here are a few of the many ways Google shapes and reinforces American news narratives:

- **Search.** Its primary search engine controls the world's awareness of everything by manipulating the results that are returned when someone wants to know something. By maintaining a list of everything you have asked about, Google's software can frequently figure out what you're thinking about. In many instances, Google has, for instance, determined a woman was pregnant before she knew it by comparing her queries over several months to those of other women.

- **News.** Its News tab, introduced in 2006 and now called Google News, is the world's largest news aggregator. It presents the news to the user with a layout similar to a newspaper, which makes it the world's largest news publication. When given a search term, News finds and high-lights articles on the topic that fit and support the dominant American news narrative on the topic as set, generally, by the *New York Times*, CNN, and other corporate news sources.

↦ **YouTube.** When Google acquired the world's biggest video aggrega-tor in 2006, it was a boon for independent media at first. Google built YouTube into the only social network that rivals Facebook in terms of active users and breadth of usage. Its golden era is over, however, and YouTube now contradicts its own original premise and mission, as we discuss below, by censoring and banning people who produce independent news.

While each of these applications has nearly unimaginable power in shap-ing the way Americans see the world, for the purpose of this book's analysis, YouTube is the most important website in the world. YouTube is where inde-pendent media flowered in the second decade of this century. With its focus on video, which is the most potent and immersive medium for storytelling, it is a fabulously empowering platform that allows anyone to set up a video channel that, with work and practice, can rival a corporate video channel in draw and significance. Simply put, it allows the free exchange of news narra-tives in a way never before possible on Earth.

Well, it used to. Censorship is the new black at YouTube. This is ironic and unfortunate given that its mission at inception was to be a Free Speech haven, a place where "you" could put anything on the "tube." YouTube now demotes its own unique user-created content and promotes videos created by corporate media news networks.

I have been stunned by the rapid pace of censorship on YouTube. In the turning point year of 2016, YouTube allowed the Sanders and Trump popu-list movements to build popular independent media channels that often suc-cessfully challenged dominant narratives. YouTube news channels offered the world truly free alternative news media. But during the Media Matters era of 2017-2019, and accelerating with the censorship of Alex Jones in 2018, Google and YouTube dramatically stepped up manipulation and propaganda on its platforms as the *#RussiaGate* and *#MeToo* narratives dominated main-stream media. As 2020 unfolded, *systemic bias* and *nefarious bias* took on whole new dimensions in Googleland. YouTube has now demoted, demonetized, and outright deplatformed hundreds of independent shows whose message someone powerful disagrees with.[8] As mentioned earlier, the show *The Highwire,* hosted by former CBS producer Del Bigtree, was summarily banned and deleted from YouTube for an episode that included interviews with prestigious scientists whose opinions on covid differed from those of the WHO. This is just one example of thousands.[9]

A Googler Blows the Whistle

You cannot have democracy without free speech. I'm a longtime progressive, and I wrote about the Sanders campaigns out of both interest and support. I'm no personal fan of Donald Trump. I'm more committed to transparency and uncovering the truth than I am to any political party or candidate. I'm more committed to open and free dialogue and the principles of Free Speech and Free Assembly than I am to ensuring one particular viewpoint is accepted as the best. So, perhaps my greatest concern today as news distribution and narrative management move fully to the internet, is that censorship is spreading. Whether it takes out more voices on the right or left, censorship is anathema to our legal traditions, to scientific inquiry, to the Enlightenment ideals enshrined in our Constitution, and to freedom itself.

I was fascinated when Google employee Zach Vorhies came forward in 2020 as a whistleblower. Vorhies was a senior software engineer at Google for eight years, a brilliant developer who worked on many of their key applications, including YouTube. In a series of interviews in 2021, followed by a groundbreaking book entitled *Google Leaks*, Vorhies revealed the extent to which Google's news and search algorithms employ tendentious bias, generally by censoring perspectives that go against corporate news narratives.[10]

The week after the 2016 election, Vorhies witnessed the Google CFO break down in tears in front of the entire company over Trump's victory. In the same "all-hands" meeting, telecast to Google's tens of thousands of employees, Sergey Brin, one of the company's founders, said he was "personally offended" by Trump's election. Then, Google CEO Sundar Pichai stood up and declared that the way voters voted was not in accordance with "our values." Pichai added that one positive thing that Google had done during the election was to use machine learning to suppress what it identified as "fake news." He promised more of that.

It is one thing for senior leadership at a major corporation to have political views and to express those on occasion. That leads to *innocent bias*, which can be problematic, but it's a normal part of life in a democracy. Everyone has an opinion and is entitled to it, including CEOs and founders.

It is another thing altogether for a corporation that today serves as the planet's dominant gateway to information to decide that, on balance, Americans had voted wrong and to promise to use its tremendous power to make them think differently. According to Vorhies, this is exactly what happened at Google in 2017. In an interview with noted independent journalist Sharyl Attkisson, Vorhies recounted the transformation he witnessed.

> **Vorhies**: I was working at YouTube in 2016, and everything was really great. But then something happened. Donald Trump won the election. And after he won the election, the company took a hard left. They decided they were going to abandon their liberal principles and start going towards an authoritarian management of their products and services.[11]

Before he resigned, Vorhies gathered documents that revealed to the world that Google and YouTube had made business decisions from the very top to remove positive news about President Trump even before he was elected. Vorhies wasn't the first whistleblower to resign from Google in this time period. Others, including Mike Wacker, who resigned, and James Damore, who was fired, also revealed an intensely one-sided political bias at Google that was bringing about manipulative algorithms in Google's applications.[12] But none of the other whistleblowers was able to produce the documents that Vorhies did.

One of Vorhies's more fascinating revelations was a set of blacklists that showed thousands of search terms that, when typed into Search or News, wouldn't return organic results but rather a set of results manipulated by Google.

> **Attkisson**: You say, "They bragged about effectively cracking down on fake news." That sounds like a good thing.

> **Vorhies**: Yeah, you would think. But when I looked at the design documents, I started to notice something very interesting. A lot of the "fake news" that they were using as examples of things that they should censor were things

involving Hillary Clinton. I was sort of apolitical, but I started to think to myself, you know, is this really "fake news?" Why is Google defining this as fake news in order to justify censorship of it? So once I realized that there was this "fake news" regimen that they were using, and it seemed political, I started looking for what that censorship execution could be. And I found it. The project was called Machine Learning Fairness.

"Machine Learning Fairness" was an internal Google project to create artificial intelligence filters on News and Search. The leaked documents showed that it was used by Google to train its filters to promote news depicting Donald Trump as a weak or inferior candidate and label as "fake news" stories that went against this narrative.

> **Vorhies**: It was in June 2019 when I realized I couldn't remain silent anymore. I had to go and disclose this to the public because it appeared Google was attempting a coup on the president.

By the middle of 2020, according to Vorhies, a concerted effort inside Google as a whole, and its subsidiary YouTube in particular, was underway to shift perceptions of the news in favor of Joe Biden and against Donald Trump. Vorhies finally resigned in disgust when he saw Sundar Pichai lie to Congress when asked whether Google maintained manual blacklists. Pichai testified to Congress: Google didn't use manual blacklists; there were no political biases in the search or news algorithms; they used no filters based on political ideology.[13]

Vorhies knew none of this testimony was true.[14]

Nevertheless, Google's narrative management that had gone on for Trump's entire term in office culminated in significant distortion of the news during the 2020 election. Independents and conservatives had already sensed a concerted effort on the part of mainstream media to attack and discredit Trump while preventing negative coverage of Joe Biden; now, they suspected the giants of social media too. It turns out these suspicions were equally well-founded.

The *coup de grace* came when Donald Trump learned of this. He promised to sue YouTube. Videos of him making this declaration were uploaded to YouTube. What do you think became of those videos?

YouTube Becomes TheyTube

Shortly after Joe Biden became president, YouTube CEO Susan Wojcicki confirmed publicly what many had long suspected. YouTube had rewritten its internal algorithms to demote independent news channels. She explained publicly that YouTube manipulated every set of search results to promote videos by corporate media sources whose slant YouTube agreed with. These promoted videos were labeled "authoritative sources." Wojcicki also explained that the new algorithms demoted videos that were not "authoritative" or that espoused "fake news" or "conspiracy theories." Those videos were now "pushed down," she said. Reversing the core principles of YouTube, Wojcicki denounced the site's own content creators:

> It's much easier to just make up content and post it from your basement than it is to ... have high-quality journalistic reporting.[15]

This was essentially a suicide note from YouTube. The founding principle was that "you" could "tube" any media you wanted and share it with the world. The reference to creating content from one's basement was precisely the criticism pundits in corporate media made about YouTube news programs, so it was stunning to hear Wojcicki use the same terms as her competitors to put down her own content creators.

The reason to visit YouTube has always been to get a *different* perspective, an *independent* perspective. No one has any trouble finding videos from corporate media. If that's the perspective one wants online, it's always available. A basic Google Search on any news topic will return dozens of MSNBC, CNN, NPR, and, usually, Fox videos. The corporate media has gotten so many things wrong over the years that many regard it not as "authoritative" but as one type of biased reporting and, frequently, propaganda. Every wrong corporate news story mentioned in this book was covered correctly by at least one of the independent sources listed in the Balanced Media Diet. YouTube has been a huge source of popular news coverage that has frequently been more truthful than what is offered in corporate media. The thirst for a different perspective has made many top independent media creators on YouTube draw viewership that surpasses corporate news television shows.

Wojcicki knows this. She also knows it isn't "easy," but, in fact, extremely difficult to create content on YouTube of sufficiently high quality to generate a substantial following. By demeaning her platform's own hard-working creators, by calling them "basement dwellers," and then by demoting their content beneath that of YouTube's competitors, the corporate media, she effectively replaced the primacy of her own product with that of her competitors'. Corporate media simply uploads content they've already broadcast from their New York and Hollywood studios and do little, if any, additional work to prepare their content for YouTube.

This corporate suicide note reflects a deep and pervasive presence of all three types of bias: *innocent bias, systemic bias*, and *nefarious bias*. Partly because of her and her colleague's personal beliefs, partly because of the parent corporation's thirst for power, and partly because of a hidden agenda, Wojcicki sacrificed some of her company's power and potential on the altar of narrative control.

Were her decisions simply financial ones, it would be elementary business strategy to encourage, boost, and support her site's powerful users—the independent news publishers and popular content creators—and bank the profits through advertising. But in the media world, as we've seen, major decisions are not merely short-term financial calculations about attention and clicks. Management of the narrative is far more valuable than attracting new users or selling ads. Wojcicki is ordering YouTube to commit hara-kiri because the larger motive of Google's parent, Alphabet, requires it. In her own words:

> So sure, we want to enable citizen journalism and other people to be able to report and other people to be able to share information and new channels, but when we're dealing with a *sensitive topic*, we have to have that information coming from *authoritative sources* so that the *right and accurate* information is viewed by our users first.[16]

Wojcicki is announcing narrative control. Her powerful social media application will force its users to see corporate media content first on "sensitive topics."[17] Any topic that users want to research and get multiple perspectives on can and will be deemed "sensitive" if it challenges dominant narratives.

I probably don't need to reiterate at this point how frequently corporate media gets important stories wrong, but let's briefly examine two cases.

⇝ **The origin of covid.** This story was buried and off-limits for a year, from March 2020 to March 2021. No doubt a "sensitive topic," at precisely the time that knowing the virus's origin would have most helped to understand and treat the disease—and potentially avert a global pandemic—YouTube demoted or banned videos investigating this scientific question. Anything that went against "authoritative sources" was suppressed. Google Search concealed important articles.[18] [19]

➻ **The 2020 election.** Independent investigative journalists were trying to get to the bottom of allegations of election fraud in several states, including Georgia, in the wake of the controversial 2020 election. YouTube banned their videos. "Authoritative" corporate media got the story deliberately wrong by alleging Trump had told the Georgia Secretary of State to "find the fraud." Trump had never said this, but the fake quote was repeated throughout corporate media nonetheless.[20] This quote had, in fact, been invented by the *Washington Post* and attributed to an anonymous source. The *Post* believed there were no recordings of the conversation, but when a recording surfaced later, it became clear that *Post* writers had concocted the quote on their own. There may or may not have been significant fraud in the 2020 election in Georgia. Trump may have made illegal phone calls. I've seen evidence both ways on this thorny question, and it's not the point of this book to settle it. What is important is that the corporate media manufactured quotes to justify a narrative, and YouTube, controlled by the new media behemoth Google, censored independent journalists questioning that narrative.[21]

Ultimately, Google's target audience is everyone seeking information, and the corporation strives to please them and to keep them coming back by providing pleasant minimalist websites and fast, useful results. What many don't realize is that the search results they see have been cleansed of information Google deems unsuitable for them and sprinkled with information they might not have requested but that Google wants them to read. If interacting like this with the world's information is not to your liking, if you would prefer to search for the truth without the blinders Google puts in place, this is an Orwellian experience. But if you appreciate it, and you want to view primarily corporate media and official government-approved versions of stories, Google and YouTube kindly provide you a pair of rose-colored glasses with which to view the world.

Facebook & Instagram
A Few Filters Between Friends

FOUNDED IN 2004 AS A SITE FOR COLLEGE FRIENDS TO FIND EACH other, share photos, and plan events, Facebook has become a global juggernaut through which a significant portion of humanity learns about the world. The world's sixth largest corporation, Facebook, renamed Meta in 2021, boasts billions of active users and is responsible for driving some 40% of global web traffic. For many people around the world, Facebook isn't a mere internet website, it *is* the internet. And that is precisely its "meta" goal: Facebook doesn't want you to have to bother with a silly old URL bar anymore that would require you to maintain knowledge of things like websites that exist outside its high walls; Facebook wants you to live in its virtual "metaverse;" Facebook wants you right where it can control and monitor your interactions with reality.

And Facebook is astonishingly good at getting what it wants.

Its target audience is everyone and anyone in the mood to connect with other human beings. And anyone in the mood just to learn what others might be thinking. This is to say, everyone, all the time. Their target is the human population.

Being ambitious isn't necessarily a bad thing; exploiting a monopoly to the detriment of customers, competitors, and society is.

Where once the sophisticated algorithms of their many applications aimed simply to circulate content amongst users that would lead them to click the 'like' button and 'engage' with the site, today, they have much grander aims: to capture and guide the thoughts of humanity. This is much like a traditional media corporation, which indeed Meta has become, only much larger. Today, about 70% of Americans use the site at least once a month, and nearly 40% say they get their news on Facebook.[22]

In the words of conservative media critic Mark Dice:

> At its onset, Facebook only showed users what their 'friends' were posting, but that changed when they added the trending module—and with this sim-

ple little box they harnessed the power to introduce their one billion users to news stories that their friends hadn't posted—stories the company feels users *should* know about, and overnight Facebook transformed from a social networking site to a news company.[23]

As a news corporation, they now selectively publish, amplify, and censor content as they see fit. This would be fine if they were regulated like a publisher, subject to defamation and antitrust law. As it is, like any other media behemoth, they lend their gargantuan power to the media's largest goal: managing news narratives.

Facebook also isn't above running its own propaganda missions. When the prospect of regulation and antitrust hearings targeting the social media giant emerged in Congress, a little-known think tank named American Edge ran ads and published opinion pieces in newspapers warning Americans that without strong technology companies, China would grow stronger and Russian cyberattacks would be more successful. Behind the scenes and the advertisements, the organization was founded by none other than Facebook.[24] Facebook was manipulating the news, but these stories and ads planted by Facebook were, of course, never flagged or suppressed.

Blowing a Different Whistle

When whistleblower Zack Vorhies came forward in 2019 to reveal how Google manipulates news and search results, many wondered whether something similar would happen at Facebook. A whistle was blown at Facebook, but it sounded quite different.

The Wall Street Journal published a series of reports in September 2021 that it titled "The Facebook Files." These were documents culled from a cache of leaks by a former Facebook executive named Frances Haugen. Haugen appeared on *60 Minutes* on October 3, 2021 and testified to Congress two days later. She was well-spoken, well-dressed, and represented by a powerful Washington law firm. What was perhaps most interesting about the revelations in the documents she leaked was that the revelations weren't very revelatory at all.

Haugen's documents showed that when designing the corporation's software, Facebook's engineering teams were often faced with a choice between making more money or preventing psychological harm to its users. In these instances, corporate executives often guided the engineers to take the path that made more money.

> The thing I saw at Facebook over and over again was there were conflicts of interest between what was good for the public and what was good for Facebook. And Facebook, over and over again, chose to optimize for its own interests, like making more money.[25]

Far from a bombshell, this was more or less the expected behavior of global mega-corporations. Publicly traded companies like Facebook are legally required to maximize profits. So what was the news here?

Certainly, studies have shown that extensive use of Facebook, particularly by children and teenagers, leads to depression and other mental health issues. But again, this was all already known. Haugen's documents also revealed the fact that certain "prominent users" of the platform received special treatment and never had their posts deleted or demoted. This, too, was at best a mild surprise.

What *was* fascinating was how Haugen and Vorhies—these two social media "whistleblowers"—were treated differently in the media. Coverage of Vorhies was scarce in general and appeared almost exclusively in smaller, independent media. What little coverage appeared in corporate media was brief and negative. He was never on *60 Minutes*. He never testified to Congress. Many Americans never heard about Vorhies at all.

Haugen was covered in glowing terms all across corporate media. NPR, *The New York Times*, MSNBC, CNN, *The Guardian,* and many more outlets trumpeted Haugen as "The Facebook Whistleblower," a selfless crusader who had resigned her job for the common good. She was featured as trending in social media for two consecutive weeks in October of 2021.[26]

Another difference was the way the two were treated by the companies they left. Google vindictively pursued Vorhies and hounded him with lawyers. Google even pushed police to raid his apartment for bogus reasons, and the raid humiliated and intimidated Vorhies; he ended up surrendering to police on a city street like a criminal.

Haugen was never intimidated, sued, nor arrested. Facebook communicated publicly and politely about her, calling her vision misguided but never attacking her personally. Haugen said she "loved Facebook," didn't want anyone to hate Facebook, and said she would happily work there again some time.

A final, key difference was their treatment by the legislative and executive branches of the federal government. Vorhies was never mentioned by any political leaders in the halls of federal power. Haugen, on the other hand, wasn't only discussed, she was invited multiple times to testify before Congress, she was asked dozens of questions and given time to reply, and she was asked to share her proposals for fixing the problems she reported.

What could explain the differences between the reception given the two "whistleblowers?" The best place to look is *the different problems* Vorhies and Haugen revealed.

Vorhies revealed the many ways Google covertly manipulates search results across its News, YouTube, and Search products; he pointed out the dangers this covert manipulation poses to Free Speech, to our political system, and to our pursuit of truthful science. He called for genuine transparency, an end to censorship, and for Google to stop manipulating information.

Haugen leaked documents revealing that Facebook did not sufficiently suppress what she termed "misinformation," "fake news," and "hate speech." The problem, according to Haugen, wasn't that there was too much censorship or manipulation of users' posts, but that there was *too little*.[27] Haugen's words in her Congressional testimony, and in the dozens of adulatory articles written about her in corporate media, called on the government and the social media giants to *increase* manipulation and censorship.

Whatever whistle it was that she was blowing, her tune was one that the government and the corporate media wanted you to hear.[28] They crave the control over the narrative that censorship and distortion grant, and Haugen's revelations provided their desires with a veneer of popular demand.[29]

Two months after her "bombshells" dropped, independent media investigations found that Haugen had been a part of Facebook's "Civil Integrity" unit, which was the unit that had managed the flow of political news in the lead-up to the 2020 election. Her unit was the very one that had coordinated the censorship of the Hunter Biden laptop story mentioned in this book's first chapter. The "Civil Integrity" unit was dissolved after Biden won the election.

I honestly don't know whether Haugen is a genuine whistleblower truly concerned that Facebook isn't sufficiently manipulating its users' posts or whether she's posing as a whistleblower at the behest of Facebook PR or government agencies to provide cover for expanding their powers. What I do know is that as the New Enlightenment unfolds, the information war grows increasingly complex. Alongside "fake news" and "fake sources," "fake whistleblowers" will be part of it.

Friends Help Friends Escape Regulation

Whatever Haugen's true aims, Facebook has rarely shied away from manipulating its users' posts or news feeds. In 2020, Facebook openly admitted to amplifying perspectives that they supported, such as articles supporting the Black Lives Matter movement and opinions favoring Joe Biden. They admitted as well that they censor "misinformation" about, for instance, the use of facemasks on children or the experimental mRNA injections if those posts don't meet their standards. Facebook steps into scientific debates and claims to identify the truth for its users; anything questioning their truth is taken down. Even if friends want to share their thoughts about these various political or scientific topics, Facebook decides what is allowed. As 2020 and 2021 unfolded, they took down millions of posts, entire sites followed by millions of people, and popular accounts that shared unapproved information.

As we'll see in Chapter 12, this is similar to, for example, MSNBC firing Phil Donahue in the lead-up to the Iraq War for expressing opinions critical of launching that war. When censorship is based on organizational priorities, it is *systemic bias;* when those priorities are hidden and support an agenda, it is *nefarious bias.*

Yet today, despite all their editorial decisions regarding what content will and will not be allowed on their site, Facebook CEO Mark Zuckerberg has maintained repeatedly before Congress that they are not, in fact, a *publisher.* Zuckerberg claims they are not responsible for the content that is posted, even though they presume to determine what is true and to censor the rest. They get to have their cake and eat it too. They get the freedom to build, defend, and exploit a monopoly around the unique and widely-used service they provide, while they also enjoy the power to manipulate, amplify, or delete things that people say and post. It's a perfect, disastrous hybrid of two legal models—the *utility* model and the *publisher* model.

The better model for regulating a massive communication corporation like Facebook would be as a *utility,* as we'll discuss later in this chapter. As *utilities*, they would get one freedom but not the other. Imagine that your phone company listened in to your conversations, and if you said something their parent corporation didn't like they ended your call and shut off your phone service?

Meta Power Metastasis

Facebook is constantly experimenting with the powers at their disposal. In one experiment, they secretly manipulated the voting behavior of hundreds of thousands of people in southern California by placing crafted notifications on users' screens at key moments in the days leading up to an election. They managed to push an additional 340,000 voters to the polls by the calculations of researchers at UC San Diego.[30] In testimony before Congress, psychologist Robert Epstein, former editor-in-chief of *Psychology Today*, warned of the tremendous power social media corporations like Google and Facebook had accrued to manipulate the thoughts of its users on issues like politics and science.[31] After his extensive research into the phenomenon, Epstein calculated that via manipulated algorithms, these social media companies could deploy "subliminal techniques" to shift as many as 15 million votes in a national election.[32]

Much like the bias at Google documented above, this power was used at Facebook in favor of the Democrats, at least as recently as 2016. Several former company employees revealed they had worked as "news curators," managing the topics in the "Trending Topics" box, which is some of the internet's most valuable and influential real estate. These "curators" removed trending items of interest to conservatives and injected topics such as overseas terrorist attacks and Black Lives Matter protests that weren't trending at all. In an article entitled "Former Facebook Workers: We Routinely Suppressed Conservative News," *Gizmodo* reported:

> Facebook workers routinely suppressed news stories of interest to conservative readers from the social network's influential "trending" news section, according to a former journalist who worked on the project...

> In other words, Facebook's news section operates like a traditional newsroom, reflecting the biases of its workers and the institutional imperatives of the corporation. Imposing human editorial values onto the lists of topics an

algorithm spits out is by no means a bad thing—but it is in stark contrast to the company's claims that the trending module simply lists "topics that have recently become popular on Facebook."[33]

Facebook was placing a firm finger on the scale of our democracy, and doing so secretly. Regardless of whom you supported for president in 2016 or 2020, or if you voted at all, this power to manipulate massive swaths of American opinion that is accruing rapidly to this Silicon Valley megacorporation poses a danger to our democracy. Even if today they favor a politician you like, that might not always be the case.

Facebook promoted articles favorable to the Black Lives Matter movement and protests but censored articles that revealed BLM co-founder Patrisse Cullors's pricey, personal real estate acquisitions.[34] Facebook banned and censored users such as Donald Trump for allegedly inciting violence,[35] but then allowed thousands of posts actually calling for violence and death to Russians[36] as the war in Ukraine began.[37] Even if you agree with some or all of the political statements Facebook made with these rules, there is no doubt it acts like a news publisher in choosing what ideas and views to allow.

Along with other pipes of the Great Wurlitzer, Facebook announced efforts in 2016 to reduce what it called "fake news." The corporation hired people who wrote code to judge every item shared on its site and rate it for "trustworthiness." They claimed their algorithms would reduce the distribution of "fake news" by up to 80%, meaning that even if a friend of yours posted something, you most likely wouldn't see the post if it was not deemed "trustworthy." They promised it would be just a few helpful filters between friends.

As we'll explore in the next chapter, this included partnerships with the shadowy Digital Forensic Research Lab (DFRL) group, a part of the Atlantic Council that purports to distinguish "true news" from "fake news" but, in fact, mostly performs narrative management. David Brock of Media Matters took credit for convincing Facebook to do this as part of his agenda to reduce the reach of conservative viewpoints.

In addition to the power Facebook has over the political and social activity—as well as the thoughts, feelings, and preferences—of its billions of users, it preserves its monopoly by actively acquiring or copying any competitors that come along. It acquired competitors Instagram in 2012, and WhatsApp in 2014, both in deals brokered at the infamous Sun Valley conference. As mentioned earlier, this is the place where social media companies, corporate media conglomerates, and CIA officials get together annually to plan the future of our media landscape.

Facebook's power is essentially CEO Mark Zuckerberg's power. He controls 58% of the corporation's voting shares.[38] Zuckerberg has complete and absolute control, and his global power is growing. With its ventures into virtual reality and remote "meta-spaces," where people come together virtually while, in fact, miles apart, it is clear his vision for the future is one in which friends and family don't frequently see each other physically, but rather, Facebook intermediates all interactions, using facial recognition and artificial intelligence to track and guide people's thoughts and feelings in the ways Zuckerberg believes are best and most profitable.

The lockdown restrictions that were put in place around the world in response to the coronavirus incomparably helped Facebook. They took the world one giant step closer to Zuckerberg's vision in which people interact primarily through technology. As more humans connect online, it provides Facebook with additional gigabytes of data about human interaction that allows them to develop their algorithms and metaverses and to deliver more and more realistic and more and more closely-surveilled virtual experiences. Far beyond mere narrative management, this trend replaces news narratives altogether with manipulated versions of reality. The power accruing to Facebook this way is unfathomable, and it will continue to accrue if the behemoth maintains its favorable, unregulated status.

Zuckerberg's enormous power has led to numerous calls to break Facebook up or, at least, regulate it like a utility. Even former co-founders have publicly bemoaned their onetime friend's unchecked monarchical power, demanding in one instance that the federal government step in and dissolve the monopoly.[39] Zuckerberg, no doubt, is using his algorithms to convince 70% of the American population that that would be a bad idea.

Twitter
Deleting Excess Characters

WHILE NOT QUITE AS POWERFUL AS GOOGLE OR FACEBOOK, TWITTER nonetheless wields formidable weapons in the management of the American news narrative. Founded in 2006 as a "microblogging" site where people could share short blurbs of text, Twitter has grown into the primary place elite professionals interact online. Twitter's sleek bluebird logo evokes friendly communication and the free spread of news and ideas. The cheerful birdie seems to chirp to you: when you send out a tweet, you join a global social conversation.

Twitter was first with its "trending" box, which appeared long before Facebook's or YouTube's. The trending box lists the ten supposedly most popular topics, tweets, or hashtags at the time, and it confers fame to those that appear there. That box was the breakthrough for the business, the game-changer, the "killer app." It made Twitter both grand and monstrous: a potent, modern, algorithmically-driven gatekeeper that decides for humanity which stories will be discussed and which ones will remain unknown.

Twitter has since become the authoritative place where politicians, journalists, athletes, corporate executives, medical experts, and movie stars interact with each other and with their fans and followers. The sheer number of users is smaller than Facebook's, but Twitter's regular users include the elite of media, politics, and Hollywood. The impact of these elite users on the national discussion is immense. Twitter is the place where CEOs comment on business developments and political leaders debate policy. Doctors, professors, and public health officials debate health issues and name-check one another.

Twitter was, in fact, President Trump's preferred method of communication with the nation, the site of his modern-day "fireside chats," where he spoke directly to the American people without the filters of the corporate media. Trump frequently shared whatever was on his mind in blunt and controversial tweets. Until he was censored.

As I was putting the finishing touches on this book, Elon Musk's aggressive bid to buy Twitter went through. An avid user of the platform, Musk has decried the company's censorship and promised a return to Free Speech as he takes over. Some have lamented the prospect of a billionaire acquiring another major media corporation. I share those concerns, but Twitter has hardly been operated benevolently by the working class. To me, Musk appears earnest in his promises, and I will watch closely in 2023 to see whether he implements the unbiased Free Speech policies he promises.

Before we get into the most important and dangerous examples of censorship on Twitter under current and past management, it's worth noting that other parts of Twitter are manipulated to amplify establishment sources and personas.

- ⟶ **Blue Checks.** In 2009, Twitter established its "verified accounts" program, whereby small blue check marks appear next to certain accounts that Twitter considers authentic and notable. It's helpful to know that a tweet coming from a famous name is not in fact coming from an imposter, but the "Blue Checks" program isn't only for ensuring authenticity. You can't get a blue check by simply confirming your identity. Blue Checks are given primarily to establishment voices and corporate media journalists.[40] The imprimatur is one way Twitter performs narrative management and suppresses independent voices. For years, you couldn't request a blue check at all, but there is now a request form. It still is not an automated process, however. Twitter decides on its own, privately, who gets "verified." No one spreading "misinformation" (as determined by Twitter) will be verified, and if you're lucky enough to be granted the coveted check, if something you say later is deemed to be out of line, your blue check will be removed even if you're still who you say you are. Musk has proposed replacing this program with paid membership.

- ⟶ **Follower Counts.** Follower counts are another way certain voices are promoted over others. Certainly, if you are able to gain thousands of organic followers, you will have a large presence on Twitter. But many celebrities "acquire" large numbers of followers through other means. Companies such as Devumi sell blocks of followers by the thousand, and countless celebrities and others participate in the gray area that

Twitter ignores where followers are purchased.[41] Twitter will then remove the fake followers from the accounts it chooses to. In 2018, *New York Times* investigations revealed that Twitter had removed fake followers from dozens of celebrity and "blue check" accounts, yet without transparency as to exactly where these accounts had come from or who had benefited. One "blue check" user, Martha Lane Fox, a Twitter board member, was given tens of thousands of extra followers, and only some of the fake ones were removed, according to the *Times* analysis.[42]

➥ **Trending Topics.** The trending topics box is another element of Twitter that is manipulated to promote approved perspectives. In one instance, MSNBC's Rachel Maddow was caught using a troll army to boost her show into the trending topics box.[43] Also, as mentioned in an earlier chapter, Twitter played a major role in the Sanders and Trump movements, whereby independent news reporters changed media narratives through sheer numbers and social media savvy. The Clinton campaign attempted to counter this by buying popularity on social media. In one instance, an anti-Sanders hashtag, #BernieLostMe, appeared in the "trending" box despite having far fewer tweets than other hashtags at the time, indicating Twitter had promoted the hashtag manually.[44]

Birds of a Feather, Silenced Together

In 2016, the Hillary Clinton campaign hired the aforementioned, notorious David Brock of Media Matters to spend a million dollars on an online trolling army to go after Bernie Sanders supporters on Twitter. The *Los Angeles Times* commented at the time:

> In effect, the effort aims to spend a large sum of money to increase the amount of trolling that already exists online ... It is meant to appear to be coming organically from people and their social media networks in a groundswell of activism, when in fact it is highly paid and highly tactical.

There was nothing good about that, but, at least, it wasn't Twitter itself attacking people. That came four years later, when Twitter joined Facebook and YouTube in silencing an exorbitant number of users and conversations.

In fact, Twitter outstripped those others and really kicked its narrative management into high gear in 2020. The bluebird preyed upon thousands of conversations, banning independent voices on politics and public health, slashing away the right to tweet from everyday people on the anti-establishment right and left. The breadth and speed of it shocked me.

In Chapter 1, we discussed Twitter's *biased* censorship of the *New York Post*'s coverage of Hunter Biden's laptop and the related Ukraine corruption scandal. The *Post*'s reporting had been clear about what was established fact and what was not (some elements of the Bidens' alleged corrupt collaboration with the Ukrainian company remained unproven), but the article added important facts. Yet on the eve of the election, it was censored. This demonstrated *nefarious bias* in Twitter's censorship, as it revealed a hidden agenda. More importantly, the event was a bellwether for the maturation of social media, marking the moment its powers of manipulation and censorship rivaled the power of establishment corporate media. Twitter's censorship of individual tweets—and then the entire account of the *New York Post*—did more to quash the story than did the *Washington Post*'s articles calling it "fake news." But even this paled in comparison to what happened next.

Censoring the President of the United States

The sun rose in a chilly sky in Washington, D.C. on the morning of January 6, 2021. Thousands of people, mostly supporters of President Donald Trump accompanied by some highly interested undercover FBI agents, rallied at the White House. President Trump appeared at a lectern and spoke to the crowd for nearly an hour and a half. He told them that the election had been fraudulent. He enumerated problems from hundreds of polling places across the country. At several points, he mentioned a planned march to the Capitol:

> I know that everyone here will soon be marching over to the Capitol building to peacefully and patriotically make your voices heard.

Trump did not accept the election results. He believed that the votes had not been counted fairly, or he wanted his supporters, at least, to believe that. He urged Congress not to certify the election that day. Whether he was correct about the election or responsible in making the speech and encouraging the march to the Capitol, certainly an elected official is permitted to question the results of an election in a modern democracy. I write this having never been a Trump supporter. Supporting free speech means precisely supporting speech one dislikes.

The speech was televised on PBS, which manipulated the narrative by running a chyron on the screen during Trump's lengthy speech, undercutting his words: "Elections experts say the election was the most secure in history."

Many Democrats would later claim Trump incited violence by making the speech, and his words would be used to justify impeachment hearings, arrests, and censorship. Critics pointed out that while he did say the march would be "peaceful," he used the word "peaceful" only once in the speech, whereas the word "fight" appeared 23 times.[45] On the other hand, the word "fight" is more common in the English language and has many more meanings than "peaceful." For instance, Trump used it five times in one sentence:

> The American people do not believe the corrupt fake news anymore. They have ruined their reputation. But you know, it used to be that they'd argue with me. I'd fight. So I'd fight, they'd fight, I'd fight, they'd fight.

Democrats and Blue News outlets used the following part of the speech to blame Trump for the violence that occurred at the Capitol later that day:

> I think one of our great achievements will be election security. Because nobody until I came along had any idea how corrupt our elections were. Most [politicians told they'd lost] would stand there at nine o'clock in the evening and say 'I want to thank you very much,' and then go off to some other life.

> But I said something's wrong here, something is really wrong. And we fight, we fight like hell, and if you don't fight like hell, you're not going to have a country anymore.

> Our exciting adventures and boldest endeavors have not yet begun. My fellow Americans, for our movement, for our children, and for our beloved country—and I say this despite all that's happened—the best is yet to come. So, we're going to walk down Pennsylvania Avenue. I love Pennsylvania Avenue. And we're going to the Capitol.

That was it. That was the dangerous, inflammatory rhetoric that supposedly incited treasonous violence and justified Trump's censorship and impeachment. That evening, Twitter banned Trump from the primary channel he had used to communicate with the nation. He was suspended permanently a day later.[46]

Facebook and YouTube[47] followed suit. Then came Instagram, Snapchat, Reddit, TikTok, and even ecommerce platform Shopify.[48] Big Tech administered the "internet death penalty" on a sitting president. It was an unprecedented show of muscle by the new kids on the media block.

Facebook CEO Zuckerberg effectively spoke on behalf of the executioners:

> We believe the risks of allowing the President to continue to use our service during this period are simply too great ... [W]e are extending the block we have placed on his accounts indefinitely.[49]

While support for the peaceful march and protests was divided pretty cleanly along party lines, the violent scenes at the Capitol that day were abhorrent to all Americans. The footage evoked chaotic scenes and attempted coups in failed states. *Why were people smashing windows in our nation's most treasured public building?*

Republicans and independents also noticed something that many Democrats probably did not: careful narrative management and biased reporting of the event. Blue News outlets, such as the *New York Times* and CNN, emphasized the injuries and a death that occurred at the Capitol while rarely mentioning undercover FBI agents who were there, the presence of a likely *agent provocateur* we discussed in Chapter 7, or the underlying purpose of the rally, which was to protest perceived election fraud. The *Times* repeatedly reported it was a riot that had caused six deaths when, in fact, only one person had died, Ashli Babbitt, and she had been shot by the police not by the protestors. There were two other deaths *outside* the Capitol: a woman who overdosed on recreational drugs on the sidewalk and a man who succumbed to a stroke during the march. Over the ensuing week, two police officers committed suicide, and two more police officers committed suicide in the months that followed. In one of the more egregious examples of bias, CNN and the *Times* reported that a fifth police officer, Brian Sicknick, had been bludgeoned to death at the Capitol when he actually died of natural causes the next day in a hospital. There were certainly many injuries sustained on all sides on that fateful day, and the violence was awful to behold, but in terms of deaths, to summarize for clarity: one gunshot death inside the Capitol at point blank range by the police, three deaths outside of the Capitol due to natural or nonviolent causes, and four suicides by police officers days or weeks later.

One difficult question facing those who believe what happened on January 6 was an insurrection is why the protestors—many of whom were gun owners—didn't bring weapons. If Trump was inciting a coup, why didn't he call on his supposed soldiers to arrive armed?

As for the undercover FBI agents, they weren't mentioned in the corporate media. Videos released by independent media, however, reveal many agents and suspected agents in attendance, including Ray Epps who is heard screaming and urging the protestors, "We have to go *into* the Capitol," to which the protestors point at him and start yelling, "Fed, Fed, Fed!"[50] As a whole, coverage of this event made many errors, and it is beyond this book's scope to establish the role of the undercover agents. Were the protestors guided only by their own rage to storm the Capitol? Or were the FBI agents present at the speech and on the march, in fact, *agents provocateurs* who pushed the marchers to become more violent and storm the Capitol? Why is Ashli Babbitt heard in recordings asking the police to request backup before she is shot and killed?[51] Why did so many police officers commit suicide afterwards? There are unfortunately more questions than answers about this troubling event.

As for social media censorship and narrative management, the event was used to accelerate sweeping censorship throughout the early 2020s. After banning leading doctors and journalists, Twitter—and then the others, in lock step—took the unprecedented step of censoring a sitting president. It is hard to review this censorship and not draw comparisons to places like Russia and Venezuela, where opposition leaders are routinely silenced. It is also difficult to devise an explanation consistent with the Constitution for preventing the nation's president from speaking his views to the electorate via the channel he wishes to use.

Twitter did it nonetheless.

Analyzing the election's legitimacy is beyond the scope of this book. I will simply say that a robust democracy should be able to withstand scrutiny, and if the simple act of questioning the results of a hotly contested election is grounds for censorship, then we are probably not living in a democracy. You might have found Trump's words to be irresponsible, or even dangerous, or perhaps you found them appropriate, or even inspiring. I am no Trump supporter, but I don't believe his words rose to the level of treason or even inflammatory speech.[52]

But the mandarins of Twitter had their *biases*, or they acted on the biases of others, and we might say they had grown trigger-happy.

Guillotines for Whistleblowers, Gallows for Scientists

The bluebird spread its wings, and Twitter censorship soared to new heights in 2021. CEO Jack Dorsey resigned and incoming CEO Parag Agrawal proved even more eager to drop the guillotine on offending users and hang "misinformation" at noon. The primary areas of censorship were a tight match for the dominant narratives of the year: political speech and public health. Some of Twitter's new rules were particularly nonsensical. Twitter unveiled policies that, for instance, banned users who "made claims contrary to health authorities."[53] Even the unfortunate denizens of George Orwell's *1984* dystopia enjoyed a modicum of free thought by comparison. This resulted in countless bans, including of sitting Congresswoman Marjorie Taylor Greene (R-GA).[54]

Another authoritarian stroke was the banning of anyone whose tweets suggested the experimental covid injections didn't stop the spread of the virus. The actual science had shown clearly for over a year that the injections did not stop the spread of the virus, which was likely why heavily vaccinated countries continued to have outbreaks well into 2022,[55] but this didn't matter to Twitter. It remained committed to the dominant narrative. Even the government-run, pharmaceuticals-funded, pro-vaccine CDC had stopped claiming the injections stopped the spread.[56] The bluebird killed tweets by thousands of users, including Harvard professor Martin Kulldorff, one of the world's preeminent epidemiologists,[57] and outright banned Dr. Robert Malone, a prominent scientist who has worked on vaccines for decades and played a lead role in the invention of the mRNA technology utilized by the injections.

Twisting the knot further, Twitter banned people for simply pointing out that Big Pharma partially funds the CDC. Drugmakers have a ridiculously vested interest in positive coverage of the vaccines, to the tune of billions of dollars.[58] When Congressman Andy Biggs (R-AZ) said precisely this—that the drugmakers are suppressing cheaper covid treatments to protect their profits—a public relations professional named Tom Elliott put Biggs' statement in a tweet. The tweet became popular, and then Elliott's business Twitter account was deleted.[59] To reiterate: congressman says something; person quotes it in a professional context; person's company gets banned. Elliott called the suspension "next-level Twitter absurdity."

> Obviously, in this case, quoting an elected leader on an issue that matters to everyone is important and newsworthy, regardless of whether you agree. (And I can't help but add that this basic point was once mainstream among progressives.)[60]

Twitter also uses a more secretive but no less pernicious form of censorship known as "shadowbanning." Users who are shadowbanned don't know they're banned; they're not actually kicked off the platform, but their tweets are quietly demoted or hidden from others. Despite countless stories proving its use anecdotally, Twitter denied for years that it secretly silenced users. Their denials were proven to be lies when a massive hack struck Twitter in July 2020.[61] The hackers managed to gain access to Twitter's internal user-management tools, and screenshots revealed administrative options such as manually reducing a user's reach or putting a topic on a "blacklist."[62] These actions are precisely "shadowbanning," and Twitter could no longer deny it.

New CEO Agrawal commented:

> One of the changes today that we see is that speech is easy on the internet. Most people can speak. Where our role is particularly emphasized is who can be heard.[63]

Shadowbanning quietly limits "who can be heard." Outright banning, on the other hand, generates backlash and can even generate positive attention for the person banned on account of the Streisand Effect mentioned earlier. "Shadowbanning" is likely much more frequently used when Twitter seeks to silence a voice inconvenient to the management of the narrative.

Yet another level of censorship arrived at Twitter late in 2021 that targeted whistleblowers and investigative journalists. The new rule called for banning leaked documents that showed government or corporate wrongdoing. The rules would prevent journalists from tweeting leaked documents and warn everyday users that a shared document might have been "obtained through hacking."[64]

Rather than assist whistleblowers, champion Free Speech, and advance the Constitution's Free Press guarantees, Twitter's new rules constrict speech and punish whistleblowers. The rules would prevent, for example, Daniel Ellsberg from tweeting the Pentagon Papers; they would even prevent or warn individuals from sharing the Pentagon Papers. Chelsea Manning's leaked documents showing the crimes of the US military would be prohibited. And perhaps most precisely, the documents that Zach Vorhies leaked that revealed the news manipulation by Google would be banned. This seemed like a death sentence for truthtellers on Twitter. But then something happened that the Twitter executives and the intelligence agents they work with couldn't have imagined.

It backfired.

Investigative journalist Max Blumenthal of *The Grayzone* tweeted in February 2021 that leaked materials implicated the BBC, Reuters, and *Bellingcat* in working with the British government to disseminate negative stories about Russia. Twitter affixed its new "hacked materials" label to Blumenthal's tweet in an effort to reduce its reach, but instead the label made the tweet more popular.[65] *The Grayzone* and *Bellingcat* were soon trending on Twitter, and readers sarcastically thanked Twitter for the new label pointing to quality journalism.[66] The Streisand Effect, whereby humanity's inner desire to know the truth cuts through censorship, drew attention to the tweet just as it had to my censored *Huffington Post* article in 2016. If every action has an equal and opposite reaction, one can expect a true flowering of the sharing of information soon, whether it's on a Twitter reinvented by Elon Musk or on a competitor committed to Free Speech.

Bluebird, Meet Mockingbird

One way we know that Operation Mockingbird not only lives on but has infiltrated the dominant media channels of today is the stunning revelation that Twitter's head of Middle East affairs is a Psychological Operations officer from the British military.

Gordon MacMillan joined Twitter in 2013 while still a member of the 77th Brigade PsyOps unit. He has worked for years placing propaganda into Twitter conversations about war, revolutions, and Middle East affairs.[67] Needless to say, MacMillan's account was never censored for deliberately spreading misinformation. When asked about the placement of a PsyOps officer into an executive position at the company, Twitter offered only: "We actively encourage all our employees to pursue external interests." You can almost hear the mockingbirds chirping. The head of the UK military, General Nick Carter, was a bit more forthcoming, saying MacMillan's placement at Twitter aids the military's "capability to compete in the war of narratives at the tactical level."[68] Carter indicated Twitter is by no means the only platform they use for distributing propaganda:

> There is no relationship or agreement between 77th Brigade and Twitter, other than using Twitter as one of many social media platforms for engagement.

Despite all its censorship and shadowbanning, Twitter strives to maintain the appearance of being a place for the free exchange of ideas. If your cherished ideas align with the news narrative of the day and can be concisely stated, Twitter remains a good place for the rapid sharing of news and opinions. You'll probably never be censored, and you'll probably never have to confront a controversial idea you dislike. But Twitter clearly will not be beaten by Facebook or YouTube when it comes to the game of manipulating trending topics and silencing voices who threaten the dominant corporate narrative.

It's important to notice the voices who are *never* censored—the ones who repeat the dominant narrative on the news of the day. They're never shadowbanned. They're never censored. Their tweets are never labeled, even if what they're saying is misleading or false. You never pay a price for misinformation if you're lying in accordance with the dominant narrative. Actual deliberate misinformation flies freely with the other birds on Twitter.

An exodus has started. This *bias* has pushed both conservatives and independents concerned about Free Speech to competitor sites like Parler, Telegram, Getter, and Gab—places where feeds are not altered by "helpful" algorithms and offer simple chronological lists of tweets and posts. These smaller sites don't rival Twitter in reach yet, but necessity is the mother of invention, and the internet does nothing if not expedite the sharing of information and the creation of new platforms.

It will be fascinating to witness the next generation of social media apps. They will likely provide the things people crave today but do not currently enjoy: privacy and freedom. The powerful social media incumbents listed in this chapter will surely attempt to acquire or squash any new competitors. But people's intrinsic drive to enjoy their inalienable rights—privacy and freedom—have toppled far more powerful establishments before.

Now, we turn to some modern examples of this new Operation Mockingbird. The social media giants employ both *systemic bias* and *nefarious bias* every day to distort the distribution of news in America, leaving us all "red, white, and blind."

9

MOCKINGBIRDS MIGRATE TO SOCIAL MEDIA

"A lie told once remains a lie, but a lie told
a thousand times becomes the truth."

Joseph Goebbels

THE GLEAMING WHITE COLUMNS OF THE SUPREME COURT SHONE IN THE sun. It was a warm July afternoon in 2020. Eleven doctors in white coats and two congressmen in suits stood behind a lectern. A small crowd of onlookers awaited the doctors' speeches, and several independent journalists with microphones were on hand to record the proceedings. No corporate media outlets were present.

"We are here," began one of the doctors, stepping to the lectern, "because we feel as though the American people have not heard from all of the expertise that's out there all across our country... We are here only to help American patients and the American nation heal."[1] Her name was Simone Gold.

Another doctor stepped forward. "I want to tell America, no one has to die.

There is a *cure* for covid... it is hydroxychloroquine, zinc, and azithromycin."

A third doctor spoke. "If it seems like there's an orchestrated attack against hydroxychloroquine, it's because there is. When have you ever heard about a medication generating this much controversy? A 65-year-old medication that's been on the World Health Organization's safe, essential list of medications for years."

The doctors were members of America's Frontline Doctors (AFD), a new organization representing doctors from all around the country who had been using a treatment of hydroxychloroquine (HCQ) and zinc to treat patients and who believed the treatment was successful but was being suppressed for financial or political reasons. This delegation of a dozen had come from all over the country to Washington D.C. to gain visibility for AFD.

Dr. Simone Gold, who is from Los Angeles, spoke first before each doctor in turn spoke for several minutes, describing their experience using the regimen to "cure covid." Many cited peer-reviewed studies. Others speculated as to why the beneficial treatment was being suppressed.

A video of the conference was uploaded by AFD to YouTube that afternoon. The video went viral and received *seventeen million* views that same day.[2] Information that wasn't appearing on corporate media was being published on the internet, via independent media, via social networks. The New Enlightenment was unfolding before our eyes.

Then, it disappeared.[3]

An Assault on the Frontlines

YouTube didn't just "push down" the video as "not authoritative." They deleted it, claiming its content went against its Terms of Service.[4] The video was labeled "fake news" and "disinformation," and it was soon nowhere to be found. *Systemic bias* was at play, likely because of the Advertisers filter on account of Big Pharma.

Whether or not you trusted Simone Gold; whether or not you believed the doctor who said she had treated 350 patients for covid, including dozens of 90-year-olds, with the HCQ + zinc treatment and not lost a single patient; whether or not you believed the nursing home facility manager who had used the treatment on his patients and staff and had successful results; whether or not you believed the doctor who declared the treatment was banned because it couldn't be patented and therefore its use would deprive pharmaceutical corporations of the billions they hoped to profit from a vaccine—whatever you believed, how could it make sense to censor these medical experts? How could it help scientific knowledge to muzzle professional doctors from sharing successful results with repurposed safe medications to fight a virus for which there was no approved treatment?

Corporate media pundits smeared the doctors over the ensuing week. It seemed to be "shoot the messenger" time. For narrative management, the *person* speaking a contrarian opinion or analysis is usually attacked rather than the opinion or analysis itself, since opposing something requires talking about it. News reports, for instance, vilified one of the doctors—Dr. Stella Immanuel, an immigrant from Cameroon with a full medical license practicing medicine in Texas. She had primitive beliefs, the media cried, about "demon sperm" and "alien DNA."[5] Rather than discuss the doctors' results and data, corporate media zeroed in on Dr. Immanuel alone and, in particular, a few sermons she had given in her other occupation as a Christian minister. The doctors were also called Trump supporters[6] in order to discredit them.[7] The CNN narrative was that Trump was clueless about science because he supported the "demon sperm" doctor,[8] and the idea was paraded mockingbird-style throughout Blue News channels for several days, indicating the presence of not just *systemic bias* but *nefarious bias* as well. MSNBC and the *New York Times*, for instance, ran pieces calling the doctor's summit "misinformation" rather than pleas for unbiased science to consider alternative treatments for covid.[9]

That was one of countless occasions of social media censorship in 2020, the year it became clear that the mockingbirds of nefarious bias had migrated to social media. To me, that year was frightening not only because of the covid pandemic but also because certain facts, opinions, and analyses were banned, particularly those appearing in independent media from heterodox scientists. In addition to suppressing treatments to the new virus, science about the lockdowns that destroyed so many world economies was similarly banned.[10]

Walking the Highwire

Two days later, a major independent news show called *The Highwire* broke the silence. Host Del Bigtree introduced the segment to his hundreds of thousands of YouTube viewers:

> The next guest that we're going to talk to may be the death blow to Facebook. Why? Because of one of the greatest censorship events that ever took place in the United States of America. We weren't afraid to talk about it. We're not going to be afraid to talk about it today. Here's a review of that incredible moment in history.[11]

And the censored video rolled on his show. Then, he interviewed Simone Gold herself live.

The next day, YouTube took down not just that episode but *The Highwire* show entirely. The independent news channel's YouTube site was deleted. Its six-figure subscriber base that it had built over many years was gone. YouTube labeled the show "misinformation" and banned it. Facebook followed suit shortly thereafter. *The Highwire* was gone.

The independent media world was put on notice about the risk journalists take in using the biased platform. Predictably, Media Matters applauded the censorship and demanded "social media platforms act responsibly and take action against dangerous ... misinformation."[12]

The Highwire's parent organization, the Informed Consent Action Network (ICAN), took a path different from the one chosen by other censored organizations: they sued both corporations based on censorship, breach of contract, and free speech.[13] They pointed out that because Congress couldn't censor *The Highwire* neither could the social media networks do so under pressure from Congress:

> Members of Congress, through threats and coercion, prevailed on Facebook and YouTube to censor ICAN. This conduct was illegal because these members of Congress would be prohibited from censoring ICAN under the first amendment right to free speech. Members of Congress could not do through Facebook and YouTube what they were prohibited from doing directly.[14]

This case made a compelling point. When Del Bigtree interviewed Dr. Gold and ran the clip of the AFD speeches at the Supreme Court, and when You-

Tube thereafter took down his entire channel, it was not only censorship but a likely violation of Free Speech, as we will discuss at the end of this chapter.

The suit was unfortunately dismissed on a technicality, but higher profile suits have been filed by other censored organizations in the ensuing months. Rumble, an uncensored competitor to YouTube, sued Google over suppressing its videos.[15] Even bigger, in July 2022, Missouri State Attorney General Eric Schmitt sued the Biden administration, alleging collusion with social media companies to censor speech that it didn't like; the suit has been joined by a dozen other states.[16] In Texas, a new law specifically preventing social media companies from censoring speech was struck down in state court but upheld on appeal and is likely headed to the Supreme Court.[17]

We'll delve deeper into this question of First Amendment violations in a moment. First, it's worth considering how YouTube's actions reduced more trust in YouTube than in *The Highwire*. These hits to YouTube's credibility are fueling the rise of new, unfiltered social media. As for Del Bigtree and *The Highwire*, the news show has only grown in stature and reach[18] on its own website in the months since it was tarred as "fake news" and taken down from Facebook and YouTube.

Throughout 2020, before and after being taken down by YouTube, *The Highwire* featured scientists, professors, and government officials with views that differed from the dominant narrative about masks, lockdowns, natural immunity, and vaccines. Personally, after adding the show to my Balanced Media Diet, I found a single episode often powerful enough to counteract an entire week of the corporate media's dominant narrative. Whether or not one agreed with all of Bigtree's guests—and I didn't—the show was clearly doing real journalism, investigating contrary views and data, performing the roles of *watchdog* and *smorgasbord* essential to the First Amendment's vision. Both democracy and science—two ideals of the Enlightenment that gave birth to our country—can only take place when contradictory viewpoints are allowed to be heard and when all assertions are subject to independent validation. For this reason, social media censorship must be seen for what it is: anathema to our system of government and a profound danger to our society.

The Ministry of Truth

Whether or not mockingbirds are still in place at mainstream corporate news outlets today, they are clearly migratory birds now, building nests inside social media.

As mentioned before, Facebook "partnered with" Media Matters in May 2018 to censor certain groups whose message did not align with the DNC news narratives. Shortly thereafter, Facebook also "partnered with" a more shadowy organization, the Digital Forensic Research Lab (DFRL).[19] The stated goal of this new partnership was to expunge certain topics, opinions, and information from the internet ostensibly to protect the integrity of US elections. The DFRL is an outgrowth of the CIA-connected Atlantic Council, a think tank based in Washington, D.C. that essentially lobbies politicians on behalf of NATO; it has extensive ties to the US military and receives significant sponsorship from major corporate entities, US intelligence agencies, and allied governments, such as Saudi Arabia. Like a modern-day Ministry of Truth tasked with identifying "fake news," "fake accounts," and "misinformation," the DFRL's task is, quite plainly, the censorship of anti-establishment discussions of important events like wars, coups, and pandemics. NATO and the Atlantic Council became two more organizations infiltrating Facebook mockingbird-style to add *nefarious bias* to news narratives.

"Censorship is the child of fear and the father of ignorance."
—Laurie Halse Anderson

Another shadowy group that might have appeared in George Orwell's *1984* is the Center for Countering Digital Hate (CCDH). This group is based in Britain and boasts ties to British intelligence services. It's responsible for some of the *nefarious bias* used by Google to financially delist independent news site *Zero Hedge* and conservative analysis site *The Federalist* in the summer of 2020.[20] These sources were not heeding the call of the mockingbirds, so they and many others were censored or "shadow-banned" in 2020.

More than the censorship obvious in the large corporate media sources, 2020 witnessed censorship of independent voices on social media. Use of the terms "disinformation" and "misinformation" exploded in 2020, as did articles by "fact checkers," groups we'll examine in the next chapter that are paid by establishment media and government organizations to appear authoritative while discrediting worrisome or inconvenient independent media reports. These groups form an important part of the "Ministry of Truth" approach to narrative management that is unfolding in this country.

The overt and covert purging of news sources, insidious "shadowbanning" of heterodox voices, and sudden "deplatforming" that took place on social media in 2020 and 2021 was probably worse than anything else that has happened to individual journalists in this young century. Still, over the past decade, the most dramatic censorship has generally been the firing of mainstream media journalists. We'll look at many instances of that in Chapter 12. Conservative voices seemed to bear the brunt of the wave of censorship and propaganda crashing down on the American media landscape in 2020 and 2021, but we'll explore censorship of voices on the left now as well.

Trimming Both Sides of the Tree

The right side of the independent media tree bore the brunt of the censorship ax leading up to the 2020 election, but by January 2021, it was evident that anti-establishment Red News wouldn't be the only side of the tree getting trimmed. Anti-establishment Blue News ran into censorship, smears, and "shadowbanning" as well. Branches of the tree fell all around.

Days after Joe Biden was inaugurated, late in January 2021, dozens of Twitter accounts[21] and Facebook pages[22] supporting the left-wing Antifa movement were summarily removed without notice. Another prominent part of the anti-establishment left media world, the World Socialist Website, was removed from Facebook.[23]

And perhaps as a result of the secretive collaborations between the Atlantic Council and the CCDH, or the many "fact-checking" websites, many leading independent voices on the left who came to prominence in 2016 were censored or banned.

This censorship will likely get worse as the policies of the Biden administration continue to disappoint those on the independent, progressive, and populist left.[24]

◈ **Jimmy Dore.** This popular commentator with a left critique of the Democratic Party built a YouTube channel with over 1 million subscribers. His follower count has been capped on YouTube, and his audience reduced on Facebook. His coverage specifically of censorship has been very good, and he takes principled stances against censorship of the right despite his clear progressive leanings.

◈ **Lee Camp.** This popular comedian has a radical left perspective[25] and was subjected to a meticulous and disingenuous smear by the *New York Times*. His social media accounts have been frozen or banned over the last two years, and his popular show called *Redacted Tonight* on the RT network has been banned on YouTube and Spotify.

◈ **Jordan Chariton.** This independent, investigative journalist with a progressive slant bravely covered the corruption surrounding the poisoning of Flint, Mich., as discussed in detail in Chapter 11, as well as the Shadow app scam that rigged the Iowa caucus to give Pete Buttigieg the edge over Bernie Sanders. His coverage of the "Capitol riots" on January 6, 2021 was taken down by YouTube.

On the right side of the spectrum, censorship of independent media was swift and sudden in 2020 and 2021, particularly around topics pertaining to election fraud, covid, lockdowns, and vaccines.

(As I list these, it occurs to me that this right-left division is less useful than it might once have been. Today, on a progressive-reactionary or authoritarian-libertarian scale, these sources might all be in a similar anti-establishment place.)

◈ **Gateway Pundit.** This popular, independent conservative news site tweeted out primary sources alleging election fraud in the 2020 election, including videos of unmarked vans in Detroit loading and unloading boxes of ballots in unofficial locations. Twitter labeled the tweets "sexually suggestive," which limited their reach, and then deleted the account with its thousands of followers.

◈ **Aaron Ginn**. This libertarian technology writer penned broadly popular articles about the likely trajectory of the covid pandemic before his articles were taken down on Medium.[26] Even his personal copy was apparently removed from his Google Docs account for containing unacceptable content.[27]

❖ **Project Veritas.** This investigative news organization, headed by James O'Keefe, was removed from Twitter after it revealed bias in Blue News networks one too many times. Twitter even deleted O'Keefe's personal account after he released video capturing CNN Technical Director Charlie Chester confessing the network had deliberately worked to remove Trump. "Look what we did, we got Trump out," Chester said. "I am 100% going to say it and 100% believe it: if it wasn't for CNN, I don't know that Trump would have been voted out." With this revelation, rather than remove CNN, Twitter removed Project Veritas.[28]

❖ **Alex Berenson.** A former *New York Times* journalist and best-selling author, Berenson was unceremoniously booted off of Twitter for "repeated violations of covid misinformation rules." He revealed on Substack the "Tweet that Did It,"[29] a tweet calling the experimental shots "therapeutics" rather than "vaccines" since they have "a limited window of efficacy, a terrible side effect profile, and must be dosed in advance of illness."[30] It was a reasonable point for debate but evidently not one Twitter or the pharmaceutical corporations could tolerate.

SOCIAL MEDIA PROTECTS YOU FROM FREE SPEECH

AN IMPORTANT QUESTION THAT WE HAVE TOUCHED ON BUT NOT FULLY answered yet is whether social media censorship amounts to violations of Free Speech under the Constitution. While *any* censorship—be it from a government, a church, or a corporation—is poisonous to democracy, science, and the larger human search for truth, the narrower question remains: does social media censorship violate the US Constitution's guarantee of Free Speech for all people?

The text of the Constitution is terse:

Congress shall make no law respecting an establishment of religion, or prohibiting the free exercise thereof; or abridging the freedom of speech, or of the press.

Many argue that social media censorship, however inconvenient or unpleasant, isn't a violation of Free Speech because it is a private corporation rather than the government itself—let alone Congressional law—censoring the citizen's opinions. I think those making this argument haven't fully considered the modern dynamics of political speech or the formidable power of the social media giants. Social media censorship violates Constitutional Free Speech protection for three reasons:

1. Social media has replaced the town square and sidewalk.

2. Social media giants enjoy and exercise monopoly power.

3. Social media companies are directly pressured by Congress.

The first point should be obvious. Even a cursory analysis of American society reveals that Google, Facebook, and Twitter have replaced the town square and the public park as the places where citizens congregate and exchange ideas. The transition to online community was occurring on its own over the past two decades before it accelerated considerably with the lockdowns and social distancing implemented during the pandemic. The Supreme Court has already called the internet "the modern public square" when deciding a 2017 First Amendment case.[31]

In the words of the ICAN lawsuit mentioned above:

> These social media platforms are the equivalent of the sidewalks of the past where Americans enjoyed the liberty of free speech. The censorship by these companies, at the behest of the government, cannot stand.[32]

The second point is that these giants wield monopoly power. Certainly, a small, medium, or even large business, such as a restaurant, retail shop, or string of chain stores isn't required to honor everyone's Free Speech rights inside its narrow confines. But today's three social media giants are different animals altogether. Their express purpose is the facilitation of discussion, and they wield monopoly power over the voices of millions.

Some might say they're not monopolies because there are three of them, plus there's Instagram, YouTube, and a handful of others. Leaving aside the fact that Facebook acquired Instagram and Google acquired YouTube, just because there are three *types* of social media doesn't mean that each corporation isn't a monopoly.

As a metaphor, consider transportation. Imagine for a moment that a single company made all the pickup trucks in the country, and that company announced one day that it was going to install recording devices in all new pickup trucks that would record and broadcast conversations to the CIA. Now, imagine that you wanted a pickup truck without the recording device.

"I'm sorry, that's all we have," the company might reply.

"You're abusing your monopoly," you might say. "How can I get a pickup truck without the recording device?"

The pickup truck company would reply, "We're not a monopoly. You can always go buy a car or a bicycle."

Yes, Google, Twitter, and Facebook all run social media operations, but their products are distinct and each controls effectively all of the market share for their product. There is no true competitor to any of them. When a competitor emerges, it is acquired (Instagram) or squashed (Parler). Furthermore, their effective monopolies enable them to manipulate the discussion to counter attempts to regulate or break them up.

Ninety percent of Americans use Google to find information. Eighty percent of Americans use Google's YouTube. Seventy percent of Americans use Facebook. Fifty percent of Americans use Facebook *daily*.[33] These are astronomical numbers that indicate monopoly power. Twitter has slightly lower usage across American society, at 35%, but its users are disproportionately the highly-educated, wealthy, and elite professionals who manage and influence national political debate.

The third point is that their sheer size and power places the tech giants in constant contact with Congress and the White House. The resulting negotiations grant the government the ability to censor opinions they don't like by proxy.

Section 230 of the 1996 Online Decency Act currently grants social media companies immunity from liability for things said on their sites.[34] This law guarantees, for instance, that Facebook can't be sued if a user posts libelous comments. The social media corporations deeply fear the repeal of this law; this makes them vulnerable to political pressure.

In the lawsuit mentioned above, ICAN alleges that Congress indeed holds repeal of Section 230 over the heads of social media giants, tacitly threatening them if they don't comply and censor offending publications, such as *The Highwire*.

This pressure and lobbying go both ways. The government needs data storage, internet services, tax revenue, and the placement of propaganda; the tech giants want tax breaks, visas for overseas workers, and billion-dollar contracts from the federal government.[35] Countless conflicts of interest arise when the tech giants lobby Congress, placing individual citizens and news organizations who happen to hold important but unpopular views in peril, and this will get substantially worse if the tech giants are continuously allowed—and compelled—to censor.

Fascism is defined as the joining of corporate and government power to oppose any countervailing power, such as that of everyday people and popular democracy. The United States is not a fascist country yet by most definitions, but this trend toward the blending of corporate and government power—including nominally private corporations manipulating and censoring information—is accelerating. This trend is a major battle in the information war we've mentioned before between the true progressives, on the one hand, who support the New Enlightenment's open flow of independent media and the greater distribution of wealth and power, and the reactionaries, on the other hand, who wish to tighten the top-down flow of information and keep wealth and power concentrated at the top.

Internal emails leaked by Google employees reveal some of the countless ways search results have been manipulated to favor government points of view. In March 2020, Google declared they would be removing from search results any news source or website promoting "conspiracy theories" or "misinformation" about covid, which was defined as anything not in line with the official WHO and CDC narrative.[36] If this wasn't already government censorship of news, it got even closer when prominent Congressman Adam Schiff (D-CA), Chairman of the House Intelligence Committee, demanded Google go further.[37]

Thereafter, in 2020, and with greater strength once Biden was in office in 2021, many Congress members called on these arbiters of information to censor news.

The issue is not that the [social media] companies are taking too many posts down. The issue is that they are leaving too many dangerous posts up.[38]

Those words came from Senator Ed Markey (D-MA). They were echoed by Congresswoman Anna Eshoo (D-CA) and many others in Congress. They revealed the pressure placed on social media companies by the party in power and indicated in unambiguous terms that the legislative branch wanted social media companies to censor certain ideas. President Biden and his press secretary, Jen Psaki, went still further, demanding the "internet death penalty" that we detailed earlier, a frightening power to contemplate in a historically free society.

The tech giants' power has become so formidable that if they distort the viewpoints available to their users, they're misleading, in effect, everyone; they're putting their finger on the scale of the public narrative. If they censor news about, say, perceptions of political candidates, they're meddling in elections. If they censor news about, say, adverse health effects of a medication, they're meddling in science. If they allow one side in an armed conflict to post violent images and words but not the other side, they're causing violence. Think of the duty of the press on a subject like the covid vaccines. It is not yet clear whether the Moderna mRNA injection, for instance, will turn out to be the modern-day penicillin or the modern-day thalidomide, or something in between, and it won't be clear for years; this is why we need science free of censorship. This is why we need today the guarantees written in our Constitution in 1789: Free Speech, Free Press, Free Religion, Free Assembly. The danger of censorship is profound. For every controversial person whom the majority demands be silenced, there's an unpopular genius we need to hear. For every Alex Jones (or Rachel Maddow), there's a Galileo.

We conclude this chapter by considering some practical solutions and regulatory approaches that address the dangers of social media censorship.

THE GIANTS AT
THE GATES

THE INTERNET REMAINS OUR GREATEST HOPE FOR BREAKING THE SPELL
of the century-old propaganda and censorship in corporate and government
media. The revolutionary powers that social media has bestowed upon us enable us to share news and analysis directly and instantly with one another.
This is bringing about a world without the filters that corporate media places
between us and reality.

Nevertheless, we must be wary. Giants guard the gate to this awakening.
Enormous tech companies stand as arbiters of our very thoughts, and they
threaten our privacy and freedom. We must become aware of the ways they
distort our knowledge of the world we live in. This is a segment of the path to
media consciousness.

Not only are these giants at the gates to the New Enlightenment filtering
the knowledge and information they provide, they are also programming us
to behave and interact in ways that enable them to harvest our choices, emotions, words, and facial expressions for their later use. As currently consti-
tuted, they have the potential to harm humanity in many ways. This is why
we as a nation must change them by dissolving their monopolies or removing
their ability to manipulate speech.

Social media also constitutes a good and important part of the New Enlightenment. Sharing information freely *is* essential for modern populist
movements, deeper democracy, individual liberty, and progressive political
activity. When building momentum for new solutions to problems, social
media is a great gift and powerful tool for the raising of both money and consciousness around public issues. The movements behind Bernie Sanders,[39]
Alexandria Ocasio-Cortez,[40] and Marjorie Taylor Greene[41]—however you feel
about each of those leaders—strengthen democracy by bringing new ideas
into the public forum.[42]

Elizabeth Warren seemed to have something different in mind when she
publicly called for criminalizing "the spread of disinformation" at a campaign
stop in 2020.[43] She wanted to target both the social media companies as well
as individual journalists advocating heterodox ideas.

We might think the solution to dishonest news reports is "fact-checking." It's a noble idea. But as we'll discover in the next chapter, "fact-checking" sites are themselves compromised and untrustworthy. At the end of the day, internet companies and government agencies need to respect first principles here: Freedom of Speech and Freedom of the Press. Readers need *media consciousness* and the permission to make up their own minds. Only by allowing all ideas—all reporting and all analyses—to be heard and discussed can we hope to attain a free, open, and just society.

Zach Vorhies leaked documents from Google disclosing that the people who work at technology companies disproportionately identify as Democrats and liberal, and so companies as a whole might be heavily liberal or favor Democrats, or both. Some Democrats might take solace in this, but it's false comfort, and people on both the left and right should understand this. Our country's first principles exist for a reason. Your party won't always be in power, so protecting basic freedoms is essential. This heavy leftward slant in tech companies endangers freedom of speech for conservatives. Peter Hasson, in his 2020 book *The Manipulators: Facebook, Google, Twitter, and Big Tech's War on Conservatives*,[44] meticulously enumerates the ways conservatives are ostracized in social media and the ways Americans' political beliefs are subtly but brilliantly manipulated by platforms like Twitter and Facebook.

On the other end of the political spectrum, and possibly more worrying, in *The Age of Surveillance Capitalism: The Fight for a Human Future at the New Frontier of Power*, Shoshana Zuboff reveals that the business model of Google, Facebook, and the other tech giants isn't to advocate for politicians or even to sell ads anymore. The goal now is to harvest every part of our human experience as data so as to advance artificial intelligence and win the race to the next technological frontier, the "metaverse."[45] Along the way, the highly developed art of propaganda is taking another leap forward. A more sophisticated kind of social programming and control is now possible through a combination of machine learning, continuous surveillance, and addictive social media platforms like TikTok and Instagram that work to manipulate our emotions and adjust our behavior. Mockingbirds in the media become unnecessary when the propaganda is hardwired into everyone's online life.

The dangers are great enough that these giants should be regulated and their powers circumscribed. Our constitutional rights to Free Speech, a Free Press, and Free Assembly must endure. As discussed in this book's Introduction, two relevant regulatory models exist for the social media giants, and we need to choose one:

1. ***Publisher.*** This regulatory model, used for instance for book publishers, allows a corporation to print only what it wants to print and to retain some intellectual property rights on what is published. The corporation is fully liable for anything illegal it publishes, such as libel. Additionally, it is subject to antitrust legislation, and because of the sensitive nature of publishing, it may not attain a monopoly in the geographical area in which it does business, usually nationwide.

2. ***Utility.*** This model, also called the "common carrier" model, is used for phone companies and cable providers. It frees a corporation from any liability for what is said over its network. This model allows monopoly market share in some instances. But the corporation may not choose who gets to speak on its network or what may be said. It simply provides to people the means for service: the antennas for the phone connections, the pipes for the water, the wires for the electricity.

Google, Facebook, and Twitter *either* get to censor and choose what to publish, *or* they get immunity from legal prosecution for what they publish. They cannot get both. What they have now is a disastrous hybrid of the two. They get to have their cake and eat it too: they get to censor or "shadowban" whatever ideas and voices they please, they get to retain intellectual property rights over what is said, and, with Section 230 of the 1996 Communications Decency Act, they are protected from liability for what users say.

Holding them in check, in theory, are "Terms of Service" agreements, but these labyrinthine contracts are in fact one more way the tech giants have seized power. These contracts do not establish clear relationships, and they are utilized to arbitrarily gag users. A study found that 91% of people don't read Terms of Service agreements before accepting them.[46] Regulating social media companies as *utilities*, as I propose here, would invalidate these unread, unreasonable, unfair contracts. A phone company could never require you to sign "service terms" that allowed them to cut off your service if you said something to a friend that the phone company disliked.

Indeed, the *utility* model is ultimately the best fit for these burgeoning behemoths. First, Americans' use of social media has grown so widespread as to be nearly as universal as our need for electricity, water, and telecommunication services; second, censorship poses profound dangers to science and democracy and must be reined in. By regulating social media corporations that attain dominant national market share as utilities, all legal speech will be permitted in these modern public squares. We will remove the responsibility—and temptation—the tech giants feel to shadowban users and censor unpopular ideas. This will protect and reinvigorate democracy and science. It will also prevent Americans from being suddenly cut off from a valuable channel for social, intellectual, and emotional connection with other human beings.

The alternative is the *publisher* model and the repeal of Section 230. This would allow the tech giants to continue to censor as they see fit—and even to carry out specific censorship requested by governments—and would open them up to lawsuits for anything harmful anyone posted on their vast networks.[47] There is little appeal to this path from either a press freedom or a free enterprise perspective. It would be jumping from the pan into the fire. Using this model would enable the government to dictate what can and cannot be said. This would increase oppression and undermine our democracy. History shows that once a government obtains control over the media, the free pursuit of science, democracy, and truth is short lived. Consider the cases of the Soviet Union, North Korea, China, and many others. The *publisher* model is, in this case, a dead-end road for a free society.

The *utility* model is the right path. It would bring a just, logical, and legal end to the nefarious exploitation of the powers of social media.

10

CHECKING FACTS AT THE DOOR

"Whoever controls the media, controls the mind."

Jim Morrison

A WEALTHY AMERICAN WOMAN WEARING A BLACK SHIRT AND BLUE scarf picked through a debris-strewn street. She stood between two white refugee tents. Looking down, she spotted a torn, pink backpack on the ground. She bent down and picked it up.

Looking into the CNN camera, she held the backpack to her nose and sniffed.

"Yes, there's definitely something..."—she wrinkled her nose—"that stinks."

She returned the backpack to the ground, having single-handedly destroyed her own media organization's news narrative. Picking through the rubble the way she did, standing there in Douma, Syria, lent credence instead to an alternative narrative.

It was April 2018, and the story presented on CNN, and on Fox, and on NPR, and on ABC was that Syrian Prime Minister Bashar al-Assad had brutally attacked his own people. Assad had allegedly dropped canisters of chemical weapons on this town as part of a civil war against the Jaysh Al-Islam rebels. The UN's Organization to Prevent Chemical Weapons (OPCW) had just sent a team to investigate the event, and their report seemed to confirm the use of chemical weapons.

The other version of the story, one not heard on corporate media, was that no such attack had happened. According to this version, rebels, who happened to be funded by the CIA, had planted the evidence of such an attack to give the *appearance* of a chemical weapons attack—in order to justify an American bombing campaign. Several things boosted the credibility of this second version of events, including the fact that two prominent members of the OPCW's team dissented strenuously from the OPCW's report, calling it a "twisted" presentation of what the team had actually found. Also supporting this narrative was the fact that Assad had firmly gained the upper hand in the civil war at that point and had no need to use chemical weapons; in fact, using chemical weapons was the one thing that US military officials had said would justify US bombing. Assad knew even the *alleged* presence of chemical weapons in neighboring Iraq, in 2003, had been sufficient pretext for a US invasion.

Tareq Haddad, a longtime writer for *Newsweek* in London, reported on these OPCW whistleblowers in his magazine. He then resigned over what he called "censorship" of the true story.[1] Robert Fisk, an award-winning foreign correspondent with a long history of independence, was on the ground in Syria and reported evidence of conventional bombing,[2] but no chemical weapons attacks.[3]

CNN only told the first version of the story. "He gassed his own people!" the hosts and military commentators declared on air,[4] insinuating it was something we couldn't and shouldn't tolerate. Like mockingbirds, other corporate media channels picked up the tune, and everywhere it was heard: Assad "gassed his own people." The *New York Times* produced a lengthy, "augmented reality," multimedia feature under the headline, "One Building, One Bomb: How Assad Gassed His Own People."[5]

And then this woman in a blue scarf sniffed a backpack on CNN.[6]

A Gas Attack That Vanished in Thin Air

Wearing no protective gear at all, casually sauntering into the site of the supposed deadly use of chemical weapons, she picked up a backpack allegedly laced with chemical agents, held it to her nose and inhaled. "Definitely something that stinks." She nodded as if to casually confirm with her untrained, bare nasal passages the work of a team of experts. There was something almost comical about how swiftly her actions destroyed the whole story she was reporting on. Who visits the site of a lethal chemical weapons attack and walks around sniffing things?

The CNN anchors said nothing, but independent media journalists pounced after the segment aired. How could the woman and the camera team know she would be able to detect an odor but wouldn't be harmed by inhaling whatever remained on the surface of that backpack? How would CNN let someone get this close without protective gear?

Why, indeed, did CNN report so uncritically the whole unproven story that Assad had gassed his own people when it made no sense that he would do so? Why wasn't the second version of the story ever mentioned? Why didn't anyone on CNN or *Newsweek* or MSNBC address the OPCW whistleblowers and the holes in the story about the gas canisters?

None of these questions are mysteries. Both *systemic bias* and *nefarious bias* were at play. In the unfortunate case of this fictional pretense for war, the five filters of *systematic bias* were all in effect, distorting some news, promoting others, and banning altogether the most contradictory viewpoints. Military pundits declaring "Assad gassed his own people" was the result of *nefarious bias,* deliberate deception with the ulterior agenda of prolonging the war.

The Dominant Narrative filter (which was "the war on terror" at the time) removed news that didn't present the Syrian government as agents of terrorism. The Elite Sources filter ensured no news counter to the CIA's declared narrative was promoted. The Avoiding Outcry filter further screened out controversy or dissent, and finally, the Advertisers and Ownership filters combined to ensure any facts or perspectives that might dissuade Americans from favoring military intervention would be either omitted altogether or presented in a dubious light.

The hidden agenda beneath the *nefarious bias* was the desire by the CIA and DoD to prolong the civil war that had begun with a CIA attempt to overthrow Assad in 2011. The Pentagon wanted to install a regime more friendly to the interests of American allies Israel and Saudi Arabia. These airstrikes escalated an ongoing proxy war with Russia that was primarily over the routing of a natural gas pipeline that was to run from the Persian Gulf to Europe. The true underlying agenda behind *nefarious bias* is rarely, if ever, mentioned in the corporate media.

Jeffrey Sachs, a Columbia University professor, managed to explain all of this in a stunning segment on MSNBC in 2018. Hosts Mika Brzezinski and Willie Geist were flummoxed as to how to respond to Sach's lucid and simple unveiling of the true agenda of the war.[7] A similar episode took place on the British television network *Sky News*. Longtime military expert Major General Jonathan Shaw was embarrassingly cut off for getting too close to the truth:

SkyNews Host: Do you think anything we've heard—from either Sergei Lavrov or indeed the Russian ambassador—has made it more difficult for the UK to launch an attack [on Syria] without putting it to Parliament?

General Shaw: Yeah, I do. But I think quite apart from all that, the debate that seems to be missing from this is, and this was actually mentioned by the ambassador: What possible motive might have triggered Syria to launch a chemical attack at this time, in this place? You know, the Syrians are winning. Don't take my word for it, take the American military's word for it. General Votel, the Head of CENTCOM, said to Congress the other day: 'Assad has won this war, and we need to face that.' And then you got last week the statement by Trump that 'America had finished with ISIL,' and that 'We'll pull out soon, very soon,' and then suddenly you get—

SkyNews Host: Ok, great, I'm very sorry, but we do need to leave it there.

And that was it, the beginning and end of that interview. General Shaw couldn't be allowed to voice one of the obvious flaws in the narrative about Assad launching gas attacks on his own people.

Mockingbirds Chirp Happily

Were the corporate media's agenda just about money or viewers or ratings or clicks, presenting both sides of this story would have been extraordinarily worthwhile. Controversy drives up ratings and increases viewership. It's always more fascinating to see both sides, to hear the debate, to get engaged in whether or not the CIA faked an entire gas attack in a foreign country. Calling out the government over its lies would be a winner for ratings and viewers every time. Here was even a major military leader willing to go on the record questioning the narrative.

But the corporate media's primary goal is the management of narratives in support of the *reactionary* agendas of their investors, owners, and advertisers. The media behemoths don't need viewers more than they need reliable control of the story and a compliant populace. Ratings and money are important, but they do not drive the media's choices in determining what stories to cover and how to cover them.

And that's why the fake chemical attack in Douma was reported to the American people the way that it was.

Seven days after the supposed attack, the US under Donald Trump unleashed a bombing campaign on the people of Syria ostensibly (as always) to help them. The victims of American military strikes are never discussed, and the deaths of Syrians at *our* hands are never worthy of mention. Just as in the case of the Weapons of Mass Distraction in Iraq, described earlier in the book, an abhorrent and unproven allegation was used in the corporate media to justify unfathomable violence.

In the months that followed, more whistleblowers came forward, providing testimony to the UN that the OPCW initial report was a coverup. The OPCW initial report had, for instance, deliberately omitted the finding of its own engineers who concluded that the canisters of gas had been manually placed rather than dropped from airplanes. In addition, Jose Bustani, the original director of the OPCW, came forward to share testimony[8] that had been blocked by the US and the UK. Still more information[9] came out via WikiLeaks.[10] The evidence became overwhelming that the attack had either never happened or had been small and manually arranged by the rebels themselves in order to justify American bombing. The BBC took the extremely rare step of retracting an entire documentary it had broadcast on the alleged attack,[11] admitting it had been "seriously flawed."[12]

The truth steadily slipped out in independent media.[13] But the damning truth[14]—that a "false flag"[15] attack[16] was reported to the American people as legitimate—was never acknowledged in the corporate media.

On the morning of April 14, 2018, the day the US, UK, and France bombed Syria, every major American newspaper covered the strikes. The top four papers—the *Wall Street Journal, New York Times, Washington Post, USA Today*—ran 18 stories in total between them on the bombing, and every single story was positive in tone. No articles recalled the disastrous invasion of Iraq, no editorials questioned the need to bomb yet another country, and no reporting existed on the flaws in the allegations of the use of chemical weapons. Just as in 2003, when the initial bombs struck Iraq, the mockingbirds were all chirping happily on that April morning.

Some things, however, were new. There were two new components of this internet news media era that hadn't existed during the buildup to the invasion of Iraq: "fact-checking" websites and "astroturf" independent news sites. These pipes of the Wurlitzer perform a valuable, new, and important role in narrative management, and we examine them in this chapter.

PROTECTING YOU FROM THE FACTS

A PROFOUND SHIFT IN AWARENESS ABOUT WORLD EVENTS IS UNFOLD-ing across our country on account of the internet and independent media. We can instantaneously hear multiple sides to each story in a way never before possible. This is steadily solving the problem of widespread bias and deception in the corporate media. If we follow something like the Balanced Media Diet proposed in this book, we can verify for ourselves that the versions of news stories that we believe to be true are, in fact, true. We can all find and consider alternatives to the news narratives we are served, we can think for ourselves, and we can cultivate the *media consciousness* that allows us to navigate the distortions.

But it can be a lot of work to read multiple versions of a story. People are busy and barely have time to read a report on the single most pressing issue of the day.

This freedom and this burden have together led to the growth of news aggregators, media ratings systems, and, most promising of all, "fact-checkers." The latter include popular sites such as PolitiFact, FactCheck, and Snopes, sites that profess to sort the truth from the lies for you. These sites publish timely pages on common questions in the news, and in effect, offer to solve the entire problem of "fake news" and *disinformation* for you: bring up a topic in the news and they'll reveal the truth.

These "fact-checking" websites have done some legitimate work in some areas of news coverage, and they should continue to do so. The problem is that they are organized and funded by the same corporate and government groups funding corporate media and corporate social media. Worse, they are handed the specific task of labeling and sorting various news accounts, making them effectively deeper purveyors of propaganda than the corporate and independent media channels they purport to "fact-check." This is the paradox of "fact-checking."

With regard to the alleged gas attack in Douma, Syria in 2018, the site PolitiFact ran two "fact-checking" reports. Neither attempted to verify that the attack had happened; both defended the mainstream corporate narrative that Assad had "gassed his own people." These were the two reports:

1. **"Red Crescent Says No Evidence of Chemical Attack in Syria's Douma."** This report made a big show of disproving something that wasn't really in contention. A report from RT, the Russian news agency, had quoted individual Red Crescent doctors on the ground who said no attack had happened. RT then ran a headline stating that the Red Crescent had found no evidence of an attack. PolitiFact didn't contact the doctors. It instead contacted the head of the Red Crescent in Beirut and determined that *as an organization* the Red Crescent had not made a statement one way or the other. PolitiFact thereby called the RT report[17] false on account of the RT report attributing doctors' statements to the organization. Politifact never talked to the doctors themselves, let alone examined the real issue of whether or not there had been a gas attack.

2. **Conspiracy claims that Syrian gas attack was 'false flag' are unproven.** From the headline, this one sounded like it was going to go after the real story. But again, PolitiFact didn't attempt to verify

anything about the gas attack itself. It checked only *claims that went against the mainstream narrative.* Much like the corporate media, PolitiFact's report demeaned reports that were dubious about the attacks as "conspiracy theories." Rather than consider them fairly, it aimed for the much lower bar of determining whether the alternative "conspiracy" story—that the attack was staged—had been proven.[18]

This second "fact-check" is particularly useful in understanding the paradox and circular logic of corporate media fact-checking. Because fact-checkers are organized and funded by the same sources as the corporate media, they primarily "fact-check" ideas, reports, and claims that *oppose* the corporate media narrative, and because they only use articles in the mainstream corporate media to determine whether those claims are true or false, they act as an additional moat around dominant media narratives.

Late in 2021, journalist John Stossel noticed that Facebook had placed "disinformation" labels on several of his investigative videos. As a result, viewership for his videos plummeted, and his revenue vanished. In response, he sued Facebook,[19] and in a fascinating court case, Facebook argued that the "fact-check" reports that they fund and use to demote and shadowban posts are just opinion.[20] It begged the question: how can a system be deemed logical that uses one set of opinions to demote, ban, and censor a different set of opinions?

Fact-Checking the Fact-Checkers

Of course, these sites don't bill themselves as opinion. The notion of a "fact-checker" that authoritatively sorts the truth from the lies is so appealing to busy people that during the confusing news environment of the early 2020s, these sites saw unparalleled traffic. With the endless pandemic, alleged election fraud, controversial vaccine mandates, and secretive Great Reset, the new era won these sites huge new audiences and made them an essential part of modern narrative management.

If we explore who funds these organizations that profess to "set the record straight," we find the same corporations that manipulate information in other parts of the American media. In an era where social media companies Google,

Facebook, and Twitter have become news publishers who censor news they deem unsafe or undesirable, it is unfortunate but perhaps unsurprising that these same companies fund the organizations that claim to determine definitively what news is true. Here's a quick look at four of the largest of these organizations:

Politifact

Founded in 2007 by the *Tampa Bay Times*, and acquired in 2018 by the Poynter Institute, Politifact received large grants in 2020 and 2021 from both Facebook and Google to identify "misinformation."[21] The Poynter Institute also receives substantial funding from pharmaceutical corporations, partisan organizations like Democracy Fund, the CIA-connected National Endowment for Democracy, the controversial Open Society Foundations run by George Soros, and the enormously powerful, pro-vaccine Bill & Melinda Gates Foundation.[22] As an organization, Politifact is made up of a handful of corporate media journalists styling themselves as referees for their profession, writing reports they're generally underqualified to write.

FactCheck

Co-founded in 2003 by a former *Wall Street Journal* journalist named Brooks Jackson and Kathleen Hall Jamieson, the founder of Annenberg Public Policy Center (APPC), FactCheck is now run out of the APPC in Philadelphia, giving it a veneer of independence. A quick look at its funding reveals that FactCheck received large grants in 2020 and 2021 similar to Politifact's from Facebook and Google to "debunk social media misinformation," and from Johnson & Johnson's Robert Wood Johnson Foundation to "correct Covid-19 disinformation and vaccine misconceptions."[23] As with Politifact, the "fact-checkers" at FactCheck are particularly dutiful when checking stories that concern the interests of the organization's funders. FactCheck has its own staff of reporters.

Snopes

This organization owns the biggest name and the most checkered history in the world of "fact-checking." Founded in 1994 by David Mikkelson, the site for years simply published Google searches on folklore and legends, such as the Loch Ness Monster and the Yeti, "debunking" outlandish claims. "The first name in fact-checking" has grown wildly from those humble roots in large part due to sizable grants from Facebook. Mikkelson got wealthy as the first to publish "facts" with the imprimatur of objectivity. Its brand luster has declined significantly in recent years. Mikkelson's penchant for lavish Las Vegas trips, embezzlement, and prostitutes[24] has landed him in court repeatedly and won him both an unsavory reputation and a messy divorce.[25] Even after run-ins with the law for falsifying business reports that enabled Snopes to pay for his hedonistic jaunts, Mikkelson still runs the company. It is now, however, 50% owned by an ad agency named Proper Media.[26] A 2021 investigation found Mikkelson guilty of over 50 instances of plagiarism.[27] Snopes has been caught taking bribes from organizations it writes about and "debunking" honest news reports about corporations it receives funding from, such as Monsanto.[28] It's unlikely such a CEO can be trusted to monitor the integrity of others, but the company still receives substantial prestige and funding from Facebook.

Science Feedback

Although not as well known as the others, Science Feedback, and its siblings Health Feedback and Climate Feedback, perform a similar role in narrative management. These sites were founded in 2015 and claim to be nonprofits, but their parent organization runs a profitable company, SciVerify, which handles the copious funds provided by Google, Facebook, and TikTok for its "fact-checking."[29] In 2020, Science Feedback was particularly active in attacking articles that examined the origin of covid.[30] An expert they regularly relied upon, the Australian virologist Danielle Anderson, was usually referred to as simply an expert in virology. But as the one foreign researcher who worked at the Wuhan lab, Anderson had a critically vested interest in the verdict on the origin of the virus. Just as Peter Daszak was regularly quoted in corporate media articles about the virus's origin without noting his central role in funding virus manipulation at the lab, Science Feedback regularly used Dr. Anderson in their "fact checking" without noting her role or her understandable desire that the origin of the virus not be traced to her lab.

Organizations such as Politifact, Snopes, and Science Feedback are unfortunately no protection against the largest sources of disinformation and propaganda that face Americans: the government and the giant media corporations that work around the clock to disseminate their reactionary agendas. Nevertheless, "fact-checking" occupies an ineluctable post in the modern mechanisms of narrative management, fortifying dominant worldviews against incursions from heretical ideas. There have been countless instances of this. Let's examine another one now.

A HOME RUN FOR PROPAGANDA

HANK AARON REMAINED A HERO TO MILLIONS OF AMERICANS UP UNTIL the day he died. "Hammerin' Hank" was a world-famous athlete, and for decades, he reigned as Major League Baseball's home run king. He lived in Atlanta, and when the experimental injections for covid were rolled out, local health officials attempted to assuage widespread doubts about the vaccines among the city's Black community by publicly administering the shots to Black leaders. On January 4, 2021, Aaron received a shot live before news cameras and microphones.[31] He smiled and said he wasn't worried. "I have no qualms about it at all."

He died about two weeks later.

No proven cause of death emerged. Whether or not the vaccine killed Aaron is not our concern here, as this is a controversial and new drug about which many things are unknown. What we're interested in is how *systemic bias* manipulated the news coverage of this important story and how "fact-checkers" checked certain facts while ignoring others.

Giant pharmaceutical corporations like Moderna, Pfizer, and Johnson &

Johnson poured billions into development of the injections and were set to make trillions if the injection turned out to be, as they claimed, "safe and effective." Inconceivable wealth was at stake: a profitable drug was potentially to be administered to the planet's entire population. *Systemic bias* was off the charts. The corporate media, for whom pharmaceuticals are the largest source of advertising, was thickly *biased* as it managed the narrative around this new drug that was experimental and without long-term safety trials. No corporate media analyst mentioned, for instance, the fraud these drug companies have engaged in throughout recent history, such as the staggering $2.3 billion settlement Pfizer paid in 2009 for pushing anti-inflammatory drug Bextra despite knowing the medication's risks.[32]

For the purposes of this book and an analysis of media manipulation, it is important to note how the CDC, the FDA, and the rest of the government immediately took the side of the drugmakers. Vaccines are a controversial topic, and I have neither sufficient expertise nor space in this book to determine whether the covid injections are "safe" or "effective." Intelligent minds clearly differ. The government manipulated the narrative overtly rather than covertly in this case, taking advantage of the Obama-era rollback of Smith-Mundt restrictions on government production of propaganda. No hidden Mockingbird manipulation was needed, although it may have been used as well. The government publicly rolled out a $1.5 *billion* propaganda campaign to "build vaccine confidence."[33] This was not to counter foreign disinformation but rather to drown out or discredit the voices of heterodox doctors and scientists attempting to participate in a national conversation.

Whatever the underlying agenda was and is, all filters of *systemic bias* were fully operational. A billion dollars buys virtually endless narrative management. Story after story praised the efficacy of the new product and tied the end of the lockdowns to their immediate and widespread uptake. But despite countless articles in both Red News and Blue News outlets that espoused the safety of the injection, doubts remained. Corporate media rarely mentioned it, but around half of Americans expressed doubts about the vaccines.[34]

And then Hank Aaron died.

Had the vaccine played a role in his death?

Enter the Fact-checkers

A FactCheck article six days after Aaron's death ran with the headline, "Fact Check: Hank Aaron's Death Attributed to Natural Causes."[35] The article began by laying out the known facts of the situation, that Aaron had received the Moderna injection and had then died seventeen days later. As proof that the two events were not connected, the author of the fact-check, D'Angelo Gore, described a phone conversation between Aaron's family and the Fulton County Medical Examiner's office that said they had no proof the death had been caused by the vaccine.

There was just one problem. No one at the Medical Examiner's office or anywhere else had actually performed an autopsy. The Examiner's office had simply offered its opinion. This inconvenient truth was nowhere in the *Fact-Check* article. Just like the corporate media stories that the piece claimed to "check," it omitted mentioning the lack of an autopsy. In truth, with no autopsy, there was no way to conclude that the vaccine injection had or hadn't played a role in his death.[36]

Maybe the injection contributed to his death, maybe it didn't. Aaron was 86. He certainly could have died of natural causes. On the other hand, there was no data for people in their 80s in the abbreviated safety trials for the Moderna injection he received,[37] the vaccine had already caused hundreds if not thousands of deaths,[38] and he did die relatively soon after receiving the shot with no clear cause of death. There wasn't sufficient evidence either way, but rather than verify and report the *actual facts*, or uncover real proof one way or the other, the "fact-check" declared that the vaccine played no role. It didn't check the facts in question but simply served as another layer of narrative control.

The idea of checking facts appeals to many Americans. Most of us are unable or unwilling to read all sides of an issue. Fact-checking also appeals to the corporate media organizations whose power derives from control of the narrative on important issues. It's thus nearly a perfect tool for narrative management. This particular "fact-check" was sponsored by the Robert Wood Johnson Foundation, which is funded by vaccine-maker Johnson & Johnson.

Writers who pen these "fact-check" articles are often unqualified to critique the claims they examine. In the case of Hank Aaron's death, which some medical doctors said could have been caused by the injection, the assignment to "check facts" was handed to a young man without any medical training named D'Angelo Gore. With a bachelor's degree in journalism, Gore has penned "fact-checks" on topics ranging from strategic petroleum reserves to Disney's tax status in Florida.[39] It was he who reviewed Aaron's death and presumed to declare the case closed. Facebook and Google then used Gore's decision to censor as "misinformation" any opinions—including those of actual doctors—that suggested the injection might have played a role in Aaron's death.

Over the past few years, since Google and Facebook took on major roles in managing the flow of news, there are almost always articles posted by these "fact-check" websites that confirm the corporate media's angle and debunk the assertions of independent media sources. Sometimes, these findings are quite helpful. Independent media is often wrong, too. But on the whole, "fact-check" companies serve primarily to confirm the corporate media's assertions and reinforce their control over the narrative. To put it plainly, "fact-checking" by the organizations listed above doesn't check whether reports, ideas, or assertions are factually true or false. Rather they *check* whether an article, claim, or statement *is in agreement with the dominant narrative.* By providing an imprimatur of objectivity, they play a powerful "meta" role in reinforcing propaganda and censorship.

Thus, "fact-check" companies serve one of the purposes of the original corporate media news stories themselves—to discredit independent media and keep corporate media organizations firmly in control of the narrative. "Fact-checking" not only is shaped by the same filters of *systemic bias* as other components of the corporate media, but through the clever guise of impartiality it provides—in many ways—an even more potent tool for the management of the narrative.

"Fact-checking" organizations now receive most of their funding from the social media corporations that are already managing the narrative alongside the corporate media. This makes *media consciousness* more difficult to attain but also more essential. These relationships between the corporate media, social media, and "fact-checkers" show how complex and sophisticated the narrative management apparatus is in the United States. There's one more important component of modern narrative management we must examine.

ASTROTURFING THE REACTIONARY AGENDA

BY NOW, IT SHOULD BE CLEAR THAT WE LIVE IN A HIGHLY SOPHISTI-
cated propaganda environment in the United States. There is a war on for our
minds. Corporate media coverage suffers from rampant *systemic bias* as well as
mockingbird-style news dissemination with *nefarious bias*. Ubiquitous "fact-
checkers" dig a second moat around the biggest new narratives. The military manipulates Hollywood movie plots[40] while Bill Gates alters television
shows[41] to maintain and expand narrative control.[42] At the annual Sun Valley
media conference, intelligence agencies meet privately with the heads of the
corporate media and social media monopolies to forge mergers and acquisitions that enable these monopolies to grow.[43]

Another way we know we're in a complex new media world is the presence
of ostensibly independent media that is tied to intelligence agencies or legacy
corporate media. The existence of these independent-looking media sources
is more evidence that the legacy corporate media channels, and even the social
media giants, no longer fully control the narrative and worry about the increasing draw and appeal of truly independent media.

This is the notion of "astroturfing." Something—a newspaper or website
or political campaign—is made to appear to be "grassroots" when it's actually a top-down fabrication by powerful reactionary interests. "Astroturf"
sources complicate our task of finding reliable independent media. The ersatz
autonomy provides an essential tool in narrative management by enabling *information laundering*, whereby dubious assertions are planted in "astroturf"
articles so that corporate media can cite them as if they originated organically
in independent reporting.

The media landscape's complexity is why I cannot—as much as I would
love to—present every reader of this book with the one, best news source
that is always honest and unbiased. Unfortunately, there is no Santa Claus.
There's no Tooth Fairy. We don't have one magical, reliable, single source of
truth about the world. Unbiased reporting does exist, but no one source *reliably* delivers it. Media sources that are great often change. Successful independent sites are often acquired (YouTube) or infiltrated (*The Intercept*) or

manipulated (Wikipedia) or purchased (*The Young Turks*) by the corporate media conglomerates or the intelligence community.

This is why a balanced media diet, a range of sources, is the best way to go, as we'll explore in Chapter 13. With a range of different perspectives, it is unlikely that essential sides of major news stories will escape your awareness, despite the censorship, propaganda, and biases in corporate—and corporate-controlled independent—media.

As I first began developing a media diet in 2016, some of my best insights and discoveries came from asking a simple question. *What sources appear to be independent but aren't?* I examined the dynamics and nature of sites' financial sponsors as well as the advertisers they promote. Here's a small sample of the "Astroturf" independent media sources I discovered.

Bellingcat

Styling itself humbly as an "independent international collective of research-ers, investigators, and citizen journalists," Bellingcat looks like an independent journalism mecca. This is how adulatory corporate media articles describe it. This is by design. Scratching the surface reveals countless conflicts of interest and a marked commitment to bolstering corporate media narratives.

Bellingcat is no small potato in the world of international news. Providing significant "independent" research on controversial topics such as the staged chemical gas attack in Douma, Syria, this website is a powerful conduit for *information laundering.* Its analysis of the Syria controversy, for instance, was used in a collaboration by none other than the *New York Times.* "We scoured a portion of the visual evidence with the investigative group, Bellingcat," the *Times* wrote in one of their many "he gassed his own people" articles.[44]

Bellingcat counts among its contributors a shockingly large number of past and present American and British intelligence agents, and it has published a far larger number of investigations into the actions of enemy states than into any actions taken by the US military, corporations, or intelligence agencies.[45] In a thoroughly-researched piece in *Monthly Review Online* in 2021, inde-pendent journalist Alan MacLeod uncovered Bellingcat's funding by Western governments and the number of former military and state intelligence officers on its staff. MacLeod's piece, "How Bellingcat Launders National Security

State Talking Points Into The Press," concludes with this:

> What we are uncovering here is a network of military, state, think-tank and media units all working together, of which Bellingcat is a central fixture. This would be bad enough, but much of its own research is extremely poor. It strongly pushed the now increasingly discredited idea of a chemical weapons attack in Douma, Syria, attacking the members of the OPCW who came forward to expose the coverup.[46]

Bellingcat's founder, Eliot Higgins, worked for over five years as a Senior Fellow at the Atlantic Council's shadowy, CIA-connected Digital Forensic Research Lab, which we discussed in the Ministry of Truth section of Chapter 9.

As for its funding, Bellingcat is largely supported by the National Endowment for Democracy (NED), a Reagan-era creation also connected to the CIA that primarily plans and undertakes regime-change operations in foreign lands. Bellingcat may do some good work, but it is hardly the independent, grassroots, investigative journalism it pretends to be. Instead, it provides a veneer of credibility to the laundering of information by intelligence agencies and makes reactionary agendas appear to be grassroots.

Wikipedia

Founded in 2001 as a decentralized global encyclopedia by entrepreneur Jimmy Wales and philosopher Larry Sanger, Wikipedia grew quickly from humble roots. It started out with a mere few dozen entries but had ten thousand user-created articles by the end of 2001, one million by the end of 2006, and five million by 2015. Today, it has over a million encyclopedic entries in each of two dozen languages and has become the default source of authoritative information for the internet. In the US alone, Wikipedia boasts over 100 million unique visitors annually—over a third of the adult, American population.[47]

Wikipedia is used heavily by Google, which does not use "fact-checking" websites the way Facebook does. The Search behemoth relies instead heavily on Wikipedia for content that is provided in "knowledge boxes" alongside search results. A study found that only one-third of Google searches result in clicks, partly because these boxes provide the information sought. Google has said it will be doing more of this—adding "context" to search results to "counteract misinformation." The idea is to guide you to the answers they believe you should see rather than let you visit the internet directly. Wikipedia has become a perfect source for Google's curated information.

Apple's Siri and Amazon's Alexa also use Wikipedia in this way. Together with Google's largesse, the money Apple and Amazon pay for this service has allowed Wikipedia's parent, Wikimedia, to rake in significant loads of cash. Annual revenue exceeded $150 million in 2021, and the company had well over $300 million in cash on hand, funds that it calls its "endowment." CEO Maryana Iskander commands a team of 500 employees, and she and senior staff take in salaries over $400,000 annually. The site is, of course, maintained using open-source software by millions of volunteers—not paid staff. Former Vice President of Engineering Erik Möller estimated the company could run on $10 million annually if needed. What could all those staff members be doing with the excess millions?

Despite its chests of cash, Wikipedia claims indigence. It holds frequent fundraisers, à la NPR, which burnish its image as a "grassroots" information source. Guilt-inducing ads pop-up regularly, like this plea in 2020:

> This Tuesday, Wikipedia really needs you. This is the 9th appeal we've shown you. 98% of our readers don't give; they look the other way ... We ask you, humbly, don't scroll away.

In 2020, Wikipedia began running ads even in some of the poorest parts of the world, such as India and Latin America, imploring readers for a few dollars.

As for its founders—Wales and Sanger—they arrived at success quite differently. Wales was an entrepreneur and financial trader in Chicago before founding Bomis, one of the internet's first pornography-focused search engines. He cultivates a "playboy of the internet" image after multiple marriages and leads a lavish lifestyle in London. Wales participates in the annual Davos and Sun Valley gatherings of the global rich. His pet peeve, it turns out, is not being called the sole founder of Wikipedia. He was caught editing his own Wikipedia biography page in 2007, deleting language about the pornography-focus of Bomis and removing references to Larry Sanger as his cofounder.

As for Sanger, he comes across as humbler than Wales. A philosopher and computer scientist by training, he first conceived of the idea of basing the partners' nascent encyclopedia on a "wiki," a term for free, collaborative, user-edited content. It's strange that Wales continues to deny Sanger's founding role, as Sanger not only conceived the original technology behind Wikipedia but also devised its original philosophy and policies. His name accompanies Wales's on the original registration of the domain name. Sanger was the only paid Wikipedia employee during its first year of existence.

Sanger left the project fairly early on and has frequently stated his objections to its current editorial approach and algorithms. Over the last few years, his criticism has sharpened. He called Wikipedia "biased propaganda" in 2021,[48] and in an interview with Fox News, he said he was "embarrassed" by what Wikipedia had become.

So, what has Wikipedia become?

For topics that are not in the news, have no bearing on the distribution of power in the world, and do not conflict with dominant news narratives, Wikipedia is a solid—often fantastic—resource for knowledge and information. If you want to know about ancient Roman smelting techniques or the geological formation of the Tierra del Fuego archipelago, for instance, Wikipedia will provide instantaneous and useful information.

For everything else, it's a tool of narrative management. Similar to the "fact checkers" mentioned above, Wikipedia forms a powerful second moat around news narratives because of its image as poor, user-generated, and objective. On any Wikipedia page that is concerned with current events or historical topics in the news, you will be hard pressed to find information contradicting dominant narratives. Pages touching on current events are often quickly locked to prevent updates by everyday people. For anything with a whiff of controversy, Wikipedia entries support the dominant narrative. Jeffery Epstein's page barely mentioned his pedophilia conviction during the decade after his initial conviction before the big media circus of 2019. The page on the origin of the coronavirus buried the theory of the lab origin and dismissed it as a "conspiracy theory." Pages on other pandemic narratives were just as bad. The Great Barrington Declaration, an epidemiological approach to covid without lockdowns supported by over 100,000 scientists, was called "dangerous."[49] Robert F. Kennedy, Jr., the famous environmentalist attorney who questioned the science behind the covid vaccines, was called "a conspiracy theorist."

Wikipedia also defends its fellow narrative managers. MeWe, a competitor to Facebook that is growing in popularity since it does not censor posts, is smeared by Wikipedia as "popular among conspiracy theorists," a place for "extreme views, like... white supremacy," and "a haven for anti-vaxxers."[50]

Like all of these "astroturf" sites, Wikipedia features abundant solid information. But if its content is user-generated, why does this humble nonprofit have such huge revenue streams? The answer is that it performs an important and lucrative role in narrative management in today's complex media world. Wikipedia might be the most dangerous site listed here because its readers don't know the true source of the information. Intelligence agencies and others with a vested interest and a hidden agenda can add or remove information anonymously. This makes it a perfect vehicle for the modern mockingbirds of *nefarious bias.*

The Young Turks

Founded by Cenk Uygur, whom we feature in Chapter 12 as a silenced independent journalist, The Young Turks (TYT) became an early YouTube success story. TYT jumped into independent media with both feet, and in 2006 it was the first daily online streaming program.[51] Uygur joined just as MSNBC was about to fire him for being too progressive. From day one, TYT took an unapologetically progressive angle to news coverage. Over the ensuing decade, it built an online progressive media powerhouse with multiple channels, dozens of shows, and $3 million in annual revenue. TYT provided support, if not an outright launching pad, for many independent, left-leaning journalists who are well known today, including Jimmy Dore, Dave Rubin, Jordan Chariton, Emma Vigeland, Kyle Kulinski, David Pakman, and Sam Seder.

During the pivotal 2016 election campaign, when independent media came of age, TYT became a home for Sanders supporters who abhorred the corporate media's incessant disinformation about their favored candidate. And then everything changed.

Jeffrey Katzenberg, a former chairman of one of the five modern corporate media behemoths, Disney, and a prominent supporter of Hillary Clinton, first provided financial support to TYT at about the same time *Huffington Post* censored me. Uygur and co-hosts Ana Kasparian and Ben Mankiewicz immediately began to talk less about Sanders. The election season continued, Clinton won the primary, and Trump defeated Clinton in the general election. Katzenberg increased his support of TYT in 2017 to the princely sum—for independent media—of $20 million.[52] TYT continued to promote itself with the same language and marketing but began increasingly to resemble, ironically, MSNBC, the network that had fired Uygur. Where once Uygur was silenced by the corporate media giants, he was now handed one of its megaphones, albeit a smaller one.

Today, TYT is a reliable Blue News outlet, a strident supporter of the loyal left side of the Democratic Party. It is no longer independent media, in this sense, as it works to manage the narrative alongside the corporate media, particularly when independent media channels question the narrative in chorus. TYT's truly independent journalists, such as Dore and Chariton, whom we highlight in this book, have long since departed. Uygur still hosts the site and provides skillful *information laundering* for Blue News talking points.

The Intercept

Pierre Omidyar, the billionaire founder of eBay, started a media corporation of his own in 2014. This company debuted with the launch of an online magazine called *The Intercept*. Omidyar's key hire was Glenn Greenwald, one of the English-speaking world's more important independent journalists. Greenwald was immediately appointed the new magazine's editor and publisher, and he brought on board Laura Poitras as a cofounder, a journalist with whom he had worked closely when helping NSA whistleblower Edward Snowden leak his revelations about domestic surveillance. Jeremy Scahill, a longtime national security writer at prominent left-leaning journal *The Nation*, was the other cofounder.

At its founding, *The Intercept* promised to be a voice for privacy, civil liberties, and government transparency. Some of its first published pieces exposed the US drone strike program[53] and revealed how a British intelligence agency sought to digitally surveil every internet user.[54] Right out of the gate, it released additional Snowden NSA documents. It appeared Greenwald had sacrificed none of his integrity to come on board the billionaire tech mogul's project. The magazine garnered praise and a reputation for courageous independent journalism, a reputation it has unfortunately but steadily lost in the ensuing years.

Unusual for a political magazine, *The Intercept's* website is black with white text. This design lends an aura of intrigue and independence. The magazine presents itself as a revealer—an "interceptor"—of secrets, as if by visiting the site you're party to intercepted intelligence. Visitors who value privacy and don't want to share their email address are instructed to get past the site's pay-wall by using their browser's "incognito" tab. *The Intercept* takes privacy and secrecy seriously, it seems. They don't expect you to know that "incognito" browser tabs don't mask your identity or IP address when you visit a website; they only prevent your own computer from storing your browsing history. Being an "interceptor" and "going incognito" provide a powerful, albeit false, visitor experience.

During its heyday in 2016, the magazine burnished its image as a voice independent of the corporate media. Articles by Greenwald, for instance, de-bunked the false narrative of the "Bernie Bros" that was used to drive support from Sanders.[55] The magazine also continued to focus on revealing misdeeds by US government and military agencies. At one point, the US Army took the rare step of singling out *The Intercept* as dangerous, forbidding soldiers from reading it.[56]

The connection to *The Nation* grew from a trickle to a river. Following Scahill were regular *Nation* contributors Naomi Klein and Lee Fang, and then Betsy Reed, longtime executive editor of *The Nation,* was made editor-in-chief of *The Intercept.*

Things changed quickly after the election of Donald Trump. The maga-zine increasingly echoed *The Nation* and more mainstream Blue News outlets in tone and substance, and its *bias* increasingly resembled those pervasive in Silicon Valley chronicled in the previous chapter. It continued to cultivate its image as a place to learn secrets and read narratives outside the mainstream.

In 2019, the magazine printed a long, circuitous, ambivalent piece about the alleged gas attacks in Syria. Written by James Harkin,[57] it muddied the waters, a bit like the *New York Times's* coverage of the Water Protectors in North Dakota. One of the primary sources that the piece relied on was Bell-ingcat.

The Intercept didn't report on Jeffery Epstein prior to his second arrest in 2019. On the Steele dossier and *#Russiagate*—a media narrative it was per-fectly positioned to discredit—its coverage wasn't substantially different from that in Blue News outlets NPR, CNN, and the *New York Times.*

Glenn Greenwald, the magazine's founder, penned an article as the 2020 election neared that was investigative, adversarial, and timely. Focusing on the Hunter Biden laptop and the Bidens' relationship to Ukraine and Burisma, the piece came out right at the time Twitter censored the *New York Post* story. Editor-in-Chief Betsy Reed read Greenwald's piece and blocked it, saying it lacked sufficient evidence. She requested Greenwald remove parts critical of Biden. Greenwald called Reed's spiking of the piece "ridiculous" and just one of many signs that the magazine he had founded had become exactly what it had set out to oppose. Rather than the aggressive "adversarial journalism" that it promised at its founding and on its masthead, and despite its cultivated aura as an independent online voice, *The Intercept* had become another Blue News outlet and lapdog to the powerful brass in the DNC. Greenwald resigned two days later, and what was left of *The Intercept*'s anti-establishment reputation went with him.[58] His cofounder Laura Poitras was fired a month later. Only Scahill, and his connections to *The Nation*, remain.

After watching these developments closely, I recommend Greenwald's independent journalism—and not *The Intercept*—in this book's Balanced Media Diet.

Bellingcat, The Young Turks, Wikipedia, *The Intercept*—a small sampling of the complex and multi-faceted "astroturf" sites, journals, and publications you'll find on the internet today. It is beyond the scope of this book to enumerate what would be an ever-changing list. A primary goal and benefit of *media consciousness* is the development of your own radar to parse independent media reporting.

SHAPING THE PAST, CONTROLLING THE FUTURE

THE PIPES OF THE GREAT WURLITZER ARE NOW PLAYED BY A DIFFERENT set of hands. Where once the agents and complicit journalists of Operation Mockingbird manually selected which of the exquisitely-tuned pipes to sound, the new master musicians have arrived: the social media giants. They have at their disposal the classical musical chords of the *New York Times* and *Washington Post*, the louder notes of Fox and MSNBC, and the steady, dulcet tones of NPR. With "fact-checkers" and "astroturf" sites, together, this marvelous instrument has a range unparalleled in history with which to blast its convincing harmonies and compelling melodies.

Like an opera in its complexity, the corporate media and social media giants bend and shape the day's news to build narratives. The hidden tools of *nefarious bias* plant and spread a poisonous story. The five filters of *systemic bias* remove conflicting perspectives. Affirmative "fact checking" lends the story a veneer of objective approbation. Finally, through *information laundering*, additional distortion on independent-looking "astroturf" sites seals the deal. It doesn't matter if the narratives are true or not. They serve their purpose as long as necessary. When they collapse, as with *#MeToo*, *#Russia-Gate*, and the "radical" Bernie Sanders, they're replaced seamlessly with the next narrative, which is blasted out and repeated until it is accepted.

Poet Muriel Rukeyser wrote, *"the universe is made of stories, not of atoms."*[59] We humans are storytelling creatures. We understand our lives through the stories we tell each other. For thousands of years prior to widespread literacy, we shared our history and cultural knowledge through spoken myths, stories, and folklore. We tend to believe what we hear if it's told in a narrative story. Societies for generations were organized around the Bible or other sacred scripture—*stories* with lessons and morals. These stories mattered to us, informed us, reminded us of where we came from, why we're here, and how to live a meaningful life.

I might take Rukeyser's words one step further: *our lives are made of narratives, not facts.* When we absorb the narratives of the corporate media—and all of us do on some level—we tell ourselves dishonest stories. We become confused and blinded. We forget what is most important to our own personal happiness and health and focus instead on reports, often distorted, about events that are important to those controlling the corporate media narratives.

Most of us already have our own beliefs and narratives about the trajectory of our lives, whether we believe in fate or destiny or not. But when it comes to our role in society and the world, in the absence of a conscious choice to tell ourselves our own narrative about what we are doing and what is worthwhile, the corporate media's narrative floods our consciousness. In the absence of alternative sources of information, we are simply overwhelmed with simple stories that instruct us what to think, what to fear, and what to long for. This is why expanding our consciousness and reclaiming the authority to decide what stories we believe is so important. This is the need for *media consciousness*.

By choosing to cover one thing and not another, the corporate media organizations and those who control them get to determine *what is important*. This is the first part of a narrative: what is included and what is excluded. Selecting what is included isn't just the ability to decide for us what is newsworthy and what isn't; this ability to tell us what is important in the present moment also confers the power to shape the past and the future. The narrative includes what it deems to be important about the past and the future and leaves out the rest.

This power also confers the power to tell us *what to be outraged about*, which in turn determines *what to be satisfied with* and *what must be defended*. We learn implicitly what isn't worth discussing, such as a genocidal war in Yemen or a series of lockdown protests in Australia, and what is important, such as a scandalous speech by Donald Trump or a confirmation hearing for a cabinet position. In this way, the corporate media today distracts us more often than it informs us. The pundits and writers don't discuss the corruption of the political parties, or the false pretenses for past wars, or the social cost of lockdowns, or government surveillance of citizens, and because of this, we don't think these things are important. We thus don't know what is truly important on any given day.

Such a confused and blind citizenry is easier to control. This is why these filters exist and have existed since, at least, the time of Edward Bernays as we will see in the next chapter. Were the propaganda not at work, were the Mockingbird system not at work, were the filters of systemic bias not at work, the media organizations would be unable to exercise this tremendous power over society's views on the world. We would have a freer and fairer society.

Humanity does not want to be at war with itself, but war is profitable and confers control of new natural resources. Human beings generally do not want other human beings to be blown up, dismembered, poisoned, or sickened. But it is quite profitable to blow people up, dismember them, poison them, and sicken them. So, people have to be convinced, cajoled, lied to, deceived, told that other beings deserve to be blown up or dismembered, told that drugs will heal them, and told that illness comes from bad people. It can be profitable to treat illness or bring peace, but even treatments and peace are more profitable if the people never quite get well or the war never quite ends.

Peace and health are the states humanity most longs for. They are also the states that are least advantageous to the drug and weapons corporations and the financial and media corporations that serve them. Neither health nor peace confers power over others nor concentrates wealth in the hands of the few.

Through media consciousness, you will see these things, and they will enrage you. And then, they will set you free. I wrote this book to show us our blindness, for it is upon noticing blindness that we learn to see.

We are awakening today in a New Enlightenment in which we are telling each other our own, better, truer stories.

WHO CONTROLS THE AGENDA?

YOU'VE GOTTEN THIS FAR, SO IF YOU DIDN'T KNOW THEM ALREADY, YOU now know the components of narrative creation and management, and you grasp the three types of media bias—innocent, nefarious, and systemic. You're probably wondering now, what is all the bias and narrative control actually *for*? What is the underlying agenda? What is it that the CIA and the corporate media propaganda machine so desperately advocate? And who exactly are these reactionaries? Who is pulling the strings and controlling the narratives?

The answers to the first few questions aren't hard to put together. As we've seen thus far in this book, the corporate media's objectives are threefold: first, capturing the attention of privileged audiences; second, selling advertising; and third, and by far most importantly, promoting the agenda of billionaires in underhanded ways. While the money made through advertising and selling subscriptions is important, the true treasure fought over by media giants is the power to create and steer the day's news narrative.

Making a catalog of the shifting agendas and narratives wouldn't be entirely useful since they change constantly, but we're taking a broad and useful snapshot. We've looked at war mobilizations, election buildups, protests and marches, and the handling of national emergencies like the covid pandemic. The agenda itself shifts month to month and year to year, but we've already explored many historical events that reveal elements of a high and often hidden agenda, and we can draw some generalizations. When the agenda is hidden, it is usually reactionary—concentrating wealth and power into fewer hands. Attacking countries abroad, reducing civil liberties at home, dividing people based on social controversies, convincing people to be scared and alone—these are things that the reactionary rich typically support but cannot openly advocate as they would run counter to our shared narrative that the United States is a free and peaceful country.

Wealthy and powerful people generally want to become more wealthy and powerful if possible. That's the core of the reactionary agenda: wealth and power. It's not so complex. Those who already have wealth and power want the crowning combination of the two: social control. Social control can prevent loss of wealth and power in the future. If it's not possible to increase their wealth and power, reactionaries obviously want to avoid losing wealth or power. At times, wars are deemed optimal paths to increasing or keeping power, wealth, or control. At other times, exploiting social issues that divide people is useful so as to prevent a mass of people from collaborating and demanding a larger slice of the wealth and abundance that the "elite"[60] enjoy.

The *progressive* political impulse seeks to share wealth and power more broadly among the population to reduce social control and to increase freedom. Despite the term's frequent misuse in corporate media, the progressive impulse always opposes reactionary forces and has done so since the signing of the Magna Carta in 1215, perhaps the birth of Western civilization's modern, progressive era. The Renaissance, the Reformation, the Enlightenment, this country's founding, the abolition of slavery, women's suffrage, civil rights have all been profound—if imperfect—events driven by the progressive impulse. The conservative impulse tends naturally to side against whichever force is ascending in a culture. During the progressive era of the 1960s and 1970s, conservatives sided with the reactionary forces. In today's era of reactionary trends like censorship, lockdowns, and forced vaccinations, many true conservatives are siding with true progressives.

In the ebb and flow between reactionary and progressive impulses, the control of a society's narrative is paramount. Thus, the arrival on the scene by thousands of independent voices countering the corporate media's one narrative poses a formidable threat to reactionaries. This is the *defining political phenomenon of our time*: the birth of the New Enlightenment and the ascendancy of reactionary forces determined to kill it.

Naming Names

As far as *who* the most wealthy and powerful reactionary billionaires are, it is beyond the scope of this book to identify specific names or groups. But since it is helpful to have a general sense of who we are talking about, let's get a sense of where true power and wealth reside. It's not really that hard to identify the globe's truly wealthy and powerful. We're not talking about executive editors at media organizations or congressmen or governors. We're not talking about those who steer powerful, quasi-government organizations like the AMA, CDC, SEC, and FDA, although the *regulatory capture* that corrupts these organizations is a major effect of the problem. For the sake of this book's probe, let's narrow the scope.

This term "elite" goes right to the top, to the most powerful people on Earth. It's only logical that those with the most wealth and power would have the most say, and that's where we'll leave it for this book. We're talking about the new tech billionaires of Silicon Valley and the old money billionaires of the Rockefeller and Rothschild families. We're talking about the establishment royalty permanently invited to the World Economic Forum in Davos, Bohemian Grove, and Sun Valley, and the people who run the largest pharmaceutical, financial, military, energy, and technology corporations.

As far as which of these billionaires pulls the most strings, that's also outside of what we're analyzing. What we do know is that when these titans get together at, say, Sun Valley, Idaho, annually, what takes place, beyond doubt, is that they and their representatives discuss their shared interests. Sometimes, they also take action as a result. That's it. Is that a conspiracy? Is that a secret plan for social control? Maybe so, maybe not. It depends on our definitions of those terms.

From an elementary analysis of the attendees and the results of the Sun Valley conference, for instance, we know billionaires meet up with one another and with CIA directors.[61] The conference frequently leads to starting or stopping mergers of powerful media corporations, such as CNN, WhatsApp, and

Instagram, or brokering the IPOs of companies like Facebook and Google. What these reactionaries are doing is planning the future of the corporate media and social media in ways that will increase their wealth and power.

For the actual editors and reporters and politicians, a great deal about what agenda to pursue is self-evident through the *systemic bias* filters. Most of what they choose *not* to say, write, or discuss is due to self-censorship. There are times when stories are overtly quashed, as we'll see in the next two chapters. There are also times when censored perspectives get through. There is creative and natural leeway built into the system to allow for the natural vagaries of history, undulations of opinion, and vicissitudes of human emotion. History's river is allowed to flow; the river's banks are sculpted.

This narrative control has become an extraordinary, polished art over the past century. Starting with the breakthroughs in psychology pioneered by people like Carl Jung and Sigmund Freud, which informed the work of Edward Bernays and Walter Lippmann in the 1920s, and onward through the twentieth century, the creation of propaganda and the management of narratives are sophisticated instruments in the hands of our society's most powerful members. In the next chapter, we take a step back to look at this history and learn how narrative control began.

11

THE CENTURY OF PROPAGANDA

"These are the times that try men's souls:
The summer soldier and the sunshine patriot will,
in this crisis, shrink from the service of their country;
but he that stands it now, deserves the love and thanks of man and woman.
Tyranny, like Hell, is not easily conquered;
yet we have this consolation with us, that the harder the conflict,
the more glorious the triumph.
What we obtain too cheap, we esteem too lightly:
it is dearness only that gives every thing its value.
Heaven knows how to put a proper price upon its goods;
and it would be strange indeed if so celestial an article
as freedom should not be highly rated."

Thomas Paine

SO WHEN DID THIS ALL BEGIN? HAS THE PRESS ALWAYS DISTORTED REAL-ity? Have we always been at the mercy of censorship and propaganda? Has humanity forever been bullied into fear, deceived into ignorance, lied into war?

Probably.

But an important transformation occurred at the outset of the twentieth century.

Some call this era we're living in the Information Century. Others say it's the Century of Technology. When the history of this epoch is written many years from now, the most compelling label for the last one hundred years will probably be the Century of Propaganda.

In 1917, a man named Edward Bernays implemented novel psychological techniques to manipulate mass opinion about World War I. It was a watershed event, and the mental makeup of this nation's citizens underwent profound change thereafter. Today, we can see that for an entire century many of our basic interpretations of political and economic reality have been consciously and scrupulously manipulated via increasingly sophisticated techniques of *bias, censorship,* and *propaganda*. The American citizenry has become "red, white, and blind."

Before we can investigate the inception of those techniques, we need to understand how we arrived at the current state of journalism—or, *the press,* as it was called in this country's early days.

THE APPEAL OF COMMON SENSE

THE NEWSPAPER, A CURIOUS INVENTION, WAS THE FIRST VEHICLE FOR regular human mass communication. Before newspapers, it was only through oratory that one could communicate with dozens of people at once, but then the audience was always limited. Everyone had to be there, and everyone had to listen at the same time.

The newspaper changed all of this, and human civilization has never been the same. The arrival of the newspaper transformed public awareness and led to an unprecedented flowering in the political and cultural conversations of the world. While there are records of government bulletins in early Roman and Chinese civilizations, the earliest publicly-distributed, recurring newspapers appeared in the seventeenth and eighteenth centuries in major European economic centers. These short bulletins generally reported merchants' daily prices for meat, grain, and other commodities, and occasionally mentioned upcoming public events or entertainment. Their use in political commentary emerged shortly thereafter and demonstrated the truly revolutionary power of the pen.

For the sake of this book, Thomas Paine is the father of independent media. In Philadelphia, in the year 1774, rather than produce a local newspaper helpful to local merchants or a journal of the ongoing decrees emanating from the court of King George III, Paine published a pamphlet advocating independence from Great Britain. The pamphlet, *Common Sense,* changed the world. Paine trumpeted in his own eloquent prose the Enlightenment ideals of democracy, free thought, and self-determination. He issued a clarion call to human potential. This profound publication crystallized opinion across the colonies. *Common Sense* was read aloud in halls, homes, and taverns across the land, and its words played no small role in bringing about this independent country of ours in 1776. *Common Sense* incidentally remains the best-selling American title in history on a proportional basis.

Similar pamphlets advocating similar ideals brought about the French Revolution a decade later. In response, the British Crown enacted harsh censorship laws at the time that suppressed the spread of enlightenment ideals and arguably prevented a similar revolution there.

Witnessing the power of the press, and the terrifying prospect of censorship, the framers of the American Constitution wrote into the First Amendment uncompromising guarantees of Free Speech and a Free Press. Independently produced pamphlets and newspapers played a critical role in attaining freedom, and it was noble and farsighted that this country's early leaders saw fit to guarantee the right of anyone to produce independent news in their young Republic rather than fear the effects that a Free Press might have on their own power.

The Free Press safeguarded in the Constitution makes no mention of "journalists," "newspapers," professional reporters, licensed writers, editors, or anything of the sort. Just as Freedom of Speech is the freedom for *anyone* to say *anything* aloud he or she sees fit to say, Freedom of the Press is the freedom for *anyone* to print and distribute *anything* they like. Libel laws would come later and define the types of personal attacks that are legal (in summary, anything *true* is fair game), but there was no intention to grant writers at, say, large newspaper or cable news networks, a set of rights for their writing more powerful than those of anyone else. Everyone's writings can be published and distributed broadly and without limit. The Freedom of Assembly allows anyone the right to *gather* a crowd for the purpose of speaking *en masse*. The Freedom of the Press guarantees anyone—regardless of profession, wealth, or station—the right to *publish* and *distribute* his or her thoughts for the benefit of our democracy and the enlightenment of the citizenry.

The Constitution's architects, having suffered years of censorship by the British, didn't add these freedoms as an afterthought. Front and center in the First Amendment, the Freedom of the Press stands right next to the Freedom of Speech, the Freedom of Assembly, and the Freedom of Religion. The Framers knew a fundamental truth of governments and human nature: the freedom to speak one's mind is essential for liberty, and the freedom to publish is inextricably linked to the freedom to speak.

Thomas Jefferson famously commented, "Left to me to decide whether we should have a government without newspapers, or newspapers without a government, I should not hesitate a moment to prefer the latter."

The Press Freedom Explosion

As the young nation entered the 1800s, printing technology and shipping modes advanced quickly. Journals and periodicals that covered local news, public events, and political commentary proliferated in number and grew in size and scope. By the middle of the 1800s, most major cities had a daily newspaper. Additional advances in ink and paper led to ever more available newspapers at ever-cheaper prices in cities around the country. The same trends were unfolding all over the world. Many newspapers became overtly political, some even playing cogent roles in revolutions. For this reason, authoritarian governments overseas often censored newspapers. In some ways, it was a flowering of new, independent media just like the one we are witnessing today. Leaps in technology brought everyday people a broader awareness of the world.

In the young United States, as the era of national growth and expansion unfolded, newspapers flourished, covering the day's events in each city, broadcasting public events, listing market prices, and shaping public opinions. The federal government guaranteed cheap "bulk rate" mail service for the sake of political communication. This further enhanced the distribution of newspapers and periodicals, enabling them to reach ever-larger audiences. Soon, major cities had multiple daily newspapers with divergent tastes, viewpoints, and coverage. The disparate journals of the time, as a whole, generally fulfilled all three essential duties of the press in a democracy—watchdog, smorgasbord, and bulletin.

Every paper had its audience and its bias.

There was no "journalism," at least not in the modern sense. No publications purported to be "neutral" on political events, and no one would have believed such pretensions anyway.

Robert McChesney, author of several books on the history and problems of corporate media, including *Rich Media, Poor Democracy*, documents quite well the *innocent bias* at the very heart of our original national media.

> The notion that journalism should be politically neutral, nonpartisan, professional, even "objective," is not much more than one hundred years old. During the first two or three generations of the Republic, such notions for the press would have been nonsensical, even unthinkable. The point of journalism was to persuade as well as inform, and the press tended to be highly partisan ... It was understood that if the government could outlaw or circumscribe newspapers, it could effectively eliminate the ability of opposition parties or movements to mobilize popular support. It would kill democracy.[1]

Such was the diversity of opinion published on a daily and weekly basis in the United States that at the time of the Civil War in the 1860s most major American cities enjoyed a wide variety of daily and weekly newspapers. Large cities all had multiple daily newspapers—some had over a dozen—each representing a known group or viewpoint. A city might have a labor newspaper, or two, an Italians' newspaper, a Catholic newspaper, a newspaper reflecting the viewpoints of the new Republican Party, and so on, and many derided the coverage of other papers. One of the nation's most important investigative journalists, Ida Wells, published investigative reports in the 1890s in *The Memphis Free Speech* that uncovered the truth about lynchings in Tennessee. Wells, who was Black, found that her reports were often called "fake news" by competing newspapers.

As the era after the Civil War gave way to the Progressive Era, it remained relatively easy to start up a new newspaper, and many came and went. Education across the states improved, and the population exploded. Each city, state, and territory boasted larger and larger literate audiences hungry for daily news.

Financially, alongside the penny or nickel each issue garnered on the street, advertising turned into a gold mine. The money made by publishing newspapers—as well as the power to be gained by persuading minds—became irresistible to the country's new wealthy businesses, and this is when things began to change. Newspaper corporations were born. Alongside the oil, railroad, and automotive corporations of the day, these growing news companies steadily acquired or founded newspapers in other cities, increasing their power and reducing the diversity of opinion available to American readers. Control of the newspaper industry at the turn of the twentieth century was beginning to fall into the hands of large, multiple-paper-owning concerns in what we could call this country's first era of media consolidation. It became difficult for small, independent newspapers to succeed since the large corporations could attract advertising across markets. Before long, all but the largest communities only had one or two dailies. This state of affairs, in which new newspapers ran into significant "barriers to entry," drew fierce criticism from the burgeoning progressive movement of the time. The Constitution's Free Press guarantee and the success of democracy were in danger, much as they are today.

McChesney describes the sentiment of the era:

> It was one thing to posit that a commercial media system worked for democracy when there were numerous newspapers in a community, when barriers to entry were relatively low, and when immigrant and dissident media proliferated widely, as was the case for much of the nineteenth century. For newspapers to be partisan at that time was no big problem because there were alternative viewpoints present. It was quite another thing to make such a claim by the late nineteenth and early twentieth centuries when all but the largest communities only had one or two newspapers, usually owned by chains or very wealthy and powerful individuals. For journalism to remain partisan in this context, for it to advocate the interests of the owners and the advertisers who subsidized it, would cast severe doubt on the credibility of the journalism.[2]

The press and the powerful have always existed in tension. This was certainly true at the turn of the twentieth century, and Progressive Era reformers like Upton Sinclair and Robert La Follette challenged concentrated corporate control of the media. Progressives were outraged at a corporate press purporting to operate for the sake of a functional democracy while raking in cash and exploiting outsized political influence. In many instances, the wealthy purchased the large urban papers in order to ensure that their preferred version of events was reported.

This era of outrage and media consolidation birthed a new type of reporting: investigative journalism. Called "muckraking" at the time, investigations into corporations' unbridled power began to expand the *watchdog* role of the media, holding the powerful to account in a new way. In 1903, a writer named Ida Tarbell began to publish a stunning series in the magazine *McClure's* entitled *The History of the Standard Oil Company*.[3] John D. Rockefeller, the richest man in the world at the time, did not take kindly to the publication of Tarbell's exquisite research. Her series recounted in grave detail the amoral business practices he had used to build Standard Oil into the towering monopoly that it was.

Rockefeller's response wasn't unlike the response of the world's richest men today—Bezos and Gates. The oil tycoon refused to publicly engage in a rebuttal and instead initiated one of the largest influence operations in American history, hiring, bribing, and buying journalists and newspapers from New York to Georgia. All the while, he branded himself a philanthropist, not unlike Gates today.

The truth has a power all its own, of course, and in this instance its power overcame the will to suppress it by the powerful. Tarbell's series became a groundbreaking book, and her writings led to the passage of antitrust legislation, a Supreme Court case, and eventually the breakup of Standard Oil itself.

The Invention of Journalism

Rockefeller and the reactionary barons of his era were aghast. They couldn't abide the thought of journalists freely publishing critical investigations. They realized they needed something even more powerful than mere ownership of newspapers. They needed to control the expansion of this new, independent media. What they came up with would set the course for the American press for the next century.

They devised "objective, professional journalism."

"Objective, professional journalism" would produce "neutral reporting" of the events of the day, they declared. This would help Americans understand the issues of the day, they said, and also justify their control of it. Because each paper would be neutral, anyone could read it and find it sufficient; because it was neutral and sufficient, a city needed only one paper; because a city needed only one paper, there would be only one owner; because there would be only one owner, that owner could be the wealthiest person or company in town or even a corporation from another state. In order for journalism to be "objective" and "professional," it would become a new profession available only to those who went to special schools, they said.

McChesney provides insight and useful facts about the era:

> Leading reformers, like Robert La Follette of Wisconsin, argued that the commercial press was destroying democracy in its rabid service to the moneyed interests. As Henry Cullen Adams put it at the time, "The press is the hired agent of a moneyed system, set up for no other reason than to tell lies where the interests are concerned." In 1919, Upton Sinclair published his opus, *The Brass Check*, which provided the first great systematic critique of the limitations of capitalist journalism for a democratic society ... In short, it was widely thought that journalism was explicit class propaganda in a war with only one side armed... Acceptance of these beliefs was very dangerous for the business of newspaper publishing, as many potential readers would find newspapers incredible, propagandistic, and unconvincing...

> Savvy publishers understood that they needed to have their journalism appear neutral and unbiased, notions entirely foreign to the journalism of the republic's first century, or their businesses would be far less profitable... Publishers pushed for the establishment of formal "schools of journalism" to train a cadre of professional editors and reporters. None of these schools existed in 1900; by 1920, all the major schools such as Columbia, Northwestern, Missouri, and Indiana were in full swing. The revolutionary and unprecedented notion of a separation of the editorial operations from the commercial affairs—termed the separation of church and state—became the professed model. The argument went that trained editors and reporters were granted autonomy by the owners to make the editorial decisions, and these

decisions were based on their professional judgment not the politics of the owners and the advertisers, or their commercial interests to maximize profit... Readers could trust what they read... Owners could sell their neutral monopoly newspapers to everyone in the community and rake in the profits.[4]

This cynical but eminently opportunistic act—the invention of "objective, professional journalism" for the sake of justifying concentrated media ownership—marks the dawn of the century of propaganda. Rockefeller founded journalism schools in order to acquire more newspapers and thereby control more of the nation's narratives. This makes him, for our sake, the father of *nefarious bias.*

The timing was perfect. Rockefeller's act, which led to the emergence of powerful journalistic institutions, coincided with the invention of propaganda and the beginning of mass psychological manipulation in the 1920s.

ONE HUNDRED YEARS OF DECEIT

STARTING A WAR IS NEVER IN THE INTEREST OF THE PEOPLE WHO WILL be asked to fight it. The poor, young men usually sent off to combat have little if anything to gain and their lives to lose. Rather, starting wars is chiefly in the interest of reactionaries, those with wealth and power, those who can command a military from afar, and those who will benefit financially from the spoils of conquest. As we've documented throughout this book, some level of dishonesty—be it subtle or overt—is nearly always necessary to assemble a willing army and a supportive populace. This was required in 1917 just as it was in 1941 and 2003.

---

*"Whether it is a democracy or a fascist dictatorship
... the people can always be brought to the bidding of the leaders.
That is easy. All you have to do is tell them they are being attacked
and denounce the pacifists for lack of patriotism, and exposing the
country to greater danger. It works the same way in any country."*
—Nazi Military Commander Hermann Goering

We could go all the way back to what was called "yellow journalism," which predates propaganda by a few decades, and examine the fake attack on the USS Maine[5] in 1898 that served as a pretext to start the "Spanish-American War." Even the name of this war implies that Spain was the aggressor, which it wasn't. William Randolph Hearst and Joseph Pulitzer's newspapers sensationalized the attack,[6] leading the country into war, inaugurating a grand American tradition of starting wars on false pretenses.

But the true origins of the American—and global—use of modern propaganda must be traced to the pivotal year of 1917, the year the United States entered World War I.

It was at this time, coinciding with breakthroughs in psychology and telecommunications, that the two men whom we will call the fathers of propaganda—Edward Bernays and Walter Lippmann—first wrote about the nature of manipulating the media and implemented mass market advertising.

As part of the buildup to joining that war, the government organized the Committee on Public Information (CPI). The CPI became a powerful propaganda apparatus, packaging, advertising, and selling the war to the American people. The war would "make the World Safe for Democracy," Americans were told. As the war commenced, and the US joined, Bernays became an integral leader of the CPI. He pioneered what appears to be the first of many scientific techniques for shaping and manipulating public opinion, which he famously dubbed the "engineering of consent."

Bernays, in particular, is a fascinating figure, a pioneer of psychological manipulation who devised countless ways to change popular opinion about things ranging from bananas to the color green. After the war, he moved into civilian life and founded an advertising firm that pioneered the field now known as public relations. He helped corporations sell a broad variety of products by applying the techniques he had learned in the CPI. He cultivated the art of manipulating the mindset of Americans toward products, people, and, most of all, ideas. He devised the campaign that made smoking cigarettes fashionable for women by manipulating the feminist movement to see cigarettes as symbols of freedom from patriarchal dominance; this worked and doubled tobacco company revenues. He established diamond rings as the symbols of marriage; this ingenuity secured billions in profits for the diamond industry. He convinced the American public that bacon and eggs was the true American breakfast. His uncle was none other than Sigmund Freud, and his knowledge of cutting-edge psychological manipulation was no coincidence.

As for wars and propaganda, Bernays's groundbreaking work at the CPI would become the blueprint upon which propaganda strategies for future wars were based. In 1919, with the American military returning home triumphant from the largest war in which it had ever fought, and American power poised to expand for the foreseeable future, Bernays became an outspoken proponent of the use of propaganda to manipulate the population.

Propaganda Will Save Us

Although he made quite a fortune off his ideas, Bernays appears to have been a true believer. He clearly viewed himself as patriotic. He advocated for the broad use of propaganda—as did many reactionaries at the time—in the earnest belief that marshaling public consciousness was necessary for stable democracy and profitable commerce.

His 1928 book *Propaganda* remains a revelation a century later. A quick read at 165 pages, the book lays out his eerily prescient vision for the use of narrative management. He proposed repeated, media-driven, psychological manipulation on a massive scale to regiment the nation's collective mind. He focused on areas of public perception, including government, politics, art, science and education. To read his opus today is to comprehend what our contemporary institutions of government and business have become:

> The conscious and intelligent manipulation of the organized habits and opinions of the masses is an important element in democratic society. Those who manipulate this unseen mechanism of society constitute an invisible government which is the true ruling power of our country.[7]

This "unseen mechanism," to Bernays's obviously brilliant mind, was a benign force.

Along with many of the ideas of his contemporary, Walter Lippmann, this formed a new field, a new practice, a new technology: the creative distortion of mass opinion. This field of practice grew to encompass not just propaganda but advertising and public relations. The field didn't simply mature over a couple of years. It was continuously refined over the ensuing century into the astonishingly sophisticated artform we see today. After Bernays established the foundation of psychological manipulation of mass opinion through narrative management, the stage was set for the growth of public relations during decades of advancement in cognitive psychology. It became a billion-dollar industry before the century was over, honed through repetition, utilized to the lucrative ends of sales and political power.

Societal storytelling itself is not bad. Large cultures *do* need shared myths and stories. A society's narrative is a potent force in steering its development, as we've explored throughout this book, and some narrative will always materialize as a nation grows and changes. This is why it is essential to be *conscious* of the narratives of the society in which one lives and to be vigilant if these narratives are artificially managed with ulterior motives.

This country's founding narrative—that "all men are created equal"—was deeply flawed since only wealthy White men could vote at the time of the nation's founding. Yet the notion encapsulated in that phrase was radically progressive and energizing; its five little words departed irrevocably from monarchy and aristocracy and set the nation on the course it has taken, bumpy as it has been, toward liberty and justice for all. The balance of the narrative asserts that government is established to "ensure domestic tranquility, provide for the common defense, promote the general welfare, and secure the blessings of liberty;" and that we all have the right to speak, assemble, petition, worship, and publish as we see fit. These creeds too have proven powerfully valid as we have slowly evolved toward their lofty ideals.

Some Americans today say it is the nation's current lack of a shared narrative that most divides us. Creating a shared narrative via propaganda, censorship, and narrative management, they say, is the best way to keep our nation at peace. Perhaps Bernays himself saw it this way. Perhaps he thought propaganda was simply a way to ensure the healthy evolution of our nation's grand project. Perhaps he sought to mold the minds of the masses with high and ethical intent.

Even if that was the case, and I'm not certain it was, the Mighty Wurlitzer is far too dangerous a machine to build and hand to a government composed of power-seeking human beings. Empowering a nation to manipulate its people's minds—rationalizing lies and celebrating deception—carries simply too great a risk. Power corrupts, even if granted benevolently. Enabling the powerful to foster and hide corruption would be to enable it to stay in power forever.

Thomas Jefferson wrote eloquently that he would prefer that the young American nation had a variety of newspapers rather than a government if it had to choose. If the narratives encapsulated in our founding documents are not enough to unite the country, the nation's new narrative must unfold organically, through millions of Americans using the freedoms of speech and press to write our shared past, present, and future. Together, we humans must tell each other stories as we always have. Propaganda won't save us. Censorship won't help us. Only speaking freely and listening to one another will forge us anew. *Media consciousness* and a Balanced Media Diet don't only allow us to understand current events better. They allow us to better hear and understand each other.

The Four Horsemen of the Mediapocalypse

The development of sophisticated propaganda in the 1920s coincided with the arrival of a brand new medium for mass communication: radio. The nation entered the era of radio and propaganda at the same time. It was also the era in which "objective, professional journalism" took root, a time in which the broad flowering of news and analysis in newspapers that had blossomed in the 1800s slowed considerably. The variety and volume of independent voices were diminishing in each city's newspapers and, now, radio stations.

Debates about the Freedom of the Press took center stage, and for the first time, government regulation intervened to protect the diversity of media voices. Because the radio spectrum is limited (unlike the paper needed to print a newspaper), the Radio Act of 1927, established the federal government as the owner of the radio spectrum and the provider of licenses to broadcasters. A new Federal Radio Commission declared that licenses would be granted based on broadcasters' promises to "serve the public interest," and that "the emphasis must be first and foremost on the interest, the convenience, and the necessity of the listening public, and not on the interest, convenience, or necessity of the individual broadcaster or the advertiser."[8] Advertising was frowned upon and opposed by listeners, but by 1930, advertising on radio was firmly established, and the growing force advertising had begun to play in the news media accelerated with the advent of radio.

In addition to the increasingly corrosive effects of advertising, and the new deceptive practice of propaganda, the increasing consolidation of media ownership behind the facade of "objective journalism" constricted the quantity and quality of news coverage in the 1920s and 1930s. Together, these were the four horsemen of a news media apocalypse galloping across the twentieth century:

1. the increasingly powerful but cloaked interests of **advertisers**

2. the disingenuous messages of **propaganda** masquerading as public relations

3. the **consolidated ownership** of media outlets in fewer hands

4. the **pretense** of "objective, professional journalism"

The countervailing force was government regulation, until it was dismantled at the end of the twentieth century. The formation of the Federal Communications Commission in 1934 promulgated the news media's most important twentieth century legal standard. The "fairness doctrine," born first out of the Mayflower Decision in 1941, codified more formally with the 1949 Broadcast Licensees Report, was the fledgling FCC's mandate that broadcasters promote "a basic standard of fairness." Along with bandwidth, licensees were assigned the duty of presenting *controversial* issues that were of interest to their communities and to devote airtime to fair and balanced coverage of those issues. Minority opinions had to be presented even if they weren't given equal time. One-sided news reports were technically illegal.

To some extent, the "fairness doctrine" simply extended the facade of "objective journalism" to radio—and eventually television—but it also paved the way for the exemplary journalism that did occur in the 1900s.

Starving for the Truth

As for the increasing presence of propaganda, one of the lowlights of corporate media at the time was the work of our favorite "paper of record," the *New York Times,* and its coverage of Russia. It seems the American media has always been congenitally allergic to reporting fairly on events concerning the globe's largest country. I say this as an American of Lithuanian extraction with no particular love of Russia's actions, particularly during the early twentieth century. What was interesting about the coverage of the Soviet Union during the 1930s is that the communist country was actually an ally of the reactionary class in America at the time. *Nefarious bias* was already rife at the time but *favoring* Russia.

In 1932, Joseph Stalin brutally forced the farms of his enormous nation into agricultural communes and collectives, transferring control of the farms to the government. In short order, brutal famines swept the land, particularly in Ukraine,[9] the Northern Caucasus,[10] and Kazakhstan.[11] Millions of farmers and peasants across the country grew desperate, found they had little to eat month after month, and slowly starved to death. The horrendous mass starvation went on throughout 1932 and 1933. Today, some refer to the man-made famines as genocide.

A *New York Times* journalist named Walter Duranty, one of the paper's most famous correspondents at the time, won a Pulitzer Prize for 13 articles that he wrote that very year analyzing the Soviet Union. Writing from Moscow, behind the Iron Curtain, he reported back to a curious nation with an "objective" journalist's credibility. He reassured America. Rather than expose the widespread suffering, he disingenuously transcribed Soviet propaganda into the pages of the *Times.* Duranty never chose to reveal the dire situation nor even directly quote any Russian citizens. "Conditions are bad, but there is no famine," he famously wrote in 1933, portraying the situation of the farmers, many of whom were literally starving to death as he wired his articles home.[12]

The Times didn't let him go until 1941. In response to calls to rescind his prize, the Pulitzer Prize committee investigated his pieces and found deception, yes, but not of a "deliberate" nature.[13] Millions of rural farmers and villagers behind the Iron Curtain died of a brutal and needless famine, and yet Americans were delivered not news, but disinformation, stamped with the imprimaturs of *The New York Times* and a Pulitzer Prize. It was neither the first nor the last time that the *Times* would splash disinformation and propaganda across its pages, of course, but it is painful nonetheless to recall the paper's defense of Joseph Stalin.

Long before the inception of Operation Mockingbird, *nefarious bias* played a major role in deceiving the American people.

A GRADUAL NARROWING OF THE CONVERSATION

BY 1945, THE MODERN ERA OF NEWS BEHEMOTHS HAD BEGUN. MOST American newspapers were owned by a dozen or so large companies that dictated what most people read: Gannett, The McClatchy Company, Hearst Corporation, Cox Enterprises, Landmark Media, Morris Communications, Tribune Company, and a few others. As for radio, and eventually television, NBC staked a large lead quickly and was by far the biggest when World War II began, rivaled only by CBS. In fact, NBC commanded such a large portion of the airwaves in 1942 that the FCC split it up. Its offshoot became... ABC.

While the four horsemen galloped through the 1950s and into the 1960s, the countervailing force of regulation survived, barely. On account of the "fairness doctrine," media corporations that gobbled up competitors were at pains to present editorial rooms that at least appeared to be independent from advertising departments. For the most part, this was a facade, but a handful of principled journalists and editors at major corporate news outlets wrote exemplary investigative pieces throughout the eras of the Cold War and the cultural upheaval of the 1960s.

It was what could be called the golden era of "objective journalism." Many journalists received significant resources to pursue their craft and enjoyed relative autonomy to investigate controversial stories and perform the *watchdog* and *smorgasbord* roles of the press. But even at its best, as we saw with the *Times'* coverage of the Soviet famines, corporate media outlets never truly opposed what Eisenhower famously called "the military-industrial complex."

Operation Mockingbird was in full swing at this time, and intelligence operations that honed the art of propaganda managed narratives with increasing precision. Every serious publication and news station seemed to support imperialist wars and the push of imperial capitalism under the guise of "free trade."

Gary Webb, a Pulitzer Prize winner and one of the many exemplary journalists of this era, explained his realizations after being run out of his profession for reporting on troubling, clandestine CIA activities in Central America:

> The reason I'd enjoyed such smooth sailing for so long hadn't been, as I'd assumed, because I was careful and diligent and good at my job. The truth was, in all those years, I hadn't written anything important enough to suppress.[14]

A final countervailing force to the horsemen was the sudden era of transparency that descended on the country after the assassinations and coups of the previous decade. As explored, the Church Committee revealed not only Operation Mockingbird but also other shocking ways the intelligence agencies were manipulating American culture. Out of this era came an important partner to the "fairness doctrine," the "cross-ownership" ban, added by the FCC in 1975. This prevented ownership by a single corporate entity of a daily newspaper and a television or radio station operating in the same market. On the meritorious grounds that narrow news media ownership is tantamount to censorship, this ban extended what passes for the golden era of corporate journalism.

The Modern World

The final decades of the twentieth century witnessed the ascendancy of television and the acceleration of corporate media consolidation. The voices were already narrowing, but a series of "media deregulation" laws passed during the Reagan administration and completed during the Clinton era pounded one nail after another into the coffin of the era of corporate "objective journalism." The year 1985 was a watershed. Reagan's FCC decided that the "fairness doctrine" had a "chilling effect" upon Freedom of Speech (for media corporations). The fairness doctrine was thus not extended to nascent cable and satellite television news networks. This ushered in the biased networks that we know today and the unfettered control of the news media by a handful of corporations. Two years later, the FCC formally repealed the fairness doctrine but maintained both the editorial and personal-attack provisions, which remained in effect until 2000.

Even more expeditious to the four horsemen of media distortion was the Telecommunications Act, signed by Bill Clinton in 1996. This was the death knell to what remained of media diversity in the country. While its proponents who worked in public relations or wrote for existing media behemoths predictably promised the act would increase competition and diversity in the news media, it did exactly the opposite. Over 4,000 radio stations were bought out, and minority ownership of television stations dropped to its lowest point since the federal government began tracking such data. Virtually every small- and medium-sized media company that preserved some modicum of diversity of perspective were swallowed up by the new supranational media conglomerates that owned not just the newspapers but the radio stations, the television stations, the popular magazines, the book publishing companies, and the movie studios.

What laws remained on the books preventing media consolidation were repealed or rewritten during Clinton's second term, and the century-long shift of control of the press from individual publishers to media corporations was complete. This further narrowed the range of voices heard in mainstream media and led to the pervasive *systemic bias* across corporate news we see today. In 2011, under Obama, all 80 remaining media rules that retained fairness doctrine language were removed. In a short 14 years, the media landscape contracted into a misshapen, top-heavy silo.

And that brings us to the current era. Within each corporate newspaper, magazine, and television show, there is some independence for individual journalists, but those who are promoted to positions of prominence are those whose opinions match those of the parent corporation's ownership. As we will examine carefully in the next chapter, those who insist on voicing opinions that are "too independent"—such as telling the truth during the buildup to a war—are fired as a matter of course. The culture of "uniformity and obedience" that we mentioned in Chapter 1 permeates the halls of the modern corporate media.

The myriad voices under countless banners that flowered at the end of the nineteenth century became *eight* giant media conglomerates at the end of the twentieth century and then *six* in 2010.[15] Today, just *five* behemoths control the majority of what Americans hear, read, and watch.[16] On topics ranging from local news to national news, from party politics to identity politics, from the culture wars to the overseas wars, what Americans know has become primarily what these corporations choose to say. Americans, that is, who still depend on corporate media for their information.

This slow, steady consolidation of newspapers and media companies at the end of the twentieth century extinguished countless, legitimate avenues of inquiry and modes of analysis. At the same time, intelligence agencies used mockingbird techniques to distribute distorted viewpoints and versions of events, manipulating the news to subvert Americans' ability to discern the truth. The events of September 11, 2001 further narrowed acceptable discourse, as journalists themselves were subject to the Bush doctrine of "you're either with us or against us" in what he called a "fight against terror." It's even easier to control the narrative when you reduce the number of voices interpreting world events. Perspectives outside the establishment narrative grew precious and scarce in corporate media. Increasingly, Americans despaired over the absence of truthful and investigative news coverage; public trust in the mainstream corporate news declined from low to very low.

The four horsemen galloped into the twenty-first century unopposed. That is, except for one little detail. A twinkle in the eye of Tim Berners-Lee at CERN in the 1980s led to a new mode of communication that would sweep the planet. It was a decentralized channel of communication, and it had the potential to revolutionize the sharing of knowledge the way that newspapers first did in the 1600s. The question was, would this new mode of communication—this world wide web of knowledge—flower? Would it support myriad independent voices? Would it reinvigorate the Freedom of the Press as envisioned by the framers of the US Constitution during the first Enlightenment? Or would it be bought and manipulated by the same power-thirsty corporations that already control the lion's share of ideas available to Americans?

These questions face our nation today, and they inspired me to write this book. As we head into the middle of the twenty-first century, we must confront them.

We turn now to a troubling event that recently asked America these very questions.

POISONING THE WELL

THE MAYOR LAID A FINGER ON A LARGE, BLACK BUTTON BUT DID NOT push it. He was standing at the control boards of a water treatment plant. His name was Dayne Walling, and the date was April 25, 2014. A dozen other local officials were assembled in the squat concrete building, looking on, waiting for Mayor Walling to push the button. The onlookers included Darnell Earley, a man recently assigned Emergency Manager of the troubled city and thereby given more power than Mayor Walling himself possessed.

The mayor led everyone in a countdown.

"Three... two... one... Go!"

With that, Walling pushed the button. The plant's pumps slowed and ground to a halt.[17] This, in turn, routed the water of the nearby Flint River into the homes of the residents of Flint, Michigan.

From that moment, it would take forty-eight hours for the water of Lake Huron—the water that Flint's residents had consumed for decades—to be fully flushed out of the city system. What was rushing toward the unsuspecting 100,000 residents of the city was a stream of polluted water, mysterious disease, government deceit, and distorted news reports.

Toxic Silence

Residents began complaining immediately. The water coming out of their faucets had an unusual color, smell, and frothiness, many said. What they didn't know, and wouldn't be told for years, was that the water was poisonous. It carried astronomical levels of toxic bacteria and heavy metals. Also, since the river water was many times more corrosive than the water pumped from Lake Huron, and since no one had bothered with corrosion control, lead leached out of the pipes and into the bloodstreams of the residents of the poor city.

Their complaints intensified, but the days turned to weeks before any coverage appeared in the local media. The first piece to appear in local media was a television news segment on May 16, 2014, *three weeks* after the switch to river water. The piece, "How Safe Is Your Tap Water?," aired on WNEM, local Channel 5. The reporter acknowledged, "TV5 has received several complaints about the smell and taste of Flint's drinking water."[18] But he went on to dispel these concerns. The piece did not raise any type of alert, formal or informal. There was no reason to be concerned.

Another week went by before the local print newspaper, the *Flint Journal,* weighed in. They interviewed a single local resident who had complaints about the water.

> "It's just weird," she said of the water coming out of her tap, which she described as murky or foamy...

That article, "State Says Flint River Water Meets All Standards but More Than Twice the Hardness of Lake Water," didn't delve any further or offer any more detailed descriptions of the water's quality. It instead discounted people's concerns.

> Initial testing of treated Flint River water shows it's meeting all quality standards set by the state...[19]

The article dismissed concerns about the water by describing it as simply "70% harder" and "higher in compounds of calcium and magnesium" than the Lake Huron water the people were used to.

The poisonous water was already giving people a serious and uncommon bacterial pneumonia called Legionnaire's disease. People were breaking out in skin rashes and losing clumps of hair. But the heavy metals—the lead in particular—were the worst: children were developing cognitive impairments and brain abnormalities. It would be many, many months before the full extent of the water's toxicity and the harm it was causing would emerge. While the callous and profiteering decision to turn a blind eye to the poisoning of the people of Flint was due to endemic corruption in Michigan state politics, the blame for the deadly delay in informing people lies squarely at the feet of the corporate media.

The Dogs that Didn't Bark

Perhaps the strangest part of the early phase of this story is that the prices citizens were paying for their water went *up*. The whole point, according to media pundits, was to help the largely poor city residents save money, but despite the water switch, citizens were asked to pay more for drinking water than in neighboring counties. The city was profiting while poisoning its people. Soon, many people couldn't afford their local water and stopped using it. This created thousands of desperately thirsty people, which led to people "stealing" water. In a stunning display of narrative management, the media focused on the putative crime of stealing—not the corruption or the poisonous water.

So many articles appeared about people "stealing water" that when the first "Boil Your Water" advisories were published by city government in August, the local media treated it as a secondary concern. Thirsty poor folks were called "thieves" who were blatantly "stealing water." With what can only be considered the flimsiest of ethics, the media ran articles quoting local government officials on only this topic. The officials complained that people who were unable to afford the bills for the water—which, despite its awful quality, had skyrocketed to an average monthly cost of $140—were finding ways to acquire water and survive. In one instance, a city employee, who happened to have a heart, regularly left a public building's outdoor faucet running, knowing that the parched locals had no other way to survive.

Although it wasn't often mentioned in media reports, yes, human beings do need water to survive. Human beings, in fact, need water far more than they need governments, newspapers, or public utilities. Local experts and media reports overlooked this. It's a common effect of the filters of *systemic bias*: corporate media shifts the focus away from negligence or crimes by elite government and corporate actors and onto minor peccadillos in the victims. Thus, the coverage spent far more time defending the expensive water system than acting as a *watchdog* for the basic human right to safe, sufficient, physically accessible, and affordable water.[20]

The *Flint Journal* ran an investigative piece on September 7, the same week as the second "Boil Water" alert. Was it about the poisonous water now piped into the homes of local residents? No. The narrative management continued. "Flint Officials Confirm 'Massive' Water Theft Investigation and Crackdown" was the title of the piece. It sounded the alarm again on water "theft." It called the problem "massive" and "growing." It featured a series of shocking quotes from the local sheriff, Robert Pickell.

I know that for people who are on fixed incomes, those that are unemployed, those that are on public assistance, it's very, very difficult to make these payments. And, that said, none of us has a right to obtain water unlawfully.[21]

Even a casual ethical philosopher would disagree with the sheriff's pronouncement. But Pickell evinced little interest in ethics. He promised a "crackdown," "arrests," and to "prosecute these people to the fullest extent of the law." That was what the media focused on—this ongoing narrative distraction about water "thieves"—while remaining nearly entirely silent on the true story, the poisoning of the population. And that's how things remained. For weeks, months, years.

The national corporate media didn't raise any significant alarm bells either. It wasn't just one metaphorical dog that didn't bark. All the dogs lay quietly snoozing.

Why was the media silent?

Horrendous waterborne diseases broke out across the city. These led to mass street protests. Finally, it was independent media rather than corporate media that uncovered the truth. The poisoning of Flint, Michigan came to light. Estimates suggest that many thousands were sickened and at least 115 people died directly and immediately from the water switch. The full, long-term mortality from the sustained poisoning will be far larger and won't be known for decades.[22]

The only good news here was the arrival of the independent media coverage as it stepped into the breach left by the increasingly biased corporate media. This heralded anew the arrival of the New Enlightenment, which will infuriate us as it informs us. The events in Flint laid bare the modern media reality in a way that few could ignore.

Drops from the Fountain of Truth

This poisoning of an American city was no innocent accident nor isolated bit of incompetence. We know this because of the work of investigative journalists who began publishing serious work on Flint in 2015. Jordan Chariton of *Status Coup,* a publication run by him and several friends in a true incarnation of the Constitution's vision of a Free Press, uncovered years of deliberate malfeasance and government cover-ups.[23] *Status Coup's* reports included bombshell revelations of systemic doctoring of water testing data. The fraud was coordinated, and it was kept secret for years. Corporate control of local media outlets was complete, and news of these coverups was filtered by thick *systemic bias*.

Even two years later, President Barack Obama did not choose to raise alarms or launch investigations but rather to calm and reassure people, as the media had been attempting to do the whole time. He did not visit Flint in 2014. Nor did he swing by in 2015. His famous visit came near the end of his presidency, in 2016, long after the crisis had made global headlines. Even at that late date, Obama declared it a "national emergency" rather than a "national disaster," which would have released enough federal funding to fix the root cause.[24] He drank a glass of water in front of television cameras and pronounced the water from Flint's pipes "drinkable, with a filter." The local media applauded rather than questioned, despite the fact that the water was literally still poisonous and would poison thousands more children and adults for years. There was no *watchdog* in the corporate media.

Shari Guertin, a resident of Flint, sued the city over the poisoning of the water, and she and her attorney told their terrible story. They won. The city appealed and tied the case up in court for years, but in 2019, an appellate court finally ruled in her favor and held the city accountable.[25] The ultimate finding of the court by Sixth Circuit Judge Richard Allen Griffin:

> Within days, residents complained of foul smelling and tasting water. Within weeks, some residents' hair began to fall out and their skin developed rashes. And within a year, there were positive tests for E. coli, a spike in deaths from Legionnaires' disease, and reports of dangerously high blood-lead levels in Flint children. All of this resulted because the river water was 19 times more corrosive than the water pumped from Lake Huron by the DWSD, and because, without corrosion-control, lead leached out of the lead-based service lines at alarming rates and found its way to the homes of Flint's residents. The crisis was predictable, and preventable.[26]

Many of these points were *still* contested in the local media even after the court's decision. The Supreme Court declined the city officials' appeal for immunity,[27] so more residents could now sue the city and state.[28]

To its immense credit, *Status Coup* stayed with the story and eventually obtained hundreds of pages of confidential government documents that revealed not only that Mayor Walling and Emergency Manager Earley knew but that Michigan Governor Rick Snyder himself had known about the poisonous water as early as October 2014. In a 2020 investigation, *Status Coup* revealed that Snyder, who is a Republican, had been advised even earlier—*a year in advance*—that such poisoning *would occur* were the river water used. They knew in advance. They did it anyway. They all got rich. Water testing data was suppressed and covered up, and those misdeeds were organized from his office.

Many Americans assume local media reporters are more independent and dutiful than their national counterparts, but local news affiliates are nearly all owned by national media conglomerates too. Local news is afflicted by exactly the same biases and filters. There are, of course, some local news journalists doing an exemplary job, but typically the best climb the corporate ladder as quickly as possible and leave local media environments.

Additional investigations finally pushed a team of government investigators to examine the Snyder administration's role. They found that the governor's office had "committed conspiracies of ongoing crimes, like an organized crime unit." A top advisor to Snyder had paid off sick Flint residents to keep them quiet. Snyder's administration had silenced a whistleblower who had sounded alarms over the water. Snyder himself pressured the Flint mayor to declare the water safe for residents. It could scarcely have been worse, and the story was concealed for years.[29]

A new state attorney general made an unusual decision in 2022 to drop racketeering charges against the government officials responsible. The independent media investigation, later picked up by the *Guardian* of London, found that incoming State Attorney General Dana Nessel, a Democrat, dropped the most damaging charges for reasons that were unclear but likely no coincidence. If convicted on the racketeering charges, not only would the damage to the political establishment have been worse, but lawsuits that residents of Flint filed against Wells Fargo and JPMorgan Chase for funding the disastrous water project could have gone forward.[30]

The story of the poisoning of Flint, Michigan continues to unfold.[31] In its complexity and horror, it provides an example of all three biases in symphonic effect. There was *innocent bias* at the start, where for a variety of personal reasons no one seemed to write about an issue that plagued mostly poor, Black people. Then, a few weeks into the crisis, we saw *systemic bias* take over:

the corporate news focused on misdeeds of the victims rather than put hard questions to people in power. Finally, after a good deal of the sordid tale was exposed, the coverup phase began, and we saw *nefarious bias* take over with a hidden agenda and deliberate concealed coordination to alter and distort the narrative.

Even more important than this demonstration of biases is how this story coexists with the dawn of the New Enlightenment and the nascent era of independent media. As this tragedy unfolded, those reading a balanced media diet were more aware of the truth about the world around them. In this case, knowing the truth made a difference in protecting one's health and well-being.

A NEW DAY IS DAWNING

THE PIPES OF THE MIGHTY WURLITZER WERE FIRST INSTALLED WITH John D. Rockefeller's disingenuous acquisition of newspapers and endowment of journalism schools. The pipes were first tuned by Bernays and Lippmann's cynically visionary work to launch the public relations industry. The pipes were finally combined into an instrument by the efforts of Frank Wisner and his CIA contemporaries. With the addition of social media, "fact checking," and "astroturf" news sites, this pipe organ has become a formidable beast to behold. It is a monster of propaganda, able to divert, distract, or drown out sources that it doesn't control. Yet, these pipes are finding they must play louder and louder to control the narratives and perspectives Americans are allowed to consider. A New Enlightenment is flowering in the minds of men and women as the internet facilitates faster and freer dissemination of original thought. The last days of the Century of Propaganda are upon us.

This disparate media environment might seem impossible to navigate, but as we've seen in this chapter, a biased, competitive, and chaotic news media is nothing new to this country. Many establishment news sources today call independent sources "fake news," and this will continue as we reach a tipping point. We've had *innocent, systemic,* and *nefarious bias* for decades. True, it has been generations since the media landscape has been quite as diverse as it is today, but when this country was founded, and throughout the 1700s, 1800s, and early 1900s, it was common for a major city to have as many as a dozen daily newspapers. Most people read only one, but it was little trouble for anyone to buy a half-dozen papers one day and get a sense of the range of debate on a particular issue. The *smorgasbord* of perspectives has helped build a society that encourages free thinking and values a diversity of opinions and interpretations.

Personally, I've had a wonderful journey these last five years discovering quality independent sources of journalism—from the dogged work of Jordan Chariton on the Flint debacle, to Caitlin Johnstone's irrepressible coverage of the Bernie Sanders campaigns, to Kim Iversen's relentless exposure of corporate media *bias* about lockdowns and vaccines, to Freddie Sayers's exquisite interviews with heterodox thinkers and scientists. I'm excited to introduce you to these and others in the Balanced Media Diet in Chapter 13.

We are entering another era like that one known to the country's founders. After a century of propaganda and consolidation, the internet's rise has pushed the pendulum back. Every viewpoint once again has its own media source. Every voice can be heard if one is interested in listening.

But two things are different this time. First, there are even more accessible sources today: you don't have to walk to the newsstand or a local library to get a dozen different opinions. You just need an internet connection. Second, and more importantly, this time around the corporate and government news organizations know the power they possess, and they are determined to keep it. They have no interest in another era of myriad media sources providing people with diverse, distinct narratives about events and ideas; they guard jealously the power that comes with controlling what ideas and perspectives are published.

The internet already presents a cornucopia of independent media options. As we examined in Chapter 4, young people already turn to independent media in numbers exponentially higher than their parents, perhaps because they have grown up with the internet and see establishment media sources as just another website, just another voice. As this New Enlightenment unfolds, many millions more will instinctively see the biases I catalog in this book. Older people are turning away in increasing numbers as well, even if with slightly less certainty.

The Death Throes of Dinosaurs

On the other hand, young and old both remain prone to reverting to "authoritative" corporate and government narratives in times of crisis. The "fact-checkers" know this. The endless pandemic, the bitterly controversial election of 2020, the proxy war in Ukraine, and much more continue to demonstrate this clearly. The corporate media behemoths know how to exploit the emotions of fear and anxiety. This is one of the primary reasons there always seems to be a crisis whenever one turns on Fox or MSNBC or CNN; when we are experiencing anxiety or fear, a part of the brain called the amygdala kicks in to prepare a "fight-or-flight" response. This cerebral response triggers the body to devote all of its resources to self-protection and thereby diminishes complex thinking and short-circuits rational thought. When we feel fear or anxiety about a crisis, we tend not to think critically and tend instead to defer to authority figures.[32]

The corporate media incessantly triggers this emotional response in its efforts to maintain control. This is part of the death throes of this old world. Use of the terms "fake news" and "misinformation" to vilify independent media is more evidence of desperation on the part of the media dinosaurs as they notice their diminishing ability to control the narrative. Desperation begets mistakes. Use of these terms is a risky proposition for the legacy news organizations, as they can boomerang. Hurling these epithets around will work sometimes, but the moment a person sees that it is *the corporate media sources themselves* that are biased, that are manipulative, that are peddling half-truths, that are spreading misinformation and propaganda, in that moment, the epithet will easily, gently, firmly land on them, and they will lose the trust of yet another viewer.

Their abysmal track record in critical times also works against the corporate media giants. From the Epstein affair to the Iraq Wars to Flint's water to the *#Russiagate* fiction, a cursory comparison reveals that your favorite establishment media source has no better track record than most independent media sources in getting stories right when it matters most. Desperately doubling down on this term "fake news" thus risks further loss of control of the media narrative. The newer terms "misinformation" and "disinformation" carry the same risks. As control of the narrative slips through their fingers, they will have to push harder against alternative narratives, and that can only mean one thing, the one thing that happens in all authoritarian countries across documented history: censorship.

We see outright censorship by the social media filters increasing every day. And we see the firing or "canceling" of journalists who stray from the narrative orthodoxy. Censorship works sometimes, for a while, but inevitably it also triggers the Streisand Effect, boosting the source and story that are censored on account of the innate human desire for truth. Indeed, many of the journalists who have been fired by these media dinosaurs for offering unacceptable perspectives are now becoming leading voices in the independent media sources that exist outside the reach of the establishment media. We turn to this very phenomenon now.

12

YOUR VIEWS ARE NO LONGER NEEDED

"To learn who rules over you, simply find out who you are not allowed to criticize."

Voltaire

IF IT IS TRUE THAT THE CORPORATE NEWS MEDIA'S PRIMARY GOAL IS TO manage news narratives to support the agenda of a reactionary oligarchy comprising the leaders of the largest corporations, a handful of billionaires, and the military-industrial complex, we would expect to find two types of evidence of this: evidence of bias in the media *advocating for* this agenda; and evidence that journalists *advocating against* this agenda have been silenced, fired, or censored.

Evidence of the first type is clear and abundantly documented throughout this book. We turn now to the second type of evidence. As it turns out, it is commonplace as well.

There is the example, of course, of *Huffington Post*'s silent, imperious censorship of my writing in 2016.

That might have seemed egregious to you, but, in fact, censorship of this kind has been far broader and deeper and gone on much longer than most Americans realize. I began monitoring the state of media in this country long before my *Huffington Post* article was taken down. I knew it might happen to me, just as I know this book might be censored or shadowbanned shortly after it's published.

I founded an online political news magazine in 2003, and its second issue focused on our nation's dwindling news sources and the ongoing consolidation that the internet was beginning to counteract. For that issue, I analyzed media ownership, and I spoke with numerous journalists in various news organizations to understand the career trajectory of the men and women in print and television news.

What I found was that many journalists enter their profession without particularly lofty principles or aspirations, and pursue their work instead with visions of fame, wealth, or power. These career journalists cultivate connections in elite circles with an almost religious zeal to advance their careers; they believe they can't afford to hold fast to any particular principles. They might not notice if they're advocating for the agenda of a reactionary oligarchy when they're only asking the most wealthy and powerful people for their opinions.

But many journalists *do* have ethics that they take quite seriously, and many will speak passionately when asked about the reason for joining their profession. They'll point out it's the only non-political job the Constitution specifically mentions and protects; they'll speak about crusading to make the world a better, more just, more civilized, and freer place. They'll know about the media's three roles as *watchdog, smorgasbord,* and *bulletin,* even if they don't use those names. In fact it was partly through my conversations with journalists that I identified these three essential roles of the press in a democracy. Many of the journalists I've personally spoken to hold their profession in high esteem—at least as an ideal—and see clearly their role in a functioning democracy. All of them acknowledged that journalism is little more than propaganda if it doesn't speak truth to power and hold elected officials and corporate executives to account. As George Orwell once said, "Journalism is printing what someone does not want printed; everything else is public relations."

A BATTLE FOR INTEGRITY

BECAUSE MANY JOURNALISTS HAVE ETHICS, THERE IS A BATTLE BE-tween, on the one hand, the integrity and ideals of individual journalists, and, on the other, the underlying agenda of corporate media propaganda. The journalist needs to be *watchdog* and speak truth to power to hold the powerful to account; corporate ownership wants to speak power to truth and thereby conceal all unfavorable facts.

This battle is evident in every corporate news organization I have examined. And power wins this battle in corporate news media virtually every time. This victory manifests often via simple hiring and promotion decisions, where *systemic bias* calls the shots. One of the less discussed drawbacks to the steep media consolidation that happened during the twentieth century is that as media corporations grew, the number of people able to write directly to readers declined. A smaller and smaller number of columnists and anchors reached a larger and larger share of the people, and the ladder one had to climb from entry-level journalist to major syndicated columnist, analyst, or anchor grew. It no longer took a single promotion or two to go from entry-level reporter to prominent writer or columnist; four or five rungs on the ladder had to be climbed. And people with the wrong outlook, the wrong focus, the wrong topic interests, or the wrong logical conclusions were simply passed over.

Focusing on the wrong things, or covering the right things but from the wrong perspective, leads nowhere in the contest for money, airtime, bylines, and career advancement. Thus, censorship of unpopular viewpoints is often done not via explicit orders but via simple, innate cultural bias, what we call *systemic bias*, the phenomenon Anand Giridharadas called "habits of mind[1]" and that George Orwell called *doublethink* in his book *1984*. People who toe the line are given a microphone; those who do not are ignored; everyone in the company witnesses the pattern.

Nonetheless, exceptions occur, stones pass through the rice sieve. Honest, brilliant journalists sometimes manage to climb the ladder with their principles intact. This happens frequently enough that direct orders are sometimes needed, such as sudden firings or abrupt demotions. Some journalists, such as Ed Schultz and Ashleigh Banfield, as discussed below, prove so successful through sheer journalistic talent that they must be explicitly blackballed for saying the wrong things from prominent perches in the media landscape.

"It is difficult to get a man to see something that his salary depends on him not seeing."
—Upton Sinclair

There are dozens of these cases. Journalists have frequently been fired for vocally opposing, or even questioning, the agenda of the ruling reactionary class. Simply taking an approach to news reporting that is insufficiently aligned with the establishment narrative often provides sufficient pretext for dismissal. The press release accompanying such a sacking will often sadly note that the journalist's words have "compromised their neutrality," and thus, they had to be fired to protect the publication's reputation. "Neutrality," in this case, means not contradicting the interests of the parent corporation

In the pages that follow, we'll meet a dozen remarkable cases who "compromised their neutrality."

Before examining this list, which is but a small sample of the many times journalists have been fired for saying the wrong thing, it's worth considering whether any journalist has ever been fired for making mistakes, "compromising their neutrality," or outright lying, if the mistake or lie *supported* the agenda of the ruling class. In other words, what happens to journalists who compromise their neutrality by vocally *supporting* the establishment narrative?

Nothing.

It turns out there are hundreds of cases of journalists simply acting as stenographers for government officials, intelligence agencies, and corporate PR flacks. In fact, *this is the norm.* Columnists and reporters write pieces every day with thin if any factual evidence but in support of mainstream narratives, often echoing one another in mockingbird fashion. They pay no price.

Even considering cases of outright *lying* in favor of the establishment narrative, it is nearly impossible to find anyone who has been fired for too enthusiastically supporting a dominant narrative.

There are a couple noteworthy cases of journalists fired for dishonest reporting in ways that neither supported nor contradicted establishment narratives. The bipolar plagiarizer Jayson Blair of the *New York Times* and the bizarre fiction-writing of Stephen Glass of *The New Republic* provide two instances. Both of those cases concern skillful liars attaining powerful positions in corporate media, but those aren't relevant for us, as their writing primarily addressed cultural issues that didn't materially support or undermine any powerful establishment narrative.

Hundreds of journalists exaggerate and tell outright lies in favor of establishment narratives, as documented throughout this book, yet I've encountered only one singular case where someone was actually fired for dishonestly advocating a perspective favored by the establishment. It is the case of Judith Miller. She was fired from the *New York Times* after penning countless pieces of propaganda masquerading as news to support the illegal invasion of Iraq in 2003. Journalists at every level wrote with the same perspective, building the case for war, but Miller crossed a line somewhere that sufficiently embarrassed the *Times*, and she was very publicly fired. Perhaps she just took the fall for the mainstream corporate media as a whole, or at least for the *Times*. Something needed to be done after the entire narrative about "Weapons of Mass Destruction" turned out to be fiction as detailed in Chapter 3.

Judith Miller. One person. The only journalist I've found who has ever been fired for getting the facts wrong in a way that supports the ruling class agenda. And even she didn't pay for her outspoken position supporting the CIA and DoD's dishonest case for war. She was discredited publicly, but she was hardly blackballed by the media behemoths. In fact, she landed on her feet and profited handsomely from the publicity. She published a book with a major publisher about her experience being fired by the *Times* and then landed jobs at the *Wall Street Journal* and Fox News. Then she won a position on the ultra-establishment, CIA-connected Council on Foreign Relations. Her career path, one might say, carries a rich aroma of Operation Mockingbird.

A GRAVEYARD OF
TRUTHTELLERS

THE PAGES THAT FOLLOW CONSTITUTE A SMALL COLLECTION OF THE journalists who have been fired, demoted, forced out, banished, or canceled by corporate media organizations for covering the news in ways that ran counter to dominant narratives. It turns out, if you tell the truth in the corporate media about the buildup to a war or about an unfavored presidential candidate, you might be fired.

Legend has it Mark Twain quipped to a dogged reporter in 1897: "The reports of my death have been greatly exaggerated." Here, the word *graveyard* is "greatly exaggerated." While most of these journalists are blackballed permanently from positions in corporate media organizations, they didn't vanish altogether as journalists but, in fact, rose again as truthtellers. Today, many lead fruitful lives of journalistic integrity at alternative and independent news organizations.

Ed Schultz (MSNBC)
Fired for covering Bernie Sanders

WITH A POPULAR, LONG-RUNNING SHOW ON MSNBC, THE HOST OF "THE Ed Show" had become an increasingly powerful progressive voice in corporate media by the spring of 2015. His show had been running for six years at that point in prominent timeslots and routinely beat CNN in the ratings, where it frequently ran opposite Anderson Cooper's show.

In May of that fateful year, Schultz flew to Burlington, Vermont and became the only television host from any of the major networks present when Bernie Sanders announced his candidacy for president in front of 3,000 supporters on the banks of Lake Champlain. Schultz interviewed Sanders at his home as well.

Schultz was preparing to air both the announcement speech and the in-person interview on his MSNBC show when he received an urgent call from

Phil Griffin, the president of MSNBC.

Griffin spoke in no uncertain terms. "You're not covering this."

Schultz responded that it was a historic moment, that it was a major presidential announcement, and that they had footage and access no other network had. Their coverage would be unique and of great public interest.

"I don't care," Griffin repeated. "You're not covering this."

Schultz didn't acquiesce quietly. But none of the footage ever appeared on MSNBC.

Schultz was one of very few corporate media hosts at the time covering labor issues. A throwback to an earlier era, he interviewed union leaders and labor-side economists. The Sanders announcement and the personal interview were not aired, but Schultz, nonetheless, covered Bernie Sanders in the weeks that followed until his show was canceled about a month later.

In an interview in 2018, months before his untimely death, Schultz gave his side of this story. His frank opinion was that both Griffin and MSNBC Chairman Andrew Lack were "connected at the hip with the DNC."

> They didn't want anybody in their primetime or their lineup supporting Bernie Sanders. They were in the tank for Hillary Clinton. And I think it was managed. And 45 days later, I was out at MSNBC... The fix was in with the mainstream media. The fix was in with managing the news and shutting down Bernie Sanders... The fix was in early on to deep-six Bernie.[2]

The case of Ed Schultz reveals both determination and a hint of desperation on the part of MSNBC. When the normal tools of narrative management aren't sufficient—and in this case with the rise of Sanders and independent media, they clearly weren't—the establishment media uses the more transparent clubs of censorship and termination.

Krystal Ball (MSNBC)
Fired for not supporting Hillary Clinton

A RISING STAR ON MSNBC, NOT YET THIRTY YEARS OLD, KRYSTAL BALL came to the network having already run for office. Ball brought a fresh perspective and personal experience from witnessing the declining fortunes working class people faced during the Obama years while she lived in East Liverpool, Ohio.

In 2014, as a host of the show *The Cycle*, where she had been host for three years, she delivered a powerful and prescient monologue concerning Hillary Clinton. The 2016 election was around the corner, and hearing Hillary Clinton's platform of, in essence, "no change," Ball urged Clinton live on MSNBC *not* to run for president. "We're now at a moment of existential crisis as a country. We're recovering slowly from the Great Recession, but as we pick our heads up at where we're heading, we don't like what we see... Don't run, Hillary," she said. "Don't run."[3]

Shortly after it aired, she was called into her boss's office to explain her perspective.

"After that," she recalled in an interview years later, "every time I was going to do another monologue on Hillary Clinton, I had to get it approved by the president of the network. That's not a normal thing."[4]

Ball's show was canceled in the summer of 2015, shortly after Ed Shultz was fired by the same network. MSNBC, it appears, was cleaning house to prepare for the 2016 primaries.

"I would do these MSNBC pieces on inequality, or the plutocracy, or Piketty, or how I thought Hillary Clinton was going to lose, and it felt very lonely," she said.[5]

Fortunately, she has survived and kept her conscience intact. Ball now has a successful daily news show *outside* of corporate media, *Breaking Points,* which is part of the Balanced Media Diet we propose in the next chapter.

Gary Webb (San Jose Mercury News)
Fired after reporting on CIA drug running

ONE OF THE FEW JOURNALISTS ON THIS LIST WHO ACTUALLY IS IN A graveyard is Gary Webb, a classically-trained, tough-nosed, old-school investigative reporter. Webb was hired off the street by the *Kentucky Post* in 1978, cut his teeth in its small newsroom, and built a career by moving on to successively larger papers. He won a Pulitzer Prize for a groundbreaking series on government corruption and landed jobs at the *Cleveland Plain Dealer* and then the *San Jose Mercury News*.

In the 1990s, he penned probably the most explosive—and most famous—investigative newspaper series of its decade, "Dark Alliance." He died in 2004 of a mysterious gunshot wound that was labelled a suicide.

"Dark Alliance" was a three-part series published when he was at the *Mercury News* in 1996, and it revealed a great deal. The CIA had supported the Nicaraguan Contras in a 1980s right-wing coup against the socialist Sandinistas; the CIA had done this by facilitating crack and cocaine importation into the United States. Most stunning of all at the time, this imported cocaine had been a primary driver of crack cocaine abuse in inner cities like Los Angeles, which in turn led to the "War on Drugs" and draconian government drug laws that criminalized and imprisoned a generation of mostly Black men.

Webb wasn't the first to write about the CIA colluding with drug smugglers, or even the first to look into how they colluded with the Nicaraguan Contras. Much of "Dark Alliance" was not, in fact, new information. The Iran-Contra Scandal had already exploded on the American political scene, revealing many of the Reagan administration's worst deeds and disclosing the media's lies to the American people about "freedom fighters" in Nicaragua. Those "freedom fighters" were, in fact, composed primarily of death squads and paramilitary troops armed with Iranian weapons and funded via cocaine money. The power of Gary Webb's writing lay in his narrative style, how he told the story in vivid but simple terms, explaining how drug running funded covert operations. He *was* the first to disclose in a national paper where the drugs ended up once they arrived on American shores.

Webb's series broke ground in one other way, as well, a harbinger of the New Enlightenment. As Nick Schou recounts in *Kill the Messenger: How the CIA's Crack-Cocaine Controversy Destroyed Journalist Gary Webb*:

> "Dark Alliance" created history in another way: it was the first major news exposé to be published simultaneously in print and on the internet. Ignored by the mainstream media at first, the story nonetheless spread like wildfire through cyberspace and talk radio. It sparked angry protests around the country by African-Americans who had long suspected the government had allowed drugs into their communities. Their anger was fueled by the fact that "Dark Alliance" didn't just show that the Contras had supplied a major crack dealer with cocaine, or that the cash had been used to fund the CIA's army in Central America—but also strongly implied that this activity had been

critical to the nationwide explosion of crack cocaine that had taken place in America during the 1980s.

It was an explosive charge, although a careful reading of the story showed that Webb had never actually stated that the CIA had intentionally started the crack epidemic. In fact, Webb never believed the CIA had conspired to addict anybody to drugs. Rather, he believed that the agency had known that the Contras were dealing cocaine, and hadn't lifted a finger to stop them. He was right, and the controversy over "Dark Alliance"—which many consider to be the biggest media scandal of the 1990s—would ultimately force the CIA to admit it had lied for years about what it knew and when it knew it.[6]

Whether or not the CIA had deliberately dumped addictive and illegal drugs into urban communities—surveys found that about 25% of Black people in those communities did believe this—what was perhaps most interesting about the entire "Dark Alliance" scandal was what happened to the career of this thorough, principled journalist after the series of articles was published.

Within two months, the *Los Angeles Times*,[7] *New York Times*,[8] and *Washington Post*[9] all swooped in to defend the CIA and attack Webb's industrious journalism. As if in a coordinated attack, these prestigious publications slung wide-ranging hit pieces at Webb, his sources, his past reporting, and his personal life. It was clearly an attempt to discredit him. Meanwhile, pieces appeared that defended the CIA. For its part, the *San Jose Mercury News* backed away from the piece rather than defend their journalist. They exiled Webb to a small regional bureau until he quit, and no other newspaper thereafter would hire Webb. The man's career effectively came to an end. His life was ruined all for making the unforgivable mistake of reporting the truth in a way that contradicted a dominant narrative. His reporting snuck through the filters of *systemic bias* one time, but no further.

Reflecting on his career shortly before his death, Webb sagely acknowledged his naivete to Kristina Borjesson in her book *Into the Buzzsaw: Leading Journalists Expose the Myth of a Free Press*, which chronicles censorship in corporate media:

> If we had met five years ago, you wouldn't have found a more staunch defender of the newspaper industry than me... I was winning awards, getting raises, lecturing college classes, appearing on TV shows, and judging journalism contests... And then I wrote some stories that made me realize how sadly

misplaced my bliss had been. The reason I'd enjoyed such smooth sailing for so long hadn't been, as I'd assumed, because I was careful and diligent and good at my job... The truth was that, in all those years, I hadn't written anything important enough to suppress.[10]

Amy Robach (ABC)
Silenced when attempting to report on Jeffery Epstein

SOMETIMES, YOU DO EVERYTHING RIGHT AS A JOURNALIST. YOU FOLlow the best traditions of your profession, you investigate wrongdoing, you question witnesses and victims, you verify corroborating evidence, and you methodically prepare a remarkable story. Sometimes, the mainstream media won't air or print the story. Not because of weak ratings, production costs, or journalistic ethics but because the story runs counter to the dominant narrative of the day—or maybe because it just makes someone in the elite look bad.

As discussed in this book's introduction, Amy Robach, co-host of ABC's *20/20* and onetime host of *Good Morning America* and MSNBC's *Weekend Today*, revealed in 2019 that she had the entire story of reactionary pedophile, sex-trafficker Jeffery Epstein in 2016, during the presidential primary. An unknown ABC News executive suppressed it. Three years later, in 2019, when the story broke all over the world, a "hot mic" on a set for ABC's *Good Morning America* caught her frustration that the story hadn't come out earlier:

> I've had the story for three years. I've had this interview with Virginia Roberts. We would not put it on the air... We convinced her to come out. We convinced her to talk to us. It was unbelievable what we had: [Bill] Clinton, we had everything. I tried for three years to get it on, to no avail.[11]

Robach said the British royal family threatened the network in a later interview, but given Epstein's connections to Clinton and Trump and Dershowitz and many other huge names in the American elite, it's unlikely ABC needed to be threatened. *Systemic bias* and the filter around Elite Sources would do the trick quietly.[12] The network's structure and the people in executive positions would instinctively prevent the creation of a new narrative this way as well as the publication of something potentially so damaging to elite sources.

Ashleigh Banfield (MSNBC)

Fired for not supporting the invasion of Iraq

UPTON SINCLAIR ONCE SAID, "IT IS DIFFICULT TO GET A MAN TO SEE something his salary depends on him not seeing."

Most journalists are simply *unable* to see the bias in the way that, say, the lead-up to a war is covered and analyzed in corporate news. But sometimes a man or woman *does* come to see and to understand something that endangers his or her salary, and sometimes that man or woman is too conscientious to lie about it. In these instances, if the lie runs counter to dominant narratives or to the objective of the news organization, the person is asked to leave—or, in certain cases, put in a tiny closet office without a phone or computer *for a year*.

In 2001, a young and promising journalist named Ashleigh Banfield won awards for her coverage on 9/11 from Ground Zero. Her work earned plaudits for her network, MSNBC, and she was promoted quickly thereafter. Banfield was sent on some of the network's most important work. At one point, she made daily appearances in various countries around the world for the nominally left-leaning media network. Her star was rising, and she became host of a show of her own entitled, "On Location," for parent company NBC News. She became an "embedded journalist" in Iraq for a short period after the initial invasion of that country in 2003. By all accounts, she was on a skyrocketing trajectory as a television news journalist.

She was invited to give a prestigious guest lecture at Kansas State University.[13] It was May of 2003, just after returning from her stint in Iraq. In her speech to the university, she questioned the media coverage of the war, coverage she had participated in providing. She questioned whether what she had done in Iraq was journalism at all, suggesting instead that serving as an "embedded journalist" was helping the government to ensure people never saw the horrible, bloody deaths suffered by hundreds of thousands of Iraqis. What was shown to viewers, she said, was insufficient.

> [It] was not journalism. Because I'm not so sure that we in America would be hesitant to do this again, to fight another war, because it looked like a glorious and courageous and successful and terrific endeavor... To truly understand what war is all about you've got to be on both sides.[14]

It didn't seem like heavy criticism of the network, but none other than Neal Shapiro, president of NBC News, singled her out.[15] The network permanently banished Banfield in an almost comical way.

"I was office-less for ten months," she recalled in an interview, remembering the small closet she was assigned.

There was no phone, no computer. For ten months. I had to report to work every day and ask where I could sit... Eventually, after ten months of this, I was given... a tape closet... They cleared the tapes out and put a desk and a TV in there... Yet they wouldn't let me leave. I begged for 17 months to be let out of my contract. If they had no use for me, [I thought], let's just part ways amicably—no need for payouts, just a clean break. And Neal wouldn't allow it. I don't know what his rationale was—perhaps he thought I would take what I felt was a very strong brand, and others felt was a very strong brand, to another network and make a success of it. Maybe that's why he chose to keep me in a warehouse. I will never forgive him for his cruelty and the manner in which he decided to dispose of me.[16]

Tareq Haddad (Newsweek)
Silenced when attempting to reveal the truth about Syria

AS DISCUSSED IN CHAPTER 10, THERE WAS ALMOST CERTAINLY NO GAS attack by Syrian President Bashar Assad in Douma, Syria in April 2018, despite the corporate media's—and the US Government's—repeated narrative that one had occurred. The story had been steadily falling apart ever since its original claims splashed across Americans' evening news. Tareq Haddad, an American-trained reporter, was working for *Newsweek* out of London. Haddad had published hundreds of articles for mainstream publications, and he prepared an article in December 2019 that pulled together the various pieces of evidence demonstrating that the Organization for the Prohibition of Chemical Weapons (OPCW) had doctored reports from its own experts.[17] Three separate whistleblowers from within the OPCW came out to protest the doctored reports, Haddad wrote, but the mainstream media ignored their voices and even labeled it a "conspiracy theory" to mention their names. No one in corporate media talked to the OPCW whistleblowers. Narrative management was in full effect.

Haddad's article was rejected numerous times by his editors at *Newsweek*. Witnessing the deadly airstrikes launched on Syria that the media justified by the alleged attack, Haddad resigned rather than swallow his disgust.[18]

Haddad penned a remarkable, eloquent, and comprehensive resignation letter. Rather than attempt to maintain his connections with the corporate media narrative managers who had censored him, he explained in detail how his Syria story was suppressed. Haddad's letter is, in fact, a heroic *tour de force* worth reading in full, as it spells out the situation we are in at the dawn of the New Enlightenment. He lists the specific steps that were taken to suppress his writing, the complaints of the OPCW whistleblowers, and then he goes deeper, describing the workings of *Newsweek* from the inside out. He names the editors who were government plants working primarily to manage narratives inside the prestigious magazine. His letter even cites Herman and Chomsky's *Manufacturing Consent*, reveals the unmistakable signs of Operation Mockingbird going on inside the mainstream publication, and exposes government and intelligence agency plants managing stories. The letter is listed in this book's endnotes, and again, I recommend reading it in its entirety. Here is an excerpt:

> The U.S. government, in an ugly alliance with those who profit the most from war, has its tentacles in every part of the media—imposters, with ties to the U.S. State Department, sit in newsrooms all over the world. Editors, with no apparent connections to the member's club, have done nothing to resist. Together, they filter out what can or cannot be reported. Inconvenient stories are completely blocked. As a result, journalism is quickly dying. America is regressing because it lacks the truth.[19]

Tareq Haddad has founded his own independent news organization and is currently reporting on the Free Speech issues at stake in the persecution and extradition of a man we will discuss at the end of this chapter, Julian Assange.

Jesse Ventura (MSNBC)

Fired for not supporting the invasion of Iraq

YET ANOTHER CASUALTY OF MSNBC'S PRO-WAR AGENDA IS JESSE VEN-
tura. A rare and compelling figure in American popular culture over the last
half-century, Ventura served in Vietnam as a Navy SEAL where he performed
underwater demolitions. Returning home after that war, he embarked on a
successful career as a professional wrestler. Born James Janos, he adopted the
sobriquet Jesse "The Body" Ventura and took on a persona that combined
a California surfer's looks with Billy Graham's flamboyance. His successful
wrestling career spanned three decades, and he eventually became a popular
television personality, commentator, and announcer for the World Wrestling
Federation as well. Ventura then moved into acting and appeared in over a
dozen major action films, such as *Predator* (1987) and *Demolition Man*
(1993). He became a modern-day corporate media renaissance man.

In 1991, Ventura entered yet another field, politics. He won a surprising
upset to become mayor of the town of Brooklyn Park in his home state of
Minnesota. A mere seven years later, in 1998, this man's already uncommon
life was transformed by its most remarkable accomplishment. As an outspoken and unapologetic political independent—a member of the fledgling Reform Party—Ventura shocked the country by winning a statewide election
and becoming the Governor of Minnesota.

His term was widely regarded as successful, and upon leaving office in
2002, Ventura was one of the most sought-after personalities in corporate
news. Networks approached him for his services as a commentator. A bidding war ensued, which MSNBC finally won by offering him over $2 million
annually, equivalent to $3 million in 2022 dollars.

"People just love this guy," MSNBC President Erik Sorenson said at the
time. "He has some kind of connection with the average guy."[20]

Despite all the efforts and all the money they spent to land him, his show
didn't last a season. After two months, MSNBC canceled it. In an interview
with the *Los Angeles Times* years later, Ventura recounted the shock he felt
when his show was killed:

It was awful. I was basically silenced. When I came out of office [as governor], I was the hottest commodity out there. There was a bidding war between CNN, Fox, and MSNBC to get my services. MSNBC ultimately won. I was being groomed for a five-day-a-week television show by them. Then, all of a sudden, weird phone calls started happening: "Is it true Jesse doesn't support the war in Iraq?"

My contract said I couldn't do any other cable TV or any news shows, and they honored and paid for the duration of it. So in essence I had my silence purchased. Why do you think you didn't hear from me for three years? I was under contract. They wouldn't even use me as a consultant!

When you live in Mexico, your houses all have names. I almost named my house "Casa MSNBC" because they bought it. I was paid like a professional athlete, and I got very wealthy. For doing nothing.[21]

He elaborated further in a subsequent interview on *The Young Turks.*

MSNBC was putting together a five-day-a-week show for me, and then all of a sudden, a phone call came to one of my subordinates, and they said, "Is it true that the Governor doesn't support the war in Iraq?" This was right as the Iraq war was... getting ready to hype up, and it turned out they wouldn't put me on the air. They paid me for all three years, they pulled my show, and I sat and collected paychecks and I couldn't say anything because my contract said I couldn't do any cable nor any news shows for three years.[22]

Similar to Banfield, above, and Donahue, below, MSNBC aggressively prevented Ventura from speaking his mind—not just on its own shows but on other networks as well.[23] In this case, they paid for his silence.

Ventura bought a house in Mexico and has gone on to a successful career in alternative media. He was hosting a popular news analysis show on RT until that channel was censored and killed in 2022. He's turned to Substack.[24]

Phil Donahue (MSNBC)

Fired for not supporting the invasion of Iraq

THE GROUNDBREAKING, WORLD-RENOWNED *PHIL DONAHUE SHOW* RAN for three decades on nationwide television, including syndication on CBS and NBC. The show deftly bridged political divides in the country by addressing controversial topics with intelligence and patience. Epitomizing the best of the golden era of "objective, professional journalism," it is widely regarded as one of the best television programs in American broadcast history. Donahue retired in 1996, but he came out of retirement in 2002 to host a new show, *Donahue*, on MSNBC. The show became the network's most popular, but it didn't even last a year.

In the frenzied media buildup to the invasion of Iraq in 2003, which we detailed in the "Weapons of Mass Distraction" section of Chapter 3, fraudulent claims about Iraq blanketed every network. Donahue meanwhile asked questions in his classic open-minded manner. In 1991, he had made no secret of his opposition to the first Iraq War, and now it seemed he was no fan of a new invasion.

Three weeks before the launch of the horrific attacks on Iraq, on February 25, 2003, Donahue's show was canceled, and Donahue was fired. The reason given was that the show had insufficient viewership. Within weeks, leaked MSNBC memos circulated by company brass revealed the true reason for his dismissal. Donahue was fired because he opposed attacking Iraq. According to the leaked memos, his show could become "a home to the liberal anti-war" masses who were protesting in the streets. Donahue would be "a difficult public face for NBC" during the war.

In Donahue's own opinion, he was fired simply because MSNBC was owned by General Electric, a war and weapons contractor who stood to make billions in profits off the war. He commented that GE "had required that we have two conservative guests on for every liberal ... and I was counted as two liberals."

Chris Hedges (New York Times)

Silenced for not supporting the invasion of Iraq

AN AWARD-WINNING JOURNALIST AND BESTSELLING AUTHOR, CHRIS Hedges spent nearly two decades as a foreign correspondent in Central America, West Asia, Africa, the Middle East, and the Balkans, reporting from more than fifty countries for *The Christian Science Monitor*, NPR, *Dallas Morning News*, and in particular the *New York Times*, where he was a foreign correspondent for fifteen years. He published numerous articles in the *Times* during the buildup to the invasion of Iraq that allowed the Bush administration to allege Iraqi involvement with 9-11. His articles guided discussion about the war across the country.

Then, he gave a commencement speech at Rockford College in May 2003. In the speech, he voiced his opposition to the war. "This *is* a war of liberation in Iraq," he told the new graduates. "But it is a war of liberation by Iraqis from *American* occupation."

The *Times* immediately issued a formal reprimand, condemning his remarks as "undermining the paper's impartiality" and forbidding Hedges from speaking further about the war. Hedges was silenced for "compromising his neutrality." Rather than abide by the proscription on speaking on the critical issue of the day, Hedges resigned.

As has been the case with many of these truthtellers banned from corporate media, Hedges has found success in independent and online media. He writes for independent online journals *Truthdig* and *ScheerPost*, teaches in a New Jersey prison, and hosts the program *On Contact* for the RT television network.

Well, he did host *On Contact* until RT America was censored and killed at the outset of the war in Ukraine, which is a proxy war between the United States and Russia. It's a shameful sign of weakness that the corporate media destroyed RT. The Balanced Media Diet in the next chapter still includes RT because a diversity of perspectives—and a diversity of biases—is essential on the path to *media consciousness*. When a corporate media journalist is fired or silenced, it is important still to hear that voice if possible.

Melissa Harris-Perry (MSNBC)

Fired for not supporting Hillary Clinton

AN INTELLECTUAL AND MEDIA DYNAMO, MELISSA HARRIS-PERRY WAS
the only tenured professor with a regular television news show in 2016. With
professorships at Princeton and Tulane under her belt, her MSNBC show
was "about race, poverty, and gender [and] operated about 20 grade levels
above the rest of television," according to Dave Wiegel of *Slate* at the time.
She built her *#Nerdland* show into one of MSNBC's most popular over the
course of four years. Then, as the election of 2016 approached, Harris-Perry,
who is Black, found her show repeatedly preempted for "other news." This
happened four weeks in a row as the primary and caucus contests between
Hillary Clinton and Bernie Sanders were beginning.

In an explosive letter to her fans and coworkers at the time,[25] she explained:

> Here is the reality: our show was taken down—without comment or discus-
> sion or notice—in the midst of an election season. After four years of build-
> ing an audience, developing a brand, and developing trust with our viewers,
> we were effectively and utterly silenced.[26]

MSNBC assigned her a slot on air, but it was to read news headlines rather
than to do her normal show. To Harris-Perry, this was an attempt to suppress
her complex analysis of the news. In an election year when MSNBC clearly
wanted simple and straightforward support for Hillary Clinton (see treatment of Krystal Ball and Ed Schultz above),[27] the historical perspective, complex analysis, and uncomfortable questions Harris-Perry brought to the table
were just too challenging. Like Schultz, she directly called out NBC News
Chairman Andrew Lack and MSNBC President Phil Griffin:

> I will not be used as a tool for their purposes. I am not a token, mammy, or
> little brown bobble head. I am not owned by Lack, Griffin, or MSNBC. I
> love our show. I want it back. I have wept more tears than I can count and I
> find this deeply painful, but I don't want back on air at any cost...
>
> I have stayed in the same hotels where MSNBC has been broadcasting in
> Iowa, in New Hampshire, and in South Carolina [for the primaries], yet I

have been shut out from coverage. I have a PhD in political science and have taught American voting and elections at some of the nation's top universities for nearly two decades, yet I have been deemed less worthy to weigh in than relative novices and certified liars. I have hosted a weekly program on this network for four years and contributed to election coverage on this network for nearly eight years.

While MSNBC may believe that I am worthless, I know better... I care only about substantive, meaningful, and autonomous work.[28]

Two days after penning this letter, on February 28, 2016, Harris-Perry was fired by MSNBC.[29] She has continued to write and teach, and she publishes regularly for *The Nation* and *Elle* magazines. She has never been hired to host another corporate media television program.

Cenk Uygur (MSNBC)
Fired for criticizing Barack Obama

CENK UYGUR PIONEERED THE MODERN MOVEMENT TOWARD INDEPEN-dent media, dedicating all his time to online news long before it was common. He hosted his own radio show and founded an internet news site—The Young Turks—in 2002 that went on to become one of the first major You-Tube success stories, amassing millions of subscribers and billions of views. Uygur's progressive politics and sharp criticism of the Iraq War, bank bailouts, and Obama's surveillance and military policies earned him a large and loyal following as a radio host on Air America and eventually attracted the interest of MSNBC.

Uygur was given an important weekday evening slot on MSNBC in 2011, and his show was immediately successful. The show's ratings went up significantly, and it began to beat CNN in its time slot, something MSNBC had struggled to do at the time. The show was an unmitigated success.

Except, that is, that Uygur was too critical "of people in power," and he refused to "play ball" with management.[30] In a monologue on The Young Turks, Uygur recounted how Phil Griffin called him into his office and told him to "tone it down."

Griffin said, 'people in Washington tell me that they are concerned about your tone ... You know, I'd love to be an outsider, outsiders are cool, but we're not. We're insiders. We are the establishment. There are two audiences. There is the audience you are trying to appeal to, the viewers. And there is management. And management is basically the club. And they want to make sure that you are cool—can play ball to be in the club.'[31]

Uygur chose not to tone it down or "play ball," and he continued doing his monologues the same way. The show's ratings continued to rise. Nevertheless, several months after this exchange with Griffin, Uygur was removed from the 6 p.m. slot. He was offered instead a contributing role on the weekends.[32] Uygur turned this down[33] and was fired.

We went in a different direction...They offered, honestly, a lot of money for that different role. I said no... I did not want to work at a place that didn't want to challenge power.[34]

Uygur went on to be only more successful as an independent media leader with The Young Turks, although as mentioned in the "Astroturfing" section in Chapter 10, he ironically chose to compromise his integrity and his network and accept lavish corporate funding in 2016.

David Wright (ABC)
Suspended for acknowledging corporate media bias

AS ESTABLISHMENT AS THEY COME, DAVID WRIGHT GRADUATED *MAGNA cum laude* from Harvard and earned a master's degree at Oxford. He first joined ABC News as a junior correspondent. Over two decades at the network, Wright became one of ABC's most seasoned and versatile correspondents, reporting from six continents, covering wars and Papal transitions, and interviewing six presidents. He was *Nightline's* lead political reporter for years, and his work has appeared on every major ABC News program.

In February 2020, while covering the New Hampshire primary that Bernie Sanders won, Wright was recorded during a conversation with other ABC News staff about the *bias* in their coverage.

I feel terrible about [the bias]. I feel that the truth suffers, the voters are poorly informed... It's like there's no upside, or our bosses don't see an upside, in doing the job we're supposed to do, which is to speak truth to power and hold people to account.[35]

He described the way the news network has changed after the acquisition by Disney.

It became a profit center, a promotion center. Like now, you can't watch *Good Morning America* without there being a Disney princess or a Marvel Avenger appearing. It's all self-promotion, promotion of [Disney], promotion of individuals within the company, as opposed to dedication to the story and a commitment to telling stories that we *need* to tell, that are maybe *hard* to tell... The commercial imperative is incompatible with news.[36]

Wright added that ABC News doesn't consider political issues or what everyday people think but rather manage narratives for prospective voters.

We need the story to move on, and so we're happy to have Buttigieg be the story last week, and we're happy to have Klobuchar as a new subject this week, and then when we're tired of her, we'll be delighted if Elizabeth Warren kicks ass in Nevada, because then we have something new to talk about.[37]

Wright mentioned *bias* against Trump, which was remarkable since he admits in the same conversation that he's a socialist and no fan of Trump.

We don't hold [Trump] to account, and we also don't give him credit for what things he does do... We're interested in three things: the outrage of the day, the investigation, and the palace intrigue of who's backstabbing whom. Beyond that, we don't really cover the guy.

As for "fake news," and what kinds of lies journalists get away with and which ones they don't, he gave an example of a mistake that was punished while indicating that much deception sails through.

A colleague of mine fucked up on Kobe Bryant, and said that all of his daughters [instead of just one] died in the helicopter crash... He got bad information and reported bad information, and he has paid the price for it, he got suspended. But you know... the fake news abounds...

I'm speaking about broadcast television. That's all I'm speaking about. ABC, CBS, NBC. And we recognize that we are dinosaurs, and we're in danger of dying... We've lost any sense of context and perspective, and it's just the urgent moment, the horse race, and the outrage from Trump.[38]

On February 26, 2020, the day after he made these remarks, Disney released a statement: "David Wright has been suspended... he will be reassigned away from political coverage when he returns."[39] The stated goal, as always, was to protect "our reputation for fairness and impartiality... to avoid any possible appearance of bias."[40] Wright had "compromised his neutrality." At the end of the conversation, he even revealed his own political leanings.

More than a Democratic Socialist, I'd consider myself a socialist. I think there should be national health insurance. I'm totally fine with reining in corporations. I think there are too many billionaires, and I think that there's a wealth gap, and that's a problem.[41]

KILL A CHICKEN
TO SCARE THE MONKEYS

AS POWERFUL AND DISTURBING AS THAT LIST OF SUPPRESSED JOURNAL-ists might be, it could go on and on. Those are just some of the more compelling cases. The articles and reports that these censored journalists would have written had they been allowed to speak would undoubtedly have offered perspectives different from the ones Americans are offered today. This is another reason independent media is on the rise. Many Americans sense that the narratives are controlled even if they don't quite know how or why.

Yet even a full list, if we could compile it here, would comprise a small percentage of the total number of journalists working in the US today. We have to consider how few journalists have the prestige and notoriety to land a hosting role on a major network, and then consider how rare it is for someone with integrity and a perspective that runs counter to the mainstream corporate news narrative to reach such a post. And then we have to consider the chilling effect that a single journalist being fired for covering the news incorrectly will have on the industry as a whole.

Think about the effect that all of these high-profile firings have had on the American media profession. There's a Chinese idiom, 杀鸡儆猴 ("kill a chicken to scare the monkeys") that suggests making a harsh example of one troublemaker to convince the others to step in line. For every Ed Schultz, Tareq Haddad, or Melissa Harris-Perry, dozens of other aspiring writers and would-be hosts wait in the wings, hoping for the prestigious job. Most of these aspirants carefully observe what makes one successful as a host or writer, and what does not. Like anyone interested in earning a promotion in his or her profession, journalists are keenly aware of what tends to get their colleagues promoted and what does not.

Consider for a moment the courage it takes to take an independent or unpopular stance in your own field or profession. At a time when the corporate media landscape is constricting, when fewer and fewer corporate journalism positions are available, it is impossible to overestimate the effect that even a small number of firings like these have had on attitudes toward topics with a whiff of controversy.

While suppressing a "chicken" like Chris Hedges or Ashley Banfield surely scared many "monkeys" in the newsrooms of American corporate media, there is a far bigger "chicken" on the media scene today. This is someone who hasn't only published honest journalism himself that undermines reactionary narratives and agendas but who has created an internet resource for people all around the world to secretly, privately, securely publish leaks and revelations on their own. The corporate media establishment has a fairly reliable hold on what corporate media journalists can and cannot publish in mainstream media. Via the rules of censorship and propaganda created by the filters of *systemic bias*—as well as via the *nefarious bias* of complicit editors, as detailed in Chapter 2—they can control quite a bit of what is heard, seen, and read by the American people. However, they have no such hold on what a citizen with a computer or phone can publish on the internet because of the work of one unusually talented Australian journalist and computer scientist, a man who has never worked in the United States.

His name is Julian Assange, and he's probably the greatest journalist of the twenty-first century.

Assange is our era's Daniel Ellsberg, Ida Tarbell, or Thomas Paine. Assange has spoken truth to power in an exemplary evocation of the First Amendment's guarantee of a Free Press. His name belongs on a short list of those who best embody New Enlightenment ideals.

The current suppression of this chicken—if they can pull it off—is meant to scare every monkey on the planet.

Julian Assange (WikiLeaks)
Arrested for publishing the truth too many times

THE FOUNDER OF THE INTERNET-BASED TRANSPARENCY ORGANIZATION WikiLeaks, Assange created software programs in 2006 that enabled anyone in the world to anonymously upload documents that he or she believed revealed important wrongdoing. Equipped with state-of-the-art encryption for security and privacy, this tool launched a global phenomenon of truthtelling, citizen journalism, and independent investigations that have included such bombshells as the video footage released by Chelsea Manning showing the US military murdering Iraqi civilians and Reuters journalists from helicopters.[42] Assange's technology resulted in countless bombshell revelations of government torture, fraud, corruption, malfeasance, murder, violence, and criminality.[43] Through WikiLeaks, the New Enlightenment shed light in a brand new way on the misdeeds of the powerful.

More than ten million documents have been leaked through the WikiLeaks site. None has ever been found to be illegitimate or a forgery.

Trained as a computer scientist, Julian Assange, an Australian citizen, is a unique case for this book. He has never worked for a corporate media outlet nor written for independent media. He's never lived in the United States. He can't be fired. Silencing him has proven far more difficult than censoring the principled, talented journalists listed above.

Nevertheless, Assange and WikiLeaks have been ruthlessly attacked in our corporate media. Again, nothing WikiLeaks has published has ever been proven to be false, fake, or less than what it appears to be. Compare this to, say, the *New York Times*, which couldn't make such a claim of integrity even for a single given month and has published propaganda that has turned out to be false for every war up to the present day.

There was a time when Assange was revered as a hero even in corporate media.[44] Initially, he was a hero to Democrats when he released the devastating "Collateral Murder" video footage of violent acts by US soldiers in Iraq. Those revelations in 2010 embarrassed Republicans George W. Bush and Donald Rumsfeld, and they interested readers and journalists across the spectrum. Assange was interviewed at the time in *Rolling Stone, Forbes,* and *Vanity Fair* as a controversial but fascinating person.[45] He sold out lecture halls around the country. He gave popular TED talks. He won the *Time* Person of the Year reader's poll in 2010 by more than 100,000 votes over distant second and third place, Recep Erdogan and Lady Gaga.[46] (*Time* instead named Facebook CEO Mark Zuckerberg Person of the Year.)

Everything changed in 2016. As with so much documented in this book, the Sanders and Trump candidacies upended the media landscape. Independent media forced its own media narratives into public consciousness. Assange released a trove of emails that year that embarrassed the DNC and damaged the campaign of Hillary Clinton. He was suddenly a hero of Republicans and an enemy to establishment Democrats.

Everyone aware of his accomplishments acknowledges that, at the least, his software deftly mixed cutting-edge encryption, peer-to-peer networking, and decoy ciphering to create an app that empowered everyday people to speak truth to power. The software doesn't only disrupt governments' abilities to lie, it disrupts corporate media's ability to manage narratives and serve as the gatekeeper to truth. This feat, more than anything else, broke new ground. By releasing documents in their entirety, sometimes without redaction, WikiLeaks puts unvarnished facts in the hands of everyday people without the legacy media's filters. Assange's critics call him egotistical and reckless; his supporters call him the greatest journalist of the twenty-first century.

From my analysis, WikiLeaks has not shown political bias. The site has released only truthful documents. Assange himself does carry his own *innocent bias,* of course, but he has released documents without fear or favor as to who the facts incriminate. Assange's opinion apparently is that corporate and government secrets are the biggest blocks to world peace. He witnessed the US annihilating Iraq in 2003 and vilifying the Iraqi government as a "regime," and in a turn of phrase, he said he hoped total transparency would bring the "annihilation of the current US regime."[47] Personally, I don't hope for the annihilation of anyone, but I do agree with him that government secrecy is one of the biggest obstacles to peace and freedom on Earth in this new century.

When WikiLeaks released the emails revealing the DNC's inner workings and the rigging of the 2016 primary for Hillary Clinton, things changed, the era of "fake news" began, and the pursuit of Assange hit another gear. Through a dubious arrest on phony sex charges in Sweden and imprisonment in London, the reactionary elite's fury with him became obvious. At first, it was unclear how the US government would silence him, as he was neither a corporate employee nor an American. But imprisonment has largely done it. The cruel and unusual suppression of Julian Assange has set a dangerous precedent for press freedom on this planet. That a journalist who is neither American nor ever worked for an American company could be held indefinitely in England and treated as a criminal by the United States for the simple act of publishing documents that embarrass powerful Americans is dangerous.[48] It threatens the New Enlightenment and endangers democracies predicated on press freedom.

So profound has WikiLeaks' impact been that a quick review of some of its most important releases is in order.[49] Many crimes we know about only because of Assange's groundbreaking organization. A summary of some highlights:

- The "Collateral Murder" footage mentioned above, leaked by former army intelligence officer Chelsea Manning. The footage shows US soldiers in Apache military helicopters shooting and killing innocent Iraqi civilians in cold blood. Soldiers are seen laughing while doing this. Helicopters circle back around to kill journalists and medical responders at the scene. The videos revealed horrible, ugly truths about the illegal invasion, further crystallizing global opinion against the war.

- Tens of thousands of additional documents from the US wars in Iraq and Afghanistan revealing murders of civilians and torture of detainees and prisoners, and the US military's coverup of these events. At least 66,000 civilian deaths were recorded in the documents, a number far larger than had been publicly admitted.

- A "Standard Operating Procedure" manual from Guantanamo Bay, revealing that prisoners were kept in squalid conditions and denied basic healthcare and even toilet paper.

- Hundreds of thousands of diplomatic messages from US officials over a fifteen year period, revealing covert military communication with Saudi Arabia that resulted in secret US bombing of Yemen and proposed bombardments of Iran.

➻ Documents revealing US efforts to spy on foreign leaders and diplomats, ranging from Chinese and German leaders to UN Secretary General Kofi Annan. Spying included obtaining credit card numbers, frequent flier numbers, and other private information.

➻ Documents revealing UK government collusion with the CIA to develop software to hack consumer devices. One goal of the Agency was to turn Samsung Smart TVs into microphones to spy on citizens via a computer virus in their set called Weeping Angel. Another goal was devising software that could hack into people's smartphones, computers, and cars to listen to conversations or obtain text messages or other data.

➻ Thousands of documents from Hillary Clinton's 2016 campaign for president, including emails among leaders in the Democratic National Committee revealing cheating and manipulation to oust Clinton's opponent in the primary, Bernie Sanders. The documents also showed fraudulent attempts by the DNC to blame those hacks on Russia.

➻ Thousands of Israeli documents revealing that country's intention to keep the Palestinian territory of Gaza on the edge of collapse by depriving its people of a functioning economy, to handle Palestinian protests with increasing violence, and to launch a new war in Lebanon.

➻ Hundreds of thousands of pager messages from government officials on the day of 9/11. The messages provided an important building block for understanding what happened on that fateful day.

➻ Thousands of emails by a climate research team at the University of East Anglia in England revealing that world temperature data was manipulated to boost the appearance of climate change. This led to a significant scientific scandal just before a climate summit in Denmark.

➻ Documents from the planning of the "Great Firewall of Australia," revealing that over half of the blocked websites were not, in fact, child porn, as had been claimed, but were actually controversial WikiLeaks entries, censored news, demoted YouTube videos, and other information that went against dominant narratives.

◆◆ Documents relating to oil trading corporation Trafigura's plan to dump toxic waste in the Ivory Coast. The documents revealed the proposed dump was based on ridiculous "science" and that the release would poison millions of people across the West African country. British newspaper *The Guardian* and several other European media companies obtained the report but said nothing because Trafigura threatened litigation. WikiLeaks then released the documents to the public, allowing the information to be known so Trafigura could be brought to justice. BBC won a prestigious media award for its belated coverage without acknowledging the role of WikiLeaks.

◆◆ The personal contact information of nearly 13,000 British National Party politicians, lawyers, doctors, and military officers, and the party's internal manifesto that indicated that the far-right party wanted to ban immigration from Muslim countries and repatriate some immigrants to "their lands of ethnic origin."

◆◆ Sarah Palin's emails, released as she was running for vice president in 2012, revealing she had used a private email account for political activity to avoid public documents laws.

◆◆ Thirty-five videos of Tibetan protests against Chinese rule in 2008 that were censored in China.[50]

◆◆ Eighty-six censored phone conversations between Peruvian politicians and oil executives in the "Petrogate" oil scandal in Peru.

◆◆ Electronic versions of unusual bibles used by Scientology and documents from Scientology leaders that revealed the drills and rituals the quasi-religious organization used to coerce its members.

◆◆ Hundreds of thousands of Sony emails released after the 2014 hack of the corporation. The emails revealed widespread corruption among top Sony officials and clandestine ties between its movie studio and the Israeli government.

◆◆ Hundreds of British Defense Manual documents that detail, perhaps ironically, how to prevent leaks of sensitive documents. Some documents specifically named WikiLeaks as a threat. The documents also warn that spying has changed. Journalists alongside foreign spies, criminals, terrorist groups, and defense staff should be, according to the documents, the first to suspect in the event of a leak.

Despite this amazing track record of serving in the press's essential *watchdog* role, politicians and pundits in the corporate media ruthlessly attack Assange and WikiLeaks. Assange has been denounced with every epithet in the book, from a lunatic and a mental health case to a sex offender and a spy, but never with credible evidence. The notion that he's a Russian spy, for instance, is completely groundless. The purported sex offenses that allegedly, coincidentally occurred just after WikiLeaks released the "Collateral Murder" footage also turned out to be groundless and were dropped by Sweden[51] before being reopened nine years later,[52] and then dropped again.[53] Charges that Assange had hacked the Icelandic Parliament were dropped when the main informant, a troubled criminal named Sigurdur Thordarson,[54] admitted to fabricating stories, embezzling funds from WikiLeaks, and accepting money from the FBI.[55] The attacks keep coming because Assange threatens the entire top-down, controlled dissemination of information that the corporate media uses to manage narratives.[56] Just as Galileo and other independent thinkers threatened the feudal lords and Catholic bishops at the outset of the first Enlightenment, Assange today is the tip of a spear threatening the modern monopoly on "the truth."

He remains in a London prison. How many government and corporate wrongdoings have remained concealed because this principled journalist remains behind bars? It's anyone's guess. The attacks on him keep coming as well, and they have intensified in Blue News outlets in the United States over the past five years.

Anchor and Pundit as Judge and Jury

One harsh set of media attacks on this independent journalist came in December of 2021, shortly after a British Court rejected Assange's request not to be extradited to the United States.[57] Two MSNBC talking heads presumed to convict Assange on air of espionage crimes. They were discussing the WikiLeaks release of the "Collateral Murder" video and other documents leaked by Chelsea Manning. Host Joe Scarborough brought former Missouri Senator Claire McCaskill on as a legal pundit, and they proceeded to lie to their viewers at least five times in less than two minutes while pronouncing Assange guilty prior to the trial.

For the sake of thoroughness, and because it's not long, here is the transcript of the entire two minutes.[58] Deliberate lies appear in UPPER CASE:

> **Scarborough:** Forget the politics of this, as a prosecutor, you're given this case and you've got a guy who's STOLEN THOUSANDS OF DOCUMENTS, pages of highly classified national security documents, RELEASED THEM TO THE WORLD, and in so doing, put the lives of US troops, of people who were working with the United States, allies, collaborators in war zones IN THE GRAVEST OF DANGER.
>
> Under any scenario, you take politics out of it, and this is an open and shut case. This is not the Pentagon Papers. THIS WASN'T *TIMES* EDITORS RIFLING THROUGH DOCUMENTS, FIGURING OUT WHAT COULD BE RELEASED AND WHAT COULDN'T BE RELEASED and explaining it. This was a guy who got stolen documents and gave them to the world.
>
> **McCaskill:** This is a pretty simple case. It's very straightforward. And the beauty of a trial, Joe, is that you narrow all of the extraneous stuff to the charges that are there against the defendant, and the charges in this case are that he was TRYING TO HACK INTO OUR MILITARY INFORMA-TION that protects not just our country, but all the men and women in uniform around the world. This is really serious stuff. Forget about the politics, the fact that both the right and the left don't like Julian Assange or love Julian Assange, depending on those circumstances being talked about, that should tell you all you need to know.
>
> This is really a guy who just VIOLATED THE LAW. And you know, I gotta laugh, if their fight against extradition is that THEY'RE WORRIED ABOUT HIS SAFETY IN PRISON, they really don't have perspective on this. There are lots and lots of people who go to federal prison who have done really worse things than Julian Assange, and they are protected in prison. I don't think he needs to worry about whether or not he'll be safe in prison. This is really just a smokescreen to try to keep him from ever being account-

able for the rule of law.

The MSNBC allegations are clear: Assange hacked into US government computers, obtained classified documents, released them to the world without vetting them, placed military people at grave risk, and, in so doing, violated US law.[59]

What they left out is that none of these allegations is true, and they knew it. These also weren't the charges in the case, and they probably knew that too. This was *systemic bias* and *nefarious bias* walking hand in hand. The underlying agenda they shared with their parent corporation was ruining a journalist who publishes truths uncomfortable to their funders and inimical to their narrative control.[60] They pushed a narrative of their own and served up to their Blue News audience an evil villain.

The actual facts of the case were not difficult to ascertain. Independent media reported on it thoroughly. Assange has never hacked into US government computers; the government has never charged him with this; and there is no evidence of this. McCaskill and Scarborough know this. Scarborough even contradicts himself a few seconds after saying Assange stole documents, saying instead Assange "got stolen documents," conflating *stealing* with *releasing* information someone else stole. The charge that he was complicit in a "hacking conspiracy" was a long linguistic leap[61] since everyone agreed to the facts: Assange had helped Chelsea Manning transfer securely via WikiLeaks the documents she wanted to release that revealed US atrocities in Iraq. That was it. It was, again, a long, linguistic leap to make this a crime. Every news organization has done this with leaked documents—arrange for them to be securely obtained, transferred, reviewed, and published.

At that point, Assange didn't simply release them en masse "to the world," as these talking heads assert, but instead did *exactly* what Daniel Ellsberg had done with the Pentagon Papers: he worked with newspapers like the *Los Angeles Times, New York Times, Guardian* in England, and *Der Spiegel* in Germany to vet which documents should be released and which should not.[62] The truth was the exact opposite of Scarborough's unproven statements. WikiLeaks had even requested that the Pentagon itself work with them[63] to ensure nothing that might directly cause loss of life[64] would be released.[65] They leaked thousands of documents so that the world and, in particular, US citizens, would know the Afghanistan war's true horrors without directly endangering lives of troops on either side. This was quality journalism, fulfilling both the *watchdog* and *smorgasbord* roles. Scarborough and McCaskill didn't want you to know that.

Those were the first two lies.

The third lie comes a few seconds later when McCaskill repeats the lie that Assange *had* hacked into military servers.

The fourth lie is asserting that the released documents put the lives of US soldiers in "the gravest of danger." This was not the case, and several military bigwigs went on record saying so. The documents WikiLeaks had chosen to release had only a "fairly modest" effect on troop safety. Three weeks after the documents were released, for instance, Pentagon spokesman Geoff Morell said, "We have yet to see any harm come to anyone in Afghanistan that we can directly tie to exposure in the WikiLeaks documents." He added later in the interview that there could be a lag "between exposure of these documents and jeopardy in the field."[66] But three months later, there was still little if any direct damage caused. Defense Secretary Robert Gates himself, a former director of the CIA, told the *Washington Post*:

> I've heard the impact of these releases on our foreign policy described as a 'meltdown,' as a 'game-changer' and so on. I think those descriptions are fairly significantly overwrought... Is this embarrassing? Yes. Is it awkward? Yes. Consequences for U.S. foreign policy? I think fairly modest.[67]

A month later, *Reuters* reported that not only had the impact on troop safety been minimal, but what danger there was had been *deliberately* played up.

> A congressional official briefed on the reviews said the administration felt compelled to say publicly that the revelations had seriously damaged American interests in order to bolster legal efforts to shut down the WikiLeaks website and bring charges against the leakers.[68]

Two years later, US officials freely conceded that they still had no evidence that the WikiLeaks releases had led to a single death.[69] Nine years after that, when Scarborough and McCaskill posed as knowledgeable experts on MSNBC, there still was no evidence.

The fifth lie deliberately distorted Assange's legal defense. McCaskill omits the true reason Assange and his lawyers are fighting extradition and then lies that he's just scared of serving time in a US prison. Leaving aside the bizarre assurances she makes that Assange would be "protected in prison," it's astonishing that this former senator, whom Scarborough brings on air as a legal expert to comment on this landmark case for global press freedoms, doesn't know the basic facts of the case. In fact, Assange's legal defense was that his alleged crimes were political in nature, that the prosecution chiefly aimed to suppress the truth, and that he was being pursued for extradition by the US government to punish him for publications about its misdeeds. His defense was political. McCaskill mentioned none of this. She omitted Assange's defense either out of rank ignorance or *bias*. Whatever the reason, she didn't want the audience to consider that the prosecution of Assange indeed *is* political in nature. Under British law, the government cannot extradite a person who is a high risk of suicide, so Assange's lawyers added to his primary defense an argument that he couldn't be extradited because his mental health had deteriorated over the ten years he'd spent in harsh detention. He wasn't worried about his personal safety in prison, but his defense mentioned the problematic possibility he might find a way to kill himself out of desperation and depression. Not only did the MSNBC commentators deliberately conceal the substance of Assange's defense, but they also misled their audience on the one small part of it they did mention.

HOMOGENIZATION OF THE NARRATIVE

FIVE ATROCIOUS LIES IN TWO MINUTES. DID ANYONE CALL THEM OUT ON it? No, not in corporate media. As we mentioned earlier, there is never a price to pay for lying in favor of establishment narratives. MSNBC's video wasn't labeled misinformation on YouTube, taken down on Facebook, or censored on Twitter. It's still up, without corrections, without a label, without a "fact check."

A viewer might wonder why no journalist with knowledge of the case was invited by MSNBC to provide a different perspective during that segment, perhaps even defend Assange as a fellow journalist. Of course, anyone at

MSNBC who might have defended Assange was likely already fired. Clearly, as Glenn Greenwald noted, the mainstream media stacked the deck against Assange in pursuit of extradition by promoting stories written by ex-security state agents to, as Senator Mnuchin announced on Twitter, "get him back on United States soil … He is our property and we can get the facts and the truth from him."[70] On August 26, 2022, he once again filed an appeal against US extradition on grounds that he faces persecution for his political opinions.[71]

To reiterate, nothing WikiLeaks has published has ever been proven false, fake, or inauthentic. Not a *single* document out of the tens of millions that have been released. Neither CNN, nor Fox, nor MSNBC, nor the *New York Times* could make that claim in any given month, let alone over the course of their decades of propaganda for wars, covert coups, "free" trade agreements, and corrupt politicians. There's never a "fact check" when you're supporting the mainstream narrative.

Only when you manage to tell a different story in corporate or social media do you find that your views are no longer needed.

By removing contrary voices, corporate media has extinguished a diversity of opinions and abandoned its essential *smorgasbord* role. The resulting homogenized narratives have cleared the way for skyrocketing advertising largesse from the giant drugmakers, weapons builders, investment banks, and energy companies. This is why corporate media continues to decline in quality but improve its bottom line—its deepening, unholy dependence on corporate cash. As independent media rises, money flows more and more heavily to the top of the corporate media ladders. Cable TV hosts and syndicated columnists are now generally millionaires talking about billionaires; each has risen in rank by playing the game, getting through the filters, colluding with high officials in the political parties, and telling lies whenever necessary. Corporate media professionals no longer have any incentive to tell the truth; they climb the ladder specifically by covering what they're told to cover from the perspective they're told to cover it.

"What does censorship reveal? It reveals fear."
—Julian Assange

This vicious cycle is hastening the unfolding of the New Enlightenment. Fewer and fewer people believe the homogenized narratives on corporate channels, but there remains no incentive for those corporate channels to change. The only path the corporate media has left is to label independent media as disinformation and censor it. But the corporate media narratives typically are less truthful than what they purport to be protecting their viewers from. This is why they continually invent new tools of narrative management—"fact checkers," "astroturf" independent media, and the brutal censorship of divergent ideas on social media. The silencing of independent opinion and analysis on corporate media is at best a temporary fix for what is deeply and permanently broken in the corporate media apparatus.

We Americans need no longer be deceived by this frantic distortion of reality. We can learn to identify the false narratives, the propaganda, and the censorship, and see through it all. We can cultivate *media consciousness* and join the New Enlightenment. We turn now to the best tool to do so: a Balanced Media Diet.

13

A BALANCED
MEDIA DIET

---

*"The smart way to keep people passive and obedient
is to strictly limit the spectrum of acceptable opinion."*

Noam Chomsky

IN THIS BOOK, WE HAVE EXPLORED MANY MECHANISMS OF NARRATIVE management. From Operation Mockingbird to *systemic bias* to social media censorship to "fact checking," these mechanisms are sophisticated, diverse, and insidious. None of us, no matter how intelligent or aware we might be, is immune to the manifold manipulation of the truth.

In this chapter, we explore what to do about it. How can we stay sane, healthy, and informed about the world in an era of such sophisticated deception?

In the last chapter, we met journalists who have been silenced, suppressed, suspended, or fired for covering current events from a perspective not aligned with dominant narratives. Many journalists of integrity have managed to keep their jobs inside corporate media, but far more have lost those jobs and now operate independently outside the walls of corporate media. We'll meet some more of them in this chapter. We'll also introduce the most important tool for gaining *media consciousness* and staying informed about current events: the Balanced Media Diet.

Our country has always produced heroic journalists who have operated outside the mainstream channels. Courageous men and women in every era, dating back to our Republic's first day, have exercised the First Amendment's protection of the press, and we as a country are infinitely better for it. Writers, researchers, and truthtellers such as Thomas Paine, Frederick Douglass, Ida Tarbell, and Daniel Ellsberg, to name a tiny few, have wielded the formidable power of the pen and instigated movements for societal change by broadening popular awareness of problems. They and their readers understood the crucial role journalism plays in a free society.

THE AMAZING INTERNET

EVERY JOURNALIST HAS USED THE MEANS AND MEDIUM MOST EFFECTIVE in his or her time. Today, truthtellers inevitably find the most powerful medium to be the internet. This world wide web is a modern miracle, easily the most powerful means of information distribution ever invented. It's a potent tool indeed for discovering and distributing truth, connecting with other humans without any central authority's approval, and instigating systemic political, scientific, or economic change. As we've learned, the internet also provides means and methods to *suppress* the truth that are also more sophisticated than such tools have ever been, and we must remember this. The internet offers different possibilities and different challenges than did the mediums of information exchange of previous eras.

In this chapter, we will meet some truthtellers and media heroes who have used the internet's marvelous power over the past decade to report news to the world and inform us of underlying truths. Each of these independent media stars has a viewpoint, an ideology, and *innocent bias*. I don't include them—or anyone else—in the Balanced Media Diet to endorse their viewpoint but to suggest that their work is valuable in a diverse and healthy diet, and to show the power of the internet to counteract the corporate media's crushing power. In constructing a Balanced Media Diet, it is highly important we balance against the nearly ubiquitous *systemic* and *nefarious bias* in corporate media, but we must also address *innocent bias* in both corporate and independent media.

"You are free to be a drunkard, an idler,
a coward, a backbiter, a fornicator;
but you are not free to think for yourself."
—George Orwell

Establishment corporate media has several enormous advantages that keep its narratives dominant. First, many citizens are too busy, overworked, anxious, depressed, confused, or scared to question the powerful narratives bellowing at them every day from televisions and social media feeds. For many of us, it's very hard to incorporate media skepticism into our busy lives. Making a living, supporting a family, keeping up with friends, and maintaining physical health are already plenty without also endeavoring to question media narratives.

Another major advantage that establishment media possesses is the use of propaganda and censorship. These techniques, as outlined in previous chapters, have been honed for decades by public relations firms and intelligence agencies, and they are highly sophisticated today in the hands of the powerful. With the ubiquity of social media reinforcing the effect of these tools, they are becoming comprehensive and omnipresent. These tools are financially expensive to implement, so they provide a perpetual edge to the corporate media giants.

Narratives are controlled through silent omission of dissenting voices and overt, mockingbird-style addition of supporting voices. CNN, for instance, can handpick its favorite talking head, amplify his or her voice, and then let social media do the rest: disseminate the pundit's perspective via hashtags while shadowbanning disagreement. Modern narrative management has progressed far beyond Operation Mockingbird.

A Thirst for the Truth

Those advantages are substantial and underscore the need to balance our media diets and take the journey to *media consciousness*. The good news is, we're doing it. People crave the truth like never before, and despite the challenges, we are finding the time in unprecedented numbers to become more broadly informed.[1] The disaster and confusion of 2020, with its divisive lockdowns, illogical mandates, censored stories, and economic devastation, prodded Americans by the millions to stop and question.[2] In increasing numbers, we thirst to figure out what exactly is going on.[3]

We now compare how stories are told in the corporate media with how they're told in independent media and find inexcusable contradictions. The use of propaganda and censorship comes with risks to media corporations' authority. A single sloppy lie that is exposed can be shared instantaneously and destroy an entire media brand's reputation. Myriad small and large deceptions came to light over the past five years that diminished corporate media's reputation as a whole. This reputation isn't likely to be quickly restored, particularly because the deceptions were not accidents that will be corrected. Corporate news and social media are propped up by money from billionaires, government agencies, and military, financial, and pharmaceutical corporations, so they don't have to produce authentic news to win viewers.[4] Independent news actually has to earn viewers with its coverage and perspective just to survive. This gives new, independent media an evolutionary edge. It is survival of the fittest. The growing thirst for truth among Americans is driving independent media to innovate, improve, and satisfy this thirst—or perish. This is a winning recipe for transforming our media landscape.[5]

George Orwell famously said, "Journalism is printing something that someone doesn't want you to print; everything else is public relations." What we are interested in with our diet is finding and supporting what Orwell called journalism. And we want to do it quickly, before they are censored on mainstream corporate media or silenced outright.

WHAT YOU'RE MISSING

MANY TOPICS THAT FASCINATE LARGE SEGMENTS OF THE AMERICAN population are rarely covered in corporate media. Here are several quick examples:

◈ **Election Fraud.** Tampering with vote counting has been going on for decades, ever since the widespread installation of electronic voting machines at the turn of the century. These machines, for flimsy ethical reasons, use proprietary, secret software and are notoriously easy to hack.[6] The three companies that make these machines[7] have close ties to one political party or the other,[8] and they all have track records of irregular or fraudulent results—market leader ES&S most of all.[9] It takes a peculiar kind of naivete to assume that no one in power would try to insert partisan code into these machines on or before election day. It's rather more reasonable to ask a different question. If the machines are easy to hack and the people in power who have won elections on those machines get to award the next contract for voting machines, is the insecure nature of the machines a feature rather than a bug? There is ample evidence that fraud has occurred multiple times,[10] and the situation has likely worsened as electronic machines have replaced pure paper voting over the last fifteen years. Yet there is no coverage of this issue in corporate media. Independent media, on the other hand, has taken up the topic with increasing vigor and begun to drive fervent political action.[11] Sharyl Attkisson, who is featured in our diet, has covered several election fraud cases[12] and reviewed *2000 Mules*, a documentary by right-leaning independent journalist Dinesh D'Souza.[13] Krystal Ball, also in our diet, provided cogent criticism of that documentary from the left.[14] Election fraud threatens to invalidate the entire basis of our democratic government. Indeed, the issue is so important and neglected in corporate media, it might be the topic of my next book. In 2021, it resulted in the election fraud protests and riots that defaced the Capitol and roiled the country. Our voting machines should use *open source* software and face such rigorous testing that calling an election into question provides a welcome opportunity to affirm the strength of our democracy. Instead, the topic is verboten.

◈ **Corporate Malfeasance.** A conflict of interest always seems to prevent corporate media from covering corporate crime and government corruption. From the now-obvious, underlying reasons for the wars in Iraq and Afghanistan; to the preventable water poisoning in Flint, Michigan; to the violent corporate militarism displayed at Standing Rock; to the criminal levels of neglect of the people of Puerto Rico after the 2017 hurricane;[15] to the suppressed science showing the dangers of giving dozens of vaccines to infants; to the longstanding effects of adding lead to gasoline;[16] to the horrendous pushing of the harmful drug Bextra by Pfizer, issues of crucial importance and widespread interest are often simply missing or, at best, selectively and briefly covered in corporate media.

◈ **Perverse Incentives.** The notion that a corporation that makes much of its profits from selling weapons would want more war in the world doesn't seem particularly controversial, but it is a fact that is almost never mentioned in corporate media coverage of politics. In the months leading up to a war, this point is strictly off-limits in mainstream news. The fact that pharmaceutical corporations make more money when there is more illness—and profit more from developing expensive *treatments* for disease rather than discovering actual *cures*—also is strictly taboo for the corporate media. These types of *perverse incentives* are treated similarly to news that is labeled with the anti-intellectual pejorative *conspiracy theory* and ignored or pushed to the margins of news coverage and political analysis.

But these incentives are real and lucrative. They are obviously running significant parts of our economy, from banks profiting from (and possibly creating) economic downturns, to antivirus computer companies profiting from (and possibly developing) malware and computer viruses; to drugmakers profiting from (and possibly encouraging) addiction; to fast food companies profiting from (and possibly fostering) obesity. This entire way of analyzing segments of our economy and politics is omitted from corporate establishment media channels as if it's too evil to discuss. Five huge corporations own the establishment media and often benefit from war, sickness, high prices, and high unemployment, so they shut out perspectives that might lead to exposing these perverse incentives. The "Deep Politics" section of the Balanced Media Diet specifically includes sources that explore these topics, and it's essential to do so to develop *media consciousness*.

◇ **What the other side sees.** Most establishment media is effectively propaganda for one side of the political spectrum. As detailed in Chapter 5, and as discussed below in the Balanced Media Diet, most American establishment media is either Red News or Blue News—"Party News"—meaning it's written and edited to appeal to, and guide the thinking of, either Republicans or Democrats. This bias distorts both *what* is covered and *how* it is covered, down to the types of questions asked and the kinds of humor and anger that are acceptable. This creates blind spots about what's happening in the world and leads to incorrect assessments of major events, such as why a war is launched or where a virus comes from, and minor events, such as why a particular piece of legislation would be good or bad for teachers or farmers. Even fairly innocuous interpretations, such as descriptions of interactions between protestors and bystanders, are always distorted depending on the subject of the protest.

As an example, when boys from a Catholic school in Kentucky stood near a Native American protester during a 2018 demonstration in Washington, D.C., one whole side of the corporate media—the Blue News side—incorrectly reported the event. They repeated it so often it became the truth for many: Nick Sandmann, a high school boy in a MAGA hat, had taunted the Native American. The truth was that the Native American had approached Nick Sandmann and taunted him.[17] The repeated distortion showed how complete the *bias* can be in our mainstream media, how pervasive thought bubbles have become, and how quickly people exposed to only one source of news can descend into groupthink.

These are some of the topics that are concealed from our consciousness if we rely on a narrow media diet.

THE REMEDY: A BALANCED DIET

SO, IS IT POSSIBLE, WITHOUT A CENTRAL AUTHORITY TELLING US WHAT is true and what is false, to gain and maintain an accurate picture of the world as each day's events unfold?

Let's not minimize what we are trying to do. This has never been possible in world history, let alone easy. Only today's technology, combined with our ever-awakening human curiosity, spiced with our evolving shared consciousness as a single human race makes this possible and compelling and worthwhile.

The answer is yes. It is possible. I have done it for five years now. I began to read more and more broadly in 2016, long before starting this book. Writing this book pushed me to go deeper and wider, and the results are unmistakable. What I can tell you is that while it is challenging to become *informed*, it's possible, it's highly rewarding, and it's easier today than it has ever been.

Not only will you become more aware of world events and learn to discern the true narratives from the false ones, but you will also begin to connect with more people across the media spectrum and up and down the socioeconomic ladder. Your opinions on political issues may or may not change, but you'll be able to understand where someone with a different opinion or different background is coming from.

As we discussed in this book's introduction, you cannot choose to opt out of the news narratives of the day. We are all "red, white, and blind." Every day, the corporate media bellows its dominant narratives at us from dawn until dusk, and even if we choose to ignore them, they still creep into our consciousness, and they still program and influence our friends and family.

The choice you have is whether or not to be *conscious* about it as you absorb media narratives. Our culture has been driven to a tipping point by partisan media sources. Becoming a conscious consumer of the news enables us to be less deceived, less manipulable, less blind, and, ultimately, champions of the underlying values we share as Americans beneath the polarized rancor of Red News and Blue News.

By *informed*, I mean having a *reasonably accurate* view of what is happening in the world beyond the reach of your own eyes and ears. You will not know everything about everything, but you will gain and maintain a reasonably accurate awareness about the things that matter most to you. There will always be *bias* in every media channel, and absolute truth is a slippery fish in every philosophical sense. But this American media landscape of ours is not so tricky or deceptive that it can't be detangled if we spend a little time with a variety of sources to hone our mental detectors of integrity and bias.

To get there, the Balanced Media Diet pushes us to explore independent media as well as corporate media, left-leaning media as well as right-leaning media, foreign news sources and domestic government propaganda, corporate PR and "native advertising," and delve, at least occasionally, into deeper systemic analysis of our political system.

Why It's Worthwhile

Reading broadly and discerning the truth from such a cornucopia of voices might sound difficult, but from my experience, a carefully chosen, balanced diet is not only manageable but also exciting and mentally invigorating. As with food, a broad diet confers intellectual vitality as well as a more accurate sense of what is going on in one's community, country, and world—and ultimately paves a path to healthier political discourse. Just as there are food additives and chemicals that will make you sick, there are dense foods that boost your immune system; just as there are fad diets that will ultimately diminish your health, there is the time-tested notion of balance that ensures a diet provides all the basic nutrients the body needs.

Eating broadly leads to a healthy appetite and physiological equilibrium; reading broadly leads to a critical mind and broader awareness.

It isn't *wrong* to simply choose one news source you like and defer to it every day, and my purpose is not to encourage judgment of people who do so. Given the busy lives we lead and the fact most Americans have little if any free time, taking this shortcut is understandable. But a diet consisting of one single food repeated over and over will lead to disease. Similarly, a media diet consisting of only one news source exclusively becomes disinformation. Even spending a little more time to consume two channels of the same food group provides a broader perspective. But given the media consolidation that transpired over the last half century, even this effort inevitably imprisons us in echo chambers with narrow views of the world and polarized beliefs. The "red, white, and blind" state cements political divisions and reinforces our blind spots.

History is replete with great tragedies that befell nations when a single group of media sources continuously deceived the majority. The Iraq War, which killed over a million innocent people and cost trillions of dollars, is one very recent such case. The Nazi Holocaust is another. Tiananmen Square. Vietnam. Stalin's famines and purges. The list is long. Rising to the challenge of reading diverse media sources is not only a worthwhile endeavor, media consciousness enhances what our minds are creating in the world. Best of all, it forces us to *sapere aude*—to think for ourselves—more deeply. These ideas inspired me when I first created a balanced set of media sources for myself, and they have inspired me to create the Balanced Media Diet proposed in this book.

Getting Started

Now that we understand where we are, how we got here, and why it's worth rising to the challenge, it's time to delve in. The Balanced Media Diet below is a guide that proposes a diverse set of media sources that will allow anyone with 30 minutes a day to become aware of the truth about current events most of the time.

First, I list the *guidelines* to follow during your initial week or two. Then, we examine the *media food groups* which I use to balance the perspectives, size, and structure of the news sources; the goal is to ensure that all media nutrients are available to our hungry minds. Finally, we delve into the forty *balanced media sources*. As a personal passion, and as part of my research for this book, I've been tracking over 200 independent and corporate news sources for the last five years. We are blessed in this country with a diverse media ecosystem. Many, many independent sources have something to offer. It was not easy to select just forty, but I strove to keep the total number manageable.

Without further ado, on the following pages are the five guidelines, the six media food groups, the diet itself, and the forty highlighted media sources of diverse nutritious value. Enjoy!

Note: This guide will be updated annually online. Prior to publishing this book, I registered both redwhiteandblind.com *and* balancedmediadiet.com. *Please find my latest recommended media diet at these sites. Technology permitting, these sites will soon allow you to customize your own media diet. The Pyramid and Chart are also both color-coded online, but since this book is printed only in black and white, the helpful colors in the Pyramid and Chart aren't visible.*

THE FIVE GUIDELINES

BEFORE WE LOOK AT THE DIET ITSELF, THERE ARE FIVE KEY POINTS TO remember when you get started. Following a Balanced Media Diet will lead fairly quickly to *media consciousness* when keeping these guidelines in mind:

1. **Do it!** The most important thing is to start. You don't have to be perfect. Go read something unfamiliar. Do it regularly. Follow a diet. View, listen, watch a diverse set of sources. I recommend following this Diet, below, but you can plan your own diverse diet if you truly commit to it.

2. **Minimize the junk.** Reduce your intake of hydrogenated oils, so to speak, the processed cheese, the high fructose corn syrup. Follow the diet I propose if you can, but if you choose a different diet, keep corporate media to ideally 25% and no more than 50% of your diet. *Nefarious* and *systemic bias* abound, and many of the insinuations are meant to distract and confuse you while denigrating other sources. If you expose yourself to repetitive, mockingbird-style narrative management, you may get the sense that something unproven is true.

3. **Be conscious.** With every source, always notice what event is deemed most newsworthy, what is being said about it, who is allowed to speak, and what emotion you are expected to feel. As your awareness grows, also consider which sources you trust most, and why.

4. **Cultivate equanimity.** Don't let your emotions be easily manipulated. Move on to the next news source before one gets you worked up. Those managing the narratives in the corporate media often aim to scare and outrage you—so that they're the ones in control of these powerful emotions. If you are always scared and outraged about the things they want you to be, your fear and anger cannot go elsewhere.

5. **Listen and engage.** Finally, interact. Once you've cultivated consciousness and equanimity, don't passively go to sleep on the real issues you will uncover as you broaden your diet. You will find meaning and inspiration as you become informed. Look before you leap, don't let your emotions be manipulated, but also do not resist the authentic promptings of your soul.

THE PYRAMID

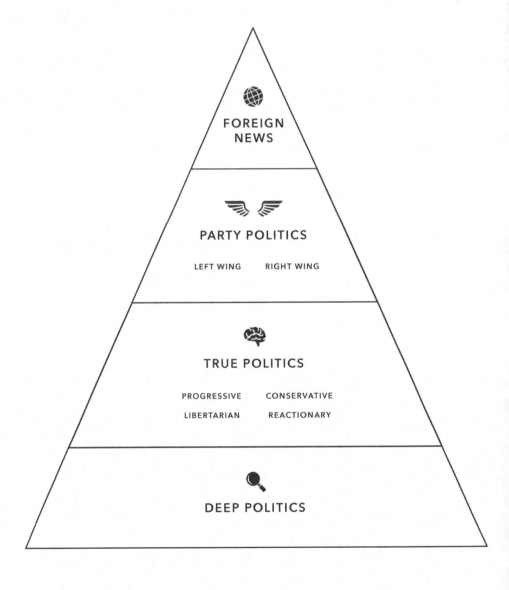

THE SIX MEDIA FOOD GROUPS

TO PROVIDE BALANCE AND ALSO ORGANIZE THE LIST OF NEWS SOURCES, I've placed them in "food groups."

Foreign News

These media sources are from other countries, including our longtime military allies, such as England, France, Germany, and Israel, as well as our frequent adversaries, such as China, Russia, Venezuela, and Iran.

> **1. Foreign News.** All news and viewpoints originating from outside the United States, particularly from non-English speaking countries. Consuming media from this group is critical for reaching an informed opinion not just as a citizen of the country but as a member of the human race. *10% of the diet.*

Party Politics

These media sources look at the daily jostling over political power among American elected officials in Washington and state capitals. They also draw battlelines over "culture war" issues such as abortion, gun control, and critical race theory. Who's placed on what congressional committees, who's approval ratings are declining, what outrageous thing was said by Donald Trump, Joe Biden, Ron DeSantis or Alexandria Ocasio-Cortez—all of this is Party Politics. These outlets imply that their type of news should be sufficient for us all: a sprinkling of hard news on top of scandals, soundbites from pundits, "infotainment" with mild news content, "hot takes" from celebrities, and one-sided analysis of events. There is usually a scandal for each party at any given time that keeps the Party Politics news cycle flowing: politicians' interactions with Russia, for instance, and—during the pandemic—who supported or flouted the official line on masks, lockdowns, and injections. These two food groups constitute 90% of corporate mainstream political news. From the *New York Times* and the *Washington Post* to Fox and MSNBC to CNN and NPR, these sources explicitly disparage other sources with labels like "misinformation" and "fake news" while implying that their own narrow perspective is the only valid one.

> **2. Republican Party Politics.** News and viewpoints that follow the daily and weekly news cycle of events, scandals, and legislation on the Republican side. Important to understanding how news is packaged to inform and outrage conservatives. Generally, the blame is placed on the other party, and there is little deeper analysis.
> *20% of the diet.*

> **3. Democrat Party Politics.** News and viewpoints that follow the daily and weekly news cycle of events, scandals, and legislation on the Democrat side. Important to understanding how news is packaged to inform and outrage liberals. Generally, the blame is placed on the other party, and there is little deeper analysis.
> *20% of the diet.*

True Politics

The next pair of media sources look beyond the parties and consider the underlying guiding political philosophies and principles that form the historical differences between conservatives and liberals, libertarians and progressives, capitalists and socialists. One way to look at the last one thousand years of Western politics is as a conflict between the three political impulses we've discussed throughout this book:

1. *progressive*, the impulse to spread wealth and power more broadly among people;

2. *reactionary*, the desire to concentrate wealth and power more narrowly; and

3. *conservative*, the aim to keep the distribution of wealth and power as it is.

The push and pull of these three drives constitute true politics. It should be mentioned that the great overarching trend—the long arc of history—has been bending in a progressive direction since the signing of Magna Carta in 1215. The terms "Radical" or "Principled" are used sometimes instead of "True" for this layer of news coverage, but the former often bears a negative connotation and the latter a positive one, so we'll mostly use "True."

> **4. Progressive True Politics.** News and analysis that will point out flaws in both parties and that will sometimes suggest that the parties agree about most things and feign disagreement. Progressive analysis includes class analysis that acknowledges that all Americans suffer when there are wars overseas, no universal healthcare, starvation wages, polluted air and water, and crippling debt. Progressive True Politics sources tend to be marginalized by Party Politics sources with these labels: "radical," "socialist," "far-left," "communist." *20% of the diet.*

> **5. Libertarian & Conservative True Politics.** News and analysis that will point out flaws in both parties and that will sometimes suggest that the parties agree about most things and feign disagreement. Libertarian perspectives include analysis of privacy and liberty that critiques the encroaching surveillance state, never-ending wars, and our shrinking set of guaranteed personal rights. Conservative perspectives include attention to founding principles and favor deliberate consideration before advocating systemic change. Words used by Party Politics sources to marginalize and silence these sources: "radical," "fascist," "alt-right," "Nazi." *20% of the diet.*

Deep Politics

This final media food group includes reporting on the political system as a whole, considering both parties and their principles, and also examining the generally allowed parameters of debate and discussion. Even a casual observer of American politics will notice that important policies remain unaffected by elections even if the party in power changes. Deep politics analyzes the political decisions and disagreements occurring in this permanent political establishment, which is called the "permanent state" or the "deep state." Deep political analysis also contemplates covert agreements between the parties, including conspiracies, both those discussed openly in the mainstream media (alleged Russian election interference; 9/11 hijackings; etc.) and those not generally discussed in the mainstream media (election fraud; faked acts of foreign aggression; assassinations; climate engineering; CIA-backed coups, etc.).

> **6. Deep Politics.** News and analysis covering our country's underlying power structures. Examining policies—even hidden ones—about things like war, energy, the money supply, and surveillance that are constructed largely by unelected officials permanently ensconced in intelligence organizations, the Pentagon, and other executive departments. Words used to marginalize and silence these sources: "paranoid," "wacky," "conspiracy theorist." *10% of the diet.*

THE SOURCES

AFTER REVIEWING HUNDREDS OF SOURCES AND USING A WEIGHTED rating to balance the selections, I recommend the following forty sources for your 2023 balanced diet. If you supplement them with other sources of your own, pay close attention to the overall balance of your diet. The sources are divided by size: *networks*, *magazines*, and *individual journalists*. The sources are also tagged with their appropriate *food group* and *viewpoint*.

NETWORKS

Al Jazeera

An international Arab news network with a full English version. Relatively open news coverage of international events. Based in Qatar, owned by a Qatari public-private partnership with majority funding from the Qatari government.

Media Food Group: Foreign Politics

Viewpoint: International, Middle Eastern, Arab

China Daily

The major English-language Chinese newspaper. *The China Daily,* or 人民日报, covers international news, with a focus on Chinese affairs. Founded and funded completely by the Chinese government and based in China. If you're concerned about foreign propaganda, please consider that all media—particularly government or corporate-funded media—is propaganda. See the description of RT, below, to be inspired to read foreign media nonetheless.

Media Food Group: Foreign Politics

Viewpoint: International, Chinese

CNN

The biggest corporate news network in the world. Currently has a Democrat bias but has shifted over the years, generally slanted against the party in the White House. Showed countless Trump rallies unedited in 2016, for instance, but then intensely critical of Trump as president. Favorable toward Biden and Democrats now. Owned by the AT&T-TimeWarner-Discovery conglomerate. Based in New York.

Media Food Group: Corporate Party Politics

Viewpoint: Democrat

Fox News

The big Republican-leaning, corporate political news network. Owned by Fox Corporation, with Rupert Murdoch as chairman and 39% ownership via a family trust.[18] Based in New York.

Media Food Group: Corporate Party Politics

Viewpoint: Republican

MSNBC

The big Democrat-leaning, corporate political news network. Originally founded through a joint venture between Bill Gates's Microsoft and GE's NBC News, which created the name: "MS-NBC." Now the DNC's favorite media titan is owned by giant media conglomerate Comcast. Based in New York.

Media Food Group: Corporate Party Politics

Viewpoint: Democrat

Newsmax

Founded in 1998, two years after Fox, by a conservative investigative reporter named Christopher Ruddy, Newsmax has grown in Fox's shadow but already commands a sizable audience among American conservatives. Trump famously noted his preference for Newsmax over Fox in 2020. Based in New York.

Media Food Group: Independent Party Politics

Viewpoint: Republican

"The first rule is to keep an untroubled spirit.
The second is to look things in the face
and know them for what they are."
—Marcus Aurelius

NPR

The government-founded, American radio network. At one point, NPR and its affiliates were primarily supported by government funding, but that was phased out during the Reagan and Clinton years—the era of media deregulation—and now they are generally supported by corporations and corporate foundations like J&J's Robert Wood Johnson Foundation. With the increased corporate underwriting, NPR has become too big and too heavily influenced by corporate forces to be considered independent. Strong establishment and Democrat bias. Based in Washington, D.C.

Media Food Group: Corporate Party Politics

Viewpoint: Democrat

One America News

Founded in 2013 at the behest of AT&T, which wanted another conservative network for its cable and satellite lineups, OAN now carries a strong Republican and, at times, anti-establishment and libertarian bias. Founder Robert Herring, a controversial, self-made millionaire, built the network with strategic, friendly coverage of Donald Trump when other networks shunned him in the early stages of the 2016 campaign. Based in San Diego.

Media Food Group: Independent Party Politics

Viewpoint: Republican

RT

A major international news network funded in part by the Russian government. We are in a never-ending Red Scare, so you're supposed to be afraid of this network, but in truth, it's a great source of alternative perspectives that will broaden your mind. It does have its bias, of course, as do all of these sources. But as you watch, think of the open-minded people in East Germany in 1970 listening to Voice of America, or the open-minded people in China today watching CNN. You're smart enough to consider unfamiliar ideas, that's the point of a media diet. In fact, as we saw in the last chapter, many of the commentators on RT are brilliant Americans who were too outspoken for the corporate media's pro-war bias: Phil Donahue, Larry King, Ed Schultz, Jesse Ventura, etc. Unfortunately, at the outset of the Ukraine proxy war between the US and Russia, as narrative management hit fever pitch prior to this new war, large corporations stepped in and killed the venerable *RT America.*[19]

Media Food Group: Foreign Politics

Viewpoint: International, Russian

Telesur

An international news network funded by a coalition of Latin American countries to counter CNN's influence. A great regular complement to an American's media diet, Telesur tends to provide alternative viewpoints with a left-leaning—at times socialist—take on international events.

Media Food Group: Foreign Politics

Viewpoint: International, Latin American (Bolivia, Cuba, El Salvador, Venezuela)

MAGAZINES & NEWSPAPERS

The Atlantic

Perhaps the epitome of a left-leaning establishment magazine, this political journal has been in print since the 1800s. After changing hands several times recently, it's now owned by the Emerson Collective, a foundation started by billionaire Laurene Powell Jobs, former Apple

CEO Steve Jobs' widow. Like the *New York Times,* it is a trendsetter for Blue News narratives. Based in Washington D.C.

Media Food Group: Independent Party Politics

Viewpoint: Democrat

The Epoch Times

A conservative-leaning, national paper, the *Epoch Times* was founded in 2000 by a graduate student, John Tang, in his basement in Decatur, Georgia. He originally reported on the repression inside his native China of his spiritual practice, Falun Gong, and attempted to expose the rampant Chinese censorship. The paper has grown considerably, particularly in the last decade, to national prominence. The clearest *bias* in its pages is firm opposition to the ever-growing power of the Chinese government. Perhaps to build up adversaries to that power, the paper tends to support nationalist movements around the world. Based in New York.

Media Food Group: Independent Party Politics

Viewpoint: Republican

MintPress News

An independent, anti-war, and anti-establishment investigative journal, *MintPress News* was founded in 2012 by Mnar Muhawesh Adley, a Minnesota journalist, because she found the American media overly supportive of wars and government surveillance. The journal has reported fearlessly ever since on these topics, and it has several groundbreaking investigations to its credit, several of which are featured in this book. Today, it's heavily attacked in corporate media with that sublime slur, "conspiracy theory." Based in Minnesota.

Media Food Group: Independent Deep Politics

Viewpoint: Nonpartisan

Consortium News

A great source for deeper analysis of the current American political situation. It was one of the first internet-based news magazines, founded by Robert Parry in 1995. Parry was the journalist who broke the Iran-Contra Scandal in the 1980s, and he is one of many journalists who have (unfortunately) been fired by corporate media for taking a step too far investigating controversial topics. Based in Virginia.

Media Food Group: Independent Deep Politics

Viewpoint: Nonpartisan

Democracy Now

A progressive television and radio show produced in New York by longtime left media personage Amy Goodman. Provides generally under-reported news on labor and social movements as well as coverage of foreign news with a focus on the effects of American sanctions and military violence. Based in New York.

Media Food Group: Independent True Politics

Viewpoint: Progressive

Global Research

Provides a trenchant critique of deep politics, focusing on the ramifications of American and Western foreign policy, American empire, terrorism, state-sponsored violence, and wars. Pulls no punches in appraising current events and American history. Based in Ottawa, Canada.

Media Food Group: Independent Deep Politics

Viewpoint: Nonpartisan

Daily Sceptic

A Britain-based review of news that questions dominant narratives. During the pandemic, they expertly questioned the justification of draconian worldwide lockdowns, offering balance for the corporate media's incessant defense of those restrictions. Great for balancing perspectives. Unfortunately, it has been a target of censorship and was demonetized by PayPal in 2022 as this book was going to print.[20] Based in London.

Media Food Group: Independent True Politics

Viewpoint: Nonpartisan

Jacobin

A socialist-leaning political magazine founded as an online magazine in 2010 by Bhaskar Sunkara, its popularity—and print edition—took off with the Sanders campaign in 2016. Sunkara's idea is to take socialist ideas out of intellectual papers and put them in a glossy, mass-appeal magazine. With a fearless attitude, the journal provides useful critiques of the Democratic Party from the left, not sparing the nominally progressive members of Congress. Based in New York, NY.

Media Food Group: Independent True Politics

Viewpoint: Progressive

New York Times ($)

Perhaps the most prestigious media organ in the world, certainly the most widely circulated Democrat-leaning paper in the country, this is the agenda-setter for left-leaning media, the "paper of record." Exhaustively reports on many international events. This news organization was also the most important asset of Operation Mockingbird, which recruited journalists to work for the CIA. Owned primarily by the American Ochs-Sulzberger family and Mexican billionaire Carlos Slim.[21] *Paywall after 3 articles.*

Media Food Group: Corporate Party Politics

Viewpoint: Democrat

The Nation ($)

Founded in 1865, this is the country's oldest weekly magazine.[22] A longtime progressive news source founded as an abolitionist journal that supported Republicans, *The Nation* is still putting out trenchant analysis and great journalism, although currently more in-line with Democrat talking points than in years past. Sometimes treads the line between Party Politics and True Politics, but lately, it offers mostly Party Politics. Based in New York. *Paywall after 6 articles.*

Media Food Group: Independent Party Politics

Viewpoint: Democrat

National Review

A traditional pillar of right-leaning thought, it was founded in the 1950s by conservative pillar William F. Buckley Jr. *National Review* has featured, critiqued, and strengthened a variety of strands of conservative thought over the decades.

Media Food Group: Independent True Politics

Viewpoint: Conservative

Reason

A leading libertarian magazine, it was founded in 1968 as a mimeographed newsletter and has grown into an important journal with a refreshing perspective on politics and culture. In a time of intense, two-dimensional political rancor, *Reason* offers a third dimension, one that is necessary when things like lockdowns and forced medical procedures are in the political discourse. Styles itself "Journal of free minds and free markets." Based in Los Angeles.

Media Food Group: Independent True Politics

Viewpoint: Libertarian

Breaking Points

A daily news show with a refreshing populist perspective and a balance of progressive and conservative thought. Co-hosts Krystal Ball (progressive) and Saagar Enjeti (conservative) analyze Beltway and national politics, and when they engage in principled debates with each other, we have a model for thoughtful political discourse. Based in Washington, D.C.

Media Food Group: Independent True Politics

Viewpoint: Bipartisan

Wall Street Journal ($)

One of the oldest American daily newspapers, and the nation's first truly national paper, the WSJ today focuses on business news but has considerable political coverage and clout too, including a famously conservative editorial page. Owned by billionaire Rupert Murdoch's News Corporation. Based in New York. *Paywall after one article.*

Media Food Group: Corporate Party Politics

Viewpoint: Republican

Your local newspaper

Stay apprised of what's going on in your town, city, and region. Practice your *bias* detectors by identifying your local paper's slant. You probably have at least two local newspapers. Regardless of perspective, the closer journalism is to where you live, the more honest it will be about the events in your local community.

Media Food Group: Corporate Party Politics

Viewpoint: Republican or Democrat

INDIVIDUAL JOURNALISTS & COLUMNISTS

Sharyl Attkisson

After three decades as a correspondent and anchor at CNN, PBS, and CBS News, Attkisson resigned from CBS in 2014, citing bias and a vanishing commitment to investigative journalism. She claimed her ability to impartially cover the Obama administration was undermined and hamstrung by the corporate networks. Today, she produces investigative news articles and a popular, 30-minute weekly news show called *Full Measure* reaching 43 million.[23] As an author, she has written three *New York Times* bestsellers, including *Slanted: How the News Media Taught Us to Love Censorship and Hate Journalism*. Attkisson's bias is nonpartisan; a dyed-in-the-wool investigative journalist, she lets the chips fall where they may.

Media Food Group: Independent True Politics

Viewpoint: Nonpartisan

Del Bigtree, The Highwire

After several years as a CBS producer on *Doctors*, Del Bigtree was approached by a doctor with information about a CDC whistleblower and a suppressed link between autism and the MMR vaccine. Bigtree left CBS and directed an acclaimed, heterodox documentary called *Vaxxed: From Cover-Up to Catastrophe* to tell the story. He set out on his own thereafter, and his weekly investigative tour de force *The Highwire* took a critical approach to the covid lockdowns, vaccines, and mask mandates, and became a runaway success as one of few news sources balancing the one-sided corporate media. The show was abruptly removed by YouTube and Facebook after interviewing scientists who suggested a lab origin to the virus. Based in Texas.

Media Food Group: Independent True Politics

Viewpoint: Nonpartisan

Rachel Blevins

Progressive news commentator who, like Phil Donahue, Ed Schultz, and Krystal Ball, was fired for being too outspoken on corporate mainstream media. Her stated goal is to "look beyond the false 'left vs. right' paradigm that is prevalent in American media" and pay attention to issues not covered elsewhere.

Media Food Group: Independent True Politics

Viewpoint: Progressive

Tucker Carlson

A conservative Fox News commentator who freely switches from toeing the party line to brashly marching to his own independent drum on current national politics. He speaks his own mind particularly on foreign policy and was one of few corporate media anchors questioning the buildup to the proxy war in Ukraine. Rumor has it, Carlson is the only news commentator that Donald Trump watches.

Media Food Group: Corporate Party Politics

Viewpoint: Republican

Jimmy Dore

A comedian by day in the tradition of George Carlin, Jimmy Dore has built a political news analysis show on YouTube that rivals in viewership many corporate media shows. He takes mainstream news stories each day and points out the propaganda and corruption of the writers, often ripping their coverage apart with trenchant analysis. He is a progressive at heart, and at times, his bias shows in his populist support for issues like ending wars, student debt cancellation, and Medicare for All, but his first passion is clearly unveiling the truth and exposing liars.

Media Food Group: Independent True Politics

Viewpoint: Progressive

Glenn Greenwald

The talented investigative journalist who provided Edward Snowden with his initial media connections to tell the world about massive American surveillance,[24] Greenwald co-founded *The Intercept* to provide censorship-free opportunities to American journalism. He then left that publication after five years when it censored him and "became its antithesis," as mentioned in the previous chapter. Greenwald, who is gay, is now based in Brazil. After *The Intercept,* he is writing independently again and reporting on issues like censorship and civil liberties better than ever.

Media Food Group: Independent True Politics

Viewpoint: Progressive

Christopher Hedges

Cogent, even caustic, left critic of capitalism, the Democrats, and our current American system, which he calls, with formidable evidence, "corporate totalitarianism." Silenced by the *New York Times* for being insufficiently supportive of the 2003 invasion of Iraq, Hedges is one of several heirs apparent to Noam Chomsky. Eminently worth listening to. Six years of his show *On Contact* have been disappeared by You-Tube.[25] He can still be found on ScheerPost.com and the Real News Network.

Media Food Group: Independent True Politics

Viewpoint: Progressive

Kim Iversen

From a successful career on several corporate radio stations to hosting an independent show of her own, Iversen has found a following with her trenchant and balanced political analysis. One of many solo video bloggers today doing excellent independent journalism, her perspective defies easy labels: she has both conservative and progressive biases, establishment and anti-establishment views. Her views depend on the issue at hand, which suggests she has that rare quality, integrity.

Media Food Group: Independent True Politics

Viewpoint: Nonpartisan

Caitlin Johnstone

Uncommonly insightful independent writer with a deep analytical perspective that is unique, Johnstone points out the flaws and corruption in both parties and explores the underlying forces directing both. She peppers her political commentary with sardonic humor, four-letter words, and occasional appeals to universal spirituality. Her bias is progressive, but she writes about deep politics, unveiling false narratives on both the left and right, and there is little partisanship in her outlook.

Media Food Group: Independent Deep Politics

Viewpoint: Progressive

Aaron Maté, The Grayzone

An independent journalist with a keen eye for uncovering media distortion in foreign affairs reporting, Maté has provided riveting clarity on many narratives explored in this book: the endless *#RussiaGate* fabrications, the alleged gas attacks in Syria, and the frequently censored genocide going on in Yemen. He's written for years for *The Nation* (above), and recently joined independent news network *The Grayzone* with fellow journalists Max Blumenthal and Anya Parampil, and perhaps unsurprisingly, British corporate media is now attempting to censor *The Grayzone*.[26]

Media Food Group: Independent Deep Politics

Viewpoint: Progressive

Andy Ngo

A conservative-leaning investigative journalist and best-selling author. The child of Vietnamese immigrants, Ngo is a courageous independent journalist who documented many of the excesses of the Antifa and Black Lives Matter protests in 2019 and 2020. He himself was beaten for filming violence and property destruction in his then-hometown of Portland, OR. He moved to the UK in 2020 on account of death threats for his reporting. Ngo is gay and writes for the *New York Post, Newsweek*, and is head editor at the *Post Millennial*, a Canadian news magazine.

Media Food Group: Independent True Politics

Viewpoint: Conservative

Joe Rogan

Probably the most popular podcast in the world, *The Joe Rogan Experience* has transformed the way many Americans see news and information. With its three-hour, free-ranging nonpartisan discussions, Rogan's show is a significant part of the currently unfolding New Enlightenment. For this reason, it is frequently attacked in corporate mainstream media. At one point, for instance, CNN played deliberately doctored clips of Rogan to make him look pale and unhealthy.[27] Important to check out at least occasionally. Based in Texas.

Media Food Group: Independent True Politics

Viewpoint: Nonpartisan

Freddie Sayers, Unherd

British journalist Freddie Sayers creates high-quality, often superb interviews. As balanced information and data on the coronavirus and lockdowns grew difficult to find in 2020, *Unherd* featured political leaders and expert scientists on all sides of the thorniest questions. Indeed, it was perhaps as un-2020 as news sources came, featuring long, thoughtful conversations rather than fearful soundbites. Sayers continues his excellent work, providing balanced and patient interviews.

Media Food Group: Foreign News

Viewpoint: Nonpartisan

Jordan Schachtel

An indefatigable independent journalist with a foreign affairs focus and a conservative slant, Schachtel left conservative network Breitbart News in 2016 on principle, alleging incessant "party-line Trump propaganda." During covid, his investigative work countering what he saw as groupthink on the lockdowns, masks, and the Capitol protests provided important perspective. Schachtel's reporting and analysis lends helpful balance to the everyday bias of corporate news.

Media Food Group: Independent True Politics

Viewpoint: Conservative

Ben Swann

A quintessential investigative journalist, Swann founded a news analysis segment called *Reality Check* and a social media channel called *Truth in Media* while working in corporate news television in Atlanta and Cincinnati. He anchored these segments for years. At one point, he won nationwide praise for pressing Obama in an interview about drone strikes. He was then suspended for investigating "Pizzagate" in 2017 and fired in 2018.[28] Now on his own, Swann founded an independent media platform, Sovren, and resurrected *Reality Check*, a show that again provides a great counterpoint to corporate media narratives.

Media Food Group: Independent True Politics

Viewpoint: Conservative

FORTY SOURCES, THIRTY MINUTES, TWENTY DOLLARS

AND THAT'S IT. FORTY SOURCES FOR A BALANCED DIET THAT WILL BUILD and develop *media consciousness.* Following this diet for a month will focus your attention, grant your mind a new outlook on events and the world, and set you on the path to understanding the political views of anyone you meet. Media consciousness is a journey, not a destination. Welcome it as a mental technique, an approach to listening, a method to keep getting smarter, a gift that keeps on giving.

Countless independent news sources are out there, of course, many of which are worth listening to at times. We could have included many more names, such as Greg Palast, Lee Camp, Matt Taibbi, Fiorella Isabel, Kyle Kulinski, Charles Eisenstein, Eva Bartlett, Bret Weinstein, Sabrina Salvati, Russell Brand, Vanessa Beeley, Dylan Ratigan, Michel Chossudovsky, Max Blumenthal, Alex Berenson, Kevin Williamson, Niko House, Dave Rubin, and many, many more. Others, unknown to me at the time of this writing, you will discover as your media journey unfolds.

A quick note on something I've barely mentioned: money. While nearly all sources selected above are free to read or view, a few have instituted a paywall; these are marked with a dollar sign ($). For these, read the number of articles allowed, then move on to the next source in the day's diet. You can also choose to pay the subscription fee, of course, but in that case, try to contribute equally to all sources you consume. Many independent journalists offer their writing for free as they attempt to build an audience but encourage donations too. I recommend devoting thirty minutes each day and twenty dollars each month. See how that feels; customize as required.

The funding of quality journalism is a complex and contentious issue, something we'll discuss in the next chapter.

THE DIET

FINALLY, THE DIET ITSELF. AFTER YEARS OF EXPLORATION AND EXPERImentation, here is what I recommend. Refer to the chart on the next page. View at least one episode or one article from each source each day.

Before you get started, pick how much time you can realistically spend. The diet has three levels to fit various lifestyles and media appetites. Thirty minutes a day will have an enormous impact on your awareness of the country and world around us. Step it up to sixty minutes or two hours if you want to accelerate your journey to *media consciousness*.

Bon Appetit!

◈ BASIC. "Conscious Citizen." (30 minutes daily)

◈ INTERMEDIATE. "Informed Journalist." (1 hour daily)

◈ EXPERT. "Media Critic." (2 hours daily)

There's a fourth option, too, for when it's time to unplug:

◈ UNPLUGGED. "On a Media Fast." (1 hour weekly)

If, after a few days, the diet seems overwhelming, I recommend focusing on certain topics. Pick one or two events or issues in the news that you care most about, and only read about those issues. For instance, let's say you care most about taxes and environmental policy. For the week, read what each source in your diet writes or says about taxes and environmental policy. The following week, you can keep the same issues, or pick new ones. The diet is balanced on a weekly basis, so it is important to stick with the same events or issues at least for one week.

It's helpful to bookmark the sites of your diet on your phone or web browser, or visit BalancedMediaDiet.com, so that you don't have to type in the addresses every time.

BALANCED DIETS

	SUNDAY	MONDAY	TUESDAY	WEDNESDAY	THURSDAY	FRIDAY	SATURDAY
BASIC (Conscious Citizen) *Example*	Your Local Newspaper	NPR	Breaking Points	RT	Your Local Newspaper	The Highwire	Fox News
	Mint Press News	Glenn Greenwald	Tucker Carlson	Kim Iversen	Consortium News	New York Times ($)	Daily Sceptic
INTERMEDIATE (Informed Journalist) *Example*	Unherd	Sharyl Attkisson	CNN	Caitlin Johnstone	Jimmy Dore	Joe Rogan	The Nation ($)
	Aaron Maté	Al Jazeera	China Daily	Newsmax	Epoch Times	Christopher Hedges	Reason
EXPERT (Media Critic) *Example*	Jordan Schachtel	Global Research	Jacobin	National Review	The Atlantic	OAN	Your Local Newspaper
	MSNBC	Wall Street Journal ($)	Ben Swann	Rachel Blevins	Andy Ngo	Democracy Now	Telesur
UNPLUGGED (Media Fast) *Example*	Your Local Newspaper			RT (or) China Daily			

BASIC
(Conscious Citizen)
30 MINUTES DAILY
Spend 30 minutes with these sources.

INTERMEDIATE
(Informed Journalist)
1 HOUR DAILY
Do BASIC then spend 30 more minutes with these.

EXPERT
(Media Critic)
2 HOURS DAILY
Do BASIC & INTERMEDIATE then 60 minutes with these.

UNPLUGGED
(Media Fast)
1 HOUR WEEKLY
Pick 2 sources from BASIC. Spend 30 minutes with each.

Legend: LOCAL NEWSPAPER · FOREIGN NEWS · PARTY POLITICS · TRUE POLITICS · DEEP POLITICS

A NEW WORLD AWAITS

YES, CORPORATE MEDIA SOURCES ARE INCLUDED IN THE BALANCED Media Diet. This is done for three reasons. First, for basic awareness: it's important to know what the dominant narratives are on both sides of the aisle. Second, for balance: some corporate media coverage is quite good despite rampant *systemic* and *nefarious bias*. Third, and most important, for cultivating *media consciousness:* viewing corporate media alongside independent media will help you identify biases and see through them—you'll begin to interpret corporate media reports by noticing not just what is being said, but *how* it's being said, *who* gets to speak, *what* is left out, and *how* the coverage wants you to feel.

We all need to find reputable sources of news, and a Balanced Media Diet is the fastest way that I have found to get there. I don't know exactly which news sources you will ultimately trust, but I do know that if you don't start from a balanced diet, you will likely end up in an echo chamber. The essential approach to all sources, both corporate and independent, is to listen, to learn, and to *consciously* identify bias.

Fast food conglomerates use advertisements to coerce us to eat one way or another. The giant media corporations would like nothing better than to convince us that the world was better when there were fewer sources, that it's inconvenient to read a diversity of news sources, and that they're best suited to determine for us which news sources are trustworthy and which are "disinformation." For instance, the *New York Times* can manipulate the coverage of Tara Reade's sexual assault allegations against Joe Biden, and it's considered in hindsight to be a "regrettable mistake," while an analysis that appears on, say, *The Highwire* about the possibility the *sars-cov-2* virus originated in a lab that makes allegations that are neither proven nor disproven—and later turn out to be true—is called "disinformation."

In the old media world, the *quality* of reporting or analysis doesn't matter, it's the *source* of reporting or analysis that determines whether news is fake or real.

It's time to leave that world behind. A Balanced Media Diet is the best and most efficient path that I have found to do so. You have endless insight and wisdom to gain, and only a little time and your blind spots to lose. What are you waiting for?

14

THE NEW
ENLIGHTENMENT

"The universe is made of stories, not of atoms."

Muriel Rukeyser

IN A SMALL COTTAGE IN MEDIEVAL STRASBOURG, JOHANNES GUTENBERG built a printing press with one small tweak. The letters could be moved. He printed a page, and then he moved the letters to print the next page. Soon, he found he could print whole books much more quickly—and cheaply—than before. He printed the first of what would become thousands upon thousands of "Gutenberg Bibles." The year was 1442, and there was no earthly way for the serfs and lords in the surrounding hills of feudal Germany and France to know the extraordinary extent to which Gutenberg's innovation would transform the world. Gutenberg himself could scarcely have imagined that he was setting into motion an irresistible force that would upend the power structures of humanity.

The invention of the movable-type press granted powers to everyday people that had until that time been the unique province of elite priests and wealthy bishops. These were the powers to read, to write, and to publish.[1]

Before long, these new powers were in the hands of the peoples of Europe, and with them came the incomparable ability to share information with one another without an intermediary authority. This dissemination of knowledge caused an unprecedented flowering of language, literacy, communication, and philosophy that over the ensuing three centuries launched what we now call the Enlightenment. The epoch ushered in modern science, art, and politics.

In 1605, in that very same city of Strasbourg, a German bookbinder named Johann Carolus printed the world's first newspaper.[2] Locals submitted to him reports of events, artisans and merchants supplied him their prices, and in a true Renaissance achievement, this talented man printed it for all in a publication called *The Account of all Distinguished and Commemorable Stories.*

The centuries that followed brought countless more breakthroughs of science and technology: telegraphs, then photographs. Telegrams, then telephones. Radio, then television. An enormous network of undersea cables was deployed over the course of a century, enabling global communication.

In 1989, working at CERN, a lab in Geneva not far from the hills of Strasbourg, an English scientist named Tim Berners-Lee wrote a computer-networking protocol similar to others at the time but with a small tweak. The letters of a word in a document on one computer server could be linked to information on another server. Berners-Lee published the first website in 1990. His site documented how to use this *hypertext transfer protocol* (HTTP) to share information.[3]

Berners-Lee had no way of knowing at the time that this new mode of linking information would sweep the planet and transform human awareness and consciousness. Within barely a year, electronic message boards popped up and personal modems arrived, allowing anyone on Earth to use HTTP to instantaneously communicate with anyone else. Within two years, websites blossomed everywhere like flowers after a lush spring rain. Web browsers arrived next, enabling anyone connected to this thing called "the internet" to share information—words and images—instantaneously with people all over the world without an intermediary authority.

No one fully understands the metamorphosis we are witnessing in global society. The internet is transforming communication, connection, and governance. It is revolutionizing science, art, and politics. It is upending the power structures of humanity.

No one fully grasps what the ability to instantly share any and every tidbit of information with the entire world means for us as a human race and as a network of spiritually conscious human beings.

What is clear is that we are in the midst of another Enlightenment.

Great Peril and Great Possibility

We are again moving away from a top-down model for the distribution of knowledge. We are shifting to a peer-to-peer model. Just as the bishops and priests of the Middle Ages clung jealously to their top-down model by which they alone could determine and dispense spiritual truth, indulgences, and salvation, the anointed editors and executives of the five giant American news corporations clutch fiercely to theirs. This modern, top-down model of determining and dispensing truth grants these giant corporations the authority to decide *what* events are covered, *how* those events are covered, and *who* gets to cover and speak about them. The media organizations—and now the social media executives—have grown accustomed to controlling the narrative we believe we are living in. Yet, the rapid distribution of knowledge, our desire to freely express ourselves, and our burgeoning instinct to question prescribed narratives are steadily pulling us away from their dominion.

The internet is shifting everything. Even Americans who don't follow a plan like a Balanced Media Diet are already informing themselves by mixing corporate establishment news with independent news that they find via social media. For the majority of Americans, the mix is shifting in only one direction—toward independent media,[4] toward bottom-up and peer-to-peer information sharing.[5] This shift is dissolving many old, institutionalized, oppressive ways of sharing power and information and birthing a new era of broader awareness. We are witnessing the crumbling of consensus reality and the birth of something new. This might sound worrisome until we realize that the consensus reality that is crumbling has often been wholly false as the examples in this book demonstrate.

It is an exciting time and a disconcerting time. It is a time of both great peril and great possibility.

The great possibility is that we are entering an era in which we create our own narratives, free from the manipulative *systemic* and *nefarious biases* of power-hungry corporations, governments, and intelligence agencies. In this benign future, we will create our news narratives based on eyewitness testimony that we share instantaneously and analyze together as a global community of diverse and engaged individuals. The veracity of our beliefs about the world around us will expand and increase as we replace censorship and propaganda with an inclusive *smorgasbord* of authentic reports.

We will also remember the cultural values that we share. As we've discussed, a society *does* need a shared story or myth to survive and thrive, but this does not require the propaganda favored by people ranging from Edward Bernays to Joseph Stalin. We Americans have sustaining stories that can connect us, bind us together, and form the backdrop to the inevitable news narratives that change with daily events. We can find our society's shared aspirational goals in our First Amendment's guarantees, in our Declaration of Independence's creed that "all [people] are created equal," and in the notion that government exists primarily to "ensure domestic tranquility" and "secure the blessings of liberty." Our nation's long, winding journey toward these goals provides a narrative that is both connecting and inspiring.

In the fifteenth century, the bishops and feudal lords decreed that no one needed information about existence beyond the gospels and history they provided. But it turned out that quite a few serfs, merchants, and artisans of feudal Europe were interested in reading the Bible themselves—and other books too. They began to *write* books as well. The nerve! The Church denounced these wayward souls as heretics, fakes, witches, blasphemers, and sinners. Yet, those wayward souls created a new world that soon dissolved the power of both the Church and feudalism.

The task of the anointed bishops and lords of our time—the editors and pundits of corporate media—is to vilify all alternative narratives as illegitimate and false. This denunciation is the entire justification for the terms "fake news" and "disinformation." They yearn to suppress peer-to-peer distribution of information and to reassert their top-down ownership of the dissemination of truth.

The great peril of our era is that they might succeed. Their powers are formidable, and their arts of deception have been refined over a full century of deployed propaganda. Mockingbird-style distribution of news narratives and the tools of *nefarious bias* have successfully engineered support for wars, hidden the actions of a serial pedophile, concealed the origins of a virus, and pushed countless other stories as needed by the manipulators whom Bernays called "the invisible government."

The peril is profound. The breathtaking advances in technology of this new era enable greater censorship, oppression, and tyranny than the world has ever seen.

This is why we must learn to identify false narratives. By following a media diet and learning to spot false narratives, we can undermine—and ultimately defeat—the reactionaries' push toward centralized, authoritative control.

How to Bake a Narrative in Five Easy Steps

The creation of narratives has been refined to an art form. By following a Balanced Media Diet, you will learn to spot narrative management and identify its five key steps:

1. Anonymous intelligence agents, government officials, or public relations officers issue a report that leads to a story in a mainstream corporate channel;

2. Other establishment channels repeat the narrative like mockingbirds;

3. The narrative is "laundered" into independent media via "astroturf" sites and magazines to lend it grassroots credibility;

4. The filters of *systemic bias* remove, reduce, and redirect viewpoints and facts that undermine the narrative;

5. Finally, opposing narratives are censored by social media corporations and "fact-checked" into oblivion by websites funded by the same news and social media corporations.

Sophisticated narrative management like this only succeeds in the absence of a Free Press. The framers of the Constitution guaranteed a Free Press specifically to create and defend a wide variety of publications that would often disagree. Together, these publications are to serve the roles of *watchdog*, *smorgasbord*, and *bulletin*, and thereby prevent systematic and authoritarian control of the news. Thus the rise of independent media is restoring a truly oppositional and informative press to our society, and thereby undermining corporate media narrative control. This is the New Enlightenment.

When independent journalists such as Kim Iverson, Glenn Greenwald, or Sharyl Attkisson interpret the day's events differently than do, say, Fox News or the *New York Times*, their alternative analyses lead to alternative—and often truer—narratives about current events. These alternative narratives are met with harsh suppression by corporate news and social media channels in an attempt to maintain unilateral control. Any independent outlet reliably providing alternative narratives is marked as "a source of disinformation" and marginalized, dismissed, or forcibly taken down. Dissenting reports are labeled "fake news" or "misinformation," or, when that's insufficient, tarred with the harsher, anti-intellectual epithet that serves as today's "blasphemer" or "witch": *conspiracy theorist*. These slurs aim to marginalize and silence not only journalists but free thinkers of all stripes who use the new, peer-to-peer models of information exchange to understand the world and arrive at deeper truths. This is the war for your mind that is raging today. Citizens increasingly want to create and share news freely while reactionaries want to centralize power and wealth more tightly into their own hands.

Searching for New Models

Part of the peril and possibility that stares at us as this battle rages is that we do not yet have a successful business model for independent media. The mythical model of "professional, objective journalism" that has reigned for a century was created by John Rockefeller and other reactionaries in the early 1900s to justify concentrated media ownership. Although some great journalism occurred during the twentieth century under this model, the blind spots built into the system slowly but steadily doomed it to the scrapheap of history. The coverage always carried *systemic bias*—if not *nefarious bias* too—and was confined within boundaries that slowly constricted over the decades. That model brought us to our current media world, which is controlled by five corporate behemoths intolerant of dissent and bent on narrative control.

The system has failed; it is dying. But the new system is not fully realized yet. Thousands of independent media voices have sprung up in a flowering New Enlightenment, but they don't yet have a functional business model, one that works for organizations both small and large without depending on corporate advertising from the giant drugmakers, profiteering banks, or weapons manufacturers. It is beyond the scope of this book to examine every potential model—there are many fascinating ideas out there—but we'll quickly examine two models that are already in practice. I propose one new idea here as well.

1. **Subscriber Supported.** This is perhaps the best and most obvious model, and it has developed organically on the internet. Sites like Substack and Supercast specialize today in empowering readers to support independent journalism via small monthly contributions. As I mentioned in the previous chapter, if everyone followed a Balanced Media Diet and then donated a few dollars each month to the sources they trusted most, we would have a functioning Free Press in no time.

2. **Advertiser Supported.** This is the model that has supported journalism throughout previous eras, including during the flowering of the original Free Press in this country in the 1700s and 1800s. It has the obvious flaw of allowing powerful business interests to buy influence—even censorship—in national news coverage. This flaw drives the potent Advertisers filter of *systemic bias* in our news today. Nevertheless, the model is not without merit. If a news source clearly and prominently names its advertisers, viewers can see whose influence is at play, and they can interpret advertising as a type of *innocent bias*. In this scenario, this model can sustain authentic journalism.

3. **Government Supported.** This is my new proposal. It has tremendous potential, but it needs to be handled carefully. The government could play a creative, supplemental role in defending and nurturing the Fourth Estate. Newspapers paid the cheapest postal rates in the 1800s precisely because the government recognized the essential role of the press in our democracy. Today, the government could step in and provide every American adult with, say, $100 in coupons to donate to news organizations of their choice. This would give citizens—not corporations—the say as to which sources receive support. Provided the government was strictly prohibited from blacklisting any news organization, a Free Press would thrive and endure under this model.[6]

Regardless of which model or models ultimately succeed, the good news is that support will be abundant. After the Sanders movement in 2015 led to the creation of alternative media on the populist left, and after the Trump election in 2016 birthed an even broader alternative news ecosystem on the right, more and more Americans are reading a broad diversity of sources, questioning the narratives pushed by the corporate media, and thinking for themselves. As the wild years of the early 2020s unfold, it matters less today whether readers have arrived at independent news from the Sanders or Trump movements. Millions have seen behind the curtain of this Wizard of Oz and no longer trust its pronouncements.

The *Times*, Fox News, the intelligence agencies, and the corporations whose words appear in the establishment media will aim to reverse this trend and extinguish any support independent media organizations find. They do not want you to think for yourself, as doing so threatens their business model and, worse, their most precious commodity: control over your beliefs and doubts, your fears and hopes, and your sense of fact and fiction.

But it's too late. Ratings for American news media have been spiraling downward for most of this century, and that has accelerated in this new decade. Already half of Americans get their news first—at least sometimes—from social media,[7] especially younger Americans.[8] A quarter of us already turn to YouTube and freely mix corporate and independent news.[9]

Phase Three of the New Enlightenment

Of course, many millions of people, particularly in our nation's older generations, remain comfortable with the top-down model of information dissemination that they grew up with. They are more easily frightened by labels like "fake news" and "conspiracy theories" that are placed on independent media because they are more mentally set in their ways and generally feel safe in the models they've known all their lives. Reassuring them about the sources they listen to—and scaring them about alternative sources—usually is not difficult.

But younger people and the many free thinkers in our older generations are already getting their news from a mix of independent and corporate media,[10] and the nationwide shift is clearly toward political independence and independent media—toward bottom-up and peer-to-peer exchanges of news, ideas, and information. Americans by the millions are losing trust in political parties with top-down models, and by extension top-down Blue News and

Red News media networks.[11]

We have already moved through three phases of the New Enlightenment and are approaching the fourth. This is my best attempt at this time to outline the early history of this new epoch:

- **"Web 1.0."** Decentralized *access* to information (1995–2005). This was the beginning of the global internet, the dawning of the New Enlightenment. Suddenly, at their fingertips, human beings had instantaneous access to roughly, by 2005, the sum total of human information. Google was the symbolic, transformative company of the era.

- **"Web 2.0."** Decentralized *creation* of information (2005-2015). Quickly, user-created content took over the internet. Social media was born. People created their own content rather than simply sharing access to information compiled by others. News articles hosted interesting comments sections that were sometimes more informative than the articles themselves. Facebook was the symbolic, transformative company of the era.

- **"Web 3.0."** Decentralized *control* of information (2015–?). The revolution in consciousness and human connection grew palpable, shaking the halls of power. Americans who had been "red, white, and blind" were opening their eyes. News corporations realized a bit late they were losing control of the story. Corporate media sites shut down their comments sections. Social media sites introduced blocking, shadowbanning, and censorship. Blockchain-based video and free-speech social media were born. It's too early to determine the transformative company of the era.

- **"Web 4.0."** Decentralized **everything.** This is what is coming. I don't know exactly when nor exactly how. It's on its way.

The one inexorable force of this New Enlightenment is decentralization. We are in an era of breathtaking technological advances and inventions that are largely pushing power downward and outward. Yet, it is not clear that decentralization and distribution of power will have the final say. The war is between the forces that, on one hand, aim to use these advances to decentralize power back to freer, smaller groups and political entities, and forces that, on the other hand, aim to centralize global power into a tiny set of reactionary hands.

A TIME WITHOUT CONSENSUS REALITY

A LOSS OF CENTRAL AUTHORITY IS DISCONCERTING. THE SENSE THAT our familiar, top-down producers of information have our best interests at heart comforts not only the older generations. We all want to believe on some level that those in authority are virtuous, especially when that authority controls something as sacred as a society's consensual truth about itself and the world.

Many of us of all generations believed in Santa Claus at one time. It was painful to open our eyes and learn the truth. This is the kind of epoch we are living in, a time of unveiling, of learning painful truths. We will all see some things and be blind to others. There is no longer one set of facts about most events that we all agree on, as people absorb reports, opinions, and commentary from various sources.[12] This presents a profound challenge both to our intellectual longing to know the truth as well as to our emotional hunger for safety and security in our communities and families. Many of us will cling to an old set of voices for as long as we can. Many will not even object when voices with unfamiliar ideas are suddenly silenced.

Censorship, propaganda, and distortion of the news are not new, as we've learned throughout this book. What is new is the speed, breadth, and depth with which this manipulation is taking over our world today, as well as the speed, breadth, and depth with which people are becoming aware of this manipulation. When the Biden administration announced its "Disinformation Governance Board" in May of 2022,[13] a certain percentage of the American population was pleased that the government intended to step in to silence independent media, but a larger percentage of the population was immediately skeptical about a government vehicle for censorship and propaganda.

I don't know precisely what's going to happen next. It's a fascinating time to be alive, to witness all this unfold, to rebel against systemic media dishonesty, and to participate in the creation of something new.

The time has come to acknowledge that the Mighty Wurlitzer of propaganda that the existing corporate media structure has disseminated over the past century harms humanity and poisons our understanding of the world.

The best state of mind today is that which Buddhists call "child's mind," a state of curiosity and openness that acknowledges what is new as simply an unknown. I hope you'll join me in this state. We will learn, by viewing events through a balanced set of perspectives, a deeper and more accurate way to perceive reality. We will engage in the work of determining what is true in the world for ourselves.

Your Turn

The distribution of information is now a two-way street. You get to share your thoughts and opinions, do your own research, and share what you find. You are now a journalist.

Others get to do the same. Trust is gained and lost as the discoveries that each person or organization present as truth are proven or disproven. This is the great experiment of science and democracy: everyone gets to participate equally, and the best ideas, theories, laws, and decisions win.

You are a contributor. Your thoughts are important. You are no longer alone in your dissent or your agreement. What you speak and what you publish are protected by the First Amendment as sacred contributions to our democratic system.

Cultural thinker Daniel Schmachtenberger calls this shared, sacred system the "Information Ecology." In defining what he calls "sensemaking," he encourages all Americans to consider deeply the source and spin of the information they encounter.[14] He advises us not to hold our silence when we see that what is reported is wrong, backwards, or not the whole picture. He also warns us not to throw out nonsense to anyone listening in the same way we wouldn't throw trash out the windows of our cars. We all share the environment in which we read, write, and share news and analysis. You, too, are a creator, a watchdog, a bulletin, a witness to the unfolding of the world.

A new era is dawning. All voices will be heard. We will not tolerate censorship of any kind, for just as was true in the Middle Ages, the lords and high priests of the modern era are terrified of losing their dominion over knowledge and truth, and they are wielding every tool and weapon they possess. They use censorship not to protect you from dishonesty but to silence truths that endanger their privilege and power. They are commandeering the new power brokers—the social media giants—to help them.

Censorship is always one of the first tools an authoritarian regime attempts to implement. Restrictions on speech grant control over the narrative that a culture or country believes about itself. Coupled with modern propaganda tools, control over the narrative grants authority over people's very thoughts. This is why the First Amendment's guarantees have never been more essential—and more of a beacon to the world—than they are today. These freedoms are direct products of the original Enlightenment, which in turn was the result of Gutenberg's printing press and the philosophical ferment it unleashed. Indeed, we could say Gutenberg's invention led directly to our guaranteed Freedom of the Press, the freedom I am exercising in writing and publishing this book. To surrender the Freedom of Speech or Press today would be to regress six hundred years as a civilization.

Defending the Freedom of Speech against censorship is not simply allowing others to share opinions with which you agree. Defending Free Speech is *allowing others to say things you absolutely despise or fear.* Views for and against Trump, Biden, Putin or anyone else must be allowed, even if they're dishonest. Not because dishonest speech is good—that's not the reason to support Free Speech—but because any authority one appoints to distinguish truth from lies will inevitably become biased and corrupted. Actual violence must always be stopped and prosecuted, of course, and speech that *directly incites violence* is already illegal under American law. Intentional *libel* of another person's character is also already illegal. Those two carve-outs exist. Silencing any other kind of speech cannot be justified in a free and modern society. Anything we can legally say offline we should be able to say online.

Most people feel uncomfortable if not a bit threatened when listening to ideas they despise or fear. This feeling unfortunately will increase in our era of uncertainty and metamorphosis. But history has shown repeatedly that we are all safer and make better collective decisions when all ideas are heard; this very insight underpins democracy and science. Listening has become challenging in this time of diminishing consensual reality, in which we have acknowledged that the existing news structure is invalid but haven't yet settled on a new one. Nevertheless, the only way out is through. When we read broadly and deeply, we tend to feel less discomfort with new ideas, and we tend to listen to others rather than attack them.

THE AWAKENING OF
MEDIA CONSCIOUSNESS

On a personal level, because this period of dissolution and reformation will not include a trusted central authority, we have to grow into the roles of generous listeners and careful speakers. Uncertainty is a difficult place for us humans on both an individual psychological level and on a societal level. Uncertainty feels dangerous, and this particular vacuum—lack of a trusted arbiter of truth—will demand we meet an increasingly large set of challenges and navigate through a vulnerable personal experience of honesty, humility, and a "child's mind" mentality. This approach will rebuild trust in one another.

It is a challenge, but there is abundant good news. Times of dissolution are times of great possibility. The advent of this internet age coincides with an evolving shared awareness of the planet and species as a whole. Never before have we known the condition of the planet and our own species with such immediacy and completeness. We are learning so much today. Human nature's cooperative side, matched in power and potential with its competitive side, is evolving and preparing us for our next state as not only stewards of our powerful species but as stewards of our precious Earth.

This moment of uncertainty will not be short, but it won't last forever. It is the darkness before the dawn, the calm before the storm, the ignorance before the Enlightenment. It is the spark of a global awakening, the emergence of a new Gutenberg, the time of a new Renaissance. It will take years. It is happening. We are awakening.

With "child's mind," everything we experience is new, interesting, an opportunity for learning, a potential avenue for exploration. This optimistic approach underpins the idea of a media diet: try reading something new every day that is unfamiliar, that scares you but intrigues you, that strikes you as wrong but is believed by a friend. With the Freedom of Speech comes the freedom to listen deeply; with the Freedom of the Press comes the freedom to read broadly. Be curious, be open. Uncertainty doesn't only bring anxiety, it also brings creativity.

We are born anew every day until we die. In setting aside the one or two voices of Truth—the one or two sources we've trusted for years—in acknowledging that they might have cleverly fed us lies, we can move into the possibility of a broader, more curious, and more perceptive awareness of the world around us. We can choose to explore. We can choose a media diet that will provide balance and stability to our navigation of the daily crises in the corporate media. This broader awareness—*media consciousness*—will bring a more balanced way of navigating the world's events. *Media consciousness* makes one less manipulable. *Media consciousness* means less sudden shock, less emotional shipwreck, less mental drifting from crisis to crisis, less anxiety, less fear. It reveals biased narratives for the distorted stories they are.

Media consciousness reveals the voices and stories about the world that are programmed in us by daily propaganda and narrative manipulation. Thus, by process of elimination, we discover which voices and stories emanate from our own authentic perception. This is when "child's mind" awakens the inner sage. This is when we begin to see more clearly.

The journey toward *media consciousness*, like the journey toward inner self knowledge, is a lifelong one that doesn't begin with ignorance and then simply end in omniscience. The journey is a winding road that steadily takes us into a more refined state of awareness. No one sees the truth all the time, but a balanced set of perspectives brings broader consciousness, and this enables us to see the actual underlying truth of current events more frequently. In this way, *media consciousness* increases our chances of knowing the truth about people, places, conditions, and events more of the time.

Finally, and perhaps most powerfully, *media consciousness* brings with it awareness of the diversity of narratives going on across the many media channels at any given time. This awareness enables us to understand the perspective of just about anyone we speak with. News narratives are used to divide us because the management of narratives is simpler when people believe the enemy to be one another rather than the ones devising manipulative stories. *Media consciousness* ends this division. It bestows insight into each narrative and thus into each person's world. It is the ultimate antidote to echo chambers and culture wars. We will know where each person is coming from, politically and socially, whether they're from the left or right, top or bottom, friend, family, or stranger. Whether it's a staunch Trump supporter or staunch Trump foe, a vaxxer or anti-vaxxer, a so-called communist or so-called fascist, we will know that viewpoint, that set of beliefs, that narrative on the world's problems. Everyone we know becomes comprehensible, knowable, reachable. We won't agree with everyone, but disagreements will be lighter, healthier, even *interesting*. Someone we disagree with becomes simply that, someone with a different viewpoint, rather than a devil from the other tribe who must be silenced or shunned.

We are social animals. We are endowed with the ability and desire to connect with one another. We yearn to tell each other our stories, and we long to listen to the stories of others. *Media consciousness*, finally, allows us to see through the deceptive facade of news narratives and to connect across the political, social, and geographical lines that divide us. This state of mutual awareness and respect of our similarities and differences, more than any single perfect news source, brings the possibility of genuine peace, freedom, and truth for all.

Epilogue

JOIN THE AWAKENING, OPEN YOUR MIND

"Sapere aude."
(Dare to think for yourself)

Immanuel Kant

I LEAVE YOU WITH FIVE THOUGHTS:

1. **The internet is amazing.** A new printing press brought us to this point, and it will also carry us through to our next phase. The journey will have twists and reveal many truths. Allow yourself to read broadly and consider the world from multiple perspectives, and the journey will be freeing and transformative.

2. **The human spirit is indomitable.** The direct exchange of truth between people across the planet is leading to a spontaneous awakening from the depths of deception in which we have lived. Many truthtellers will surface. You might be one of them. They will often be mocked or vilified, but they will sprout nonetheless like flowers in the cracks in the censorship pavement.

3. **The Streisand Effect is real.** We have a mechanism in our minds that abhors concealment and craves transparency. Like an innate immune system, this psychological drive dictates that when we learn that certain information is concealed or suppressed, we will seek it, replicate it, and share it. The human spirit longs for truth as the body longs for air. This longing makes the New Enlightenment unstoppable.

4. **A media diet is a gift to the mind.** Conscious consumption of news, like the conscious consumption of food, is possible and essential. You don't eat the same food your entire life. Similarly, a media diet doesn't have to be perfect or be followed forever, but doing it will engage your mind, healthfully challenge your assumptions, and reset your mental sense of the world you actually live in.

5. **Listen to friends and family.** Freedom enables genuine listening. Through the phenomena now unfolding, we can learn broadly and deeply about global events. We can see through manipulated narratives. We can overcome "confirmation bias." We can understand the viewpoints of others. This final act—understanding others' viewpoints—enables us not only to connect with each other but to respect one another's differences. This respect is what will inspire us to define and protect one another's freedom to live, love, and prosper independently. We can do this today. There is no need to wait a moment longer.

ACKNOWLEDGEMENTS

IT'S A DELIGHTFUL TASK TO RECALL THE PEOPLE WHO HELPED ME WRITE, edit, and publish this book. May those whose names I've accidentally left out forgive me.

First, without the editing, coaching, and assistance of Maria Lewytzkyj-Milligan, this book would likely still be in its first draft. Thank you, Maria, from the bottom of my heart, for all of your amazing work throughout writing, revising, sourcing, footnoting, and revising again.

Jessica Kleinman was ridiculously patient with me, and her creative instincts and facility with typesetting give this book's text its flow and beauty. Jason Anscomb did an amazing job with the cover and was unflinchingly flexible with his time as we iterated through designs and titles.

My profound thanks to the "alpha readers" who read the manuscript first. They encouraged me where the book was going in the right direction and warned me where it was heading off into the wilderness. Dan Burfoot, Brian Fair, Michael Bedar, and Lynne Michelson: *Thank you*. Later, in 2022, the "beta readers" provided invaluable insights and suggestions. Kenn Burrows, Vicki Estrella, Reuben Sandler, Kellita Maloof, and Andrew Thomas: *Thank you*.

I would like to thank my sister, Wendy Heilbut, now in her own legal practice, for registering the key trademarks and providing early lawyerly thoughts. My new neighbor, Steve Rohde, moved in up the hill just in time to provide me with other valuable lawyerly thoughts as well as insights into our dear, lasting treasure, the First Amendment.

I would like to stop the presses—and the moving vans—to thank the brilliant Ashley Rindsberg, who found time during an international move to pen a compelling foreword. Please rush out and find *The Gray Lady Winked* wherever fine books are sold—you will be enthralled, horrified, and enlightened.

Peggy Duffield, you might know me better than I know myself. Your coaching these last ten years has unlocked potential I didn't know I had. Can you believe we're here now, writing and reading an Acknowledgements page for a book that not long ago was just an idea, a fantasy, a figment of our imaginations?

Zack Vieira, thank you for being so many things—a friend, a fellow rower, a tenant, a burner, a musician—and the designer of the logos and early design ideas that led to this cover. Nick Boule, your video editing for the Red, White & Blind channel has taken another fantasy of mine into reality.

I would like to thank Dalyn Miller and Jimmy Dwyer at DMPG for their unstinting publicity work and for placing me on podcasts where I get to live out my dream of talking to people about these issues so near to my heart.

My sweet gratitude to the excellent folks in Sebastopol at Hippizzazz and HopMonk, eateries that I haunted for days while revising this manuscript.

To everyone who has commented on my blog and on social media: *thank you*. Many of you—Scott Bendure, Kevin Christaldi, Jim Brasunas, Rachel Altman, Bjorn Remmers, Loree Sandler, Anne Buzzard, et al.—provided important advice when I was selecting the cover, author photo, and subtitle.

Finally, and most deeply of all, I would like to thank my beautiful wife, Pamela Brasunas, for caring for our amazing Corin and for allowing me the time to bunker out of sight for long stretches of time. Writing is, ultimately, a solitary craft. Without your love, support, and vision, my dear, I wouldn't have been able to write a single word.

NOTES

IT IS A UNIQUE CHALLENGE TO PROVIDE SOURCES IN A BOOK LIKE THIS. A news source that I criticize in one place might be used as corroboration and support in other places. For this reason, I have endeavored to cite a broad variety of sources from all across our media landscape—a veritable Balanced Media Diet of citations.

Website links are current as of October 2022.

Introduction

1. Many of the men do deny involvement, and Virginia awaits a true day in court. Dershowitz, for his part, wrote a book attempting to refute the charges: Dershowitz, Alan. *Guilt by Association: The Challenge of Proving Innocence in the Age of #MeToo.* Hot Books. New York, NY. 2019.

2. "All Aboard The 'Lolita Express': Flight Logs Reveal the Many Trips Bill Clinton and Alan Dershowitz Took On Pedophile Jeffrey Epstein's Private Jet With Anonymous Women." *Daily Mail,* January 22, 2015. www.dailymail.co.uk/news/article-2922773

3. Trump flew on the Lolita Express many times in the 1990s, but he seems to have broken with Epstein in the early 2000s and even kicked him out of his house at one point. Crane-Newman, Molly and John Annese. "Trump Took Several Trips on Epstein's Jet: Flight Logs." *New York Daily News,* December 20, 2021. www.nydailynews.com/new-york/nyccrime/Ny-maxwell-trump-flight-logs-20211221-zcroqrt42rex7mld73yx6nyh7a-story.html

4. Kevin Spacey, John Glenn, Yitzhak Perlman, George Mitchell, etc. Villarreal, Daniel. "Bill Clinton Went to Jeffrey Epstein's Island With 2 'Young Girls,' Virginia Giuffre Says." *Newsweek,* July 30, 2020. www.newsweek.com/bill-clinton-went-jeffreyepsteins-island-2-young-girls-virginia-giuffre-says-1521845

5. The *New York Times* ran two articles on Epstein across the entirety of 2005 and 2006. Most national outlets ran none. One piece flattered Epstein's lavish lifestyle, the other mildly questioned his lenient sentence. Landon, Thomas Jr. "Working for Top Bosses on Wall St. Has Its Perks." *New York Times,* February 5, 2005. www.nytimes.com/2005/02/05/business/

working-for-top-bosses-on-wall-st-has-its-perks.html. Goodnough, Abby. "Questions of Preferential Treatment Are Raised in Florida Sex Case." *New York Times,* September 3, 2006. www.nytimes.com/2006/09/03/us/03epstein.html

6. Grigoriadis, Vanessa. "Billionaires Are Free." *New York,* October 26, 2006. www.nymag. com/guides/money/2006/23463/

7. Trotter, JK. "Flight Data From Jeffrey Epstein's Private Jets Show a Lavish Travel Schedule As the Walls Closed In." *The Insider,* Jul 12, 2019. www.insider.com/jeffrey-epsteins-private-jet-flight-data-2019-7

8. Giuffre, Virginia Roberts. *The Billionaire's Playboy Club.* Draft of memoir, unsealed court document. archive.org/details/billionaires-playboy-club_20210502_0041

9. "Leaked ABC News Insider Recording Exposes #EpsteinCoverup 'We Had Clinton, We Had Everything.'" *Project Veritas,* November 5, 2019. www.youtube.com/watch?v=3lfwkTsJGYA

10. Brown, Julie K. "Perversion of Justice: How a Future Trump Cabinet Member Gave a Serial Sex Abuser The Deal of a Lifetime." *Miami Herald,* November 28, 2018. www.miami-herald.com/news/local/article220097825.html

11. Keek, Jorge. "The Breakdown of All the Newest Ghislaine Maxwell Claims." *Film Daily,* August 10, 2020. filmdaily.co/obsessions/true-crime/ghislaine-maxwell-claims/

12. Colen, Aaron. "Frustrated ABC News Anchor Caught On Hot Mic Saying Network Suppressed Epstein Story for Years." *Blaze,* November 5, 2019. www.theblaze.com/news/frustrated-abc-news-anchor-caught-on-hot-mic-saying-network-suppressed-epstein-story-for-years

13. Nathan, Sara. "ABC Bosses Scramble After Amy Robach's Comments About Jeffrey Epstein Leak." *New York Post,* November 5, 2019. pagesix.com/2019/11/05/abc-bosses-scramble-after-amy-robachs-comments-about-jeffrey-epstein-leak

14. Brown, Julie K. *Perversion of Justice: The Jeffrey Epstein Story.* Dey Street Books. New York, NY. 2021.

15. Schindler, John R. "It Sure Looks Like Jeffrey Epstein Was a Spy—But Whose?" *The Observer,* July 10, 2019. observer.com/2019/07/jeffrey-epstein-spy-intelligence-work

16. Folkenflik, David. "A Dead Cat, A Lawyer's Call And A 5-Figure Donation: How Media Fell Short On Epstein." *NPR,* August 22, 2019. www.npr.org/2019/08/22/753390385/a-dead-cat-a-lawyers-call-and-a-5-figure-donation-how-media-fell-short-on-epstei

Chapter 1: Uniformity and Obedience

1. Frischknecht, Friedrich. "The History of Biological Warfare." *European Molecular Biology Reports,* June 4, 2003. www.ncbi.nlm.nih.gov/pmc/articles/PMC1326439

2. Clark, David P. and Nanette J. Pazdernik. "Biological Warfare: Infectious Disease and Bio-terrorism." *Biotechnology,* July 24, 2015. www.ncbi.nlm.nih.gov/pmc/articles/PMC7150198

3. Tungul, Jade. "Inside the US Government's Top-Secret Bioweapons Lab." *Business Insider,* Apr 11, 2021. www.businessinsider.com/us-government-tests-deadly-chemical-warfare-agents-utah-2019-10

4. Qiu, Jane. "How China's 'Bat Woman' Hunted Down Viruses From SARS to the New Coronavirus." *Scientific American,* June 1, 2020. www.scientificamerican.com/article/how-chinas-bat-woman-hunted-down-viruses-from-sars-to-the-new-coronavirus1

5. See Qiu, above.

6.Jacobsen, Rowan. "Inside the Risky Bat-Virus Engineering That Links America to Wuhan." *MIT Technology Review,* June 29, 2021. www.technologyreview.com/2021/06/29/1027290/gain-of-function-risky-bat-virus-engineering-links-america-to-wuhan

7. Guterl, Fred. "Dr. Fauci Backed Controversial Wuhan Lab With U.S. Dollars for Risky Coronavirus Research." *Newsweek,* April 28, 2020. www.newsweek.com/dr-fauci-backed-controversial-wuhan-lab-millions-us-dollars-risky-coronavirus-research-1500741

8. Branswell, Helen. "NIH Awards $7.5 Million Grant to Ecohealth Alliance, Months After Uproar Over Political Interference." *Stat News,* August 27, 2020. www.statnews.com/2020/08/27/nih-awards-grant-to-ecohealth-alliance-months-after-uproar-over-political-interference

9.Daszak, Peter, Charles Calisher, Christian Drosten, et al. "Statement in Support of the Scientists, Public Health Professionals, and Medical Professionals of China Combatting Covid-19." *The Lancet,* February 19, 2020. www.thelancet.com/journals/lancet/article/PIIS0140-6736(20)30418-9/fulltext

10. See Daszak, above.

11. Bentley-York, Jacob. "Nearly All Lancet Scientists Who Publicly Trashed Covid Lab Leak Theory Have Links to Wuhan Research, Report Says." *The Sun,* September 11, 2021. www.the-sun.com/news/3642216/lancet-scientists-links-wuhan-research-report-says/

12. For instance: Husseini, Sam. "Peter Daszak's EcoHealth Alliance Has Hidden Almost $40 Million in Pentagon Funding and Militarized Pandemic Science." *Independent Science News,* December 16, 2020. www.independentsciencenews.org/news/peter-daszaks-ecohealth-alliance-has-hidden-almost-40-million-in-pentagon-funding

13. "The Proximal Origin of SARS-CoV-2." *Nature.* March 17, 2020. www.nature.com/articles/s41591-020-0820-9

14. Brumfiel, Geoff and Emily Kwong. "Virus Researchers Cast Doubt on Theory of Coronavirus Lab Accident." *NPR,* April 23, 2020. www.npr.org/sections/goatsandsoda/2020/04/23/841729646/virus-researchers-cast-doubt-on-theory-of-coronavirus-lab-accident

15. Firozi, Paulina. "Tom Cotton Keeps Repeating a Coronavirus Fringe Theory That Scientists Have Disputed." *Washington Post,* February 17, 2020. www.washingtonpost.com/politics/2020/02/16/tom-cotton-coronavirus-conspiracy

16.Stevenson, Alexandra. "Senator Tom Cotton Repeats Fringe Theory of Coronavirus Origins." *New York Times,* February 17, 2020. www.nytimes.com/2020/02/17/business/media/coronavirus-tom-cotton-china.html

17. Sanger, David. "Pompeo Ties Coronavirus to China Lab Despite Spy Agencies' Uncertainty." *New York Times,* May 3, 2020. www.nytimes.com/2020/05/03/us/politics/coronavirus-pompeo-wuhan-china-lab.html

18. Godoy, Maria. "Group Whose NIH Grant for Virus Research Was Revoked Just Got a New Grant." *NPR,*

August 29, 2020. www.npr.org/sections/goatsandsoda/2020/08/29/907237520/group-whose-nih-grant-for-virus-research-was-revoked-just-got-a-new-grant

19. Alex Paterson & Brennan Suen. "Joe Rogan Spreads Unfounded Conspiracy Theory That Covid-19 Started in a Lab." *Media Matters,* September 23, 2020. www.mediamatters.org/joe-rogan-experience/joe-rogan-spreads-unfounded-conspiracy-theory-covid-19-started-lab

20. Castro-Chavez, Fernando. "COVID-19: Hypothesis of the Lab Origin Versus a Zoonotic Event Which Can Also Be of a Lab Origin." *Global Journal of Science Frontier Research.* Volume 20, Issue 3. 2020. globaljournals.org/GJSFR_Volume20/2-Anticovidian-v-2-COVID-19.pdf

21. Bigtree, Del. "Covid Origin Controversy Reignited." *The Highwire,* April 2, 2021. the-highwire.com/videos/covid-origin-controversy-reignited

22. Durden, Tyler. "Is This the Man Behind the Global Coronavirus Pandemic?" *Zero Hedge,* January 29, 2020.

23. Hawkins, Derek. "Twitter Bans Zero Hedge Account After It Doxxed a Chinese Researcher Over Coronavirus." *Washington Post,* February 1, 2020. www.washingtonpost.com/technology/2020/02/01/twitter-zero-hedge-coronavirus

24.Murdock, Jason. "Twitter Suspends Account of Chinese Virologist Who Claimed Coronavirus Was Made in a Lab." *Newsweek,* September 16, 2020. www.newsweek.com/twitter-suspends-dr-li-meng-yan-wuhan-lab-coronavirus-covid19-1532193

25. See Brumfiel, above.

26. *The Highwire,* April 2, 2021. See Bigtree, above.

27. Baker, Nicholson. "The Lab-Leak Hypothesis." *New York Magazine,* January 4, 2021. nymag.com/intelligencer/article/coronavirus-lab-escape-theory.html

28. Quay, Steven and Richard Muller. "The Science Suggests a Wuhan Lab Leak." *Wall Street Journal,* June 6, 2021. www.wsj.com/articles/the-science-suggests-a-wuhan-lab-leak-11622995184

29. Regalado, Antonio. "No One Can Find The Animal That Gave People Covid-19." *Technology Review,* March 26, 2021. www.technologyreview.com/2021/03/26/1021263/bat-covid-coronavirus-cause-origin-wuhan

30. Jacobsen, Rowen. "Inside the Risky Bat-Virus Engineering That Links America to Wuhan." *Technology Review*. January 29, 2020. www.technologyreview. com/2021/06/29/1027290/gain-of-function-risky-bat-virus-engineering-links-america-to-wuhan

31. Chan, Alina and Matt Ridley. *Viral: The Search for the Origin of Covid-19*. Harper Perennial. New York. 2022.

32. "*New York Times* Rushed To Publish Studies Favoring Covid Market Theory According to Molecular Biologist." *Rising*, March 9, 2022. youtu.be/mZfNDQwWWJE

33. Downey, Caroline. "Flashback: Fauci Has Freudian Slip, Starts to Say U.S. Collaborated With 'Chinese Communists' on Gain-of-Function Research." *National Review*, January 3, 2022. news.yahoo.com/flashback-fauci-freudian-slip-starts-224055885.html

34. Fu, Angela. "Dr. Anthony Fauci Calls Sen. Rand Paul's Claim That NIH Funded Risky Virus Research at Wuhan Lab 'Preposterous.'" *Poynter*, May 11, 2021. www.poynter.org/reporting-editing/2021/dr-anthony-fauci-calls-sen-rand-pauls-claim-that-nih-funded-risky-virus-research-at-wuhan-lab-preposterous

35. Hains, Tim. "Fauci: Attacking Me Is Attacking Science." *Real Clear Politics*, June 9, 2021. www.realclearpolitics.com/video/2021/06/09/fauci_attacking_me_is_attacking_science.html

36. Kakutani, Yuichiro. "NYT Quietly Scrubs Chinese Propaganda." *Washington Free Beacon*. August 4, 2020. freebeacon.com/media/nyt-quietly-scrubs-chinese-propaganda

37. Downey, Caroline. "NIH Admits to Funding Gain-of-Function Research in Wuhan, Says EcoHealth Violated Reporting Requirements." *National Review*, October 21, 2021. www.nationalreview.com/news/nih-admits-to-funding-gain-of-function-research-in-wuhan-says-ecohealth-violated-reporting-requirements

38. Dunleavy, Jerry. "Fauci Shut Down Lab Leak Theory Despite Scientists Lending It Credence, Emails Show." *Washington Examiner*, January 11, 2022. www.washingtonexaminer.com/policy/healthcare/fauci-shut-down-lab-leak-theory-despite-scientists-lending-it-credence-emails-show

39. Ruskin, Gary. "FOI Documents on Origins of Covid-19, Gain-of-Function Research and Biolabs." *US Right to Know*, April 8, 2022. usrtk.org/biohazards/foi-documents-on-origins-of-sars-cov-2-risks-of-gain-of-function-research-and-biosafety-labs

40. Tinker, Ben. "Fauci Says Natural Origins Theory of Coronavirus Is Still the Most Likely." *CNN*, July 17, 2021. www.cnn.com/2021/07/17/politics/fauci-covid-natural-origins-theory/index.html

41. Marquardt, Alex and Jeremy Herb. "US Intelligence Community Review Does Not Determine Origin of Covid-19." *CNN*, August 27, 2021. www.cnn.com/2021/08/27/politics/us-intelligence-covid-origins-report/index.html

42. Ladden-Hall, Dan. "Lancet Report Claiming COVID Could Have Come From U.S. Lab Met With Uproar." *Daily Beast*, September 15, 2022. news.yahoo.com/lancet-report-claiming-covid-could-132931783.html

43. Zimmer, Carl and Benjamin Mueller. "New Research Points to Wuhan Market as Pandemic Origin." *New York Times*, February 27, 2022. www.nytimes.com/interactive/2022/02/26/science/covid-virus-wuhan-origins.html

44. Morris, Emma-Jo and Gabrielle Fonrouge. "Smoking-Gun Email Reveals How Hunter Biden Introduced Ukrainian Businessman to VP Dad." *New York Post*, October 14, 2020. nypost.com/2020/10/14/email-reveals-how-hunter-biden-introduced-ukrainian-biz-man-to-dad

45. Griffith, Keith. "Twitter Unlocks New York Post's Main Account Following Two-Week Free Speech Stalemate Over Hunter Biden Articles After the Big Tech Goliath Censored Them." *Daily Mail*, October, 30 2020. www.dailymail.co.uk/news/article-8899105/Twitter-buckles-unlocks-New-York-Posts-main-account-two-week-stalemate.html

46. Solomon, John. "Joe Biden's 2020 Ukrainian Nightmare: A Closed Probe Is Revived." *The Hill*, April 1, 2019. thehill.com/opinion/white-house/436816-joe-bidens-2020-ukrainian-nightmare-a-closed-probe-is-revived

47. Perloff, James. "Council On Foreign Relations." *The New American,* July 23, 2009. thenewamerican.com/council-on-foreign-relations

48. Vogel, Kenneth. "Trump, Biden and Ukraine: Sorting Out the Accusations." *New York Times,* September 22, 2019. www.nytimes.com/2019/09/22/us/politics/biden-ukraine-trump.html

49. See Vogel, above.

50. Rid, Thomas. "Insisting That the Hunter Biden Laptop Is Fake Is a Trap. So Is Insisting That It's Real." *Washington Post*, October 20, 2020. www.washingtonpost.com/outlook/2020/10/24/hunter-biden-laptop-disinformation

51. Risen, James. "Joe Biden, His Son and the Case Against a Ukrainian Oligarch." *New York Times*, December 8, 2015. www.nytimes.com/2015/12/09/world/europe/corruption-ukraine-joe-biden-son-hunter-biden-ties.html

52. Fearnow, Benjamin. "Hunter Biden Emails Have 'Nothing to Do' With Russian Disinformation, National Intelligence Director Says." *Newsweek*, October 19, 2020. www.newsweek.com/hunter-biden-emails-have-nothing-do-russian-disinformation-national-intelligence-director-says-1540255

53. Bertrand, Natasha. "Hunter Biden Story Is Russian Disinfo, Dozens of Former Intel Officials Say." *Politico*, October 19, 2020. www.politico.com/news/2020/10/19/hunter-biden-story-russian-disinfo-430276

54. "Hunter Biden's New Hilarious Answer About His Laptop." *Jimmy Dore Show*, April 3, 2021. www.youtube.com/watch?v=epw4CTdtZQc

55. Schreckinger, Ben. *The Bidens: Inside the First Family's Fifty-Year Rise to Power.* Grand Central Publishing. New York, New York. 2021.

56. Post Editorial Board. "Washington Post, New York Times Finally Admit Hunter's Laptop Is Real—But Only To Protect Joe Biden Some More." *New York Post*, April 2, 2022. nypost.

com/2022/04/01/new-york-times-finally-admit-hunters-laptop-is-real-but-only-to-protect-joe-biden

57. Bond, Shannon. "Facebook and Twitter Limit Sharing 'New York Post' Story About Joe Biden." *NPR*, October 14, 2020. www.npr.org/2020/10/14/923766097/facebook-and-twitter-limit-sharing-new-york-post-story-about-joe-biden

58. Greenwald, Glenn. "New Proof Emerges About the Hunter Biden Laptop: a Definitive Account of the CIA/Media Fraud." *System Update*, September 2, 2021. www.youtube.com/watch?v=I31O5_X4P1Y

59. Lubold, G. Strobel, W. "Russian Spy Unit Paid Taliban to Attack Americans, U.S. Intelligence Says." *Wall Street Journal*, June 27, 2020. www.wsj.com/articles/russian-spy-unit-paid-taliban-to-attack-americans-u-s-intelligence-says-11593214584

60. Savage, C., Schmitt, E., & Schwirtz, M. "Russia Secretly Offered Afghan Militants Bounties to Kill Troops, U.S. Intelligence Says." *New York Times*, June 26, 2020. archive.is/RJOQS

61. Nakashima, E., DeYoung, K., Ryan, M. Hudson, J. "Russian Bounties to Taliban-Linked Militants Resulted in Deaths of U.S. Troops, According to Intelligence Assessments." *Washington Post*, June 28, 2020. www.washingtonpost.com/national-security/russian-bounties-to-taliban-linked-militants-resulted-in-deaths-of-us-troops-according-to-intelligence-assessments/2020/06/28/74ffaec2-b96a-11ea-80b9-40ece9a701dc_story.html

62. Johnstone, Caitlin. "This Russia-Afghanistan Story Is Western Propaganda at Its Most Vile." *Greanville Post*, July 3, 2020. www.greanvillepost.com/2020/07/03/this-russia-afghanistan-story-is-western-propaganda-at-its-most-vile

63. Greenwald, Glen. "Liz Cheney Lied About Her Role in Spreading the Discredited CIA 'Russian Bounty' Story." *Substack*, May 14, 2020. greenwald.substack.com/p/liz-cheney-lied-about-her-role-in

64. Rawnsley, Adam. "U.S. Intel Walks Back Claim Russians Put Bounties on American Troops." *Daily Beast*, April 15, 2021. www.thedailybeast.com/us-intel-walks-back-claim-russians-put-bounties-on-american-troops

65. Dilanian, K. & Memoli, M. "Remember Those Russian Bounties for Dead U.S. Troops? Biden Admin Says the CIA Intel is not Conclusive." *NBC News*, April 15, 2021. www.nbcnews.com/politics/national-security/remember-those-russian-bounties-dead-u-s-troops-biden-admin-n1264215

66. American Press Institute. "What Is the Purpose of Journalism?" www.americanpressinstitute.org/journalism-essentials/what-is-journalism/purpose-journalism

67. Fadul, J. A., Estoque, R. S. *A Textbook for an Introductory Course in Sociology.* Lulu. Raleigh, United States. 2010.

68. Greenwald, Glenn. "Julian Assange Loses Appeal: British High Court Accepts U.S. Request to Extradite Him for Trial." *Substack*, December 10, 2021. greenwald.substack.com/p/julian-assange-loses-appeal-british

69. The warnings come when telling her viewers that social media isn't censoring *enough*, such as on May 4, 2021 and August 27, 2021. "Transcript: The Rachel Maddow Show, 5/4/21."

Rachel Maddow Show. www.msnbc.com/transcripts/transcript-rachel-maddow-show-5-4-21-n1266364 and Transcript: The Rachel Maddow Show, 8/27/21." *Rachel Maddow Show.* www.msnbc.com/transcripts/transcript-rachel-maddow-show-8-27-21-n1277999.

70. Warzel, Charlie. "Don't Go Down the Rabbit Hole." *New York Times,* February 18, 2021. www.nytimes.com/2021/02/18/opinion/fake-news-media-attention.html

Chapter 2: A History of Lies

1. "An Impeachable Offense? Bush Admits Authorizing NSA to Eavesdrop on Americans Without Court Approval." *Democracy Now,* December 19, 2005. www.democracynow.org/2005/12/19/an_impeachable_offense_bush_admits_authorizing

2. *Protecting Our Civil Liberties: The Core of Democracy,* July 25–26, 2003 conference. www.grassrootspeace.org/PDFfiles/GCCTraprockConference.pdf

3. Hersh, Seymour. "Huge C.I.A. Operation Reported in U.S. Against Antiwar Forces, Other Dissidents in Nixon Years." *New York Times,* December 22, 1974. www.nytimes.com/1974/12/22/archives/huge-cia-operation-reported-in-u-s-against-antiwar-forces-other.html

4. Hersh, Seymour. "C.I.A. Is Linked to Strikes in Chile That Beset Allende." *New York Times,* September 20, 1974. www.nytimes.com/1974/09/20/archives/cia-is-linked-to-strikes-in-chile-that-beset-allende.html

5. Hersh, Seymour. "Kissinger Called Chile Strategist." *New York Times,* September 15, 1974. www.nytimes.com/1974/09/15/archives/kissinger-called-chile-strategist-covert-cia-activities.html

6. Hersh, Seymour. "C.I.A. Said to Have Asked Funds for Chile Rightists in '75." *New York Times,* October 21, 1974. www.nytimes.com/1974/10/21/archives/cia-said-to-have-asked-funds-for-chile-rightists-in-73-a.html

7. Operation Mockingbird is sometimes confused with Project Mockingbird, a related covert operation whereby intelligence agents wiretapped journalists' phones in the 1960s. This was ostensibly done to identify sources of leaked information but also obtained forthcoming coverage before it was published.

8. Bernstein, Carl. "The CIA and the Media: How America's Most Powerful News Media Worked Hand in Glove with the Central Intelligence Agency and Why the Church Committee Covered It Up." *Rolling Stone,* October 20, 1977. Retrieved at: www.carlbernstein.com/the-cia-and-the-media-rolling-stone-10-20-1977

9. Church Committee Final Report, Vol 1: Foreign and Military Intelligence, p. 455 www.intelligence.senate.gov/sites/default/files/94755_I.pdf

10. Ginzberg, Gary. "A Complicated Life Frank G. Wisner, Sr.." *Advisors Magazine,* December 3, 2019. www.advisorsmagazine.com/trending/23537-a-complicated-life-frank-g-wisner-sr

11. Adams, Sandi. "Operation Mockingbird – What Was It? CIA Mind-Control and Propaganda." July 18, 2020. sandiadams.net/operation-mockingbird-what-was-it-cia-mind-control-and-propaganda

12. Wilford, Hugh. *The Mighty Wurlitzer: How the CIA Played America*. Harvard University Press. London, United Kingdom. 2008. pp226-7.

13. Davis, Deborah. *Katharine the Great: Katharine Graham and the Washington Post*. Harcourt Brace Jovanovich. New York, NY. 1979. p 138-9.

14. See Bernstein, above.

15. See Bernstein, above.

16. Goodman, Amy and David. *Static: Government Liars, Media Cheerleaders, and the People Who Fight Back*. Hyperion. New York, New York. 2006. p. 95.

17. See Bernstein, above.

18. The full final report is at: www.andrew.cmu.edu/user/rp3h/lansberry/Church_Committee_I.pdf.

19. See Bernstein, above.

20. Horrock, Nicholas. "CIA to Stop Enlisting Agents From the Press and Church." *New York Times*, February 12, 1976. www.nytimes.com/1976/02/12/archives/cia-to-stop-enlisting-agents-from-the-press-and-the-church-cia-to.html

21. Shane, Scott. "That Time the C.I.A. Tried to Recruit Me: Our National Security Reporter on Covering Spies." *New York Times*, February 14, 2018. www.nytimes.com/2018/02/14/insider/are-spies-like-us-a-national-security-reporter-says-yes-and-no.html

22. This quote has been almost entirely scrubbed from the internet, but it's still captured in a video on Operation Mockingbird by author Mark Dice. The quote starts at 1:35. Dice, Mark. "Operation Mockingbird: The CIA's Covert Media Manipulation Program" *YouTube,* June 21, 2021. youtu.be/3KY0ktXAuvc

23. Norton, Ben. "Vanderbilt Oligarch Heir Anderson Cooper Worked at CIA in College." *Grayzone*, February 25, 2020. thegrayzone.com/2020/02/25/vanderbilt-anderson-cooper-cia-college

24. Bishop, Tom. "US Psychological Warfare Experts Worked at CNN and NPR During Kosovo War." *World Socialist Website*, April 18, 2000. www.wsws.org/en/articles/2000/04/cnn-a18.html

25. "Why Were Government Propaganda Experts Working On News at CNN?" *Fairness and Accuracy in Reporting*, March 27, 2000. fair.org/take-action/action-alerts/why-were-government-propaganda-experts-working-on-news-at-cnn

26. Borger, Julian. "CNN Let Army Staff Into Newsroom." *Guardian*, April 11, 2000. www.theguardian.com/world/2000/apr/12/julianborger

27. See Norton, above.

28. Mazzetti, Mark and Borzou Daragahi. "U.S. Military Covertly Pays to Run Stories in Iraqi Press." *Los Angeles Times*, November 30, 2005. www.latimes.com/archives/la-xpm-2005-nov-30-fg-infowar30-story.html

29. Barstow, David. "Behind TV Analysts, Pentagon's Hidden Hand." *New York Times*, April 20, 2008. www.nytimes.com/2008/04/20/us/20generals.html

30. "Pentagon Sets Sights On Public Opinion." *Associated Press*, August 5, 2010. www.nbcnews.com/id/wbna29040299

31. Thayer, Joziah. "Birds of a Feather Flock Together Under the Mockingbird's Wing - DD19 Entree." *Hive Blog*, 2020. hive.blog/deepdives/@wedacoalition/birds-of-a-feather-flock-together-under-the-mockingbird-s-wing-dd19-entree

32. "European Media Writing Pro-US Stories Under CIA Pressure - German Journalist." *RT*, October 18, 2014. newtube.app/user/yabba/EESpFOz

33. See *RT*, above.

34. Tracy, James. "English Translation of Udo Ulfkotte's 'Bought Journalists' Suppressed?" *Information Clearinghouse*, August 1, 2017. www.informationclearinghouse.info/47560.htm

35. Valania, Jonathan. "L.A. Times Disowns Reporter Outed as a CIA Collaborator." *Huffington Post*, September 5, 2014. www.huffpost.com/entry/la-times-disowns-reporter_b_5770388

36. Silverstein, Ken. "The CIA's Mop-Up Man: L.A. Times Reporter Cleared Stories With Agency Before Publication." *Intercept*, September 4, 2014. theintercept.com/2014/09/04/former-l-times-reporter-cleared-stories-cia-publication

37. See Valania, above.

38. Maté, Aaron. "The Rise and Fall of the 'Steele Dossier': A Case Study in Mass Hysteria and Media Credulity." *Nation*, January 11, 2021. www.thenation.com/article/politics/trump-russiagate-steele-dossier

39. Greenwald, Glenn. "The Inspector General's Report on 2016 FBI Spying Reveals a Scandal of Historic Magnitude: Not Only for the FBI but Also the U.S. Media." *Intercept*, December 12, 2019. theintercept.com/2019/12/12/the-inspector-generals-report-on-2016-fb-i-spying-reveals-a-scandal-of-historic-magnitude-not-only-for-the-fbi-but-also-the-u-s-media/

40. Mangan, Doug. "Trump-Russia Steele Dossier Analyst Igor Danchenko Pleads Not Guilty in FBI Lie Case Prosecuted by John Durham." *CNBC*, November 10, 2021. www.cnbc.com/2021/11/10/trump-russia-dossier-analyst-igor-danchenko-arraigned-in-fbi-lie-case-.html

41. Dore, Jimmy. "Another RussiaGate Source Arrested for Lying!" *Jimmy Dore Show*, November 5, 2021. youtu.be/ JtWtpQ67BRI

42. "Dirty Tricks by Clintons Shaped Liberal Opinion and News Coverage of Trump for Years." *Washington Examiner*, November 17, 2021. www.washingtonexaminer.com/opinion/

editorials/dirty-tricks-by-clintons-shaped-liberal-opinion-and-news-coverage-of-trump-for-years

43. Hudson, John. "U.S. Repeals Propaganda Ban, Spreads Government-Made News to Americans." *Foreign Policy*, July 14, 2013. foreignpolicy.com/2013/07/14/u-s-repeals-propaganda-ban-spreads-government-made-news-to-americans

44. Cushing, Tim. "'Anti-Propaganda' Ban Repealed, Freeing State Dept. To Direct Its Broadcasting Arm at American Citizens." *TechDirt*, July 15, 2013. www.techdirt.com/2013/07/15/anti-propaganda-ban-repealed-freeing-state-dept-to-direct-its-broadcasting-arm-american-citizens

45. Countering Foreign Propaganda and Disinformation Act. S.3274 — 114th Congress (2015-2016). www.congress.gov/bill/114th-congress/senate-bill/3274

46. Swann, Ben. "U.S. Can Legally Propagandize Its Own Citizens." *Reality Check*. August 14, 2018.

47. Goldenziel, Jill and Manal Cheema. "The New Fighting Words?: How U.S. Law Hampers the Fight Against Information Warfare." *Journal of Constitutional Law*, November 2019. This is a naive and gullible piece dressed up as a serious academic consideration; the authors make the outrageous suggestion that because of Russian attempts to interfere in our political debate we should roll back American guarantees of Free Speech and privacy.

48. A partisan but decent rendition here: Hamilton, John and Kevin Kosar. "Sad! A Brief History Of White House Propaganda From Teddy Roosevelt To Donald Trump." *The Bulletin of Atomic Scientists,* November 12, 2020. thebulletin.org/2020/11/sad-a-brief-history-of-white-house-propaganda-from-teddy-roosevelt-to-donald-trump

49. "Senate Select on Intelligence Volume 2: Russia's Use of Social Media with Additional Views." November 10, 2020. www.intelligence.senate.gov/sites/default/files/documents/Report_Volume2.pdf

50. Maté, Aaron. "New Studies Show Pundits Are Wrong About Russian Social-Media Involvement in US Politics." *The Nation*, December 28, 2018. www.thenation.com/article/archive/russiagate-elections-interference

51. Stein, Jeff. "Study: Hillary Clinton's TV Ads Were Almost Entirely Policy-Free." *Vox,* March 8, 2017. www.vox.com/policy-and-politics/2017/3/8/14848636/hillary-clinton-tv-ads

52. Constitutional Rights Foundation. "Gutenberg and the Printing Revolution in Europe." Winter 2009. www.crf-usa.org/bill-of-rights-in-action/bria-24-3-b-gutenberg-and-the-printing-revolution-in-europe

53. History of Spain. "The Spanish Inquisition III." August 9, 2021. historyofspain.es/en/video/the-spanish-inquisition-iii

54. CIA record #104-10406-10110. "Countering Criticism of the Warren Report." (PSYCH. 1967) conspiracy-theories.eu/countering-criticism-of-the-warren-report-psych-1967

55. deHaven-Smith, Lance. *Conspiracy Theory in America*. University of Texas Press. Austin, Texas. 2013.

56. Orwell, G. *Nineteen Eighty-Four*. Penguin. London, United Kingdom. 1949.

57. "The Danger is Now: International Blasphemy Rights Day 2021." *Center for Inquiry,* September 30, 2021. centerforinquiry.org/news/the-danger-is-now-international-blasphemy-rights-day-2021

58. Smith, A. (1827). *An Inquiry Into the Nature and Causes of the Wealth of Nations*. University Press for T. Nelson and P. Brown. Edinburgh, United Kingdom.

59. Beaumont, Peter. "Afghanistan Papers Detail US Dysfunction: 'We Did Not Know What We Were Doing.'" *The Guardian*, December 14, 2019. www.theguardian.com/us-news/2019/dec/14/afghanistan-papers-detail-us-dysfunction-we-did-not-know-what-we-were-doing. But it was worse than that. Craig Whitlock's book *The Afghanistan Papers* (Simon & Schuster, 2021) recounts the drugs and corruption that actually ruled the war while the US government and media presented a different picture.

60. Kitman, Jamie Lincoln. "The Secret History of Lead." *The Nation*, March 2, 2000. www.thenation.com/article/archive/secret-history-lead

61. Remembering the Phoebus Cartel: "This is Why We Can't Have Nice Things." *Veritaseum*, March 26, 2021. youtu.be/j5v8D-alAKE

62.Mann, Brian. "Four U.S. Companies Will Pay $26 Billion To Settle Claims They Fueled The Opioid Crisis." *NPR Morning Edition*. www.npr.org/2022/02/25/1082901958/opioid-settlement-johnson-26-billion

Chapter 3: Bias, Innocent or Nefarious

1. "Former CIA Agent John Stockwell Talks about How the CIA Worked in Vietnam and Elsewhere." *King Rose Archives*. Interview: February 7, 1983. Retrieved: June 28, 2021. youtu.be/NK1tfkESPVY?t=103

2. Cohen, Mitchel. "How Bush Sr. Sold the Gulf War." *Counterpunch*, December 28, 2002. www.counterpunch.org/2002/12/28/how-bush-sr-sold-the-gulf-war

3. See Cohen, above.

4. Tisdall, Simon. "Superpowers Unite on Iraq." *The Guardian*, August 3, 1990. www.theguardian.com/world/1990/aug/03/iraq.davidhirst

5. Holland, Joshua. "The First Iraq War Was Also Sold to the Public Based on a Pack of Lies." *Bill Moyers Show*, June 27, 2014. billmoyers.com/2014/06/27/the-first-iraq-war-was-also-sold-to-the-public-based-on-a-pack-of-lies

6. Regan, Tom "When Contemplating War, Beware of Babies in Incubators." *Christian Science Monitor*, September 6, 2002. www.csmonitor.com/2002/0906/p25s02-cogn.html

7. See Regan, above.

8. Stein, Jonathan and Tim Dickinson. "Lie by Lie: A Timeline of How We Got Into Iraq." *Mother Jones*, September 2006. www.motherjones.com/politics/2011/12/leadup-iraq-war-timeline

9. Too many to list. A quick sample:

Gordon, Michael & Judith Miller. "Threats And Responses: The Iraqis; U.S. Says Hussein Intensifies Quest for A-Bomb Parts." *New York Times*, September 8, 2002. www.nytimes. com/2002/09/08/world/threats-responses-iraqis-us-says-hussein-intensifies-quest-for-bomb-parts.html

Burns, John. "The World; How Many People Has Hussein Killed?" *New York Times*, January 26, 2003. www.nytimes.com/2003/01/26/weekinreview/the-world-how-many-people-has-hussein-killed.html

Rice, Condoleeza. "Why We Know Iraq Is Lying." *New York Times*, January 23, 2003. www. nytimes.com/2003/01/23/opinion/why-we-know-iraq-is-lying.html

"Iraqi Scientist Says U.S. Unlikely to Find Biological Weapons." *New York Times*, April 29, 2003. www.nytimes.com/2003/04/29/international/middleeast/iraqi-scientist-says-us-unlikely-to-find-biological.html

Miller, Judith. "Aftereffects: Germ Weapons; Leading Iraqi Scientist Says He Lied to U.N. Inspectors." *New York Times*, April 27, 2003. www.nytimes.com/2003/04/27/world/aftereffects-germ-weapons-leading-iraqi-scientist-says-he-lied-to-un-inspectors.html

10. Pollack, Kenneth. "Saddam's Bombs? We'll Find Them." *New York Times*, June 20, 2003. www.nytimes.com/2003/06/20/opinion/saddam-s-bombs-we-ll-find-them.html and Miller, Judith. "Aftereffects: Prohibited Weapons; Illicit Arms Kept Till Eve of War, An Iraqi Scientist Is Said to Assert." *New York Times*, April 21, 2003. www.nytimes.com/2003/04/21/world/aftereffects-prohibited-weapons-illicit-arms-kept-till-eve-war-iraqi-scientist.html

11. Miller, Judith. "Threats And Responses: Chemical Weapons; Iraq Said To Try To Buy Antidote Against Nerve." *New York Times*, November 12, 2002. www.nytimes. com/2002/11/12/world/threats-responses-chemical-weapons-iraq-said-try-buy-antidote-against-nerve-gas.html

12. Miller, Judith. "Defectors Bolster U.S. Case Against Iraq, Officials Say." *New York Times,* January 24, 2003. www.nytimes.com/2003/01/24/world/threats-responses-intelligence-defectors-bolster-us-case-against-iraq-officials.html

13. Imperial War Museums. "5 Photographs From the Day the World Said No to War." www. iwm.org.uk/history/5-photographs-from-the-day-the-world-said-no-to-war

14. United States Congressional Serial Set, Serial No. 14878, Senate Reports Nos. 343-373. (n.d.). (n.p.): Government Printing Office.

15. Woodward, B.. *Plan of Attack*. Simon & Schuster. London, UK. 2012.

16. Powell, C. Remarks to the United Nations Security Council. [speech video recording]. February 5, 2003.

17. Before the Senate Select Committee on Intelligence of the United States Senate., US Senate Select Committee on Intelligence, 108th Cong. (2003) (testimony of Robert Mueller III.) February 11, 2003. www.intelligence.senate.gov/hearings/current-and-projected-national-security-threats-united-states-february-11-2003

18. Interesting to note that coverage of the Ukraine debate 20 years later was so similar. No anti-war voices on MSNBC or CNN. Rendall, Steve. "Amplifying Officials, Squelching Dissent." *Fairness and Accuracy in Reporting (FAIR)*, May 2003. fair.org/extra/amplifying-officials-squelching-dissent

19. Stiglitz, Joseph and Linda Bilmes. *The Three Trillion Dollar War*. W. W. Norton, New York, NY. 2008. Nobel Prize economists estimate the true cost to the United States for the Iraq War.

20. Black, Crofton, Abigail Fielding-Smith and Jon Ungoed-Thomas. "$540 Million Covert PR Ops in Iraq for Pentagon." *The Sunday Times,* October 2, 2016. www.thetimes.co.uk/article/lord-bell-ran-540m-covert-pr-ops-in-iraq-for-pentagon-m5js07xtr

21. Norton, Ben. "U.S. Paid P.R. Firm $540 Million To Make Fake Al-Qaida Videos in Iraq Propaganda Program." *Salon*, October 3, 2016. www.salon.com/2016/10/03/u-s-paid-p-r-firm-540-million-to-make-fake-al-qaida-videos-in-iraq-propaganda-program

22. "Misperceptions, the Media and the Iraq War: Study Finds Widespread Misperceptions on Iraq." *World Public Opinion Survey,* October 2, 2003. web.archive.org/web/20061008020042/http://www.worldpublicopinion.org/pipa/articles/international_security_bt/102.php

23. Piller, Charles and Doug Smith. "Unintended Victims of Gates Foundation Generosity." *Los Angeles Times,* December 16, 2007 www.latimes.com/nation/la-xpm-2007-dec-16-la-na-gates16dec16-story.html

24. See Piller, above.

25. Martin, Michel. "Bill Gates Weighs In on 'How To Avoid A Climate Disaster' With New Book." *NPR*, March 14, 2021. www.npr.org/2021/03/14/977215406/bill-gates-on-new-book-how-to-avoid-a-climate-disaster

26. MacLeod, Alan. "Documents Show Bill Gates Has Given $319 Million to Media Outlets." *MintPress News*, November 15th, 2021. www.mintpressnews.com/documents-show-bill-gates-has-given-319-million-to-media-outlets/278943

27. See MacLeod, above.

28. Schwab, Tim. "While the Poor Get Sick, Bill Gates Just Gets Richer." *Nation*, October 5, 2020. www.thenation.com/article/economy/bill-gates-investments-covid

29. See MacLeod, above.

30. "Gates Foundation, Viacom Partner to Insert Educational Messages Into Television Programming." *Philanthropy News Digest,* April 3, 2009. philanthropynewsdigest.org/news/gates-foundation-viacom-partner-to-insert-educational-messages-into-television-programming

31. Brenan, Megan. "Americans Remain Distrustful of Mass Media." *Gallup*, September 30, 2020. news.gallup.com/poll/321116/americans-remain-distrustful-mass-media.aspx

32. McKennett, Hannah, and John Kuroski. "The Gulf of Tonkin Incident: The Lie That Sparked the Vietnam War." *All That Is Interesting*, September 10, 2019. allthatsinteresting.com/gulf-of-tonkin

33. Paterson, Pat, Lieutenant Commander, U.S. Navy. "The Truth About Tonkin." *Naval History Magazine*, Volume 22, Number 1. February 2008. www.usni.org/magazines/naval-history-magazine/2008/february/truth-about-tonkin

34. Faulder, Dominic. "US Bombing of Cambodia—Still Counting the Dead." *The Irrawaddy*, Volume 9, Number 8. October 2001. www2.irrawaddy.com/article.php?art_id=2412

Chapter 4: It's Not About the Money, It's About the Money

1. Brasunas, Tony. "Please Recognize Your Privilege If You Can Afford 8 Years of Hillary Clinton and the Status Quo." *Huffington Post*, April 1, 2016. www.huffpost.com/entry/please-recognize-privilege-8-years-of-hillary-clinton_b_9591922

2. Brasunas, Tony. "Only Voter Suppression Can Stop Bernie Sanders." *Huffington Post,* April 26, 2016. www.huffpost.com/entry/only-voter-suppression-can-stop-bernie-sanders_b_9780128

3. Brasunas, Tony. "Is Democracy Dead in California?" *Huffington Post*, June 28, 2016. www.huffpost.com/entry/is-democracy-dead-in-california_b_5772c94fe4b04650f1505de2

4. Brasunas, Tony. "Exit Polls Are the Thing Wherein to Catch the Conscience of Elections." *Huffington Post*, July 5, 2016. www.huffpost.com/entry/exit-polls-are-the-thing-wherein-to-catch-the-conscience_b_5772e818e4b00eaa47881646

5. Brasunas, Tony. "The Deeper Reason Many Intelligent Progressives and Independents Will Not Support Hillary Clinton." *Medium,* originally *Huffington Post,* July 19, 2016. tonybrasunas.medium.com/the-deeper-reason-independents-and-progressives-will-not-support-hillary-clinton-db79a10b23c7

6. See Brasunas, above.

7. In 2003, Barbara Streisand attempted to censor a photo of her lavish Malibu home that an aerial photographer had placed in a document about the California coastline. Prior to her attempts to remove the photo from the internet, it had only been downloaded six times. Her demand that it be removed resulted in widespread media coverage and over 400,000 downloads of the photo. Cacciottolo, Mario. "The Streisand Effect: When Censorship Backfires." *BBC News.* June 15, 2012. www.bbc.com/news/uk-18458567

8. Sottile, Chiara and Daniel Medina. "Pipeline Protesters Say Police Nearly Blew Off Woman's Arm." *NBC News*, November 22, 2016. www.nbcnews.com/storyline/dakota-pipeline-protests/pipeline-protesters-decry-excessive-force-after-woman-s-arm-blown-n687326

9. The movement began in April and attracted national attention in independent media, but corporate media, including *NPR* and *New York Times,* did not send anyone to Standing Rock

until late August. CNN coverage was done by a local affiliate. NBC published one notable interview and sent in reporters at the end of October.

10. Moynihan, Colin. "Cause of Severe Injury at Pipeline Protest Becomes New Point of Dispute." *New York Times,* November 24, 2016. www.nytimes.com/2016/11/24/us/dakota-pipeline-sophia-wilansky.html?_r=0

11. "Statement by Father of Sophia Wilansky, Critically Injured at NoDAPL Action." *Indian Country Today,* November 22, 2016. indiancountrytoday.com/archive/statement-by-father-of-sophia-wilansky-critically-injured-at-nodapl-action-p64B2D_NrU2BsLdPqtZtig

12. *Reclaiming Native Truths. Changing the Narrative About Native Americans: A Guide for Allies.* June, 2018. rnt.firstnations.org/wp-content/uploads/2018/06/MessageGuide-Allies-screen.pdf

13. "Trust in Mass Media Returns to All-Time Low." *Gallup,* September 17, 2014. news.gallup.com/poll/176042/trust-mass-media-returns-time-low.aspx

14. "Americans Remain Distrustful of Mass Media." *Gallup,* September 30, 2020. news.gallup.com/poll/321116/americans-remain-distrustful-mass-media.aspx

15. Bedard, Paul. "US 'Trust' In News Is World's Lowest, Trump Loss Killed 'Interest.'" *Washington Times,* June 23, 2021. www.washingtonexaminer.com/washington-secrets/us-trust-in-news-is-worlds-lowest-trump-loss-killed-interest

16. Enjeti, Saagar. "US Has Lowest Trust in Media of Entire Free World. A New Order Must Replace It." *Breaking Points,* June 24, 2021. www.youtu.be/n5qbW_JcHPQ

17. Flood, Brian. "CNN Has Shed More Than Half Its Viewers Since Biden Took Office." *Fox News,* April 16, 2021. www.foxnews.com/media/cnn-viewers-biden-took-office-staggering-60-percent-in-key-demo

18. The network averaged just 548,000 viewers during the week of January 3, a dizzying drop from the nearly 2.7 million viewers the same week in 2021. Anderson, Natasha. "Tuning out! Viewership at Scandal-Plagued CNN Plummets by as Much as 90%." *Daily Mail,* January 12, 2022. www.dailymail.co.uk/news/article-10394997/CNN-loses-nearly-90-advertiser-coveted-demographics-overall-total-audience.html

19. Pengelly, Martin. "Chris Cuomo Fired by CNN for Helping Brother Andrew Fight Sexual Misconduct Charges." *Guardian (London),* December 5, 2021. www.theguardian.com/media/2021/dec/04/chris-cuomo-fired-cnn-brother-andrew-sexual-misconduct-charges

20. Smith, Emily. "Chris Cuomo Allegedly Blasted Janice Dean as 'That Fox Weather Bitch' in Smear Plot." *New York Post,* December 10, 2021. nypost.com/2021/12/10/chris-cuomo-allegedly-blasted-janice-dean-as-that-fox-weather-bitch

21. Enjeti, Saagar. "Millions Turn Off Mainstream News as New Journalism Rises." *Rising,* April 23, 2021. www.youtu.be/K5E8Us2vL7Y

22. Tracy, Marc. "Public Radio Group Criticizes New York Times Over 'Caliphate' Correction." *New York Times,* January 12, 2021. www.nytimes.com/2021/01/12/business/public-radio-group-criticizes-new-york-times-over-caliphate-correction.html

23. Al-Arian, Laila. "Caliphate: How the New York Times' Islamic State Scoop Unraveled." *Middle East Eye*, January 15, 2021. www.middleeasteye.net/big-story/new-york-times-caliphate-debacle-deeper-problems

24. Kakutani, Yuichiro. "NYT Quietly Scrubs Chinese Propaganda." *Washington Free Beacon*, August 4, 2020. freebeacon.com/media/nyt-quietly-scrubs-chinese-propaganda

25. Schachtel, Jordan [Tweet] *Twitter*, June 16, 2020. twitter.com/jordanschachtel/status/1272993411168075776

26. Feiner, Lauren. "Amazon Is the Most Valuable Public Company in the World After Passing Microsoft." *CNBC*, Jan 7 2019, www.cnbc.com/2019/01/07/amazon-passes-microsoft-market-value-becomes-largest.html

27. Herman, E. S., Chomsky, N.. *Manufacturing Consent: The Political Economy of the Mass Media*. Knopf Doubleday Publishing Group. United Kingdom. 2011.

28. Hersh, Seymour. "The Killing of Osama bin Laden." *The London Review of Books*, May 21, 2015. www.lrb.co.uk/the-paper/v37/n10/seymour-m.-hersh/the-killing-of-osama-bin-laden

29. Sarlin, Benjamin. "The Man Who Knew Cheney's Secrets." *Daily Beast*, July 14, 2009. www.thedailybeast.com/the-man-who-knew-cheneys-secret

30. "Ten Bombshell Revelations From Seymour Hersh's New Autobiography." *Zero Hedge*, August 8, 2018. www.zerohedge.com/news/2018-08-02/ten-bombshell-revelations-seymour-hershs-new-autobiography

31. Ackerman, Spencer and Ed Pilkington. "Obama's War on Whistleblowers Leaves Administration Insiders Unscathed." *Guardian (London)*. March 16, 2015. www.theguardian.com/us-news/2015/mar/16/whistleblowers-double-standard-obama-david-petraeus-chelsea-manning

32. I have been unable to confirm whether it was the publisher or Hersh himself who canceled the book, as Hersh has given indications both ways. As someone who has spent years researching and writing books, it is hard to imagine voluntarily spiking one's own book without significant external pressure.

33. Brand, Russell. "Epstein, Gates & Mainstream Media's Conspiracy of Silence." youtu.be/eGsZMYiF20g

34. "Noam Chomsky on Propaganda, Interview With Andrew Marr." *The Big Idea*, BBC, February 14, 1996. youtu.be/GjENnyQupow

35. "Anand Giridharadas: How Bias Actually Works at MSNBC, New York Times." *Rising*, May 11, 2020. www.youtube.com/watch?v=11WDbwZfiw8

Chapter 5: Red News, Blue News, Fake News, True News

1. Polls in the spring and summer of 2015, such as this CNN poll, typically showed him 60+ points behind Clinton: i2.cdn.turner.com/cnn/2015/images/04/20/cnnorc-2016poll04202015.pdf

2. Sunkara, Bhaskar. "Ep. 12: Bhaskar on Bernie: Talking Democratic Socialism With Jacobin Editor Bhaskar Sunkara." 2019. www.berniesanders.com/podcast/ep-12-bhaskar-bernie-talking-democratic-socialism-jacobin-editor-bhaskar-sunkara

3. Johnson, Adam. "Washington Post Ran 16 Negative Stories on Bernie Sanders in 16 Hours." *FAIR*, March 8, 2016. fair.org/home/washington-post-ran-16-negative-stories-on-bernie-sanders-in-16-hours

4. Vavreck, Lynn. "The Ad That Moved People the Most: Bernie Sanders's 'America.'" *New York Times*, December 30, 2016. www.nytimes.com/2016/12/30/upshot/the-campaign-ads-that-moved-people-the-most.html

5. Norton, Ben. "New York Times Busted for Anti-Bernie Bias: The Iconic, Clinton-Endorsing Newspaper Slyly Edits Article To Smear Sanders." *Salon.* March 16, 2016. www.salon.com/2016/03/16/new_york_times_busted_for_anti_bernie_bias_the_iconic_clinton_endorsing_newspaper_slyly_edits_article_to_smear_sanders

6. Sainato, Michael. "WikiLeaks: New York Times Propped Up Clinton, Subverted Sanders." *Observer*, October 13, 2016. observer.com/2016/10/wikileaks-new-york-times-propped-up-clinton-subverted-sanders/

7. Taibbi, Matt. "How the 'New York Times' Sandbagged Bernie Sanders." *Rolling Stone,* March 15, 2016. www.rollingstone.com/politics/politics-news/how-the-new-york-times-sandbagged-bernie-sanders-189129

8. Halper, Katie. "PBS Taps Journalist With Anti-Sanders Bias To Help Moderate Debate." *FAIR*, December 17, 2019. fair.org/home/pbs-taps-journalist-with-anti-sanders-bias-to-help-moderate-debate

9. "Hillary Clinton Email Archive." *WikiLeaks*, March 16, 2016. wikileaks.org/clinton-emails/

10. Email entitled "From time to time I get the questions in advance." WikiLeaks, March 12, 2016. wikileaks.org/podesta-emails/emailid/5205

11. Biddle, Sam. "WikiLeaks Emails Show DNC Tried To Get Someone To Pin Down Sanders Jewish/Atheist Leaning To Win 'Percentage Points' in KY and WV." *The Intercept,* July 22, 2016. theintercept.com/2016/07/22/new-leak-top-dnc-official-wanted-to-use-bernie-sanderss-religious-beliefs-against-him

12. Email entitled "New Ways." *WikiLeaks*, March 8, 2015. wikileaks.org/podesta-emails/emailid/4097

13. Ernst, Douglas. "WikiLeaks Reveals Clinton Camp's Work With 'Very Friendly and Malleable Reporters.'" *Washington Times*, October 21, 2016. www.washingtontimes.com/news/2016/oct/21/wikileaks-reveals-hillary-clinton-camps-work-with-

14. Pfeiffer, Alex. "Hill's Shills: Leaks Have Exposed Journalists In Clinton's Corner." *Daily Caller*, October 11, 2016. dailycaller.com/2016/10/11/hills-shills-leaks-have-exposed-journalists-in-clintons-corner

15. Email entitled "Follow-up Media Call." *WikiLeaks*, January 13, 2015. wikileaks.org/podesta-emails/emailid/44903

16. Email entitled "Friday Strategy Call at 8:00 AM ET." *WikiLeaks*, April 23, 2015. wikileaks.org/podesta-emails/emailid/1120

17. Debenedetti, Gabriel. "They Always Wanted Trump." *Politico*, November 7, 2016. www.politico.com/magazine/story/2016/11/hillary-clinton-2016-donald-trump-214428/

18. Email entitled "[AGENDA & MEMO] Friday Strategy Call at 8:00 AM ET." *WikiLeaks, April 23, 2015.* wikileaks.org/podesta-emails/emailid/1120

19. "Trump Got 15 Times More Coverage in 2015 Than Bernie." *Tyndall Report, Common Dreams*. www.commondreams.org/views/2016/12/03/how-media-iced-out-bernie-sanders-helped-donald-trump-win

20. "Voters Outraged As Media Accused of Falsely, Preemptively Crowning Clinton." *Common Dreams*, June 6, 2016. commondreams.org/news/2016/06/06/voters-outraged-media-accused-falsely-preemptively-crowning-clinton

21. Wasserman, Edward. "Murder by Media: The Dean Scream." *Miami Herald*, February 21, 2005. ewasserman.com/2005/02/21/murder-by-media-the-dean-scream

22. The term used was generally "official volunteers," but these weren't just people who supported the campaign. This was one half of each state's specific allotment of attendees; they were credentialed along with each state's delegates to enter the convention.

23. Lapowsky, Issie. "Twitter Attacks Clinton's Record With #WhichHillary." *WIRED*, February 25, 2016. www.wired.com/2016/02/whichhillary

24. Hanley, Brian. "Anti-Hillary Clinton Hashtag Breaks the Internet Two Days Before South Carolina Primary." *Huffington Post*, February 25, 2016. www.huffpost.com/entry/anti-hillary-clinton-hash_b_9322034

25. Garofalo, Michael. "Clinton Campaign to Bernie: Drop Your Negative Tone and Maybe Hillary Will Debate You in NY." *Salon*, March 29, 2016. www.salon.com/2016/03/28/clinton_campaign_to_bernie_drop_your_negative_tone_and_maybe_hillary_will_debate_you_in_ny

26. Golshan, Tara. "Bernie Sanders's Fans Show Hillary Clinton What Negative 'Tone' Is Really Like." *Vox*, March 30, 2016. www.vox.com/2016/3/30/11332820/tonedownforwhat-bernie-sanders-tone-hillary-clinton

27. Meyer, Robinson. "Here Comes the Berniebro." *Atlantic*, October 17, 2015. www.the-atlantic.com/politics/archive/2015/10/here-comes-the-berniebro-bernie-sanders/411070

28. Greenwald, Glenn. "The 'Bernie Bros' Narrative: a Cheap Campaign Tactic Masquerading As Journalism and Social Activism." *The Intercept*, January 31, 2016. theintercept.com/2016/01/31/the-bernie-bros-narrative-a-cheap-false-campaign-tactic-masquerading-as-journalism-and-social-activism/

29. Rappeport, Alan. "From Bernie Sanders Supporters, Death Threats Over Delegates." *New York Times*, May 16, 2016. www.nytimes.com/2016/05/17/us/politics/bernie-sanders-supporters-nevada.html

30. Kurtzleben, Danielle. "Women And The Generational Divide Between Hillary Clinton, Bernie Sanders." *NPR*, February 1, 2016. www.npr.org/2016/02/01/465144857/women-and-the-generational-divide-between-hillary-clinton-bernie-sanders

31. Parkinson, Hannah Jane. "Click and Elect: How Fake News Helped Donald Trump Win a Real Election." *Guardian*, November 14, 2016. www.theguardian.com/commentisfree/2016/nov/14/fake-news-donald-trump-election-alt-right-social-media-tech-companies

32. Dewey, Caitlin. "Facebook Fake-News Writer: 'I Think Donald Trump Is in the White House Because of Me.'" *Washington Post*, November 17, 2016. www.washingtonpost.com/news/the-intersect/wp/2016/11/17/facebook-fake-news-writer-i-think-donald-trump-is-in-the-white-house-because-of-me

33. Sydell, Laura. "We Tracked Down a Fake-News Creator in the Suburbs. Here's What We Learned." *NPR*, November 23, 2016. www.npr.org/sections/alltechconsidered/2016/11/23/503146770/npr-finds-the-head-of-a-covert-fake-news-operation-in-the-suburbs

34. Smith, David. "Donald Trump Hints at Assassination of Hillary Clinton by Gun Rights Supporters." *Guardian*, August 10, 2016. www.theguardian.com/us-news/2016/aug/09/trump-gun-owners-clinton-judges-second-amendment

35. Graves, Lucia. "This Is Donald Trump at His Lowest Yet: A Man Hinting at Murder." *Guardian*, August 9, 2016. www.theguardian.com/commentisfree/2016/aug/09/donald-trump-second-amendment-quote-hillary-clinton

36. Corasaniti, Nick and Maggie Haberman. "Donald Trump Suggests 'Second Amendment People' Could Act Against Hillary Clinton." *New York Times*, August 9, 2016. www.nytimes.com/2016/08/10/us/politics/donald-trump-hillary-clinton.html

37. Dougherty, Jill. "The Reality Behind Russia's Fake News." *CNN*, December 2, 2016. www.cnn.com/2016/12/02/politics/russia-fake-news-reality/index.html

38. Timberg, Craig. "Russian Propaganda Effort Helped Spread 'Fake News' During Election, Experts Say." *Washington Post*, November 24, 2016. www.washingtonpost.com/business/economy/russian-propaganda-effort-helped-spread-fake-news-during-election-experts-say/2016/11/24/793903b6-8a40-4ca9-b712-716af66098fe_story.html

39. See Sydell, above.

40. "Trump to CNN Reporter: You Are Fake News." *CNBC*, January 11, 2017. www.cnbc.com/video/2017/01/11/trump-to-cnn-reporter-you-are-fake-news.html

41. Chambers, Francesca and Keith Griffith. "VP Pence Says He and Trump Support a 'Free and Independent Press' - But They'll Call the Media Out When Reporters Play 'Fast And Loose With the Facts.'" *The Daily Mail*, February 20, 2017. www.dailymail.co.uk/news/article-4243152/Pence-fr.html

Chapter 6: Managing the Narrative

1. Ta, Linh. "Bernie Sanders Leads Register/CNN/Mediacom Iowa Poll." *Iowa Capital Dispatch*, January 10, 2020. iowacapitaldispatch.com/2020/01/10/bernie-sanders-leads-register-cnn-mediacom-iowa-poll

2. Lerer, Lisa and Reid Epstein. "Democratic Leaders Willing to Risk Party Damage to Stop Bernie Sanders." *New York Times*, March 2, 2020. www.nytimes.com/2020/02/27/us/politics/democratic-superdelegates.html

3. Martin, Jonathan. "'Stop Sanders' Democrats Are Agonizing Over His Momentum." *New York Times*, April 16, 2019. www.nytimes.com/2019/04/16/us/politics/bernie-sanders-democratic-party.html

4. Brigham, Bob. "'I Feel Like Christmas Was Canceled': Political Junkies Shocked by Spiking of Iowa Caucuses Poll." *Raw Story*, February 1, 2020. www.rawstory.com/2020/02/i-feel-like-christmas-was-cancelled-political-junkies-shocked-by-spiking-of-iowa-caucuses-poll

5. Lee, MJ. "Bernie Sanders Told Elizabeth Warren in a Private 2018 Meeting That a Woman Can't Win, Sources Say." *Washington Post*, January 13, 2020. www.cnn.com/2020/01/13/politics/bernie-sanders-elizabeth-warren-meeting/index.html

6. Bloomberg Politics. "Sen. Sanders Says He Never Told Warren A Woman Couldn't Win." January 14, 2020. youtu.be/oI7Ivo2gie0

7. See Lee, above.

8. Herndon, Astead and Jonathan Martin. "Warren Says Sanders Told Her a Woman Could Not Win the Presidency." *New York Times*, January 13, 2020. www.nytimes.com/2020/01/13/us/politics/bernie-sanders-elizabeth-warren-woman-president.html

9. See Bloomberg video, above.

10. See Bloomberg video, above.

11. Taibbi, Matt. "CNN's Debate Performance Was Villainous and Shameful." *Rolling Stone*, January 15, 2020. www.rollingstone.com/politics/political-commentary/january-democratic-debate-2020-cnn-bernie-sanders-elizabeth-warren-938365

12. CNN Chyrons During January 2020 CNN Democratic Nominee Debate. [Tweet] *Twitter*, January 14, 2020. twitter.com/ninaturner/status/1217299524370206720

13. This 2020 Iowa debacle was so fascinating, troubling, and revealing that I took the time to investigate deeply. Please learn more with my 7000-word piece: Brasunas, Tony. "The Complete Story: What Really Happened in Iowa." *Medium*, February 10, 2020. tonybrasunas.medium.com/the-complete-story-what-really-happened-in-iowa-ab1d12d3d0e2

14. The deception extends to the headline here, saying Sanders trails when the newsworthy development was that he had pulled into a lead: "Sanders Climbs, Now Nearly Tied With Biden Among Registered Voters: Reuters Poll." *CNBC*, January 17, 2020. www.cnbc.com/2020/01/17/sanders-climbs-now-tied-with-biden-among-registered-voters-reuters-poll.html

15. See Reuters poll, above.

16. Lindorff, Dave. "CNN's Sanders Hit Piece Doesn't Pass the Smell Test." *FAIR,* January 13, 2020. fair.org/home/cnns-sanders-hit-piece-doesnt-pass-the-smell-test

17. Collins, Sean. "Talking About the Warren and Sanders Handshake Keeps Us From Having To Talk About Sexism." *Vox,* January 15, 2020. www.vox.com/policy-and-politics/2020/1/15/21066949/elizabeth-warren-bernie-sanders-handshake-democratic-debate-sexism

18. Spencer, Keith. "There Is Hard Data That Shows 'Bernie Bros' Are a Myth." *Salon*, March 9, 2020. www.salon.com/2020/03/09/there-is-hard-data-that-shows-bernie-bros-are-a-myth

19. Jilani, Zaid. "'Bernie Bro' aggression is actually political engagement." *Forward,* February 27, 2020. forward.com/opinion/440613/senator-sanders-reframe-the-bernie-bro-narrative-as-the-lifeblood-of

20. Bekiempis, Victoria. "Outcry After MSNBC Host Compares Sanders' Nevada Win to Nazi Invasion." *The Guardian*, February 24, 2020. www.theguardian.com/us-news/2020/feb/23/msnbc-chris-matthews-sanders-nevada-win-nazi-invasion

21. "Watch MSNBC Meltdown Amid Bernie's Nevada Victory." *NowThis News*, February 24, 2020. youtu.be/gZ43aTu9Grg

22. Mak, Tim. "How Russia Is Trying to Boost Bernie Sanders' Campaign." *All Things Considered, NPR*, March 5, 2020. www.npr.org/2020/03/05/812186614/how-russia-is-trying-to-boost-bernie-sanders-campaign

23. Barnes, Julian E. and Sydney Ember. "Russia Is Said to Be Interfering to Aid Sanders in Democratic Primaries." *New York Times,* February 21, 2020. www.nytimes.com/2020/02/21/us/politics/bernie-sanders-russia.html

24. Stracqualursi, Veronica and Devan Cole. "Pete Buttigieg Claimed Victory in Iowa Before Any Results Were Reported." *CNN*, February 4, 2020. www.cnn.com/2020/02/04/politics/pete-buttigieg-iowa-caucus/index.html

25. Stewart, Emily and Ella Nilsen. "Pete Buttigieg Claims Victory in Iowa Before the Results Are In." *Vox,* February 4, 2020. www.vox.com/2020/2/4/21122122/pete-buttigieg-iowa-victory-speech

26. Malone, Clare. "That Last, Unreleased Des Moines Register Poll of Iowa Really Did Show Biden in Fourth." *FiveThirtyEight*, February 3, 2020. fivethirtyeight.com/live-blog/iowa-caucus-2020-election-live/#254963

27. See Stewart, above.

28. Hunter, Carol. "From the Editor: Des Moines Register, Partners Cancel Release of Iowa Poll After Respondent Raises Concerns." *Des Moines Register*, February 1, 2020. www.desmoinesregister.com/story/news/2020/02/01/des-moines-register-cnn-cancels-release-iowa-poll-over-respondent-concerns/4637168002

29. Dwilson, Stephanie Dube. "Shadow & the Iowa Democratic Caucus App: 5 Fast Facts You Need to Know." *Heavy*, February 4, 2020. heavy.com/news/2020/02/shadow-iowa-democratic-caucus-app

30. "Cyber Experts Weigh In on the App That Crashed the Iowa Caucus." *CBS News.* February 5, 2020. www.youtube.com/watch?v=YbZ8zLH6T1A

31. See Brasunas, above.

32. "DNC Claims Right to Select Presidential Candidate." *Project Censored.* October 4, 2017. www.projectcensored.org/9-dnc-claims-right-select-presidential-candidate

33. Chariton, Jordan. "DNC: We Can Legally Choose Candidate Over Cigars in Back Room." *The Young Turks,* May 1, 2017. medium.com/theyoungturks/dnc-we-can-legally-choose-candidate-over-cigars-in-back-room-e3026730e252

34. McClennen, Sophia A. "The DNC's Elephant in the Room: Dems Have a Problem — It's Not Donald Trump." *Salon,* May 13, 2017 www.salon.com/2017/05/13/the-dncs-elephant-in-the-room-dems-have-a-problem-its-not-donald-trump
Riotta, Chris. "Was the Election Rigged Against Bernie Sanders? DNC Lawsuit Demands Repayment for Campaign Donors." *Newsweek,* May 15, 2017. www.newsweek.com/bernie-sanders-rigged-hillary-clinton-dnc-lawsuit-donald-trump-president-609582

35. Project Censored. "The Top 25 Censored Stories Of 2016-17." 2017. www.projectcensored.org/category/the-top-25-censored-stories-of-2016-2017/page/4

36. Chariton, Jordan. "Why Democrats Are Full of Sh*t on Voting Rights." *Status Coup,* July 9, 2021. statuscoup.substack.com/p/why-democrats-are-full-of-sht-on

37. See Hunter, above.

38. Shiver, Phil. "The Final Des Moines Register Poll—The One They Decided Not To Release—Shows Joe Biden In Fourth Place." *The Blaze,* February 3, 2020. www.theblaze.com/news/final-des-moines-register-poll-biden-fourth

39. Coverage in corporate media was overwhelmingly positive about Buttigieg during the campaign. His military experience was painted as brief but dutiful and dangerous. Rarely, and only in passing, was it mentioned that he worked with the CIA and other intelligence agencies:

Maddow, Rachel. "Interview with Pete Buttigieg." *MSNBC,* April 4, 2019. www.msnbc.com/transcripts/rachel-maddow-show/2019-04-15-msna1219976

Zeleny, Jeff. "Buttigieg Wields His Military Credentials: 'It's Not Like I Killed Bin Laden,' but It Was Dangerous." *CNN,* May 17, 2019. www.cnn.com/2019/05/17/politics/buttigieg-military-service-2020/index.html

40. Rubinstein, Alexander. "Media Darling Pete Buttigieg Was in Unit That Worked With CIA in Afghanistan." *The Grayzone*, February 7, 2020. thegrayzone.com/2020/02/07/pete-buttigieg-cia-afghanistan

41. "Hear Buttigieg's Reaction to Latest Iowa Results." *CNN*, February 7, 2020. edition.cnn.com/videos/politics/2020/02/07/pete-buttigieg-iowa-caucus-lead-new-hampshire-town-hall-2020-vpx.cnn

42. Hackney, Deanna. "Review Largely Blames Iowa Caucus Problems on Democratic National Committee." *CNN*, December 13, 2020. www.cnn.com/2020/12/12/politics/iowa-caucus-review/index.html

43.Helmore, Edward. "Once the Scourge of Democrats, Former Republican Plays Tough For Hillary Clinton." *The Guardian*, November 29, 2014. www.theguardian.com/world/2014/nov/29/david-brock-former-republican-hitman-hillary-clinton

44. Gold, Hadas. "Media Matters to Pivot Away From Focus on Fox News, As It Names New President." *Politico*, December 6, 2016. www.politico.com/blogs/on-media/2016/12/media-matters-announces-new-president-and-new-direction-232228

45. These slurs are used against independent voices on the left too, such as this piece attacking Alex Rubinstein and Jimmy Dore: Ross, Alexander Reid. "These 'Dirtbag Left' Stars Are Flirting With the Far Right." *Daily Beast,* March 9, 2021. www.thedailybeast.com/these-dirtbag-left-stars-are-flirting-with-the-far-right

46. Samuel, Terence and Nancy Barnes. "NPR Launches Disinformation Reporting Team." *NPR,* July 15, 2022. www.npr.org/sections/npr-extra/2022/07/15/1111727112/npr-launches-disinformation-reporting-team

47. "Democracy Matters: Strategy for Action." *Media Matters*, 2017. www.documentcloud.org/documents/3440721-337535680-Full-David-Brock-Confidential-Memo-on

48. Dore, Jimmy. "NBC & Google Team Up To Censor Conservative News." *Jimmy Dore Show*, June 18, 2020. www.youtube.com/watch?v=Y4JGwR10UCA

49. Scherer, Michael. "Hillary Clinton's Bulldog Blazes New Campaign Finance Trails." *Time,* September 10, 2015. time.com/4028459/david-brock-hillary-clinton-media-matters/

50. CDA Section 230: "No provider or user of an interactive computer service shall be treated as the publisher or speaker of any information provided by another information content provider" (47 U.S.C. § 230).

51. Holzberg, Melissa. "Facebook Banned 1.3 Billion Accounts Over Three Months To Combat 'Fake' And 'Harmful' Content." *Forbes,* March 22, 2021. www.forbes.com/sites/melissaholzberg/2021/03/22/facebook-banned-13-billion-accounts-over-three-months-to-combat-fake-and-harmful-content

52. Robertson, Adi. "Facebook has banned nearly 1,000 'militarized social movements,' documents reveal." *The Verge,* October 12, 2021. www.theverge.com/2021/10/12/22722885/facebook-militarized-social-movements-banned-internal-list-leak

53. Bell, K. "Facebook has banned 3,000 accounts for COVID-19 and vaccine misinformation." *Engadget*, August 18, 2021. www.engadget.com/facebook-removed-3000-accounts-covid-vaccine-misinformation-184254103.html

54. Ingraham, Laura. "Ingraham Reacts to Time Article Revealing Driving Forces Behind Biden's Win." *Fox News*, February 5, 2021. www.youtube.com/watch?v=0cw03E2eoQU

55. Ball, Molly. "The Secret History of the Shadow Campaign That Saved the 2020 Election." *TIME*, February 4, 2021. time.com/5936036/secret-2020-election-campaign

56. Vorhies, Zach and Kent Heckenlively. *Google Leaks: A Whistleblower's Exposé of Big Tech Censorship*. Skyhorse. New York, New York. 2021.

57. Bose, Nandita and Elizabeth Culliford. "Biden Says Facebook, Others 'Killing People' by Carrying COVID Misinformation." *Reuters*, July 16, 2021. www.reuters.com/business/healthcare-pharmaceuticals/white-house-says-facebooks-steps-stop-vaccine-misinformation-are-inadequate-2021-07-16

58. See Bose, above.

59. Lemon, Jason. "Video of Biden Saying Vaccinations Prevent Covid Resurfaces After Infection." *Newsweek*, July 21, 2022. www.newsweek.com/joe-biden-2021-video-saying-vaccinations-prevent-covid-resurfaces-1726900

60. Ball, Krystal and Saagar Enjeti. "Outrage After Biden Pushes Internet Death Penalty for 'Misinformation.'" *Breaking Points*, July 19, 2021. www.youtube.com/watch?v=4ACNDoqlr_o

61. See Ball, above.

62. Swann, Ben. "On Masks, Facebook Fact-Checkers Bought and Paid for by Gates Foundation." Reality Check, August 31, 2020. podtail.com/en/podcast/reality-check-with-ben-swann/facebook-fact-checkers-bought-and-paid-for-by-gate

63. *Gaslight*. 1944, Metro-Goldwyn-Mayer. George Cukor, director. The film depicts a young woman whose husband attempts to rob her of her wealth while slowly manipulating her into believing she is insane.

64. "Dr. Anthony Fauci Talks With Dr Jon LaPook About Covid-19." *60 Minutes*, March 8, 2020. www.youtube.com/watch?v=PRa6t_e7dgI

65. Good Morning America. "Realities of Facemasks in Fight Against Coronavirus Exposure." *ABC News*, Feb 27, 2020. www.youtube.com/watch?time_continue=309&v=pZiGJUbxqww

66. See *60 Minutes*, above.

67. Lazzarino, Antonio Ivan, et al. "Covid-19: Important Potential Side Effects Of Wearing Face Masks That We Should Bear In Mind." *British Medical Journal*, May 21, 2020. www.bmj.com/content/369/bmj.m2003

68. Ross, Katherine. "Why Weren't We Wearing Masks From the Beginning? Dr. Fauci Explains." *TheStreet*, June 12, 2020. www.thestreet.com/video/dr-fauci-masks-changing-directive-coronavirus

69. Chamberlain, Samuel. "Fauci Emails Show His Flip-Flopping on Wearing Masks To Fight Covid." *New York Post,* June 3, 2021. nypost.com/2021/06/03/fauci-emails-show-his-flip-flopping-on-wearing-masks-to-fight-covid

70. KEEL 710 AM. "We Were Lied to About Facemasks and COVID-19." July 23, 2020. 710keel.com/we-were-lied-to-about-facemasks-and-covid-19

71. Ball, Krystal and Saagar Enjeti. "Fauci Admits Government Lied About Masks To Preserve Supplies." *Rising,* June 18, 2020. www.youtube.com/watch?v=_2MmX2U2V3c

72. It would take pages to document all the media coverage of flip-flops on covid policies. A survey:
Harsanyi, David. "Fauci Is Not Your God." *National Review,* February 22, 2021. www.nationalreview.com/2021/02/fauci-is-not-your-god
Olson, Tyler. "Fauci's Mixed Messages, Inconsistencies About COVID Masks, Vaccines and Reopenings Come Under Scrutiny." *Fox News,* February 23, 2021. www.foxnews.com/politics/faucis-mixed-messages-inconsistencies-about-covid-19-masks-vaccines-and-reopenings-come-under-scrutiny
Specter, Michael. "How Anthony Fauci Became America's Doctor." *The New Yorker,* April 10, 2020. www.newyorker.com/magazine/2020/04/20/how-anthony-fauci-became-americas-doctor
Chamberlain, Samuel. "Fauci Emails Show His Flip-Flopping on Wearing Masks To Fight Covid." *New York Post,* June 3, 2021. nypost.com/2021/06/03/fauci-emails-show-his-flip-flopping-on-wearing-masks-to-fight-covid/
Jankowicz, Mia. "Fauci Said Government Held Off Promoting Face Masks Because It Knew Shortages Were So Bad Even Doctors Couldn't Get Enough." *Business Insider,* June 15, 2020. www.businessinsider.com/fauci-mask-advice-was-because-doctors-shortages-from-the-start-2020-6

73. Maté, Aaron. "MSNBC's Rachel Maddow Sees a "Russia Connection" Lurking Around Every Corner." *The Intercept,* April 12 2017. theintercept.com/2017/04/12/msnbcs-rachel-maddow-sees-a-russia-connection-lurking-around-every-corner

74. Rosas, Julio. "Rachel Maddow Theorizes Russian Attack on Power Grid During Polar Vortex: 'What Would You and Your Family Do'." *Mediaite,* January 31, 2019. www.mediaite.com/tv/rachel-maddow-theorizes-russian-attack-on-power-grid-during-polar-vortex-what-would-you-and-your-family-do

75. Maté, Aaron. "The End of Russiagate." *Le Monde,* May 2019. mondediplo.com/2019/05/02russiagate-end

76. Dore, Jimmy. "Final Nail in Russiagate Coffin: CrowdStrike Admits 'No Evidence.'" *Jimmy Dore Show,* May 11, 2020. www.youtube.com/watch?v=WRoTGlQ4JMA

77. Seitz, Amanda. "FBI Reviewed Cybersecurity Firm's Evidence in 2016 DNC Election Hack." *Associated Press,* September 26, 2019. apnews.com/article/archive-fact-checking-7657130451

78. Maté, Aaron. "The Failed Russiagate Playbook Can't Stop Bernie Sanders." *The Nation,* February 25, 2020. www.thenation.com/article/politics/bernie-sanders-russiagate

79. Dunleavy, Jerry. "Obama Spy Chief And Other Top Officials Had No Direct Evidence Of Trump-Russia Collusion: Transcripts." *Washington Examiner,* May 7, 2020. www.washingtonexaminer.com/news/obama-spy-chief-and-other-top-officials-had-no-direct-evidence-of-trump-russia-collusion-transcripts

80. Enjeti, Saagar. "Obamagate Is Real and the Media Can't Just Ignore It." *Rising,* May 12, 2020. www.youtube.com/watch?v=co_JQuttDa8

81. Trump later pardoned Flynn too, but the unexpected dropping of charges happened first: Singman, Brooke. "DOJ Drops Case Against Michael Flynn, In Wake Of Internal Memo Release." *Fox News,* May 7, 2020. www.foxnews.com/politics/drops-doj-case-against-michael-flynn-in-wake-of-internal-memo-release

82. See Maté in *Le Monde,* above.

83. Goldman, Adam and Charlie Savage. "Authorities Arrest Analyst Who Contributed to Steele Dossier." *New York Times,* November 4, 2021. www.nytimes.com/2021/11/04/us/politics/igor-danchenko-arrested-steele-dossier.html

84. Farhi, Paul. "The Washington Post Corrects, Removes Parts Of Two Stories Regarding The Steele Dossier." *Washington Post,* November 12, 2021. www.washingtonpost.com/lifestyle/style/media-washington-post-steele-dossier/2021/11/12/f7c9b770-43d5-11ec-a88e-2aa4632af69b_story.html

85. Cohen, Marshall. "The Steele Dossier: A Reckoning." *CNN,* November 18, 2021. edition.cnn.com/2021/11/18/politics/steele-dossier-reckoning/index.html

86. MacLeod, Allan. "The Utility of the RussiaGate Conspiracy New McCarthyism Allows Corporate Media To Tighten Grip, Democrats To Ignore Their Own Failings." *FAIR,* July 27, 2017. fair.org/home/the-utility-of-the-russiagate-conspiracy

87. Enjeti, Saagar. "Media Faces 'Extinction Level Event' As Russiagate, #MeToo Implode." *Rising,* May 11, 2020. www.youtube.com/watch?v=HCSdDKsxo34

88. See Enjeti, above.

89. A feather in its cap, independent media program *Rising* (back when Enjeti and Ball were hosts) was the first news outlet to interview Reade after she made her allegations public. Corporate media ignored the issue altogether, but independent media wrote articles. *Rising* let Reade tell her own story. "Joe Biden Accuser Tara Reade Speaks Out." *Rising,* Mar 26, 2020. www.youtube.com/watch?v=ZmVUQ7ii3_4

90. "Megyn Kelly Interviews Biden Accuser Tara Reade." *Associated Press,* May 7, 2020. www.youtube.com/watch?v=Y4Mgpj4t7ZU

91. The story remains contested by Clinton, but upon investigation, I find Broaddrick's allegations persuasive. For a reasonable, middle-of-the-road presentation of the facts: "Is Juanita Broaddrick Telling the Truth?" *Slate,* March 3, 1999. slate.com/news-and-politics/1999/03/is-juanita-broaddrick-telling-the-truth.html

92. Ball, Krystal. "Krystal Ball Blasts Media for Entitled Meltdown Over Megyn Kelly Interview With Tara Reade." *Rising,* May 8, 2020. www.youtube.com/watch?v=SypnUFeKUrw

Chapter 7: The Pipes of the Mighty Wurlitzer

1. Quite a bit has been written about the incident in independent media from both military and media perspectives if one is willing to dig. A more nuanced angle than I was able to appreciate at the time: "The EP-3 collision: 2001 and 201?" *Asia Sentinel*, Mar 29, 2013. www. asiasentinel.com/p/the-ep-3-collision-2001-and-201

2. Wong, Natalie. "Hong Kong Activist, Writer 'Kong Tsung-Gan' Confirms That's Only a Pen Name." *South China Morning Post*, August 15, 2020. www.scmp.com/news/hong-kong/society/article/3097523/hong-kong-activist-writer-kong-tsung-gan-confirms-thats-only

3. Blumenthal, Max. "Western Media's Favorite Hong Kong 'Freedom Struggle Writer' Is American Ex-Amnesty Staffer in Yellowface." *Grayzone*, August 8, 2020. thegrayzone. com/2020/08/08/hong-kong-western-media-yellowfacing-amnesty

4. Dore, Jimmy. "Mainstream Media Caught Using Fake Sources!" *Jimmy Dore Show*, August 17, 2020. www.youtu.be/pdN3wkdZsA8

5. Romboy, Dennis. "Utah Activist in Capitol Riot Sold His Video to CNN, NBC for $35k Each, Court Docs Say." *Deseret News*, February 17, 2021. www.deseret.com/utah/2021/2/17/22287763/activist-capitol-riot-video-sold-nbc-cnn-35k-each-john-sullivan-federal-charges

6. Eustachewich, Lia. "Who Is John Sullivan, Accused Provocateur Charged in Capitol Riot?" *New York Post*, January 15, 2021. nypost.com/2021/01/15/who-is-john-sullivan-accused-provocateur-charged-in-capitol-riot

7. Blumenthal, Max. "Chaos Agent: Right-Wing Blames US Capitol Riot on Notorious Instigator Banished by Black Lives Matter." *Grayzone*, January 12, 2021. thegrayzone. com/2021/01/12/chaos-agent-right-wing-us-capitol-riot-black-lives-matter

8. "The New York Times Announces First Narrative Nonfiction Podcast, 'Caliphate' With Rukmini Callimachi." *Investors New York Times*, March 10, 2018. investors.nytco. com/news-and-events/press-releases/news-details/2018/THE-NEW-YORK-TIMES-AN-NOUNCES-FIRST-NARRATIVE-NONFICTION-PODCAST-CALIPHATE-WITH-RUKMINI-CALLIMACHI/default.aspx

9. Al-Arian, Laila. "Caliphate: How The *New York Times*' Islamic State Scoop Unraveled." *Middle East Eye*, January 15, 2021. www.middleeasteye.net/big-story/new-york-times-caliph-ate-debacle-deeper-problems

10. Folkenflik, David. "'New York Times' Retracts Core Of Hit Podcast Series 'Caliphate' On ISIS." *NPR*, December 18, 2020. www.npr.org/2020/12/18/944594193/new-york-times-retracts-hit-podcast-series-caliphate-on-isis-executioner

11. Rindsberg, Ashley. *The Gray Lady Winked*. Midnight Oil Publishers. Hungary. 2021.

12. The *Times* will publish endless nuanced pieces on a neoliberal trade pacts but will ultimately reveal their true position: "A Pacific Trade Deal." *New York Times*, November 5, 2013. www.nytimes.com/2013/11/06/opinion/a-pacific-trade-deal.html

13. Craig Whitlock lays out the basics of drugs, corruption, and government deception in his worthwhile 2021 book named after the leaked papers. Lee Camp goes deeper and lays asunder the true agenda of the war and enumerates (with some profanity) the lies told to the American people about it for nearly two decades. Whitlock, Craig. *The Afghanistan Papers.* 2021, Simon & Schuster. Camp, Lee. "The War in Afghanistan Is a Fraud (and Now We Have Proof)." *Consortium News,* January 10, 2020. consortiumnews.com/2020/01/10/the-war-in-afghanistan-is-a-fraud-and-now-we-have-proof

14. One of the more anti-intellectual pieces to grace the pages of a major newspaper told readers "critical thinking… isn't helping." Warzel, Charlie. "Don't Go Down the Rabbit Hole." *New York Times,* February 18, 2021. www.nytimes.com/2021/02/18/opinion/fake-news-media-attention.html

15. Krugman, P. "$2000 stimulus checks bad policy." [Tweet]. *Twitter,* December 23, 2020. twitter.com/paulkrugman/status/1341784874181603330

16. Sirota, David. "The Thumb on the Scale." *The Lever,* November 8, 2021. www.levernews.com/the-thumb-on-the-scale

17. This piece the *Times* corrected, although not until after the damage was done: Medina, Jennifer. "Bernie Sanders Retracts Endorsement of Cenk Uygur After Criticism" *New York Times,* December 13, 2019. www.nytimes.com/2019/12/13/us/politics/bernie-sanders-cenk-uygur.html

18. A typical assault on independent media here: Belluz, Julia and John Lavis. "Joe Rogan Is a Drop in the Ocean of Medical Misinformation." *New York Times,* February 8, 2022. www.nytimes.com/2022/02/08/opinion/joe-rogan-health-misinformation-solutions.html

19. Zinoman, Jason. "An American Comic on a Russian Channel: What He Avoids Speaks Volumes." *New York Times,* June 7, 2017. www.nytimes.com/2017/06/07/arts/television/trump-russia-comedy-redacted-tonight-lee-camp.html

20. Ball, Krystal and Saagar Enjeti. "New York Times Blatantly Admits Cover-Up At Biden Campaign Request." *Rising,* April 14, 2020. www.youtube.com/watch?v=63yeQ1GCzIY

21. Rosen, Christine. "The Case of Taylor Lorenz." *Commentary Magazine,* April 2021. www.commentary.org/articles/christine-rosen/taylor-lorenz-clubhouse-woke-journalism

22. Takala, R. "New York Times Reporter Locks Twitter Account After Falsely Accusing Tech Entrepreneur of Using a Slur." *Mediaite,* February 8, 2021. www.mediaite.com/news/ny-times-reporter-locks-twitter-account-after-falsely-accusing-tech-entrepreneur-of-using-a-slur

23. Rogan, Joe. "NY Times Writer Criticizes Tulsi Gabbard." *Joe Rogan Experience,"* January 21, 2019. www.youtube.com/watch?v=xpurFfcSNfU

24. Stephens, Brett. "Bernie's Angry Bros." *New York Times.* January 31, 2020. www.nytimes.com/2020/01/31/opinion/sanders-bernie-bros.html

25. Rappeport, Alan. "From Bernie Sanders Supporters, Death Threats Over Delegates." *New York Times,* May 16, 2016. www.nytimes.com/2016/05/17/us/politics/bernie-sanders-supporters-nevada.html

26. Bowles, Nellie. "The Pied Pipers of the Dirtbag Left Want to Lead Everyone to Bernie Sanders." *New York Times*, February 29, 2020. www.nytimes.com/2020/02/29/us/politics/bernie-sanders-chapo-trap-house.html

27. Spencer, Keith. "There Is Hard Data That Shows 'Bernie Bros' Are a Myth." *Salon*, March 9, 2020. www.salon.com/2020/03/09/there-is-hard-data-that-shows-bernie-bros-are-a-myth

28. "Number of Twitter followers of Democratic candidates for the 2020 U.S. presidential election." www.statista.com/statistics/1037466/twitter-followers-democratic-presidential-candidates

29. See Spencer, above.

30. Ellefson, Lindsey. "Fox News Ends 2021 as Most-Watched Basic Cable Channel for Sixth Straight Year." *The Wrap*, December 29, 2021. www.thewrap.com/cable-news-2021-ratings-fox-news-msnbc-cnn

31. "Misperceptions, the Media and the Iraq War." *PIPA/Knowledge Networks Poll,* October 2, 2003. web.stanford.edu/class/comm1a/readings/kull-misperceptions.pdf

32. Melton, Melissa. "We'll Know Our Disinformation Program Is Complete When Everything the American Public Believes Is False." *ConspiracyAnalyst*, January 13, 2015. conspiracyanalyst.org/2015/01/13/cia-flashback-well-know-our-disinformation-program-is-complete-when-everything-the-american-public-believes-is-false

33. Katz, A.J.. "Top Cable News Shows of 2021: Tucker Carlson Tonight Is No. 1 in All Measurements for First Time Ever." *Ad Week*, January 3, 2022. www.adweek.com/tvnewser/top-cable-news-shows-of-2021-tucker-carlson-tonight-is-no-1-in-all-categories-for-first-time-ever/496940

34. Sheth, Sonam. "Fox News Won a Court Case by 'Persuasively' Arguing That No 'Reasonable Viewer' Takes Tucker Carlson Seriously." *Business Insider*, September 24, 2020. www.businessinsider.com/fox-news-karen-mcdougal-case-tucker-carlson-2020-9

35. Egan, Matt. "GE Gets a Badly Needed Win in Iraq." *CNN*, October 22, 2018. www.cnn.com/2018/10/22/business/ge-iraq-power-siemens

36. "GE Signs Power Agreements Worth Over $1.2 Billion With Iraq." *Reuters*, August 19, 2020. www.reuters.com/article/us-ge-iraq/ge-signs-power-agreements-worth-over-1-2-billion-with-iraq-idUSKCN25F2SM

37. Working with Glenn Greenwald, Matt Orfalea created a video montage of Nicole Wallace's deceptions. "Viral Video of MSNBC Host's Lies." May 22, 2022. youtu.be/ZbfQZki-YZXk

38. Concha, Joe. "Judge Dismisses One America News Defamation Lawsuit Against Rachel Maddow." *The Hill*, May 23, 2020. thehill.com/homenews/media/499294-judge-dismisses-one-america-news-defamation-lawsuit-against-rachel-maddow

39. Greenwald, Glenn. "A Court Ruled Rachel Maddow's Viewers Know She Offers Exaggeration and Opinion, Not Facts." Jun 22, 2021. greenwald.substack.com/p/a-court-ruled-rachel-maddows-viewers

40. In the judge's words: "Maddow's show is different from a typical news segment where anchors inform viewers about the daily news."

41. "MSNBC Admits Maddow Not a Real Source Of Information." *Breaking Points*, June 24, 2021. www.youtu.be/k-AnC_7lhfE

42. "Panel Reacts to Joe Rogan Endorsement of Bernie Sanders." *Rising*, January 24, 2020. youtu.be/fZwTEbDEQF4

43. MSNBC seems to have removed the video, but it can be found elsewhere, such as at "Rachel Maddow's Non-Stop Covid Lies." *Jimmy Dore Show*, December 31, 2021. www.youtu.be/qWLc8dHW0T4

44. There are no studies showing the vaccines stop transmission of the virus, and there weren't any when Maddow made her statements. There are abundant studies showing that the injections have no effect on transmission, and abundant studies, such as this one, showing the injections *somewhat* reduce transmission without stopping it: Eyre, David W., et al. "Effect of Covid-19 Vaccination on Transmission of Alpha and Delta Variants." *New England Journal of Medicine*, February 24, 2022. www.nejm.org/doi/full/10.1056/nejmoa2116597

45. Concha, Joe. "Larry King Hits CNN: 'Stopped Doing News' To Focus on Trump." *The Hill*, November 8, 2018. thehill.com/homenews/media/415669-larry-king-hits-cnn-stopped-doing-news-to-focus-on-trump

46. Vaishampaiyan, Akshay. "Larry King on RT: U.S. Talk Show King Joins Russian Network." *Mic*, May 30, 2013.www.mic.com/articles/45265/larry-king-on-rt-u-s-talk-show-king-joins-russian-network

47. Edwards, Jim. "10 Amazing Facts About Pfizer's $2.3B Bextra Settlement." *CBS News*, September 2, 2009. www.cbsnews.com/news/10-amazing-facts-about-pfizers-23b-bextra-settlement

48. CNN ran several pieces at the time of the settlement in 2009, but in the thirteen years afterwards CNN has only mentioned Pfizer's wrongdoing once—in the last sentence of a piece in 2012 reporting that the BP settlement for the Deepwater Horizon oil spill had broken the Bextra settlement's record.

49. Dore, Jimmy. "'Pfizer Intentionally Deceived and Defrauded' – US Justice Department." *Jimmy Dore Show*, January 24, 2022. www.youtu.be/IS3RvTglJ3s

50. Darcy, Oliver. "Right-Wing Media Pushed A Deworming Drug To Treat Covid-19 That The FDA Says Is Unsafe For Humans." *CNN Business*, August 23, 2021. www.cnn.com/2021/08/23/media/right-wing-media-ivermectin/index.html

51. Too many studies to cite. "Use of Ivermectin Is Associated With Lower Mortality in Hospitalized Patients With Coronavirus Disease 2019." http://journal.chestnet.org/article/S0012-3692(20)34898-4

52. www.nobelprize.org/prizes/medicine/2015/press-release

53. Burnett, Erin. "Podcast Host Joe Rogan Announces Positive Covid-19 Test." *CNN Out Front*, September 1, 2021. www.cnn.com/videos/media/2021/09/01/joe-rogan-podcast-positive-covid-ebof-sot-vpx.cnn

54. Dore, Jimmy. "CNN Lied About Joe Rogan, Admits Dr. Sanjay Gupta!" *Jimmy Dore Show*, Oct 16, 2021. www.youtube.com/watch?v=4yiigLK8t0g

55. See Dore, above.

56. O'Keefe, James. "CNN Director Admits Network Engaged in 'Propaganda' to Remove Trump from Presidency." *Project Veritas*, April 13, 2021. www.youtu.be/Dv8Zy-JwXr4

57. Iversen, Kim. "CNN Caught on Camera Admitting To Pro-Democrat Propaganda." April 13, 2021. www.youtu.be/i76G3MV0pOM

58. Greenwald, Glenn. "Due Process, Adult Sexual Morality and the Case of Rep. Matt Gaetz." April 11, 2021. greenwald.substack.com/p/due-process-adult-sexual-morality

59. Fandos, Nicholas. "The Matt Gaetz Investigation: What We Know." *New York Times*, April 2, 2021. www.nytimes.com/2021/04/02/us/politics/matt-gaetz-investigation.html

60. Bauder, David. "CNN President Resigns After Relationship With Co-Worker." *ABC News*, February 2, 2022. abcnews.go.com/Business/wireStory/cnns-zucker-resigns-relationship-worker-82626299

61. Hutton, Christopher. "CNN President Jeff Zucker Resigning Over Undisclosed Relationship With Employee." *Washington Times*, February 02, 2022. www.washingtonexaminer.com/news/jeff-zucker-resign-cnn

62. National Public Radio Consolidated Financial Statements: Years ended September 30, 2021 and 2020. media.npr.org/documents/about/statements/fy2021/National%20Public%20Radio%20-%20Consolidated%20Financial%20Statements%20-%20S2120.pdf

63. Hensley, Scott. "Johnson & Johnson To Pay $2.2 Billion In Marketing Settlement." *NPR*, November 4, 2013. www.npr.org/sections/health-shots/2013/11/04/242989557/risperdal-johnson-johnson-to-pay-2-2-billion-in-marketing-settlement

64. Petras, James. "The Ford Foundation and the CIA: A Documented Case Of Philanthropic Collaboration With the Secret Police." *The Unz Review*, December 15, 2001. www.unz.com/jpetras/the-ford-foundation-and-the-cia/

65. Lerro, Bruce. "Left Gatekeepers Through the New Left: Monitored Rebellion." *Dissident Voice*, May 19, 2020. dissidentvoice.org/2020/05/left-gatekeepers-through-the-new-left-monitored-rebellion

66. Saunders, Frances Stonor. *Who Paid the Piper: The CIA and the Cultural Cold War.* pp134-135. Granta Books. London, England. 1999.

67. Hollar, Julie. "Here's the Evidence That the Corporate Media Says Is Missing of Washington Post's Bias Against Sanders." *FAIR*, August 15, 2019. fair.org/home/heres-the-evidence-corporate-media-say-is-missing-of-wapo-bias-against-sanders

68. Shenoy, Rupa. "Young Iowa Climate Activists Turn Political." *Public Radio International, The World.* February 3, 2020. theworld.org/file/2020-02-03/young-iowa-climate-activists-turn-political

69. Zinoman, Jason. "An American Comic on a Russian Channel: What He Avoids Speaks Volumes." *New York Times,* June 7, 2017. www.nytimes.com/2017/06/07/arts/television/trump-russia-comedy-redacted-tonight-lee-camp.html

70. Simon, Scott. "A Look At RT's 'Redacted Tonight.'" *NPR Weekend Edition,* December 16, 2017 www.npr.org/2017/12/16/571305374/a-look-at-rts-redacted-tonight

71. In response to NPR's hit piece and unwillingness to interview him live, Camp wrote a brilliant satirical takedown of NPR's propaganda. Camp, Lee. "How To Create NPR's Propaganda – As Seen In a Hit Piece Against Me." *World Against War,* December 2017. worldbeyondwar.org/lee-camp-create-nprs-propaganda-seen-hit-piece

72. Bishop, Tom. "US Psychological Warfare Experts Worked at CNN and NPR During Kosovo War." *World Socialist Website*, April 18, 2000. www.wsws.org/en/articles/2000/04/cnn-a18.html

73. Harper, Jennifer. "Rush Limbaugh, Michael Savage, Sean Hannity Named Top 'Streaming' Talk Show Hosts." *Washington Times,* January 9, 2020. www.washingtontimes.com/news/2020/jan/9/rush-limbaugh-michael-savage-sean-hannity-named-to

74. Fleury, Michelle. "Amazon Boss Jeff Bezos Buys Washington Post for $250m." *BBC News,* August 6, 2013. www.bbc.com/news/av/business-23582797

75. Konkel, Frank. "The Details About the CIA's Deal With Amazon." *The Atlantic,* July 17, 2014. www.theatlantic.com/technology/archive/2014/07/the-details-about-the-cias-deal-with-amazon/374632

76. La Monica, Paul. "News Corp. Wins Fight for Dow Jones." *CNN*, August 1, 2007. money.cnn.com/2007/07/31/news/companies/dowjones_newscorp

77. See Warzel, above.

78. Biddle, Sam. "Make Mark Zuckerberg Testify." *Intercept*, September 11, 2017. www.theintercept.com/2017/09/11/make-mark-zuckerberg-testify

Chapter 8: Censorship Central

1. Nunez, Michael. "Former Facebook Workers: We Routinely Suppressed Conservative News." *Gizmodo,* May 9, 2016. gizmodo.com/former-facebook-workers-we-routinely-suppressed-conser-1775461006

2. Noam Chomsky. "Manufacturing Consent: Noam Chomsky and the Media." Accessed at *wikiquote*. quotepark.com/quotes/2067311-noam-chomsky-if-you-believe-in-freedom-of-speech-you-believe-i

3. Statcounter. "Search Engine Market Share Worldwide, Jan-Dec 2020." gs.statcounter.com/search-engine-market-share/all/worldwide/2020

4. Globally, it trails only BBC, CNN, *New York Times*, and MSN.com. Majid, Aisha. "Top 50 News Sites in the World." *Press Gazette,* March 2, 2022. pressgazette.co.uk/most-popular-websites-news-world-monthly/2

5. Nesbit, Jeff. "Google's True Origin Partly Lies in CIA and NSA Research Grants for Mass Surveillance." *Quartz*, December 8, 2017. qz.com/1145669/googles-true-origin-partly-lies-in-cia-and-nsa-research-grants-for-mass-surveillance

6. Ahmed, Nafeez. "How The CIA Made Google: Inside the Secret Network Behind Mass Surveillance, Endless War, and Skynet." *Medium*, January 22, 2015. medium.com/insurge-intelligence/how-the-cia-made-google-e836451a959e

7. Edwards, Jim. "Social Media Is a Tool of the CIA. Seriously." *CBS News*, July 11, 2011. www.cbsnews.com/news/social-media-is-a-tool-of-the-cia-seriously

8. Phillips, Jack. "YouTube Deletes CPAC's Video About Trump's Lawsuit, Group Can't Upload Content." *Epoch Times*, July 11, 2021. www.theepochtimes.com/mkt_breakingnews/youtube-deletes-cpacs-video-about-trumps-lawsuit-group-cant-upload-content_3896374.html

9. Alexander, Julia. "More Than 17,000 YouTube Channels Removed Since New Hateful Content Policy Implemented." *The Verge,* September 3, 2019. www.theverge.com/2019/9/3/20845071/youtube-hateful-content-policies-channels-comments-videos-susan-wojcicki

10. Vorhies, Zach and Kent Heckenlively. *Google Leaks: A Whistleblower's Exposé of Big Tech Censorship*. Skyhorse. New York, New York. 2021.

11. Attkisson, Sharyl. "Big Tech Whistleblower." *Full Measure*, January 11, 2021. fullmeasure.news/news/cover-story/big-tech-censorship-part-1

12. O'Neil, Tyler. "Google Manager Told Whistleblower: 'We Need to Stop' Fake News Because "That's How Trump Won.'" *PJ Media*, March 11, 2019. pjmedia.com/news-and-politics/tyler-o-neil/2019/03/11/google-manager-fake-news-and-hate-speech-are-how-trump-won-the-election-n64342

13. "Google CEO Sundar Pichai Testifies on Data Collection." CSPAN, December 11, 2018. youtu.be/WfbTbPEEJxI

14. Fellow whistleblower Mike Wacker corroborated Vorhies revelations about blacklists. Wacker, Mike. "Google's Manual Interventions in Search Results." July 2, 2019. medium.com/@mikewacker/googles-manual-interventions-in-search-results-a3b0cfd3e26c

15. Parker, Tom. "YouTube CEO: It's Easy To 'Make Up Content and Post It From Your Basement' So We Boost "Authoritative Sources." *Reclaim the Net*, April 8, 2021. reclaimthenet.org/youtube-ceo-basement-authoritative-sources

16. See Parker, above.

17. Dore, Jimmy. "YouTube CEO Admits Suppressing Independent News." *Jimmy Dore Show*, April 24, 2021. www.youtube.com/watch?v=3l6praw8JUg

18. Pichai, Sundar. "Coronavirus: How we're helping." Company Blog Announcement. March 6, 2020. blog.google/inside-google/company-announcements/coronavirus-covid19-response

19. Tweet by Author Aaron Ginn on July 18, 2021: "Google is reading what you host in Google Docs. They deleted and removed access to my personal copy of *Evidence over Hysteria: COVID-19*. Free is never free." www.twitter.com/aginnt/status/1416860936946823185

20. Soave, Robby. "Trump Never Told Georgia's Lead Election Investigator To 'Find the Fraud.'" *Reason*, March 15, 2021. reason.com/2021/03/15/trump-find-the-fraud-media-wrong-anonymous-source-call

21. "YouTube Bans New Videos Claiming US Election Fraud." *AFP*, December 9, 2020. www.yahoo.com/now/youtube-bans-videos-claiming-us-172957890.html

22. Gramlich, John. "10 Facts About Americans and Facebook." *Pew Research*, May 16, 2019. www.pewresearch.org/fact-tank/2019/05/16/facts-about-americans-and-facebook

23. Dice, Mark. *The True Story of Fake News*. p 151. Resistance Manifesto. San Diego, CA. 2017.

24. Anderson, Natasha. "Facebook's 'Fake News': Social Media Giant Planted Op-Eds in Newspapers and Ran TV Ads Across the US Via Shadowy Lobbying Group." *Daily Mail*, May 18, 2022. www.dailymail.co.uk/news/article-10827743/How-Facebook-planted-op-eds-newspapers-TV-ads

25. "Facebook Whistleblower Frances Haugen: The 60 Minutes Interview." *YouTube*, October 3, 2021. www.youtube.com/watch?v=_Lx5VmAdZSI

26. Zakrzewski, Cat, Cristiano Lima, and Will Oremus. "Facebook Whistleblower Frances Haugen Tells Lawmakers That Meaningful Reform Is Necessary 'For Our Common Good.'" *Washington Post*, October 5, 2021. www.washingtonpost.com/technology/2021/10/05/facebook-senate-hearing-frances-haugen

27. This is also supported by a documentary *Inside Facebook: Secrets of the Social Network* that was released by an undercover investigative journalist: Statt, Nick. "Undercover Facebook Moderator Was Instructed Not To Remove Fringe Groups Or Hate Speech." *Verge*, July 17, 2018. www.theverge.com/2018/7/17/17582152/facebook-channel-4-undercover-investigation-content-moderation

28. Birnbaum, Emily, and Leah Nylen. "House Antitrust Leaders Meet With Facebook Whistleblower." *Politico*, October 21, 2021. www.politico.com/news/2021/10/21/house-antitrust-leaders-meet-with-facebook-whistleblower-516556

29. Allyn, Bobby. "Here Are 4 Key Points From the Facebook Whistleblower's Testimony on Capitol Hill." *NPR*, October 5, 2021. www.npr.org/2021/10/05/1043377310/facebook-whistleblower-frances-haugen-congress

30. Kiderra, Inga. "Facebook Boosts Voter Turnout." UC San Diego News Center, September 12, 2012. ucsdnews.ucsd.edu/pressrelease/facebook_fuels_the_friend_vote

31. Testimony to the Judiciary Subcommittee. July 16, 2019. vimeo.com/352617228

32. Watson, Paul Joseph. "Psychologist: Big Tech Will Use 'Subliminal Methods' To Shift 15 Million Votes on Election Day." Summit News, March 10, 2020. summit.news/2020/03/10/psychologist-big-tech-will-use-subliminal-methods-to-shift-15-million-votes-on-election-day

33. See Nunez, above.

34. Flood, Brian and Joseph Wulfsohn. "Facebook Blasted for Censoring Report on BLM Co-Founder's Pricey Real Estate." *Fox News,* April 16, 2021. www.foxnews.com/media/facebook-censoring-black-lives-matter

35. Bowden, John. "Nick Clegg Says Facebook Sets a Red Line on Inciting Violence in Wake of Trump Ban." *The Independent,* June 6, 2021. www.independent.co.uk/news/world/americas/us-politics/clegg-facebook-trump-ban-violence-b1860557.html

36. Vengattil, Munsif and Elizabeth Culliford. "Facebook Allows Ukraine War Posts Urging Violence Against Invading Russians, Putin." *Reuters,* March 10, 2022. news.yahoo.com/exclusive-facebook-instagram-temporarily-allow-211146449.html

37. Dore, Jimmy. "Facebook OKs Violent Speech – But Only Against Russians." *Jimmy Dore Show,* Mar 12, 2022. www.youtu.be/YoZl_gwysrY

38. Olson, Parmy. "Zuckerberg Still Has Too Much Control of Facebook." *Bloomberg News,* February 17, 2022. www.bloomberg.com/opinion/articles/2022-02-17/zuckerberg-still-has-too-much-control-of-facebook

39. Hughes, Chris. "It's Time to Break Up Facebook." *New York Times,* May 9, 2019. www.nytimes.com/2019/05/09/opinion/sunday/chris-hughes-facebook-zuckerberg.html

40. Shroff, Kaivan. "Why Who Gets Twitter's Little Blue Check Matters." WBUR, June 28, 2021. www.wbur.org/cognoscenti/2021/06/28/twitter-verification-blue-check-yashar-ali-kaivan-shroff

41. Confessore, Nicholas, Gabriel J.X. Dance, Richard Harris And Mark Hansen. "The Follower Factory." *New York Times,* January 27, 2018. www.nytimes.com/interactive/2018/01/27/technology/social-media-bots.html

42. Confessore, Nicholas, Gabriel J.X. Dance, Richard Harris. "Twitter Followers Vanish Amid Inquiries Into Fake Accounts." *New York Times,* January 31, 2018. www.nytimes.com/interactive/2018/01/31/technology/social-media-bots-investigations.html

43. "Rachel Maddow Busted Using Multiple Fake Twitter Accounts To Boost Mentions Of Her Show." theblacksphere.net/2013/03/rachel-maddow-busted-using-multiple-fake-twitter-accounts-to-boost-mentions-of-her-show. Original blog post here: freerepublic.com/focus/f-news/2992736/posts

44. See Dice, above.

45. "Trump Used 'Fight' Or 'Fighting' 20 Times in Rally Speech, Dean Says." *Associated Press,* February 10, 2021. www.pbs.org/newshour/politics/democrats-use-rally-footage-to-argue-incitement

46. Feiner, Lauren. "Twitter Bans Trump, Says Plans for Jan. 17 Armed Protests Are Circulating." CNBC, January 8, 2021. www.cnbc.com/2021/01/08/twitter-permanently-suspends-trumps-account.html

47. Sargent, Kayla. "YouTube Joins Other Big Tech Platforms, Censors President Donald Trump." Media Research Center, January 13th, 2021. www.newsbusters.org/blogs/free-speech/kayla-sargent/2021/01/13/youtube-joins-other-big-tech-platforms-censors-president

48. Hall, Alexander. "Six Tech Platforms Censor Trump or Supporters Over DC Riot." Media Research Center, January 8th, 2021. www.newsbusters.org/blogs/free-speech/alexander-hall/2021/01/08/six-tech-platforms-censor-trump-or-supporters-over-dc

49. MetaNewsRoom. Twitter, January 7, 2021. twitter.com/metanewsroom/status/1347211647245578241

50. Dore, Jimmy. "Did FBI Instigate The January 6 Riots?" *Jimmy Dore Show,* September 21, 2022. youtu.be/--fTF7zhk4g

51. Hanneman, Joseph. "Ashli Babbitt Pleaded With Police To Call for Backup Moments Before She Was Shot and Killed." *Epoch Times,* January 19, 2022. www.theepochtimes.com/ashli-babbitt-dramatically-confronted-police-for-not-stopping-rioters_4220583.html?utm_source=partner&utm_medium=internal

52. I'm not a lawyer, but the "inciting imminent violence" standard of *Brandenberg v. Ohio* seems clear. Trump's speech should be protected unless it led to imminent violence (ie before the police could arrive). I just don't see it. Calling the election fraudulent was certainly distasteful to many, but Trump called for a peaceful march. Moreover, the police had ample time prior to the protest's arrival at the Capitol.

53. "Covid-19 Misleading Information Policy." December 2021. help.twitter.com/en/rules-and-policies/medical-misinformation-policy

54. Greene's personal account was banned after she tweeted anti-lockdown opinions and data about vaccine injuries. "Twitter Bans Personal Greene Account for Covid Misinformation." *Politico,* January 2, 2022. www.politico.com/news/2022/01/02/twitter-bans-greene-covid-526362

55. Gutman-Wei, Rachel. "The Pandemic of the Vaccinated Is Here." *The Atlantic,* December 9, 2021. www.theatlantic.com/health/archive/2021/12/fully-vaccinated-omicron-infections/620953
Estrin, Daniel. "Highly Vaccinated Israel Is Seeing A Dramatic Surge In New COVID Cases. Here's Why." *NPR,* August 20, 2021. www.npr.org/sections/goatsandsoda/2021/08/20/1029628471/highly-vaccinated-israel-is-seeing-a-dramatic-surge-in-new-covid-cases-heres-why

56. "Vaccines Work." www.cdc.gov/coronavirus/2019-ncov/vaccines/effectiveness/work.html

57. Boyd, Scott. "Harvard Epidemiologist Martin Kulldorff Locked Out by Twitter Over Confirmed Face Mask Realities." *Freedom First Network,* May 15, 2021. freedomfirstnetwork.com/2021/05/harvard-epidemiologist-martin-kulldorff-locked-out-by-twitter-over-confirmed-face-mask-realities

58. Griffin, Riley. "Pfizer Boosts Forecast for Vaccine Sales to $33.5 Billion." Bloomberg, July 28, 2021. www.bloomberg.com/news/articles/2021-07-28/pfizer-expects-covid-vaccine-sales-to-top-33-billion-this-year

59. Howe, Caleb. "Twitter Suspends Grabien Media for Sharing Video, Quote of Republican Rep. on Fox News." Mediaite, January 1, 2022. www.mediaite.com/online/twitter-suspends-grabien-media-for-sharing-video-quote-of-republican-rep-on-fox-news/amp

60. Ellliott, Tom. [Tweet] *Twitter*, December 31, 2021. twitter.com/tomselliott/status/1476978027267510277?ref_src=twsrc%5Etfw

61. Goodin, Dan. "Twitter Lost Control of Its Internal Systems To Bitcoin-Scamming Hackers." *Ars Technica*, July 15, 2020. arstechnica.com/information-technology/2020/07/twitter-lost-control-of-its-internal-systems-to-bitcoin-scamming-hackers

62. Bicheno, Scott. "Massive Twitter Hack Reveals Evidence of Shadow Banning Tools." *telecoms.com*, July 16, 2020. telecoms.com/505597/massive-twitter-hack-reveals-evidence-of-shadow-banning-tools

63. Skelding, Conor and Jon Levine. "New Twitter CEO Raises Free-Speech Worries." *New York Post*, December 4, 2021. nypost.com/2021/12/04/new-twitter-ceo-parag-agrawal-raises-free-speech-concerns

64. Binder, Matt. "Twitter Is Now Adding a Controversial 'Hacked Materials' Warning Label To Tweets." *Mashable*, February 23, 2021. mashable.com/article/twitter-hacked-materials-warning-label

65. Dore, Jimmy. "Twitter's Suppression Makes Article Go Viral." *Jimmy Dore Show*, February 25, 2021. www.youtube.com/watch?v=xQfGVpU1Eg0

66. See Binder, above.

67. Cobain, Ian. "Twitter Executive for Middle East Is British Army "Psyops" Soldier." *Middle East Eye*, September 30, 2019. www.middleeasteye.net/news/twitter-executive-also-part-time-officer-uk-army-psychological-warfare-unit

68. Gilbert, David. "A Senior Twitter Exec Has Been Moonlighting in the British Army's Information Warfare Unit." *Vice*, September 30, 2019. www.vice.com/en/article/ywa5m7/a-senior-twitter-exec-has-been-moonlighting-in-the-british-armys-information-warfare-unit

Chapter 9: Mockingbirds Migrate to Social Media

1. This video can still be found with persistent searching. "We Have Been Lied To: American Doctors Address Covid Misinformation At Scotus Press Conference." www.bitchute.com/video/zr04GsUupOwk

2. Bokhari, Allum. "Facebook, Google/YouTube, Twitter Censor Viral Video of Doctors' Capitol Hill Coronavirus Press Conference." *Breitbart News*, July 27, 2020. www.breitbart.com/tech/2020/07/27/facebook-censors-viral-video-of-doctors-capitol-hill-coronavirus-press-conference

3. Schwartz, Ian. "Facebook and YouTube Ban Video of Doctors Talking COVID, Silenced Doctors Hold Press Conference." *RealClearPolitics*, July 28, 2020. www.realclearpolitics.com/video/2020/07/28/facebook_and_youtube_ban_video_of_doctors_talking_covid_silenced_doctors_hold_press_conference.html?spotim_referrer=recirculation

4. Passantino, Jon and Oliver Darcy. "Social Media Giants Remove Viral Video with False Coronavirus Claims that Trump Retweeted." *CNN Business*, July 28, 2020. www.cnn.com/2020/07/28/tech/facebook-youtube-coronavirus/index.html

5. Andrews, Travis M. and Danielle Paquette. "Trump Retweeted a Video With False Covid-19 Claims. One Doctor in It Has Said Demons Cause Illnesses." *Washington Post,* July 29, 2020. www.washingtonpost.com/technology/2020/07/28/stella-immanuel-hydroxychloro-quine-video-trump-americas-frontline-doctors

6. "Misleading Virus Video, Pushed by the Trumps, Spreads Online." *New York Times,* July 28, 2020. www.nytimes.com/2020/07/28/technology/virus-video-trump.html

7. Zadrozny, Brandy and Ben Collins. "Dark Money and PAC's Coordinated 'Reopen' Push Are Behind Doctors' Viral Hydroxychloroquine Video." *NBC News*, July 28, 2020. www.nbcnews.com/tech/social-media/dark-money-pac-s-coordinated-reopen-push-are-behind-doctors-n1235100

8. Stracqualursi, Veronica. "Trump Promotes a Doctor Who Has Claimed Alien DNA Was Used in Medical Treatments." *CNN,* July 29, 2020. www.cnn.com/2020/07/29/politics/stella-immanuel-trump-doctor

9. Frenkel, Sheera and Davey Alba. "Misleading Virus Video, Pushed by the Trumps, Spreads Online." *New York Times,* July 28, 2020. www.nytimes.com/2020/07/28/technology/virus-video-trump.html

10. It wasn't until January 2021 that corporate media allowed this science to be examined openly, with stories in Newsweek and Fox News: Colarossi, Natalie. "COVID Lockdowns May Have No Clear Benefit vs Other Voluntary Measures, International Study Shows." *Newsweek*, January 14, 2021. www.newsweek.com/covid-lockdowns-have-no-clear-benefit-vs-other-voluntary-measures-international-study-shows-1561656
Best, Paul. "Mandatory Lockdowns May Not Be Any Better at Controlling COVID-19 Than Less Restrictive Measures, Study Finds." *Fox News,* January 15, 2021. www.foxnews.com/health/coronavirus-lockdowns-may-have-no-clear-benefit-vs-voluntary-measures-interna-tional-study-says

11. "The Frontline Doctor Who Went Viral." *The Highwire,* July 29, 2020. thehighwire.com/videos/the-frontline-doctor-who-went-viral

12. Johnson, Timothy. "YouTube Terminates Anti-Vaccine Figure Del Bigtree's Account After He Pushed Dangerous Coronavirus and Vaccine Misinformation." *Media Matters*, July 30, 2020. www.mediamatters.org/coronavirus-covid-19/youtube-terminates-anti-vac-cine-figure-del-bigtrees-account-after-he-pushed

13. Informed Consent Action Network. "ICAN Files Opposition To Facebook and You-Tube's Motion To Dismiss Its Censorship Lawsuit." June 26, 2021. www.icandecide.org/ican_press/ican-files-opposition-to-facebook-and-youtubes-motion-to-dismiss-its-censorship-lawsuit

14. See Informed Consent Action Network, above.

15. Greenwald, Glenn. "Court Rejects Google's Attempt to Dismiss Rumble's Antitrust Lawsuit, Ensuring Vast Discovery." July 30, 2022. greenwald.substack.com/p/court-rejects-googles-attempt-to

16. Iversen, Kim. "Biden and Fauci Sued For Coercing Big Tech To Censor Dissent." *Rising,* July 14, 2022. www.youtube.com/watch?v=M9jkITpnDp4

17. Ozimek, Tom. "Court Rules Against Social Media Companies in Free Speech Censorship Fight." *Epoch Times,* September 17, 2022. www.theepochtimes.com/court-rules-against-social-media-companies-in-free-speech-censorship-fight_4737140.html

18. Informed Consent Action Network. Facebook post, November 23, 2020. www.facebook.com/ICANdecide/posts/1928482153958446

19. Atlantic Council's Digital Forensic Research Lab Partners With Facebook To Combat Disinformation in Democratic Elections. *Atlantic Council,* May 17, 2018. www.atlantic-council.org/news/press-releases/atlantic-councils-digital-forensic-research-lab-partners-with-facebook

20. Bokhari, Allum. "Report: Google Financially Blacklists ZeroHedge, Threatens the Federalist Over Comment Sections." *Breitbart,* June 16, 2020. www.breitbart.com/tech/2020/06/16/google-financially-blacklists-the-federalist-and-zerohedge-at-the-behest-of-nbc-leftist-nonprofit

21. "With Biden in Office, Twitter Shuts Down Antifa Accounts That Have 71K Followers." *Law Officer News,* January 22, 2021. www.lawofficer.com/with-biden-in-office-twitter-shuts-down-antifa-accounts-that-have-71k-followers

22. Cathell, Mia. "Here Are the Antifa Groups Facebook Has Banned and the Ones That Are Still Active." *Post Millennial,* August 20, 2020. thepostmillennial.com/here-are-the-antifa-groups-facebook-has-banned-and-here-are-the-ones-it-hasnt

23. "Facebook Escalates Attack on Socialist Left." *World Socialist Website,* January 25, 2021. www.wsws.org/en/articles/2021/01/25/pers-j25.html

24. Krystal Ball and Rachel Bovard. "Kyle Kulinski: Previewing the Hellish Future of MSNBC in the Biden Era." *Rising,* August 4, 2020. www.youtube.com/watch?v=SC8bXEm xI5k&list=TLPQMTIwODIwMjAB9s7g52eFaA&index=3

25. Maté, Aaron. "Lee Camp on Bernie Sanders Smears," *The Grayzone,* March 8, 2020. www.youtube.com/watch?v=JiSaEc58uUc

26. "Aaron Ginn." *CensorTrack,* March 20, 2020. censortrack.org/case/aaron-ginn

27. Ginn tweeted on July 18, 2021: "Google is reading what you host in Google Docs. They deleted and removed access to my personal copy of *Evidence over Hysteria: COVID-19.* Free is never free." www.twitter.com/aginnt/status/1416860936946823185

28. Schemmel, Alec. "SILENCED! Twitter Suspends Project Veritas Founder James O'Keefe Permanently." *Media Research Center,* April 15, 2021. www.newsbusters.org/blogs/free-speech/alec-schemmel/2021/04/15/silenced-twitter-suspends-project-veritas-founder-james

29. Berenson, Alex. "Goodbye Twitter. I Am Officially Suspended." Substack Personal blog. August 28, 2021. alexberenson.substack.com/p/goodbye-twitter

30. Pariseau, Gabriela. "Twitter 'Permanently Suspended' Alex Berenson for Alleged Misinformation." *Media Research Center*, August 30th, 2021. www.newsbusters.org/blogs/free-speech/gabriela-pariseau/2021/08/30/censored-twitter-permanently-suspended-alex-berenson

31. This unanimous decision also prevented state governments from banning anyone—even sex offenders—from social media platforms, calling Facebook and Twitter Americans' "principal sources for knowing current events, checking ads for employment, speaking and listening in the modern public square, and otherwise exploring the vast realms of human thought and knowledge." Packingham v. North Carolina, 137 S. Ct. 1730, 1737 (2017).

32. See Informed Consent Action Network, above.

33. Gramlich, John. "10 Facts About Americans and Facebook." *Pew Research Center*, June 1, 2021. www.pewresearch.org/fact-tank /2021/06/01/facts-about-americans-and-facebook

34. "Section 230: The Most Important Law Protecting Internet Speech." *Electronic Frontier Foundation*. www.eff.org/issues/cda230

35. Owens Jeremy C. "Why Governments Are Giving Billions in Tax Breaks To Apple, Amazon and Other Tech Giants." *MarketWatch*, October 14, 2016. www.marketwatch.com/story/why-governments-are-giving-billions-in-tax-breaks-to-apple-amazon-and-other-tech-giants-2016-10-13

36. Pichai, Sundar. "Coronavirus: How we're helping." Company Blog Announcement. March 6, 2020. blog.google/inside-google/company-announcements/coronavirus-covid19-response

37. "Schiff Urges Google, YouTube, Twitter to Inform Users Who Interact With Coronavirus Misinformation." *Congressional Press Release*, April 30, 2020. schiff.house.gov/news/press-releases/schiff-urges-google-youtube-twitter-to-inform-users_who-interact-with-coronavirus-misinformation

38. DeCosta-Klipa, Nik. "Mark Zuckerberg Tells Ed Markey How Facebook Will Respond to Posts by Donald Trump That Undermine the Election." *Boston Globe*, October 28, 2020. www.boston.com/news/politics/2020/10/28/mark-zuckerberg-ed-markey-facebook-respond-donald-trump-election-posts

39. Flegenheimer, Matt, Rebecca R. Ruiz, Nellie Bowles. "Bernie Sanders and His Online Army." *New York Times*, February 22, 2020. www.nytimes.com/2020/01/27/us/politics/bernie-sanders-internet-supporters-2020.html

40. Stanage, Niall. "The Memo: No, Really—What if Alexandria Ocasio-Cortez Runs for President?" *The Hill*, July 29, 2022. thehill.com/homenews/house/3578887-the-memo-no-really-what-if-alexandria-ocasio-cortez-runs-for-president

41. Ball, Molly. "On the Campaign Trail With Marjorie Taylor Greene." *Time*, June 14, 2022. time.com/6186463/marjorie-taylor-greene-interview-georgia

42. Jilani, Zaid. "'Bernie Bro' Aggression Is Actually Political Engagement." *Forward*, February 27, 2020. forward.com/opinion/440613/senator-sanders-reframe-the-bernie-bro-narrative-as-the-lifeblood-of

43. Polumbo, Brad. "Criminalizing Free Speech Online? Elizabeth Warren Has a Plan for That." *Washington Examiner*, January 29, 2020. www.washingtonexaminer.com/opinion/elizabeth-warren-unveils-dystopian-fighting-disinformation-plan-criminalizing-free-speech-online

44. Hasson, Peter J. *The Manipulators: Facebook, Google, Twitter, and Big Tech's War on Conservatives.* Regnery Publishing. Washington, D.C. 2020.

45. Zuboff, Shoshana. *The Age of Surveillance Capitalism: The Fight for a Human Future at the New Frontier of Power.* Public Affairs. New York, New York. 2019.

46. Berreby, David. "Click To Agree With What? No One Reads Terms Of Service, Studies Confirm." *The Guardian*, March 3, 2017. www.theguardian.com/technology/2017/mar/03/terms-of-service-online-contracts-fine-print

47. Morrison, Sara. "How the Capitol Riot Revived Calls To Reform Section 230." *Vox*, January 11, 2021. www.vox.com/recode/22221135/capitol-riot-section-230-twitter-hawley-democrats

Chapter 10: Checking Facts at the Door

1. We will get into Haddad's case in great detail in Chapter 12. Macleod, Alan. "Newsweek Journo Quits After Editors Kill Report on Syria Chemical Attack Scandal." *MintPress News,* December 9 2019. www.mintpressnews.com/newsweek-tareq-haddad-quits-syria-douma-opcw/263292

2. Fisk, Robert. "The Search for Truth in the Rubble of Douma – And One Doctor's Doubts Over the Chemical Attack." *The Independent*, April 17, 2018. www.independent.co.uk/voices/syria-chemical-attack-gas-douma-robert-fisk-ghouta-damascus-a8307726.html

3. Dore, Jimmy. "CNN Reporter Sniffs 'Poison' on Air." *Jimmy Dore Show*, April 26, 2018. www.youtube.com/watch?v=Mydfue-vF90

4. El Sirgany, Sarah and Hilary Clarke. "Gassed Where They Had Hidden, Syrian Families Killed In Minutes." *CNN*, April 9, 2018. www.cnn.com/2018/04/09/middleeast/syria-douma-victims-intl

5. Browne, Malachy, Christophe Koettl, et.al. "One Building, One Bomb: How Assad Gassed His Own People." *New York Times*, June 25, 2018. www.nytimes.com/interactive/2018/06/25/world/middleeast/syria-chemical-attack-douma.html

6. See Dore, above.

7. MSNBC has taken down the episode, but it's preserved online, including in a worthwhile *Jimmy Dore Show* episode: Dore, Jimmy. "Professor Stuns MSNBC Panel on Syria." *Jimmy Dore Show*, April 18, 2018. www.youtu.be/O2TRzA2ezk

8. "Ex-OPCW Chief Jose Bustani Reads Syria Testimony That US, UK Blocked at UN." *The Grayzone*, October 5, 2020. www.youtube.com/watch?v=ZgIDlgD_txM

9. Niemuth, Niles. "New WikiLeaks Documents Expose Phony Claims of 2018 Syria Chemical Weapons Attack." *World Socialist Website,* December 16, 2019. www.wsws.org/en/articles/2019/12/16/chem-d16.html

10. "OPCW Douma Docs." *WikiLeaks*, 2019. wikileaks.org/opcw-douma

11. "BBC Admits Syria Chemical Attack Documentary Had 'Serious Flaws.'" *The Cradle*, September 6, 2021. thecradle.co/Article/news/1666

12. "Flanagan. Padraic. BBC Admits Syria Gas Attack Report Had Serious Flaws in 'Victory for Truth' After Complaint by Peter Hitchens." *Daily Mail*, September 4, 2021. www.dailymail.co.uk/news/article-9958679/BBC-admits-Syria-gas-attack-report-flaws-complaint-Peter-Hitchens.html

13. Cobban, Helena. "Did Assad Really Use Chemical Weapons in Douma?" *Lobe Log*, June 11, 2019. lobelog.com/did-assad-really-use-chemical-weapons-in-douma

14. Dore, Jimmy. "BBC Host Tries Censoring Truth on Syria." *Jimmy Dore Show*, April 26, 2018. www.youtube.com/watch?v=2pwXfHyTlCo

15. Maté, Aaron. "New Leaks Shatter OPCW's Attacks on Douma Whistleblowers." *The Grayzone*, February 11, 2020. thegrayzone.com/2020/02/11/new-leaks-shatter-opcws-attacks-douma-whistleblowers

16. Dore, Jimmy. "Syrian Gas Attack Was Staged, Leaked Documents Reveal." *Jimmy Dore Show,* May 22, 2019. www.youtube.com/watch?v=FLRQSfSKoJo

17. Greenberg, Jon. "False: Red Crescent Says No Evidence of Chemical Attack in Syria's Douma." *Politifact*, April 13, 2018. www.politifact.com/factchecks/2018/apr/13/antiwarcom/syrian-red-crescent-did-not-deny-chemical-attack-d

18. Gillin, Joshua. "Conspiracy Claims That Syrian Gas Attack Was 'False Flag' Are Unproven." *Politifact*, April 7, 2017. www.politifact.com/article/2017/apr/07/unproven-online-theories-doubting-syrian-gas-attac

19. Lucas Nolan. "John Stossel Sues Facebook Alleging Defamation Over 'Fact-Check' Label." *Breitbart*, September 24, 2021. www.breitbart.com/tech/2021/09/24/john-stossel-sues-facebook-alleging-defamation-over-fact-check-label

20. "Facebook Admits the Truth: 'Fact Checks' Are Really Just (Lefty) Opinion." *New York Post*, December 14, 2021. nypost.com/2021/12/14/facebook-admits-the-truth-fact-checks-are-really-just-lefty-opinion

21. The Poynter Institute PolitiFact. "Who Pays for PolitiFact?" January, 2022. www.politifact.com/who-pays-for-politifact

22. The Poynter Institute. "Poynter's Top Funding Sources." April 2022. www.poynter.org/major-funders/#1632843888743-52666069-9ec9

23. Factcheck.org. "Our Funding." www.factcheck.org/our-funding

24. Goodman, Alana. "Facebook 'Fact Checker' Who Will Arbitrate on 'Fake News' Is Accused of Defrauding Website To Pay for Prostitutes." *Daily Mail*, December 21, 2016. www.dailymail.co.uk/news/article-4042194

25. Patrick, Jim. "'Fact-Checking' Snopes Co-Founder David Mikkelson Accused of 'Daily Sex Assaults' by Second Wife." *Law Enforcement Daily*, September 30, 2021. www.lawenforcementtoday.com/fact-checking-snopes-co-founder-david-mikkelson-accused-of-daily-sex-assaults-by-second-wife

26. Streitfeld, David. "For Fact-Checking Website Snopes, a Bigger Role Brings More Attacks." *New York Times*, December 25, 2016. www.nytimes.com/2016/12/25/technology/for-fact-checking-website-snopes-a-bigger-role-brings-more-attacks.html

27. Jones, Dean Sterling. "The Co-Founder of Snopes Wrote Dozens of Plagiarized Articles." *Buzzfeed News*, August 27, 2021. www.buzzfeednews.com/article/deansterlingjones/snopes-cofounder-plagiarism-mikkelson

28. Groundbreaking blogger Vani Hari found that Snopes came after her for writing negatively about Monsanto's RoundUp: Hari, Vani. "Do You Trust Snopes? You Won't After Reading This." foodbabe.com/do-you-trust-snopes-you-wont-after-reading-how-they-work-with-monsanto-operatives

29. Science Feedback. Partners, Funders & Donors. www.sciencefeedback.co/partners-funders-donors

30. Such as: "Viral New York Post Article Perpetuates the Unfounded Claim that the Virus that Causes Covid-19 is Manmade." www.sciencefeedback.co/evaluation/viral-new-york-post-article-perpetuates-the-unfounded-claim-that-the-covid-19-virus-is-manmade

31. Warren, Michael and Ron Harris. "Hank Aaron, Civil Rights Leaders Get Vaccinated in Georgia." *Associated Press*, January 5, 2021. apnews.com/article/georgia-andrew-young-hank-aaron-coronavirus-pandemic-atlanta-2f32ea8b2067d85202b2d22665fde739

32. Department of Justice Press Release. "Justice Department Announces Largest Health Care Fraud Settlement in Its History." September 2, 2009. www.justice.gov/opa/pr/justice-department-announces-largest-health-care-fraud-settlement-its-history

33. Facher, Lee. "The White House Is Set To Unveil a Wide-Reaching, Billion-Dollar Campaign Aimed At Convincing Every American To Get Vaccinated." *STAT*, March 15, 2021. www.statnews.com/2021/03/15/white-house-unveil-a-wide-reaching-billion-dollar-campaign-convincing-every-american-to-get-vaccinated

34. Tyson, Alec, Courtney Johnson & Cary Funk. "U.S. Public Now Divided Over Whether To Get COVID-19 Vaccine." *Pew Research*, September 17, 2020. www.pewresearch.org/science/2020/09/17/u-s-public-now-divided-over-whether-to-get-covid-19-vaccine

35. Gore, D'Angelo. "Hank Aaron's Death Attributed to Natural Causes." *Factcheck.org*, January 28, 2021. www.factcheck.org/2021/01/scicheck-hank-aarons-death-attributed-to-natural-causes

36. Kennedy Jr., Robert. "National Media Pushes Vaccine Misinformation—Coroner's Office Never Saw Hank Aaron's Body." *Defender, Children's Health Defense*, February 12, 2021. childrenshealthdefense.org/defender/national-media-vaccine-misinformation-hank-aaron

37. No phase of the clinical trials provided data on safety or efficacy for people over 80, and Aaron was 86. The analysis of the largest data set, the Phase 3 trials, included data on adults over 65 and indicated that as adults aged, efficacy and safety declined. "Safety and Immunogenicity of SARS-CoV-2 mRNA-1273 Vaccine in Older Adults." *New England Journal of Medicine*, December 17, 2020. www.nejm.org/doi/full/10.1056/NEJMoa2028436

38. There were 1,400 reported deaths in the Vaccine Adverse Events Reporting System (VAERS) at the time, a number that surpassed 30,000 in 2022. It is the only publicly available data on vaccine deaths in the US. Some believe these numbers undercount vaccine deaths; others believe they overcount deaths. openvaers.com/covid-data

39. www.factcheck.org/author/dangelo-gore/

40. "Here are 410 Movies Made Under the Direct Influence and Supervision of the Pentagon." *The Free Thought Project*, August 7, 2018. www.thefreethoughtproject.com/here-are-410-movies-made-under-the-direct-influence-and-supervision-of-the-pentagon

41. "Gates Foundation, Viacom Partner To Insert Educational Messages Into Television Programming." *Philanthropy News Digest*, April 3, 2009. www.philanthropynewsdigest.org/news/gates-foundation-viacom-partner-to-insert-educational-messages-into-television-programming

42. Dice, Mark. "One of Hollywood's Biggest Secrets Finally Revealed." *YouTube*, February 17, 2022. www.rumble.com/vtlopa-entertainment-liaison-offices-in-depth-report.html

43. Dice, Mark. "The Sun Valley Conference: Where Mainstream Media, Social Media, and CIA Meet To Coordinate Agendas." *YouTube*, April 15, 2016. www.youtube.com/watch?v=XL4WkMhDemQ

44. Browne, Malachy, Christoph Koettl, Anjali Singhvi, et al. "One Building, One Bomb: How Assad Gassed His Own People." *New York Times*, June 24, 2018. www.nytimes.com/interactive/2018/06/25/world/middleeast/syria-chemical-attack-douma.html

45. Maté, Aaron. "Bellingcaught: Who Is the Mysterious Author of Bellingcat's Attacks on OPCW Whistleblower?" *Grayzone*, March 24, 2021. thegrayzone.com/2021/03/24/author-bellingcat-opcw-whistleblower

46. MacLeod, Alan. "How Bellingcat Launders National Security State Talking Points Into the Press." *MintPress News*, April 9, 2021. www.mintpressnews.com/bellingcat-intelligence-agencies-launders-talking-points-media/276603

47. "comScore Ranks the Top 50 U.S. Digital Media Properties for January 2015." February 24, 2015. web.archive.org/web/20150317071240/http://www.comscore.com/Insights/Market-Rankings/comScore-Ranks-the-Top-50-US-Digital-Media-Properties-for-January-2015

48. "Wikipedia Co-Founder: I No Longer Trust the Website I Created." *Unherd*, July 14, 2021. www.youtu.be/l0P4Cf0UCwU

49. Stieber, Zachary. "NIH: Check Out Wikipedia To See Why Great Barrington Declaration Is 'Dangerous.'" *Epoch Times,* December 24, 2021. www.theepochtimes.com/nih-check-out-wikipedia-to-see-why-great-barrington-declaration-is-dangerous_4176405.html

50. "MeWe." en.wikipedia.org/wiki/MeWe Quoted on June 1, 2022.

51. Flomenbaum, Adam. "Why the Young Turks Launched a Facebook-Native Show." *Ad Week*, February 24, 2015. www.adweek.com/lostremote/why-the-young-turks-launched-a-facebook-native-show/50404

52. Sprangler, Todd. "Jeffrey Katzenberg's WndrCo Invests in TYT Network As Part of $20 Million Round." *Variety*, August 8, 2016. variety.com/2017/digital/news/young-turks-jeffrey-katzenberg-wndrco-funding-1202518938

53. "The Drone Papers." theintercept.com/drone-papers

54. Gallagher, Ryan. "Profiled - From Radio To Porn, British Spies Track Web Users' Online Identities." *The Intercept*, September 25, 2015. theintercept.com/2015/09/25/gchq-radio-porn-spies-track-web-users-online-identities

55. Glenn, Greenwald. "The 'Bernie Bros' Narrative: a Cheap Campaign Tactic Masquerading As Journalism and Social Activism." *The Intercept*, January 31, 2016. theintercept.com/2016/01/31/the-bernie-bros-narrative-a-cheap-false-campaign-tactic-masquerading-as-journalism-and-social-activism

56. Gallagher, Ryan. "U.S. Military Bans The Intercept." *The Intercept*, August 20, 2014. theintercept.com/2014/08/20/u-s-military-bans-the-intercept

57. Harkin, James. "Douma Chemical Attacks and the Fog of Syria's Propaganda War." *The Intercept,* February 9 2019. www.theintercept.com/2019/02/09/douma-chemical-attack-evidence-syria

58. Nelson, Steven. "Glenn Greenwald Quits The Intercept Over 'Censorship' of Hunter Biden Article." *New York Post*, October 29, 2020. nypost.com/2020/10/29/glenn-greenwald-quits-the-intercept-over-hunter-biden-article

59. Rukeyser, Muriel. "The Speed of Darkness." 2006. www.poetryfoundation.org/search?query=The+Speed+of+Darkness

60. I don't love the word "elite," as it implies a superiority in talent or skill, such as an elite musician, programmer, or scientist . Reactionaries are often inferior when judged purely on talents and skills.

61. NPR puts a positive spin on this closed-doors convention of media, government, and intelligence brass: Gura, David. "Moguls, Deals And Patagonia Vests: A Look Inside 'Summer Camp For Billionaires.'" *NPR Morning Edition*, July 5, 2021. www.npr.org/2021/07/05/1012587989/moguls-deals-and-patagonia-vests-a-look-inside-summer-camp-for-billionaires

Chapter 11: The Century of Propaganda

1. McChesney, R. W. (2003). The Problem Of Journalism: A Political Economic Contribution To An Explanation Of The Crisis In Contemporary Us Journalism. *Journalism Studies*, 4(3), 319. www.tandfonline.com/doi/abs/10.1080/14616700306492

2. See McChesney, above.

3. Tarbell, Ida. "The History of the Standard Oil Company." *McClure's*, November 1903. www.google.com/books/edition/McClure_s_Magazine/THvhO1HipFEC?hl=en&gbpv=1

4. See McChesney, above.

5. Perloff, James. "Spanish-American War: Trial Run for Interventionism." *The New American,* August 10, 2012. www.thenewamerican.com/trial-run-for-interventionism

6. Kashatus, William. "This Was a Real 'Fake News' Story – And It Landed Us in a War." *History News Network,* February 26, 2018. www.historynewsnetwork.org/article/168374

7. Bernays, Edward. *Propaganda*. Horace Liveright, Inc. New York, NY. 1928.

8. Federal Communications Commission v. Pottsville Broadcasting Co. U.S. Supreme Court, Legal Information Institute, 1940. www.law.cornell.edu/supremecourt/text/309/134

9. "The Kazakh Famine of 1930-33 and the Politics of History in the Post-Soviet Space." *Woodrow Wilson Center*, March 26, 2012. www.wilsoncenter.org/event/the-kazakh-famine-1930-33-and-the-politics-history-the-post-soviet-space

10. Perović, Jeronim. "Highland Rebels: The North Caucasus During the Stalinist Collectivization Campaign." *Journal of Contemporary History,* April 2016. pp. 234-260. www.jstor.org/stable/24671839

11. Holocaust and Genocide Studies. "Holodomor: The Ukrainian Genocide." *University of Minnesota.* cla.umn.edu/chgs/holocaust-genocide-education/resource-guides/holodomor

12. "New York Times Statement About 1932 Pulitzer Prize Awarded to Walter Duranty." *New York Times.* www.nytco.com/company/prizes-awards/new-york-times-statement-about-1932-pulitzer-prize-awarded-to-walter-duranty

13. See *New York Times* statement, above.

14. Schou, Nick. *Kill the Messenger: How the CIA's Crack-Cocaine Controversy Destroyed Journalist Gary Webb.* PublicAffairs. New York, New York. 2006.

15. Louise, Nickie. "These 6 Corporations Control 90% of the Media Outlets in America." *Tech Startups*, September 18, 2020. techstartups.com/2020/09/18/6-corporations-control-90-media-america-illusion-choice-objectivity-2020

16. When Viacom and CBS merged in 2019 (for a second time) and became what is now known as Paramount, we were left with just five megacorporations controlling the conduits of the media: Disney-ABC; Comcast-NBC; Paramount-CBS; NewsCorp-Fox; and Warner-CNN.

17. Adams, Dominic. "Closing the Valve On History: Flint Cuts Water Flow From Detroit After Nearly 50 Years." *Michigan Live*, April 25, 2014, www.mlive.com/news/flint/2014/04/closing_the_valve_on_history_f.html

18. Goheen, Wesley and Gino Vicci. "How Safe Is Your Tap Water?" *WNEM Channel 5*, May 16, 2014. www.wnem.com/news/how-safe-is-your-tap-water/article_61de20f7-3007-5c40-b2b4-89cc49a64f3b.html

19. Fonger, Ron. "State Says Flint River Water Meets All Standards but More Than Twice the Hardness of Lake Water." *Flint Journal*, May. 23, 2014. www.mlive.com/news/flint/2014/05/state_says_flint_river_water_m.html

20. In fact recognized by the UN as a human right on July 28, 2010.

21. Young, Molly. "Flint Officials Confirm 'Massive' Water Theft Investigation, Crackdown." *Michigan Live*, September 17, 2014. www.mlive.com/news/flint/2014/09/flint_officials_confirm_massiv.html

22. Ruble, Kayla and Jacob Carah. "Flint Water Crisis Deaths Likely Surpass Official Toll." *Frontline, PBS*. July 24, 2018. www.pbs.org/wgbh/frontline/article/flint-water-crisis-deaths-likely-surpass-official-toll

23. Chariton, Jordan and Jenn Dize. "Michigan's Ex-Gov. Rick Snyder Knew About Flint's Toxic Water—and Lied About It." *VICE*, April 16, 2020. www.vice.com/en/article/z3bdp9/michigans-ex-gov-rick-snyder-knew-about-flints-toxic-waterand-lied-about-it

24. Egan, Paul, and Todd Spangler. "President Obama Declares Emergency in Flint." *Detroit Free Press*, January 16, 2016. www.freep.com/story/news/local/michigan/2016/01/16/president-obama-declares-emergency-flint/78898604

25. Salamacha, Becca. "Supreme Court declines to hear Flint, Michigan, officials' appeal over water crisis." *Jurist*, January 22, 2020. www.jurist.org/news/2020/01/supreme-court-declines-to-hear-flint-michigan-officials-appeal-over-water-crisis

26. See Salamacha, above.

27. Romo, Vanessa. "Supreme Court Allows Flint Water Lawsuits To Move Forward, Officials Not 'Immune.'" *NPR*, January 21, 2020. www.npr.org/2020/01/21/798331185/supreme-court-allows-flint-water-lawsuits-to-move-forward-officials-not-immune

28. See Salamacha, above.

29. Chariton, Jordan. "Flint Water Cover-Up: More Details From Our Stunning Story." *Status Coup*, July 22, 2021. www.youtube.com/ridg4N2Ag6o

30. Chariton, Jordan and Charlie LeDuff. "Revealed: The Flint Water Poisoning Charges That Never Came To Light." *The Guardian*, January 17, 2022. www.theguardian.com/us-news/2022/jan/17/flint-water-poisoning-charges

31. In 2021, a federal judge finally awarded $626 million in settlements of claims. Egan, Paul. "Federal Judge Gives Final Approval to $626.25M Settlement in Flint Water Crisis." *Detroit Free Press*, November 10, 2021. www.freep.com/story/news/local/michigan/flint-water-crisis/2021/11/10/federal-judge-approves-settlement-flint-lead-poisoning-case/5556131001

32. Hoy, Toni. "The Amygdala: Function & Psychology of Fight or Flight." *BetterHelp*, April 14, 2022. www.betterhelp.com/advice/psychologists/the-amygdala-function-psychology-of-fight-or-flight

Chapter 12: Your Views Are No Longer Needed

1. "Jimmy vs. Anand Giridharadas!" *Jimmy Dore Show*, May 14, 2020. www.podgist.com/the-jimmy-dore-show/jimmy-vs-anand-giridharadas/index.html

2. Dore, Jimmy. "Ed Schultz Death: What MSNBC Won't Tell You." *Jimmy Dore Show*, July 7, 2018, www.youtube.com/watch?v=syVTtJge__8

3. Kilpatrick, Connor. "Krystal Ball is the Anti-Rachel Maddow Bernie Fans Have Been Waiting For." *Jacobin*, December 19, 2019. www.jacobinmag.com/2019/12/krystal-ball-rising-the-hill-msnbc

4. See Kilpatrick, above.

5. See Kilpatrick, above.

6. Schou, Nick. *Kill the Messenger: How the CIA's Crack-Cocaine Controversy Destroyed Journalist Gary Webb*. Nation Books. New York, New York. 2006. pp8-9.

7. Schou, Nick. "Ex-L.A. Times Writer Apologizes For "Tawdry" Attacks." *LA Weekly*, May 30, 2013. www.laweekly.com/ex-l-a-times-writer-apologizes-for-tawdry-attacks

8. "The New York Times Wants Gary Webb To Stay Dead." *The Nation*, October 10, 2014. www.thenation.com/article/archive/new-york-times-wants-gary-webb-stay-dead

9. "WPost's Slimy Assault on Gary Webb." *Consortium News*, October 18, 2014. consortiumnews.com/2014/10/18/wposts-slimy-assault-on-gary-webb

10. Borjesson, Kristina. *Into The Buzzsaw: Leading Journalists Expose The Myth Of A Free Press*. Prometheus. New York, New York. 2004.

11. Colen, Aaron. "Frustrated ABC News Anchor Caught on Hot Mic Saying Network Suppressed Epstein Story for Years." *Blaze*, November 5, 2019. www.theblaze.com/news/frustrated-abc-news-anchor-caught-on-hot-mic-saying-network-suppressed-epstein-story-for-years

12. Folkenflik, David. "A Dead Cat, a Lawyer's Call, and a Five-Figure Donation: How Media Fell Short on Epstein." *All Things Considered*, August 22, 2019. www.npr.org/2019/08/22/753390385/a-dead-cat-a-lawyers-call-and-a-5-figure-donation-how-media-fell-short-on-epstei

13. Banfield, Ashleigh. "Landon Lecture Series on Public Affairs." *Kansas State University*, April 24, 2003. www.k-state.edu/landon/speakers/ashleigh-banfield/video.html

14. Banfield, Ashleigh. "Landon Lecture at Kansas State University Transcript." *American Rhetoric*, April 24, 2003. www.americanrhetoric.com/speeches/ashleighbanfieldlandonksu.htm

Red, White & Blind

A

15. Dumas, Timothy. "Truth and Consequences: Meet Ashleigh Banfield. She Spoke Out About TV War Coverage and Paid a High Price. Would She Do It Again?" *New Canaan-Darien Magazine*, February 2009. web.archive.org/web/20150217090152/http://www.newcanaandarienmag.com/n/January-2009/Truth-and-Consequences/index.php?cparticle=1&siarticle=0#artanc

16. Ariens, Chris. "I Will Never Forgive Him for His Cruelty and the Manner in Which He Decided to Dispose of Me." *Adweek*, February 11, 2009. www.adweek.com/tvnewser/i-will-never-forgive-him-for-his-cruelty-and-the-manner-in-which-he-decided-to-dispose-of-me/23865/

17. Dorman, Sam. "Newsweek Reporter Quits, Claiming Outlet 'Suppressed' Story on Global Chemical Weapons Watchdog." *Fox News*, December 7, 2019. www.foxnews.com/media/newsweek-reporter-tareq-haddad-quits

18. MacLeod, Alan. "Inside Journalist Tareq Haddad's Spectacular Departure from *Newsweek*." *MintPress News*, December 20t 2019. www.mintpressnews.com/newsweek-journalist-tareq-haddad-quits-corruption-journalism/263667

19. Haddad, Tareq. "Lies, *Newsweek* and Control of the Media Narrative." December 14, 2019. www.tareqhaddad.com/investigation-lies-newsweek-and-control-of-the-media-narrative-first-hand-account

20. "Jesse Ventura's Talk Not Cheap for MSNBC." *Globe & Mail*, February 10, 2003. www.theglobeandmail.com/arts/jesse-venturas-talk-not-cheap-for-msnbc/article18284415

21. Collins, Scott. "Jesse Ventura Searches for Coverups." *Los Angeles Times*, November 29, 2009. www.latimes.com/archives/la-xpm-2009-nov-29-la-ca-conversation29-2009nov29-story.html

22. Uygur, Cenk. "Jesse Ventura: MSNBC Tried To Shut Me Up." *Huffington Post*, May 9, 2010. www.huffpost.com/entry/jesse-ventura-msnbc-tried_b_492237

23. Roper, Eric. "Jesse Ventura Says MSNBC Nixed His Show for Not Supporting Iraq War." *Minneapolis Star-Tribune*, November 30, 2009. www.startribune.com/ventura-says-msnbc-nixed-his-show-for-not-supporting-iraq-war/78150302

24. Van Oot, Torey. "Jesse Ventura Turns to Substack." *Axios*, June 1, 2022. www.axios.com/local/twin-cities/2022/06/01/jesse-ventura-substack-newsletter

25. Smith, Jamil. "Melissa Harris-Perry's Email to Her #nerdland Staff." *Medium*, Feb 26, 2016. medium.com/@JamilSmith/melissa-harris-perry-s-email-to-her-nerdland-staff-11292bdc27cb#.a53n1i5n7

26. Byers, Dylan. "MSNBC's Melissa Harris-Perry Walks Off Show in Protest." *CNN*, February 27, 2016. money.cnn.com/2016/02/26/media/melissa-harris-perry-msnbc/index.html

27. Weigel, David. "Melissa Harris-Perry and Rand Paul Agree on One Thing: Hillary Clinton's 'Appalling Choice.'" *Slate*, February 11, 2014. slate.com/news-and-politics/2014/02/melissa-harris-perry-and-rand-paul-agree-on-one-thing-hillary-clinton-s-appalling-choice.html

28. See Smith, above.

29. Folkenflik, David. "MSNBC Fires Host Melissa Harris-Perry Over Controversial Memo." *NPR*, March 9, 2016. www.npr.org/2016/03/09/469837015/msnbc-fires-host-melissa-harris-perry-over-controversial-memo

30. "Cenk Uygur, MSNBC Differ on Why He Left." *Politico*, July 21, 2011. www.politico.com/blogs/onmedia/0711/Cenk_Uygur_MSNBC_differ_on_why_he_left.html

31. Corcoran, Michael. "Uygur Out at MSNBC: Another Progressive Show Canceled for Political Reasons." *FAIR*, November 1, 2011. fair.org/extra/uygur-out-at-msnbc

32. Mirkinson, Jack. "Cenk Uygur on Leaving MSNBC: Network Told Me To 'Tone It Down,' Didn't Want To 'Challenge Power'" *HuffPost*, July 21, 2011. www.huffpost.com/entry/cenk-uygur-msnbc-leaving_n_905415

33. "Rejecting Lucrative Offer, Cenk Uygur Leaves MSNBC After Being Told To 'Act Like an Insider.'" *Democracy Now*, July 22, 2011. www.democracynow.org/2011/7/22/rejecting_lucrative_offer_cenk_uygur_leaves

34. "Why Cenk Uygur Left MSNBC - Part 1." *The Young Turks*, July 20, 2011. youtu.be/HrKKkGl3TnY

35. Clark, Chrissy. "ABC's David Wright Admits Network Doesn't Care About News." *The Federalist*, February 26, 2020. thefederalist.com/2020/02/26/watch-abcs-david-wright-admits-network-doesnt-care-about-news

36. See Clark, above.

37. See Clark, above.

38. See Clark, above.

39. Farhi, Paul. "ABC News Suspends Correspondent David Wright After Comments About Trump Coverage, Socialism, in Project Veritas Sting." *Washington Post*, February 26, 2020. www.washingtonpost.com/lifestyle/media/abc-news-suspends-correspondent-david-wright-after-project-veritas-sting/2020/02/26/764efc06-5849-11ea-9b35-def5a027d470_story.html

40. Miller, Hayley. "Journalists Slam ABC News for Suspending David Wright After Project Veritas Sting." *Huffington Post*, February 26, 2020. www.huffpost.com/entry/abc-news-suspends-david-wright-project-veritas_n_5e569234c5b62e9dc7db547d

41. See Clark, above.

42. "Leaked U.S. Video Shows Deaths of Reuters' Iraqi Staffers." *Reuters*, April 5, 2010. www.reuters.com/article/us-iraq-usa-journalists-idUSTRE6344FW20100406

43. Weir, Alison. "Remembering the Crimes of the Powerful Exposed by WikiLeaks' Julian Assange." *MintPress News*, April 22, 2019. www.mintpressnews.com/remember-the-crimes-of-exposed-by-julian-assange/257652

44. Lagan, Bernard. "International Man of Mystery." *Sydney Morning Herald*, April 10, 2010. www.smh.com.au/technology/international-man-of-mystery-20100409-ryvf.html

45. "The Iraq Archive: The Strands of a War." *New York Times*, October 23, 2010. www.nytimes.com/2010/10/23/world/middleeast/23intro.html

46. Friedman, Megan. "Julian Assange: Readers' Choice for TIME's Person of the Year 2010." *Time*, December 13, 2010. newsfeed.time.com/2010/12/13/julian-assange-readers-choice-for-times-person-of-the-year-2010

47. Keating, Joshua. "How WikiLeaks Blew It." *Foreign Policy*, August 16, 2012. foreign-policy.com/2012/08/16/how-wikileaks-blew-it

48. Gura, David. "WikiLeaks Founder May Have Blood on His Hands, Joint Chiefs Chairman Says." *NPR*, July 30, 2010. www.npr.org/sections/thetwo-way/2010/07/30/128868663/wikileaks-founder-may-have-blood-on-his-hands-joint-chiefs-chairman-says

49. "WikiLeaks: Document Dumps That Shook the World." *BBC News*, April 12 , 2019. www.bbc.com/news/technology-47907890

50. Sweney, Mark. "WikiLeaks Defies 'Great Firewall of China.'" *Guardian*, March 19, 2008. www.theguardian.com/media/2008/mar/19/digitalmedia.tibet

51. Bruton, F. Brinley, Mo Abbas and Corky Siemaszko. "Julian Assange: Sweden Drops Rape Investigation Into WikiLeaks Founder." *NBC News*, May 19, 2017. www.nbcnews.com/news/world/julian-assange-sweden-drops-rape-investigation-wikileaks-founder-n761986

52. Mackey, Robert. "Sweden Reopens Investigation of Julian Assange for Rape, Complicating U.S. Extradition." *Intercept*, May 13, 2019. theintercept.com/2019/05/13/sweden-reopens-investigation-julian-assange-rape-complicates-u-s-extradition

53. Griffiths, Frank. "Julian Assange Appeals To UK Court Against Extradition To US." *Associated Press*, July 1, 2022. apnews.com/article/technology-london-espionage-extradition-julian-assange-415fc4d82b1e02a2c42f1a68e13fb4b9

54. Alexandersson, Bjartmar Oddur and Gunnar Hrafn Jónsson. "Key Witness in Assange Case Admits To Lies in Indictment." *Stundin*, June 26, 2021. stundin.is/grein/13627/key-witness-in-assange-case-admits-to-lies-in-indictment

55. Gregoire, Paul. "Key US Witness Admits To Falsifying Evidence Against Assange in Return for Immunity." *Sydney Criminal Lawyers*, March 7, 2021. www.sydneycriminallawyers.com.au/blog/key-us-witness-admits-to-falsifying-evidence-against-assange-in-return-for-immunity

56. Youssef, Nancy. "Officials May Be Overstating the Danger from WikiLeaks." *McClatchy*, September 25, 2013. www.mcclatchydc.com/news/special-reports/article24602194.html

57. Greenwald, Glenn. "Julian Assange Loses Appeal: British High Court Accepts U.S. Request to Extradite Him for Trial." *Substack*, December 10, 2021. greenwald.substack.com/p/julian-assange-loses-appeal-british

58. Glenn Greenwald rolls the footage and lays out the lies one by one in an episode of his podcast *System Update*. I've summarized here his scrupulous reporting on this ridiculous MSNBC segment, but it is worth viewing his video in its entirety: "The Real Disinformation Agents: Watch As NBC Tells 4 Lies in a Two-Minute Clip." *System Update*, December 16, 2021. youtu.be/6TizS6SPeSI

59. Gura, David. "WikiLeaks Founder May Have Blood on His Hands, Joint Chiefs Chairman Says." *NPR*, July 30, 2010. www.npr.org/sections/thetwo-way/2010/07/30/128868663/wikileaks-founder-may-have-blood-on-his-hands-joint-chiefs-chairman-says

60. Ottenberg, Eve. "The Biden-Trump Persecution of Julian Assange." *Counterpunch*, August 19, 2022. www.counterpunch.org/2022/08/19/the-biden-trump-persecution-of-julian-assange

61. Lee, Micah. "Crumbling Case Against Assange Shows Weakness of "Hacking" Charges Related to Whistleblowing." *The Intercept*, September 30, 2020. theintercept.com/2020/09/30/assange-extradition-cfaa-hacking

62. Goodwin, Bill. "Assange Revelations Among Most Important In US History, Says Daniel Ellsberg." *Computer Weekly*, 17 Sep 2020. www.computerweekly.com/news/252489159/Assange-revelations-among-most-important-in-US-history-says-Daniel-Ellsberg

63. Nakashima, Ellen. "Pentagon: Undisclosed WikiLeaks Documents 'Potentially More Explosive.'" *Washington Post*, August 11, 2010. voices.washingtonpost.com/checkpoint-washington/2010/08/pentagon_undisclosed_wikileak.html

64. Holden, Michael. "WikiLeaks Acted in Public Interest, 'Pentagon Papers' Leaker Tells Assange Hearing." *Reuters*, September 16, 2020. www.reuters.com/article/britain-assange-idINKBN26725L

65. Pleming, Sue. "Pentagon tells WikiLeaks: 'Do right thing.'" *Reuters*, August 5, 2010. www.reuters.com/article/us-afghanistan-wikileaks/pentagon-tells-wikileaks-do-right-thing-idUSTRE6744AO20100805

66. Connoly, Katie. "Has release of WikiLeaks documents cost lives?" *BBC*, December 1, 2010. www.bbc.com/news/world-us-canada-11882092

67. Whitlock, Craig. "Gates: Warnings of WikiLeaks fallout overblown." *Washington Post*, November 30, 2010. voices.washingtonpost.com/checkpoint-washington/2010/11/the_obama_administration_has_w.html

68. Hosenball, Mark. "US Officials Privately Say WikiLeaks Damage Limited." *Reuters*, January 18, 2011. www.reuters.com/article/wikileaks-damage/us-officials-privately-say-wikileaks-damage-limited-idUSN1816319120110118

69. Pilkington, Ed. "Bradley Manning Leak Did Not Result in Deaths by Enemy Forces, Court Hears." *The Guardian*, July 31, 2013. www.theguardian.com/world/2013/jul/31/bradley-manning-sentencing-hearing-pentagon

70. Greenwald, Glenn. "NBC News Uses Ex-FBI Official Frank Figliuzzi to Urge Assange's Extradition, Hiding His Key Role." *Substack*, January 2, 2021. greenwald.substack.com/p/nbc-news-uses-ex-fbi-official-frank

71. Assange Defense. "Julian Assange Files His Perfected Grounds of Appeal." August 26, 2022. assangedefense.org/press-release/julian-assange-files-his-perfected-grounds-of-appeal

Chapter 13: A Balanced Media Diet

1. Worden, Kristin, et al. "Many Americans Are Unsure Whether Sources of News Do Their Own Reporting." *Pew Research*, December 8, 2020. www.pewresearch.org/fact-tank/2020/12/08/many-americans-are-unsure-whether-sources-of-news-do-their-own-reporting

2. Van Kessel, Patricia, et al. "In Their Own Words, Americans Describe the Struggles and Silver Linings of the COVID-19 Pandemic." *Pew Research*, March 5, 2021. www.pewresearch.org/2021/03/05/in-their-own-words-americans-describe-the-struggles-and-silver-linings-of-the-covid-19-pandemic

3. McGreal, Chris. "Broken and Distrusting: Why Americans Are Pulling Away From the Daily News." *The Guardian*, July 17, 2022. www.theguardian.com/us-news/2022/jul/16/americans-avoid-news-reuters-survey

4. Gottfried, Jeffrey, et al. "Americans See Skepticism of News Media as Healthy, Say Public Trust in the Institution Can Improve" *Pew Research*, August 31, 2020. www.pewresearch.org/journalism/2020/08/31/americans-see-skepticism-of-news-media-as-healthy-say-public-trust-in-the-institution-can-improve

5. Stocking, Galen, et al. "Many Americans Get News on YouTube, Where News Organizations and Independent Producers Thrive Side by Side." *Pew Research*, September 28, 2020. www.pewresearch.org/journalism/2020/09/28/many-americans-get-news-on-youtube-where-news-organizations-and-independent-producers-thrive-side-by-side

6. Princeton Professor Andrew Appel has demonstrated this repeatedly:
"Hacked Vote." learngerman.dw.com/en/i-hack-and-i-vote/a-16363925
Wofford, Ben. "How to Hack an Election in 7 Minutes." *Politico,* August 5, 2016. www.politico.com/magazine/story/2016/08/2016-elections-russia-hack-how-to-hack-an-election-in-seven-minutes-214144
Additionally, work by author Bev Harris and engineer Bennie Smith resulted in a bombshell video disclosing voting machines can award fractional votes to hide fraud. Recommended viewing:
Harris, Bev. "Fraction Magic - Detailed Vote Rigging Demonstration." *Black Box Voting*, October 31, 2016. youtu.be/Fob-AGgZn44
Bloomberg wrote up their work in a rare instance of corporate media coverage:
Riley, Michael and Jordan Robertson. "The Computer Voting Revolution Is Already Crappy, Buggy, and Obsolete." *Bloomberg Businessweek*, September 29, 2016. www.bloomberg.com/features/2016-voting-technology/?leadSource=uverify%20wall
In 2018, at a convention, children didn't hack an actual live election—that would be illegal—so instead they hacked replicas, in mere minutes: Collier, Kevin. "An 11-Year-Old Changed The Results Of Florida's Presidential Vote At A Hacker Convention. Discuss." *BuzzFeed News*, August 11, 2018. www.buzzfeednews.com/article/kevincollier/voting-hackers-defcon-failures-manufacturers-ess

7. Wilkie, Jordan. "'They Think They Are Above the Law': The Firms That Own America's Voting System." *Guardian*, April 22, 2019. www.theguardian.com/us-news/2019/apr/22/us-voting-machine-private-companies-voter-registration

8. Goodkind, Nicole. "Mitch McConnell Received Donations from Voting Machine Lobbyists Before Blocking Election Security Bills." *Newsweek*, July 26, 2019. www.newsweek.com/mitch-mcconnell-robert-mueller-election-security-russia-1451361

9. Huseman, Jessica. "The Market for Voting Machines Is Broken. This Company Has Thrived in It." *ProPublica*, October 28, 2019. www.propublica.org/article/the-market-for-voting-machines-is-broken-this-company-has-thrived-in-it

10. I recommend starting with these two excellent books on the 2004 election, the first election featuring widespread use of electronic voting machines:
Fitrakis, Robert, Steven Rosenfeld, and Harvey Wasserman. *What Happened in Ohio: A Documentary Record of Theft And Fraud in the 2004 Election.* New Press, 2006.
Miller, Mark Crispin. *Fooled Again: How the Right Stole the 2004 Election and Why They'll Steal the Next One Too (Unless We Stop Them).* Basic Books, New York, NY. 2005.

11. Whittaker, Zack. "Senators Demand To Know Why Election Vendors Still Sell Voting Machines With 'Known Vulnerabilities.'" *TechCrunch*, March 27, 2019. techcrunch.com/2019/03/27/senators-security-voting-machines

12. "Attkisson, Sharyl. "Democrats Coordinated Illegal Ballot Collection Scheme in Arizona, Say Prosecutors." July 24, 2022. sharylattkisson.com/2022/07/democrats-coordinated-illegal-ballot-collection-scheme-in-arizona-say-prosecutors

13. Attkisson, Sharyl. "Summary of '2000 Mules,' the Documentary About 2020 Election Fraud." May 25, 2022. sharylattkisson.com/2022/05/summary-of-2000-mules-the-documentary-about-2020-election-fraud

14. Ball, Krystal. "Krystal Ball Dismantles Dinesh D'Souza's '2000 Mules' Election Fraud Movie." *Breaking Points,* May 12, 2022. youtu.be/3z1GcQla3qQ

15. Hernández, Areliz, et al. "Hurricane Maria and Its Aftermath Caused a Spike in Puerto Rico Deaths, With Nearly 3,000 More Than Normal." *Washington Post*, August 28, 2018. www.washingtonpost.com/national/study-hurricane-maria-and-its-aftermath-caused-a-spike-in-puerto-rico-deaths-with-nearly-3000-more-than-normal/2018/08/28/57d6d2d6-aa43-11e8-b1da-ff7faa680710_story.html

16. Kitman, Jamie Lincoln. "The Secret History of Lead." *The Nation*, March 2, 2000. www.thenation.com/article/archive/secret-history-lead

17. Hains, Tim. "Nick Sandmann: The Truth In 15 Minutes." *Real Clear Politics*, February 3, 2019. www.realclearpolitics.com/video/2019/02/03/nick_sandmann_the_truth_in_15_minutes.html

18. Gawande, Amar. "Who Owns Fox News 2022: The Company That Changed Media." *Who Owns,* July 28, 2022. itsknows.com/who-owns-fox-news

19. Facebook, YouTube, and TikTok, as well as DirectTV, Dish Network, Roku, and SlingTV all banished RT from their networks, depriving the network of both exposure and revenue: Nickinson, Phil. "Dish and Sling TV also drop Russia Today channel." *Digital Trends,* March 4, 2022. www.digitaltrends.com/movies/sling-tv-dish-rt-america

20. Evans, Owen. "PayPal Shuts Down Free Speech Union and The Daily Sceptic Accounts." *Epoch Times,* September 21, 2022. www.theepochtimes.com/paypal-shuts-down-free-speech-union-and-the-daily-sceptic-accounts_4744529.html

21. Hughes, Jason. "Mexican Billionaire Carlos Slim Becomes *New York Times'* Largest Single Shareholder." *The Wrap,* January 14, 2015. www.thewrap.com/mexican-billionaire-carlos-slim-becomes-new-york-times-largest-single-shareholder

22. Rondon, Michael. "How America's Oldest Magazines Are Modernizing (and Monetizing) Their Archives." *Folio,* November 13, 2014. archive.foliomag.com/how-america-s-oldest-magazines-are-modernizing-and-monetizing-their-archives

23. Sarto, Dan. "The Brand Gallery Creates Show Package for Sinclair's 'Full Measure With Sharyl Attkisson'." *Animation World Network,* October 30, 2015. awn.com/dev/vfxworld/the-brand-gallery-creates-show-package-for-sinclairs-full-measure-with-sharyl-attkisson

24. "GAP Client Edward Snowden Speaks To German Press: 1/26/14 Transcript." ARD, [interview] whistleblower.org/press/gap-client-edward-snowden-speaks-german-press-12614-transcript

25. Hedges, Chris. "Chris Hedges: Digitally Disappeared; YouTube Has Deleted Six Years of My Show." *Pressenza,* March 30, 2022. www.pressenza.com/2022/03/digitally-disappeared-youtube-has-deleted-six-years-of-my-show

26. Klarenberg, Kit. "Intelligence Operative Confirms British Gov't Is Targeting The Grayzone." *The Grayzone,* August 24, 2022. thegrayzone.com/2022/08/24/intelligence-british-govt-grayzone

27. Dore, Jimmy. "AP's Colossal Joe Rogan Fact Check Fail." *Jimmy Dore Show,* February 4, 2022. www.youtu.be/i0tc18x4C6c

28. Ho, Rodney. "CBS46's Ben Swann Fired After Attempt To Bring Back Reality Check." *Atlanta Journal-Constitution,* January 29, 2018. www.ajc.com/blog/radiotvtalk/cbs46-ben-swann-fired-after-attempt-bring-back-reality-check/NeAW6LA1crpuxoGqmszkKP

Chapter 14: The New Enlightenment

1. To be clear, this was the first *metal* movable type printing press. There is evidence a *ceramic* movable-type printer was invented in China as early as 1090, but its success in printing books is unclear, as no printed materials have survived that were printed with ceramic movable type.

2. Norman, Jeremy. "Johan Carolus's 'Relation,' the First Printed European Newspaper or Newsbook." *History of Information.* www.historyofinformation.com/detail.php?id=34

3. CERN. "A Short History of the Web." home.cern/science/computing/birth-web/short-history-web

4. McGreal, Chris. "Broken and Distrusting: Why Americans Are Pulling Away From the Daily News." *The Guardian,* July 17, 2022. www.theguardian.com/us-news/2022/jul/16/americans-avoid-news-reuters-survey

5. Stocking, Galen, et al. "Many Americans Get News on YouTube, Where News Organizations and Independent Producers Thrive Side by Side." *Pew Research*, September 28, 2020. www.pewresearch.org/journalism/2020/09/28/many-americans-get-news-on-youtube-where-news-organizations-and-independent-producers-thrive-side-by-side

6. If this idea seems unwieldy or unconventional, and I could write a whole chapter on it, consider it akin to voting. Each citizen gets one vote in each election, and each citizen gets enough coupons to slightly influence the coverage of the news.

7. "Social Media and News Fact Sheet." September 20, 2022. *Pew Research Center*. www.pewresearch.org/journalism/fact-sheet/social-media-and-news-fact-sheet

8. Shearer, Elisa. "More Than Eight-in-Ten Americans Get News From Digital Devices." *Pew Research*, January 12, 2021. www.pewresearch.org/fact-tank/2021/01/12/more-than-eight-in-ten-americans-get-news-from-digital-devices

9. See Stocking, above.

10. See Shearer and Stocking, above.

11. Jones, Jeffrey. "Millennials, Gen X Clinging To Independent Party ID." *Gallup*, August 18, 2022. news.gallup.com/poll/397241/millennials-gen-clinging-independent-party.aspx

12. See Stocking, above.

13. Greenwald, Glenn. "Homeland Security's 'Disinformation Board' Is Even More Pernicious Than It Seems." *Substack*, May 4, 2021. greenwald.substack.com/p/homeland-securitys-disinformation

14. Schmachtenberger, Daniel. "The War on Sensemaking." *Rebel Wisdom*, August 19, 2019. youtu.be/7LqaotiGWjQ